The French
Second Republic
A Social History

The French Second Republic

A Social History

ROGER PRICE
Lecturer in European Studies
University of East Anglia

B. T. Batsford London

To Heather, Richard and Siân
To my Mother and in memory
of my Father

First published 1972
© Roger Price 1972
7134 1117 1

Printed and bound in Great Britain by
C. Tinling and Co. Ltd, Prescot, Lancs
for the publishers B. T. Batsford Ltd,
4 Fitzhardinge Street, London W1

Contents

Preface

As will be obvious to any reader, this work owes a great debt to the works of a number of historians, and in particular to Mm. Armengaud, Bastid, Le Bras, Chalmin, Chatelain, Chevalier, Daumard, Dupeux, Duveau, Gille, Girardet, Gossez, Labrousse, Loubère, Marcilhacy, Pierrard, Soboul, Tudesq, Vidalenc, Vigier.

I would like to express my gratitude also to Peter Kemmis Betty of B. T. Batsford Ltd and to the librarians and archivists of the Archives nationales, Archives historiques du Ministère de la Guerre, Bibliothèque nationale, Paris Préfecture de Police, British Museum, University of East Anglia and the University College of Wales, Swansea, and especially to Miss D. K. Dale of the inter-library loans service at the latter; and to Miss J. Wilson and Miss J. Matthews who typed part of the manuscript.

To J. C. Rees of the Department of Politics at Swansea and Dr Stephen Wilson at East Anglia I owe ideas and stimulation, to my old friends Robert and Jane Frugère care and consideration whilst away from home.

My main debts are to my father and mother and to my wife without whose constant help and tact this book could never have been written.

R.P.

Chronology

1848	February 23	Revolution in Paris
	February 24	Abdication of Louis-Philippe
		Provisional government established
		Universal suffrage procliamed
	March 16	Demonstration by conservatives
		Demonstration by left-wing elements
	April 23	Election of Constituent Assembly
	May 15	Demonstration by left-wing elements
	June 22–26	June insurrection
		Cavaignac government
	December 10	Election of Louis-Napoléon Bonaparte as President of the Republic
1849	April	Expeditionary Corps sent to Rome
	May	Election of Legislative Assembly
	June 13	Demonstration against the Roman expedition
1850	March	Loi Falloux on education
		Left-wing electoral victories
	May	Law restricting franchise
1851	July	Failure of attempts to secure conservative constitutional reform
	December 2	*Coup d'état*
	December 14	Plebiscite
1852	November 20–21	Plebiscite on Empire
	December 1	Proclamation of Napoléon III as Emperor of the French

INTRODUCTION

France in the 1840s was a society undergoing economic and social transition. The process of industrialization was becoming more rapid due to the stimulus of railway construction. Agriculture still, however, predominated, both in terms of its contribution to the national income and because the vast majority of Frenchmen still depended upon it, either directly as landowners, farmers or labourers, or indirectly as industrialists, merchants or workers whose markets and employment depended upon the prosperity and purchasing power of the rural population.

In this situation a revolution occurred towards the end of February 1848 caused by a combination of circumstances which created a crisis of confidence in the existing political regime, leading some men to overthrow it and those who had formerly been its staunchest defenders to stand by and watch it disappear.

The explanation of these events and of the subsequent course of affairs must be based on the structure of French society at this particular time. By comparison with the period from 1789 to 1793 the political scene was characterized by the passing of power to more and more conservative men. The situation did not seem to demand extreme action by the new republican government. There were no invading armies bent on restoring the old regime and, more significantly, no Frenchmen were prepared to defend it. Louis-Philippe had not represented principles worthy of sacrifice. His role from 1830 had been to preserve order and help create the preconditions for the acquiring and enjoyment of wealth. His fall indicated his failure and the ending of his *raison d'être*. Those things which men would have been prepared to defend—the wealth which gave them security and status were not under serious attack.

In a society in which most men either possessed property, however small, or could genuinely hope to possess, in which relatively few yet felt without hope or in danger of being dispossessed, it was not an easy matter to mount an attack on wealth and its representatives.

Established values had not been sufficiently shaken. There were no convincing alternatives to established social forms.

The Provisional Government created immediately after the revolution was an amalgam of the most popular republican figures. They were able to install themselves in Paris because there was no organized group able to pose an alternative. The republic seemed proper in a situation in which the 'people' had overthrown a monarch.

Unexpectedly assuming power these men had no clear ideas, no plans. They were middle class with a genuine sympathy for the poor but also a contempt and fear for the unwashed and illiterate. Moreover, they could rely on the rest of France to support them against revolutionaries in Paris. For the first time the provinces were prepared to defy the capital. Not only were there real differences of interest and of political consciousness but the speed of the dialogue between Paris and the provinces had been increased as the means of communication developed. Inhabitants of rural areas and provincial towns could be more aware of events in Paris, could exert a more genuine influence on national politics where they not only elected representatives, through the process of universal suffrage introduced immediately after the revolution, but if necessary could rush to Paris by railway to protect these representatives.

Paris was less assertive than formerly, the provinces less receptive. Industry was developing but as yet it had not created a factory proletariat but something more akin to peasants in factories, subdued by their misery and without the hope of a better future which is a pre-requisite for sustained action.

The dominant political force was conservative but an interesting feature of the Second Republic was the growth of a rural and small town radicalism which appeared all the more dangerous because it was concentrated in particular regions. This occurred in the most economically backward areas amongst men who found their economic status and thence their social status threatened by the developing forces of market agriculture and industrial capitalism. This also was a will to defend the *status quo* but these were regions in which the *status quo* differed from that elsewhere.

The mass of Frenchmen wanted to preserve the existing social forms for which they could visualize no alternative. Universal suffrage backed by the threat and use of force guaranteed them their own way once their political leaders could agree on the means. The absence of agreement between leading politicians, however, prevented repressive action determined enough to satisfy insecure conservatives. These politicians could not forget the habits of parliamentary politics.

The exaggerated hopes of the more dissatisfied part of the community in the general elections of 1852, the exaggerated fears of other parts, continued economic crisis and social unrest, created an uncertain situation in which one man could pose as the potential saviour of society. This man possessed a hallowed name and the assuredness generally lacking in political figures. His appeal had already been proven by his election in December 1848 as President of the Republic. He wanted to unite France and he could be trusted to crush disorder. The history of the Second Republic is the history of revolution in Paris followed by reaction elsewhere – a reaction beginning with the first election under universal suffrage in April 1848, consummated finally after long argument over means, by a military *coup d'état* in December 1851.

It is paradoxical that a republic which began with the introduction of universal suffrage should end with a plebiscite approving the creation of an Emperor, that the greater involvement of the masses in politics would end with their approval of the dictatorship of one man. The general desire for social order and certainty led, as before in French history, to submission to military rule, but never more clearly had the willingness of the rich and the comfortable to renounce political power for economic security been revealed. In many respects the basic outline of political allegiances in subsequent French history was created in these four years 1848–52. The poor felt themselves thrust out from society by the brusque crushing of their aspirations after the June insurrection of 1848 and the *coup d'état* in December 1851. The wealthy would ever after be hostile to demands for social reform and frightened of all change. Those who were neither rich nor poor would as always gravitate towards one extreme or another as their interests took them. The important thing is that men previously had hoped and believed it possible to bridge the gulf between rich and poor, now increasingly the poor could look only towards social revolution, the rich to repression by the administrative machine, church and army. These habits would take long to break, the suspicions remain strong in France today.

The process by which the political and social groups favouring radical change were overwhelmed by conservative and reactionary elements will be traced through the major and often the minor events of this period, from the revolution of February 1848 and the short-lived period of euphoria which succeeded it to the brutal insurrection of June – a conservative victory which did not bring the feeling of security with it – to the election of Louis-Napoléon Bonaparte in December 1848 and the subsequent competition between the new President and the old politicians for the support of all those who opposed change, a competition interrupted by occasional alliances called for by the resurgence of the radical left, but which it was increasingly obvious that conservatives were tiring of, wanting as they did not parliamentary debate but dictatorship.

I

Structure of a Society

This present work sets out to be a social history of France in the period of acute crisis of the mid-nineteenth century. It will, particularly in the earlier chapters, at times proceed by means of a critique of Karl Marx's essays on the Second Republic – an approach adopted because it was felt that such criticism of what were and are extremely influential works would facilitate the rejection of pre-conceptions still sometimes held about the nature of French society and institutions in this period.

Marx interpreted French history in terms of classes or fractions of classes. This is the product of his personal view of what are the most important factors involved in historical causation. The officials of the *Statistique de la France* and of the Paris Chamber of Commerce, upon whose work this first chapter is to a large extent based, possessed different ideas in this respect. For them the dividing line between employer and employee was often less important than the factor of participation in production within the same industry. Comparison between their statistical data and Marx's categories is thus difficult. Indeed comparison between any two official surveys of French society is difficult because of the lack of adequate definition of the categories used and the probability that over time the practical definition of these categories did in fact change.[1] At best the censuses and enquiries of the nineteenth century provide us with a generalized picture of society and its development, a picture which is, however, certainly adequate, to compare with Marx's broad description of French society drawn in terms of four basic classes – bourgeoisie, petty bourgeoisie, peasantry and proletariat.

France was essentially an agricultural country, its industry being in a clearly undeveloped condition compared with that of Britain.

There were only a few great industrial centres, with Paris as the most important - for Marx the proletarian city of France *par excellence*.[2]

What anyway was this proletariat? In place of definition which is lacking we can refer the reader to the *Communist Manifesto* adding that this is rather an idealized conception, or to the various volumes of *Das Capital* where the abiding impression is of the proletarian as being the individual submerged in large-scale factory production. Revolution is certainly constantly portrayed as emerging from an urban society where production and the working class is organized in large-scale units. To what extent was this Parisian proletariat employed in the factory? Or perhaps is Marx using the word in a sense differing from his normal usage? It would seem probable that with his book-derived knowledge and his practical experience of the city he must have known the character of its economic life.

On this latter contemporary statistics are revealing. Consider first the results of the enquiry of the Paris Chamber of Commerce made during 1847-1848.[3] First the forms of employment (see table opposite).[4]

The major employing industries were those attending to the material needs of the Parisian population in the form of food, clothing, furniture and housing, or otherwise the typically Parisian luxury industries – groups of activities traditionally engaged in on a small scale. The figures indicate relative importance in terms of numbers employed.

Paris was the centre of administration, trade, finance and communications, but because of its concentration of population and of wealth tended to be too expensive for large workshops and factories, for entrepreneurs unwilling or unable to pay more than elsewhere for sites, in rent and wages. It acted rather as the centre for the disposal of goods produced in France and because of its large population provided the largest market for consumer goods such as food and clothing and also for high quality luxury goods. According to the economist Audiganne, in 1847 only 318 workshops in the department of the Seine used mechanical power or employed more than twenty workers. Only about 30,000 workers were employed in these, with countless more employed in smaller and more technically primitive workshops.[5] The statistical chart produced opposite is in fact the best proof of this. The scale of production was small and its form is best described as artisanal.

Whatever the arbitrariness involved in separating industrial workers from artisans, it is quite clear that the Parisian was far more

6

NUMBER OF PRODUCERS

	Employing more than 10 workers	2 to 10	A single worker or working alone	Total	Total no. of workers
Food and drink	113	2,066	1,494	3,673	10,428 (7,947 men)
Building	873	2,300	888	4,061	41,603 (33,533 men)
Furniture	856	2,605	2,252	5,713	36,184 (28,509 men)
Clothing and shoes	1,739	8,547	18,930	29,216	90,064 (29,941 men)
Textiles	698	1,244	1,857	3,799	36,685 (10,920 men)
Skins and leather	102	233	91	426	4,573 (4,201 men)
Coach building, saddlery and military equipment	279	700	274	1,253	13,754 (10,531 men)
Chemicals and ceramics	212	460	587	1,259	9,737 (6,455 men)
Metal, engineering and metal products	545	1,469	1,090	3,104	24,894 (21,926 men)
Precious metals and jewellery	432	1,081	879	2,392	16,819 (10,810 men)
Coopers and basket-makers	85	785	691	1,561	5,405 (3,992 men)
Articles de Paris	833	2,510	2,781	6,124	35,679 (17,542 men)
Printing and paper	350	1,116	769	2,235	16,705 (10,877 men)
Total	7,117	25,116	32,583	64,816	342,530 (197,184 men)

likely to have been the latter than the former. Marx labels all workers proletarians. In applying this to Paris he uses it in what for him is an abnormal manner. The significance of the difference between the industrial factory worker and the artisan employed at skilled work in a small workshop or room of his own home will become more

7

evident later. Even much later in the century observers would stress not the element of change over the years, but that of continuity; thus the economist Lavollée writing in the *Revue des Deux Mondes* in 1865 – 'What characterizes above all else Parisian industry is the extreme division of labour, the variety and small scale. Large factories are few and far between, small workshops are very numerous; there is nothing to resemble the character of factory towns where several large factories each employ hundreds and thousands of workers at the same work. ...'[6] This resembles Audiganne's conclusions concerning Parisian industry in 1847.

The owners of workshops and shopkeepers were distinguished from the workers by the fact of possession of property, whether in the form of business premises, or stock of goods, or both, and in the greater likelihood of owning their living accommodation. But obviously there was much in common between the patron working alone or with a small number of employees, the small shopkeeper dependent on working-class customers, and these latter themselves. This emphasizes the artificiality and arbitrariness of social categorization and indicates part of the reasoning behind the methodological approach involved in this history by which an attempt will be made to stress the fragility of the dividing lines between defined social groups.

Be this as it may, a generalized view of Parisian society as a whole is necessary. This is provided for the period of the Second Republic by Adeline Daumard in her *La Bourgeoisie parisienne de 1815 à 1848*. Using the results of the Chamber of Commerce Enquiry of 1847, corrected by means of various other statistics, Mlle Daumard divides the population of Paris into the following categories:

	Percentage of total
Proprietors, *rentiers*	8
Liberal professions and clerks	7
Commercial professions	8
Industrial professions	11
Milieux populaires	56
Soldiers	10

She assumes that the bourgeoisie will be found amongst the top 34 per cent and proceeds further with the assumption that domestics will be limited, if not exclusively, then largely, to bourgeois households; this in fact being a part of the definition of this class by way of life. The census report of 1846 indicated 46,466 households with domestics, and Mlle Daumard calculates on the basis of an average of four people for each bourgeois household that in 1846 the Parisian population included 185,000 bourgeoisie, 17·5 per cent of the total population.[8] On the basis of these figures it is perhaps fair to assume that the proportion of the population being neither bourgeois, military nor appertaining to the *milieux populaires* and labelled commonly petty bourgeois made up the remaining 16·5 per cent of the population.

In place of non-existent statistics we have to rely on such local studies as that by Mlle Daumard of Paris, which utilized sources like the registration of declarations after decease and notaries' archives.[9] As did Mlle Daumard we must attempt to escape the narrow limits of definition of social groups in terms of occupation or the faculty of ownership or non-ownership of some material property or professional skills, and whilst always taking those vitally important factors into account consider also general way of life, and attitude towards life, the latter particularly as reflected by reaction over time to specific changing events. Even so it is necessary to use certain basic concepts as tools of analysis and to divide the Parisian, and subsequently the French, population into basic groups. The categories used in this chapter are those which have been already successfully used in social analysis, though definition and use may vary between analysts. Thus Daumard accepts the existence of a bourgeoisie, and a petty bourgeoisie as did Marx. Her definition is more nuanced than the latter's, in that she places the most successful and more wealthy members of professions involved in agriculture, industry, commerce and finance, etc., among the ranks of the upper bourgeoisie; the moderately successful are also classed by their total existence, including here political ineligibility during the July monarchy, and increased contacts with the *milieux populaires* as variously middle middle and lower middle class, including for example lesser government officials, doctors, lawyers, industrial and commercial entrepreneurs and shopkeepers, whilst the manual labourers or those whose living standards, taxes, lack of property and of security associated them with manual labourers are considered together as belonging to the *milieux populaires*. There might be some doubts concerning the one social group which is adequately identified in Marx's historical essays, the *lumpenproletariat*, composed of 'decayed roués with dubious means of subsistence and of dubious origin, alongside ruined and adventurous offshoots of the bourgeoisie . . . vagabonds, discharged soldiers, discharged jailbirds, escaped galley slaves, swindlers, mountebanks, *lazzaroni*, pickpockets, tricksters, gamblers, *procureurs*, brothel keepers, porters, *literati*, organ grinders, rag-pickers, knife grinders, tinkers, beggars – in short, the whole indefinite, disintegrated mass, thrown hither and thither, which the French term *la bôhème*.'[10] This is a definition of a social group above all in terms of way of life and reflects to a great extent contemporary opinion. Louis Chevalier in his work *Classes laborieuses et classes dangereuses à Paris pendant la première moitié du XIXe siècle'*, shows the confusion in the bourgeois mind between these two classes. He quotes Balzac's *La Fille aux yeux d'or* – 'Certainly one of the most terrible spectacles one can witness is the general aspect of the Parisian people. Emaciated, wrinkled, sallow and dried up, they are horrible to look upon . . . men whose distorted, eager faces distil through every pore the thoughts, the desires, the poison that is seething in their brains. . . .'[11] This is a picture of a separate world, of a different form of humanity. The tendency is to confuse poverty and criminality, and indeed the one might often lead, from desperation, to the other. Chevalier emphasizes how contemporary literature saw particular occupational groups as especially susceptible to crime. A reading of Balzac, Hugo and Sue is sufficient support for this. The attitudes of men like de Tocqueville to the mobs of 1848 is one of fear as of a new barbarism. To contemporary opinion the ragpicker and the beggar exemplified pauperism and desperation. It has been necessary to depart from statistics because none are available. It can only be said that contemporaries saw this *lumpenproletariat*, and described and defined it in a manner similar to that of Marx. In a large city, the centre of immigration, with insufficient accommodation and often with inadequate employment opportunities, misery was inevitable. Misery breeds crime. Crime for many becomes an occupation. These elements occupationally and in their attitudes to life separate themselves from other more cohesive groupings.

Having described the occupational character of Paris, it becomes necessary to consider that of France as a whole and first that of urban France, of secondary importance numerically, but of great significance in terms of political and ideological movements.

First, what was the numerical relationship of the urban population to the total population?

According to the census report of 1872 the urban population, defined as the total population living in towns with at least 2,000 inhabitants, was 11,214,017 compared with a rural population of

24,888,904.[12] Development from 1846 had taken the following form:[13]

Population	1846	1851	1856	1861	1866	1872
	%	%	%	%	%	%
Urban	24·42	25·52	27·31	28·86	30·46	31·06
Rural	75·58	74·28	72·69	71·14	69·54	68·94

The trend indicated here is that of a slow urbanization becoming more rapid in the decade of the 1860s. The practical value of the definition of 'urban' might be questioned. Obviously life in a town with a population of somewhere around 2,000 will differ greatly from that in a great metropolis like Paris. Further question might be thrown on the value of the statistics if one thinks for example of the difference between a small mining town and a similarly sized but differently structured small market town. However, the statistics above can be enlarged upon using the conclusions of the old but still useful work of Adna Ferrin Weber, *The Growth of Cities in the Nineteenth Century*. For France Weber concludes that urban growth was largely medium and large city growth, in fact that normally the larger the city the faster the growth, linking this with the rate of industrial development.[14] This is illustrated by the following chart showing the percentage increase in population of various sizes of towns:[15]

% of total population	1801	1851	1872	1891
100,000+	2·8	4·6	9·1	12·0
20–100,000+	3·9	6·0	6·7	9·1
10–20,000+	2·8	3·8	4·4	4·8
Total 10,000+	9·5	14·4	20·2	25·9

As Weber also uses the results of the census of 1872 comparison between our first set of figures above and these is possible and supports the view that if many of the people regarded by the statistician as urban dwellers did in fact live in a mixed urban-rural environment, the tendency, whatever the falsification of statistics due to the secession of much of Alsace and Lorraine, was still towards a more rapid concentration in large, more totally urban areas, with all the significance that this must have for social structure and general attitudes towards life.

Most of the French urban population however, and this is worth emphasizing, continued to live in relatively small communities – in 1851 4,827,355, that is 54 per cent of the total urban population, lived in towns with between three thousand and ten thousand inhabitants.

The results of the census of 1851[16] revealed 1,331,260 individuals engaged in *grande industrie*.[17] By 1872 this figure had fallen to 1,276,825, both figures including those engaged in mining.[18] The decline in numbers, surprising at first sight, being explained by the loss of most of Alsace and Lorraine, two of the most highly developed industrial areas. Even at the latter date the average unit of production included in the category *grande industrie* employed only about nineteen workers, whilst the average for all industrial establishments reduced itself to about five,[19] and this after the great era of industrial expansion during the Second Empire. Urban France as Paris then, as regards industrial development, was involved essentially in small-scale production.

More significant to our study than this question of averages is the degree of concentration, the development especially of the basic heavy industries such as textiles, coal and metallurgy, and of the areas in which such activities were centred. Marx places his hopes for revolution in the future on the development of 'modern industry'.[20] In a few years time he would suggest that 'steam, electricity, and the self-acting mule were revolutionaries of a rather more dangerous character than even citizens Barbès, Raspail and Blanqui'.[21] It was particularly on the departments of the Paris Basin, of the north-east and the east that he must have pinned his hopes. But Marx does use the word 'proletariat' in two senses. He pins his revolutionary hopes on the proletarians of Paris and of the new, developing industrial areas. It has already been stressed that the Parisian worker was rather the artisan than factory worker. Might there not be a basic fault in an analysis which, using certain categories tends, either for convenience's sake or because of inadequate definition, to include within a particular category what does not entirely belong there. There is the possibility that the simplification involved in the lumping together of the factory worker and the Parisian artisan will result in a false image of French society for the reader, and in mistakes of interpretation by Marx himself.

Returning then to the original point concerning heavy industrial development; here again it would be possible to use statistics to illustrate the dominance of particular areas and the consequent creation in them of pockets in which a factory proletariat was at least numerically significant. Consider just one as indicative. The Enquiry of 1847 into the industries of the north-east and east, the main regions of development, revealed that in the twenty-one departments of north-east France, there were 6,844 industrial establishments (2,377 in the Nord alone), employing 377,685 men, women and children (106,620 in the Nord), that is an average of about 55 per establishment (45 in the Nord).[22]

For the entire area of eastern France the average unit considered employed 35 workers.[23] Concentration then was greatest in the north-east in towns like Lille and Mulhouse rather than in the east as in Lyon, where the technical difficulties involved in mechanizing the production of silk restricted concentration.

This statistical survey can be filled out only by considering the process of industrial development. What is necessary is an outline of this development to help explain and illustrate a changing social structure.

One writer has listed the preconditions for industrialization as follows: resource utilization, financial organization, transport facilities, a property relationship, suitable labour, developed exchange relationships, freedom from traditional bonds and restraints, a general mobility, political order to provide a degree of certainty of a return on investment, 'a minimum value consensus', motives and enterprise.[24] It would be pointless to consider each one of these within the French context but it might be worthwhile to highlight the factors seen by economic historians as restricting economic development so as to gain a first insight into a community mentality.

It could be said that in France technical knowledge and even the legal forms for industrial expansion existed but that men were reluctant. This psychological factor is important. Not only were the workers, whether peasants or artisans, reluctant to enter the oppressive factory, but the more fortunate, wealthier sections of the population were reluctant to eschew the security of state funds for their investments, for the possibly greater gains but with the greater risks of industrial investment. In addition many manufacturers would not have wished this, being concerned through individualism and family pride to preserve their entrepreneurial independence even at the risk of stagnation.

This psychological factor however is not all. Consider for example the relatively slow growth of French population. There was less need to modernize techniques where demand increased only slowly and high duties protected against foreign competition. The slow expansion of Parisian and provincial banks and the cautious attitude towards industrial investment which they shared, restricted the more adventurous industrialists forcing them, as Balzac's character César Birotteau, sometimes to have recourse, when the banks refused to extend credit, to the usurer with whom 11 per cent was a fairly low rate of interest. According to Roger Priouret the small French banker in the first half of the nineteenth century had the mentality of a usurer, whilst the large had that of a financier of the *ancien régime*. He supports this by quoting James de Rothschild who, perhaps regretting his involvement in railway finance, observed that 'There are three ways to ruin oneself: cards, women and engineers. The first two are more agreeable, but the third is more certain.'[25]

The development of heavy industry, as has already been indicated, took place largely in the Paris Basin, north-east and east for various reasons, including for example accessibility to raw materials, communications, etc., but the seemingly most important factor was availability of capital. Consider two examples – the department of the Nord with an old commercial tradition whose profits provided capital permitting the development of textiles and with the use of steam power, of mining; then in the east the textile industries of Alsace. Here capital was available from the more adventurous Swiss banking houses. Other major developments, namely of the railways and the inter-dependent development of metallurgy, were supported by financiers initially probably because of state guarantees to railway companies which gave an unusual degree of security to industrial investment. Once involved there was a need for continued investment to maintain or increase profitability. Perhaps also financiers quickly acquired a sense of power and a taste for the prestige involved in directing large and important enterprises. As far as metallurgy and mining were concerned high initial capital investment and the reciprocal dependence together with the recurring need to finance modernization encouraged both concentration and integration and such companies as the mining Compagnie d'Anzin and the metallurgical group Chatillon-Commentry serve as prime examples of the new industrial capitalism.

But even in this highly capitalized sector, if by the end of the Empire the production of iron using charcoal had been practically eliminated, in 1848 much of production remained primitive although the industry was changing rapidly under the impulse of railway construction.

Even if the banks had been more willing to provide funds, and this did in fact increasingly occur from the railway boom of the 1840s, though normally with extreme caution, the banks themselves were restricted by the withdrawal of money from circulation through investment in government loans, and by the emphasis on thrift in peasant communities dominated by the notion of purchasing land at almost any price. Indeed the peculiar existence of the French peasant has been blamed, not simply for this, in itself of great significance, but also for the slow development of an urban labour force. Bertrand Gille blames the Revolution of 1789 for destroying many large estates and increasing the security of possession of the peasant.[26]

The peasant limited the size of his family, and the extent of his purchases, of his demand, in order to save. He desired to avoid the factory at all costs. Only with the decline of rural, domestic industry and other forms of supplemental employment necessary to the existence of the poor peasant and landless labourer could the industrial labour force be substantially increased, but this must be a slow process, if increasingly gathering momentum, because of the factors considered above.

During the July Monarchy, however, significant change was occurring. First in the field of transport – roads and canals were improved, and railway construction encouraged actively by the government.

The existence of a large market and the possibility of large-scale production obviously depended on transport facilities. Thus in the 1840s one of the most important elements for industrialization was coming into existence, and in so doing gave a vital impulse to metallurgy and engineering and indirectly to all manner of other industries, increasing the size of their markets and intensifying the competition for them; both factors demanding concentration.

The limitations to this must however be emphasized. Consider below the construction of railway lines.[27]

1840	497 kilometres in existence
1850	3,080 kilometres in existence
1860	9,525 kilometres in existence
1870	17,929 kilometres in existence

The July Monarchy saw the beginning of a trend which was to be developed during the Second Empire and this was true of most sectors of primary industrial development, of metallurgy, engineering and textiles. In 1847 5,153,000 tons of coal and lignite were produced in France, in 1869 13,464,000,[28] at the same time iron and steel production increased by 32 per cent and that of pig iron by 100 per cent.[29] The number of steam engines used in industry increased from 525 developing 900 h.p. in 1832 to 4,853 (62,000 h.p.) in 1847,[30] and to 27,958 of 341,000 h.p. by 1870.

By contrast with the period of the July Monarchy that of the Second Empire enjoyed an inflation due to the development of Australian and Californian gold mines which stimulated investment. By this time above all a basis for further development had been created, experience had done something to reduce the psychological restrictions and encourage that attitude often labelled Saint-Simonian. And yet, as the figures on population structure and size of productive unit in 1872 show, there was throughout this period a great deal of continuity at least in statistical, organizational and even topographical terms if perhaps not to the same extent in popular attitudes. Above all during the period of the Second Empire must be noted the extension of financial and legal facilities, in the latter case easing the formalities involved in the creation of joint stock companies and partnership with limited liability, previously largely restricted in practice to the field of public utilities, and of the railway network, and the continued concentration of the basic industries. Here was a continuation of tendencies apparent in the 1840s but intensified by the fact that a growing exploitation of the individual worker by lowering wages (diluting the labour force or increasing hours, so as to maintain profits and competitiveness) had by about 1848 become far more difficult because of the natural limits of human endurance, and productivity could only be increased subsequently by mechanization. The whole period of the July Monarchy, Second Republic and Second Empire would seem to be that which Rostow has labelled 'take-off' into an industrial economy, but it remained unfulfilled even at the end of the century in the sense that in France agriculture remained more important than in any other manufacturing country and that in 1881 two-thirds of the population lived in the country or in small market towns. Change and continuity – but in terms of social structure above all continuity.

There were essentially three types of industrial workers, each reflecting a particular stage in the development of production. First, the artisan working in a small workshop who remained the typical French worker, even if his contribution to the national product was as a proportion increasingly reduced. Second, the workers in villages partly engaged in agriculture, partly in industrial work under the domestic system, and their possibly even more unfortunate compatriots the urban domestic workers deprived of the benefits of agriculture. Lastly, the factory workers and miners reflecting the development of capitalism from its more commercial beginnings to a mechanized, large-scale form of production.

French industry was geared essentially towards the consumer market rather than capital goods. The most significant example of industrial development was the textile industry. This also was by far the most important industrial employer of labour. Here too were most evident the variations in technique, and here existed all three of the basic types of labour noted above.

Consider Lille, viewed by contemporaries as the prime example of an industrial town. An estimated 50,000 people in the 1850s were dependent on factory production, were in the normal Marxist sense proletarians. But even here about 89,000 were dependent on more primitive forms of manufacture,[31] and if there were some examples of large-scale production in the field of spinning the average labour force of a mill tended to be about 150.[32]

This at least is more properly *grande industrie* than most of the productive units so defined by official statisticians. In addition, the trend towards concentration was clearly evident particularly during the frequent crises of the 1830s and 1840s when the smaller productive units tended to fade away whilst the larger, anxious to maintain a share of diminished markets, sought to reduce costs and prices by technical innovation and an increasing scale of production.[33] The economic crisis was a vital factor encouraging concentration in all spheres of the economy, and it is worth remembering that perhaps ten of the eighteen years of the July Monarchy were years of economic depression.

As our earlier figures have shown the French industrial worker was normally to be found in the workshop using production tools rather than machines. Various reasons have already been suggested for this, and to them it is only necessary to add here the technical difficulties involved in the mechanization of weaving and silk manufacture in textiles. The most important causes were, it needs to be reaffirmed, poor communications and a consequently restricted market which made in many cases further capital investment unnecessary even if capital had been available.

The other form of production considered was that of the domestic workers producing goods for a merchant and payed at a piece-rate. Competitiveness with machine production was possible because of the low wages paid to a worker who could in the country eke out his existence by cultivating a small plot of land or working as an agricultural labourer at harvest, or in the towns have recourse to municipal or private charity. The relatively high production costs of French industry during what was still an initial period of development, sheltered by high duties against foreign competition, also helped preserve the competitiveness of domestic industry. The decline of this latter was however evident throughout the nineteenth century with significant economic consequences in respect of the creation of an adequate industrial labour force.

If there was variation within a city like Lille in the forms of production, between regions differences are even more apparent. In textiles between the relatively advanced forms of production in Lille and Mulhouse for example, and that of Haute-Normandie where the merchant rather than the manufacturer was dominant. In Paris and Lyon the artisan dominated; in Lille, Mulhouse and Le Creusot the factory worker.

All these were however large urban areas and the majority of the French urban population lived in small towns closely linked with the surrounding countryside. It will be necessary to consider the differing mentalities not only between Parisian artisans and Lille factory workers, but between these two and the industrial workers of such departments as the Isère and Vaucluse, and Hautes and Basses-Alpes, areas of importance in our political narrative – of the latter, the report of a Commission of Enquiry established as part of the general enquiry into industry and agriculture of 1848, revealed an unchanging environment where the demand for cloth was regulated by the prosperity of agriculture, where its producers were essentially artisans catering for the needs of the local population.[34] Basses Alpes in its geographical isolation might be regarded as an extreme example but it does reveal the opposite pole of industrial development or non-development, to that of Lille; it reveals a contrasting environment for the worker to that of Le Creusot or Paris. In between there were departments like the Loire with about a quarter of its population engaged in industry in 1850 but, with the exception of coal mining, engaged in small-scale and declining ribbon making, or ironmongery,[35] or the department of the Eure, tenth in importance in the value of industrial production in 1850 where the major industry, textiles, was increasingly concentrated but existed side by side with artisanal production almost medieval in character.[36]

Variation is what is everywhere noticeable in the environment of groups involved in industry and commerce. This fact will have to be taken constantly into consideration in a subsequent analysis of political reactions. The technical form of production, the consequent everyday activity and relationships, are elements constituting part of the total social environment, are variables which must inevitably influence the character of other variables such as the formation and composition of social groups, their attitude to their environment and their activity to preserve or change this. In considering the industrial development of France it might be possible to conclude, tentatively, that France in 1848 was composed of a number of societies united by elements of a common cultural and political history, differentiated by variations in social structure, with the degree of unity or difference between these seen as the product of the development of communications each with the other and particularly with the cultural and marketing centre of Paris. Similarity of social structure will increase with time and railways.

Marx, within the limited scope of an essay, failed to emphasize these differences in the urban sphere. By contrast he did, however, place some stress on the different political reactions of peasants to the *coup d'état* of 1851 as the product of differing physical conditions of existence. If his brief comments on industrial development emphasize its limitations and ignore the fundamental differences between the Parisian artisan and the provincial artisan and factory worker and the differences between these last two, his comments on the rural scene are more extensive and might appear at least in this respect of variation to be more perceptive,[37] and to be especially significant in the analysis of what was still an agricultural country.

He is essentially concerned with one social group – the peasantry engaged in inefficient non-market production becoming poorer with the land and the weight of its debts. In this respect he paints a uniform picture.

The statistical image, however, shows a lesser degree of uniformity. The census of 1851 had twelve categories for its analysis of the population engaged in agriculture, from proprietors themselves engaged in cultivation, to farmers renting land, sharecroppers, day labourers, foresters and variations on these including the many day labourers who also owned some land.[38] If Marx is correct in assuming that the great majority of the population is rural, he is not in also assuming that these are mainly 'free landowners'.[39] The figures of 1851, whatever the much commented on inaccuracy of this particular census, indicate only 6,698,536 owners of land amongst 14,318,476 individuals directly engaged in agriculture.[40] A large part of the rural population were therefore not peasants in the true sense of the word.

The vital strand of Marx's analysis concerns the parcellation of land with its consequent effect on peasant property lust and social attitudes which is as much forseen as described.

The process of parcellation is impossible to deny. Consider the table drawn by Georges Dupeux on the basis of the land tax. The increased proportion of small assessments indicates parcellation.[41]

Assessment	1826 Number	%	1842 Number	%	1858 Number	%	Indices base 100 in 1826
20 francs and below	8,024,987	77·94	8,873,951	77·09	10,464,757	79·63	130
21 to 30	663,237	6·44	791,711	6·88	821,852	6·26	124
31 to 50	642,345	6·24	744,911	6·47	758,876	5·78	118
51 to 100	527,991	5·13	607,956	5·28	609,562	4·65	115
101 to 300	335,505	3·26	375,860	3·26	368,631	2·81	110
301 to 500	56,602	0·55	64,244	0·56	59,842	0·46	106
501 to 1000	32,279	0·31	36,862	0·32	37,333	0·29	114
1001+	13,447	0·13	16,346	0·14	15,870	0·12	118
	10,296,693	100·0	11,511,841	100·0	13,118,723	100·0	127

These figures indicate an increase in the total number of those assessed, and indeed an increase in all categories, but with the relative proportion of those assessed at 20 francs or below almost continually increasing and that of those assessed above continually decreasing. In numerical terms the number of holdings assessed at 20 francs or below increased by over two million in the period under consideration. Albert Soboul, accepting Dupeux's figures, concluded that because one individual might own several holdings the number of landowners might be estimated to be 6·5 million in 1826, and 7·5

million in 1850.[42] More significant are the figures, again derived from
Dupeux, which reveal the size of holdings assessed. Here the earliest
figures available are for 1884.[43]

Categories	Number of holdings	Area involved (ha.)	Percentage of total number of holdings	of total area
Below 50 ares	6,597,843	1,147,804	46·90	2·31
50 ares to 1 hectare	1,987,480	1,426,785	14·12	2·88
1 to 5 hectares	3,735,173	8,647,714	26·54	17·50
5 to 10 hectares	892,887	6,254,142	6·36	12·67
10 to 20 hectares	476,843	6,629,491	3·38	13·42
20 to 50 hectares	261,829	7,866,769	1·84	15·95
50 to 75 hectares	50,230	3,044,065	0·36	6·17
75 to 100 hectares	23,273	2,015,752	0·16	4·08
100 to 200 hectares	31,567	4,338,240	0·22	8·79
Over 200 hectares	17,676	8,017,542	0·12	16·23
	14,074,801	49,388,304	100·00	100·00

Henri Sée categorized agricultural holdings in the following
manner: 'very small' as less than one hectare; 'small' as composing
from one to ten hectares; 'medium' from ten to forty hectares;
'large' from forty to one hundred; and 'very large' over one hundred
hectares.[44] Applying these categories to the above table it is possible
to conclude that 61.02 per cent of French landholdings in 1884 were
very small, 32·90 per cent small, about 5·22 per cent of medium size,
0·52 per cent large, and 0·34 per cent very large. This certainly tends
to support Marx's description of parcellation leading to the decreasing
size of the peasant land-holding. 35·27 per cent of the agricultural land was contained in holdings of above 50 hectares and if
13,700,000 holdings are smaller than 20 hectares, the 400,000 which
are greater occupy roughly the same amount of land. These two
major groupings each occupied about half the land of France. This
indicates a polarization of wealth and poverty in the agricultural
sector similar to that analysed by Marx in the industrial. This is
compatible with Marx's analysis of agricultural development except
for one vital fact, that this analysis reflecting Marx's revolutionary
concerns is of the development of small-scale agriculture and presents

a rather one-sided view of the French rural scene. If half the French land is farmed on a larger scale and presumably more efficiently, then how does the smallholding not only continue to exist but increase in numbers whilst competing with large-scale units? Either, as Marx suggests, the smallholding is sufficiently self-supporting to be able to ignore the market for agricultural products, or it is sufficiently efficient, perhaps due to specialization, to compete. This question must be examined, and in doing so it might be wise to avoid, as in the preceding analysis of industrial development, generalizations concerning the whole of France.

Large farms existed especially in the north and north-west, in Normandy, Picardy, the Ile de France, the valleys of the Loire and Seine, the Nivernais and Languedoc and the basin of the Garonne. They were far less common in the east, in Brittany, the Massif Central, Alpine region and Pyrenees. To highlight the importance of variation it is worthwhile to consider the differences between large- and small-scale agriculture rather on the basis of regions containing both than on a national level. To do this two areas which have been the subject of detailed study have been selected and the analysis which follows will follow closely that of the historians involved.[45]

First the work of Christianne Marcilhacy, which considers the department of Loiret in 1850. She divides it according to natural divisions into five parts: the Beauce, in the north-west of the department covering 21 per cent of its area is rich land, at this time specializing in cereal production, where, if in each canton there were a small number of large farms, the average was 20 hectares worked by a peasant proprietor and his family with the aid of migrant labour during the harvest. This peasant was relatively wealthy both in terms of area of land owned and of its product, and moreover concerned himself with the improvement of his land, for example with the use of fertilizers.

The second area, that of the forest of Orléans, was obviously different in character, excluding almost entirely peasant property. What existed was backward due to the isolation of the few peasant communities. Similarly the Gâtinais Orléanais, less densely forested but with inadequate cultivated land for its population and a large proportion of propertyless labourers and others owning a small piece of land which required that they find another occupation to supplement the income from it.

Crossing the department is the Val de Loire where parcellation had been taken to an extreme, with most holdings having less than two hectares. Here there were few landless labourers and in spite of the small size of the holdings the proprietors, engaged primarily in vine growing, enjoyed, at least in 1850, a high degree of prosperity.

The last division of Loiret was part of the area known as the Sologne, covering 18 per cent of the department, an area of sandy heath and woodland interspersed with lakes. This was primarily an area of large property but used as much for hunting as cultivation due to the poorness of the soil. The few peasant proprietors and the larger number of sharecroppers and labourers enjoyed very poor standards of life, although under the Second Empire drainage of the marshes and the improvement of communications was to lead to a substantial improvement.

This department might serve as a prime example of variation due essentially to geographical factors, but also it must be emphasized to inadequate communications restricting the spread of new ideas and techniques and limiting agriculture except in the Beauce largely to subsistence farming. The Beauce provided an example of a flourishing agriculture created by good soil, relatively good communications providing access to markets and ideas, and the will to apply these ideas, the desire not simply to extend the area of land owned but to improve the fertility of this land. The difference in farming techniques and life between the Beauce and Sologne was extreme but highlights the variations within a social group commonly labelled peasants.

The study of the Alpine Region by Philippe Vigier provides added material for this emphasis on differences within the agricultural sector and for a subsequent definition of the social groups present.

The area concerned, covering the departments of the Hautes and Basses-Alpes, Drôme, Isère and Vaucluse was supremely agricultural, with in 1851 73 per cent of the active population engaged in agriculture. Here medium and small-sized property dominated but with large farms important especially in the low country.

In this latter area there was evidence of a process even further developed in Flanders, namely the development of commercial agriculture. Production was not for local needs but for urban markets with crops of wheat, silk, garance and vines, supplying in particular Marseille and Lyon. The size of productive units was relatively large and techniques advanced. The number of peasant proprietors was relatively small compared with the number of labourers, share-croppers, renting farmers and mixtures of these. This development

B

was not due simply to geographical factors but to good communications and large markets which not only demanded particular crops but also supplied the capital necessary for the application of improved farming techniques. In the lowland area of the Alpine Region the farmer was, as the industrialist, dependent on the workings of supply and demand, and was subject to all the consequent uncertainty.

Ignoring a middle zone of hills and plateaux of general transition, the highland area is especially worth considering. Here existed the indebted, impoverished peasant, here existed the extremes of parcellation described by Marx. This was the economy of the eighteenth century. Production was not specialized but was a poly-culture designed to supply the needs of the producer and local population, with a maximum amount of cultivation, almost in spite of the soils, because of continued fear of famine.

For the peasant or labourer in such an area the only means of improving both security and standards of existence would be through the purchase of land and Vigier estimates that between 1826 and 1848 the number of holdings assessed for the land tax increased by 22·4 per cent, that is by about 1 per cent per year.[46]

Parcellation occurred through the purchase of large farms by urban speculators and their subdivision into small lots which could easily be sold at a relatively high price in an area of rural overpopulation. In contrast to Marx's account of the impoverishment of agriculture the Chamber of Commerce at Vaucluse reported in 1835 that agricultural standards were continually improving largely because of the sub-division of the land which, in making small proprietors of former labourers, gave them the will to work. Furthermore the general conclusion of Vigier, in the sense that the large estates subdivided were normally those worst cultivated, and that subdivision therefore contributed to the improvement of agriculture in many cases, especially where the small-holders tended to follow the example of rich scientific farmers, is worthy of consideration, but this latter is true rather of the lowlands than of the isolated mountainous region, deprived, as the Sologne, of both ideas and markets and as part of a vicious circle, of the capital to be derived largely from production for the market.

In the lowlands a commercial, money economy supplied the peasant or labourer with the resources to purchase land. In the mountains often the initial purchase sum or even the payments spread over a long period could be acquired only from the local moneylender and this person in a backward region was of social and political importance. But indebtedness is often a reflection of increasing prosperity – the initial will to borrow and the presumed ability to maintain the repayments at a high rate of interest reflects both confidence in the future and an existing pecuniary surplus once the bare needs of subsistence have been provided for. Vigier's account of the period of the July Monarchy supports this.[47] However, if economic conditions change and expectations are not fulfilled the existence of debt will worsen an already possibly miserable situation. It is possible that Marx generalized from the experience of sections of the French agricultural community at a particular period, namely the crisis period from 1846, whilst we have here opposed a generalization based on a more prosperous era. Again variation, on this occasion over a limited period of time, but which indicates that parcellation could mean increased prosperity and with improved communications and crop specialization would benefit many smallholders whilst impoverishing and eliminating many others.[48]

One last fact must be stated concerning the Alpine mountain areas and indeed all areas of intense parcellation. Many small proprietors were forced to earn part of their living as agricultural labourers, or even in industry, often domestic in nature. In the particular region under consideration and other isolated areas seasonal migration was extensive. Equally significant was a dependence on common land and forest rights providing pasture for animals and building and heating materials. It was the assault on these traditional rights, and the decline in the opportunities for domestic or migratory labour as industrial production became more mechanized and required a permanent labour force, and later the slow mechanization of agriculture, that above all else created rural poverty, this, rather than parcellation, which was one of a number of variables in the peasants' economic situation. Before the changes in the other variables listed above, parcellation probably contributed to increased prosperity in the countryside. With these changes many smallholders found themselves forced to rely on a landholding inadequate to provide for a family's existence. In time permanent migration was to result along a pattern already prevalent in the department of the Nord where industrial development both absorbed surplus agricultural labour and helped create that surplus.

Marx is guilty of excessive generalization and simplification concerning such factors as parcellation and the misery it caused, which might obviously lead to the misinterpretation of a specific historical situation. More especially he understimates the complexity of an agricultural economy, a complexity which the above regional descriptions were intended to emphasize. On the basis of these, what generalizations can be made to effectively compare with Marx's?

According to one contemporary self-affirmed Marxist historian there was in 1848 not one class of peasantry but a number of classes.[49] Rural society varied between the capitalist exploitation of the Nord with its polarization, at least in relative terms, between the large-scale proprietor or farmer and the agricultural labourer, and the masses of small proprietors found in the Alpine mountains. In between these two extremes the variations are countless. All we can do is list the social groups continually present and assert that the social structure of various areas will provide numerous variations in the relative proportions of each of the social groups present.

To take first the peasantry, difficult to define precisely, but including certainly all the owners of less than ten hectares and most of those owning land earlier classified as medium in extent, particularly in the latter case if we accept Vigier's delineation which ascribes to property which is neither owned by aristocrats nor peasants the title of bourgeois property and clarifies this by adding that by bourgeois he means the inhabitants of an urban settlement most of whose revenue is derived from a non-agricultural profession.[50] This accords also with our emphasis on the importance of style of life as an element in the definition of social groups. Peasants were then the poverty stricken smallholders of the Sologne, the far more wealthy vignerons of the Loire Valley whose holdings were even smaller, the peasants of the Alpine highlands whose standard of life was somewhere between these but whose environment and problems were totally different. Peasants also were many of those involved in commercial agriculture in the valleys of the Alpine region with all the significance of their attachment to capitalist development. Peasants were the prosperous farmers of the Beauce and the far less prosperous if often more large-scale farmers of the west.

It is impossible to agree with Soboul's division of the peasantry into a relatively rich and a poor peasantry, particularly with his emphasis on regional nuances.[51] Additionally it must be agreed that in the course of agricultural development the rich tended to strengthen their position whilst the struggle for continued existence as peasant landowners by the poor became increasingly more difficult and less successful. According to a contemporary estimate by the agronomist Joigneaux there were 980,000 materially comfortable peasants and 4,150,000 poor in the late 1840s.[52]

It was the rich peasant and non-peasant proprietor who supported the movement towards the enclosure of common land and the protection of the forests from over-use, the poor, dependent on their common rights and on the traditional rights in the forest, who opposed these existing tendencies on the basis of custom and an ideal of the future, but essentially from necessity.

This then might be considered as a vital factor to be retained for further development. At least in economic terms it might be argued that social conservatism is a product of the individual's belief in continued and increasing prosperity, radicalism a product of discontent expressing itself in either a defensive or more aggrandizing manner. This is the significance of Marx's distinction between the conservative and revolutionary peasant, and Soboul's between the rich and the poor. The latter corrects or at best develops an element only implicit in the former. But if economic variation can be reduced to these two basic terms – rich and poor, and possible behavioural tendencies advanced from these this is to ignore the total environment within which both rich and poor exist, and in accepting the significance of total environment we admit extreme regional variation again. This is something which can only be fully discussed in the context of socio-political development in the period under discussion. Here we can only go on to observe the existence of other, non-peasant social groups within the rural scene which might influence peasant behaviour and exert a considerable socio-political influence themselves; but again the extent and nature of this influence must be left for subsequent discussion, and we proceed with a mere enumeration of these factors of rural life.

Consider first the ownership of the largest of estates. It has been estimated that of the 387 tax payers assessed for over 5,000 francs in 77 departments 266 were nobles or had pretensions to nobility in 1840.[53] This group, part of that element of the population labelled by A. J. Tudesq '*les grands notables*', was the leading element of an aristocracy fairly clearly definable by way of life and social psychology. The great notabilities for Tudesq were those whose wealth, social functions and prestige gave them an influence over the development of national life. Less significant nationally but important locally were the other proprietors with large estates (i.e. over 40 hectares). It might generally be said that these were all either aristocrats or members of the urban bourgeoisie. In 1862 there were 154,167 such large landholdings.[54] Assuming that these belonged sometimes to the same people and in the proportion of 100 holdings per sixty people,[55] then there were about 92,500 owners of large (in the relative sense) estates. To sub-divide these into bourgeois or aristocratic ownership is impossible, as it is to calculate what part of the medium-sized estates belonged to aristocrats or urban bourgeoisie or peasants. Although many of these estates were bought for the purpose of investment and to gain the prestige attached to ownership of land it is worthwhile re-emphasizing that the large estates were often centres for agricultural progress where farmed in part by the owner himself. The dominance of agricultural improvement societies by large land-owners, often, from the period of the July Monarchy, by aristocrats who had withdrawn from political life on the inception of the new regime, is evidence of this.

The last major element involved in the rural scene was the small market town or village, and here particularly those groups normally labelled middle and petty bourgeois – the doctor, veterinary, notary, innkeeper, school teacher, minor official or artisan. These were often the sources of ideas, they had the prestige of education and posses-sions. Their economic role is indicated by their function, except for the fact that the usurer too was usually bourgeois and often the notary. The significance of these and particularly of the usurer will become clear as we consider the development of the Second Republic. It will differ between areas according to urban development and variations of social structure.

The rural scene was changing – but only slowly. As with industry, communications and capital were the vital factors – accessibility to ideas and markets, the financing of improvement. As with industry, change began to be noticeable during the July Monarchy but with the most significant developments occurring only under the Second Empire and even then the routine of rural life strongly resisted change. The transition from a self-sufficient to a market economy took a long time, its major features included the application of science to agriculture, the introduction of machines or on a lower level of the scythe to replace the sickle, the replacement of subsistence farming producing a small surplus for the local market by specialized com-mercial farming. Different areas were affected to differing extents but these trends were all in favour of the richer exploiter of the land.

During the Second Empire the emigration of the poorest peasant proprietors and of the surplus labourers tended to become permanent and for the first time an adequate industrial labour force began to come into existence. Yet the powers of resistance of the French peasant were great and through slow improvement of cultivation, and deliberate limitation of the size of his family, he sought to maintain himself. The most significant thing about French social development between 1840 and 1870 was the lack of change in social structure. If industrialization involves sectorial re-location, that is a shift from agricultural to non-agricultural activities, then the census of 1872 which reveals 68·94 per cent of the population to be rural, compared with 75·58 per cent in 1846, indicates only slow change.[56] Of equal significance perhaps is another conclusion of this census report which claimed that 62·89 of the total active population had some form of property however unimportant, some sort of material stake in the existing society.[57] Marx exaggerated the necessity for the decline in numbers of the smallholding peasantry under economic pressure and possibly also its growing will for revolutionary social change, but that is another question. Marx simplified, or ignored the problem of distinctions within the French industrial working class and the significance of regional variations in rural life and social structure, though correctly emphasized the significance of communications for rural life. Essentially Marx exaggerated the pace of industrial and agricultural change though not consistently and often only implicitly. Whether he did or not seems to have depended on whether at a particular moment he had hopes for a new revolutionary outbreak or whether his analysis required an explanation of the failure of revolution to occur.

In the latter case he turned to a viewpoint later to be more clearly expressed in the first volume of *Capital*, namely that 'the transformation of the individual and scattered means of production into socially concentrated means of production, the transformation of the pygmy property of the many into the titan property of the few, the expropriation of the great masses of the people from the land, from the means of subsistence, and from the instruments of labour ... comprises the prelude to the history of capital,'[58] and to revolution. This concentration had most certainly not occurred in France. Marx was aware of this but emphasized the significance of the elements for change in French economic development. The statistical review in this chapter suggests that his emphasis was exaggerated.

Under consideration from this point will be factors which 'reveal themselves much less through statistical documentation than through the observation of human behaviour, carried on over a long period, or in the favourable conditions offered by a political revolution, especially where accompanied by an economic crisis,'[59] i.e. a period of social tension, ideal for the laying bare of men's deepest hopes, ambitions and fears, for the revealing of the various facets of social psychology.

II

Condition of a Society: 1847

Ruling Circles

The simplest characterization of the regime which ruled France from 1830 to 1848 is found in *The Eighteenth Brumaire of Louis Bonaparte* where in discussing the royalists during the Second Republic Marx writes that 'One section, the large landowners, had ruled during the Restoration and was accordingly Legitimist. The other, the aristocrats of finance and big industrialists, had ruled during the July Monarchy and was consequently Orleanist', adding that 'The high dignitaries of the army, the university, the church, the bar, the academy and of the press were to be found on either side, though in various proportions.'[1]

The general picture gained from his essays is of a regime constantly in financial difficulties and dependent consequently on the providers of credit, on the great financiers.[2] This was the bourgeois monarchy although 'it was not the French bourgeoisie that ruled under Louis-Philippe, but one faction of it: bankers, stock-exchange kings, railway kings, owners of coal and iron mines and forests, a part of the landed proprietors associated with them – the so-called finance aristocracy'.[3] Here the notion of the financier is given a far broader meaning and seems to include the wealthiest members of society, those most prominent in economic life. Indeed as Marx proceeds to add, the industrial bourgeoisie proper were part of the official opposition[4] and this due to the relative underdevelopment of French industry producing a situation in which 'French industry does not dominate French production; the French industrialists, therefore, do not dominate the French bourgeoisie.'[5]

This was the rule of the wealthy who had created a regime through which their interests, and above all the facilities necessary for the creation of wealth were protected and provided. It was tainted for

Marx with the smell of corruption, of oppression and of exploitation.

The Marxian picture is one that has been acceptable to many historians, and was that of many contemporaries. De Tocqueville likened the July Monarchy to an 'industrial company all of whose operations are designed to benefit the shareholders.'[6]

According to Marx political power and the social influence, which is an essential part of it, are based on economic power, on the material and financial resources controlled by the ruling group in society. It is possible therefore to begin by considering the elements of economic power and whether in fact social power more generally was based on these.

Emphasis was placed in the last chapter on the significance of regional variations in economic development, on the existence of a large number of fairly distinct societies within France. In line with this it is the sources of local power as a pre-requisite for national power which will first be considered.

The basic idea behind this approach is the view that at a local level the great landowners dominated the smaller, the tenants and agricultural labourers; the manufacturer and merchant, his employees; that power was conferred by possessions. These two possessing groups had a conscious aim, namely to preserve and extend their possessions and way of life. Wealth conferred upon them the privilege of access to leisure, to education, to ideas and to easy organization. Organization and a conscious purpose made the exercise of repression possible. Wealth also conferred prestige in the eyes of the other social groups which shared in the possession of material goods and in the awareness of the benefits of this and which tended to subordinate jealousy to respect, though this might vary – respect increasing with the felt need for the protection of possessions. The less wealthy were often in addition directly clients of the more wealthy, as in the obvious case of shopkeepers.

In a society based upon private property the fundamental threat to the stability of social structure must come from those to whom property has come to seem unattainable, but only when this notion is coupled with the belief that the existing social structure is not eternal and when an ideal exists which might serve as a basis for organization due to shared assumptions. Without an ideal, protest if it occurred could only be limited, both in respect of the numbers involved in it and in its aims. It could only seek improvement of material conditions within the existing society, without directly threatening its power structure. The July Monarchy was an epoch in which conscious purpose and the effective wielding of power was the preserve of the wealthy and declined an intensity as the constituent elements of society grew less wealthy. It was an epoch in which because of the limits to economic development and especially to that of communications the personal influence of the wealthy individual was a vitally important power factor within the area in which his wealth was known, and from which it was derived. Additionally, if the social attitudes of the wealthy and of the educated – and for many of the latter wealth was only relative compared with the absence of possession amongst the poor – tend to be in a general manner national, the growth of opposition to their social domination amongst the masses in our period occurred essentially on a local level and more significantly occurred in some locales and not in others, for reasons which can only be explained by consideration of regional factors.

The most obvious means of considering in whose hands local power lay is first to look at the structure of the Chamber of Deputies. This will reveal some significant facts concerning the social structure of French society during the July Monarchy taking into account of course the limited franchise, which is in itself indicative of a social hierarchy, of the power of the privileged to maintain this hierarchy and of the inability of other social groups to oppose it.

A recent study of the social composition of the Chamber of Deputies after the election of 1846 reveals that of consistent government supporters 36 per cent were nobles or had pretensions to nobility, and 15 per cent were *grande bourgeoisie*, that is great financiers or industrialists, 25 per cent were less wealthy urban bourgeoisie and 20 per cent rural bourgeoisie. The percentages for the non-Legitimist opposition are different in respect of the larger proportion of bourgeoisie of all kinds but especially urban bourgeoisie included within it, but in 1846 the Chamber was substantially pro-government.[7] The very level of the requisite qualifications for candidature made it essential that candidates be men of relative wealth. More significant, though, is the fact that in 1846 84 per cent of the deputies were elected by less than 400 votes.[8] An election in such conditions must obviously be different from that involving a mass electorate and must clearly depend to a large extent on personal contacts and influences.

This political aspect of social existence is revealing of society as a

33

whole. The representatives of an area in both the Chamber and in the departmental council were generally representatives of a small group of men with wealth, the most influential of whom have been labelled by Tudesq '*les grands notables*' and the totality of whom were the notables, notable because of the factors which distinguished them from the masses, these including wealth and ownership of land, or occupation as a functionary or a member of the liberal professions. A simple distinguishing feature is that the notable did not work with his hands.

Political conflict, where the politically involved were limited by law and illiteracy, tended to be between personalities rather than about politics, at least outside the large cities where a more numerous electorate made it essential to appeal to ideals as well as interests, and some localities where the conflict between the aristocracy and other notables labelled bourgeoise continued and ideals of monarchy and Church were brought into play, though not, it must be noticed, basic concepts of society.

If the notables in rural areas, and this means most of France, possessed one common characteristic it was ownership of land. In this respect at least at the local level and in respect of the deputies elected in 1846 the term 'bourgeoisie' is something of a misnomer if it is defined, as it does tend to be in Marxist theory, in terms of the urban capitalist. If the bourgeoisie dominated Orleanist France, and even this cannot be taken for granted, it should be noted that of government supporters in the Chamber only 25 per cent are categorized as urban by the Higonnets. Similarly, when Tudesq considered the background of 85 presidents of *conseils généraux* he found that if 32 were functionaries or former functionaries, 14 lawyers, 15 merchants, bankers or industrialists, and only 22 landed proprietors without other occupation, then all 85 owned land and 21 were nobles.[9]

This is interesting proof of the prestige of land, a not surprising fact given the prevalent psychology in a society based upon private property in which wealth and escape from the harshness of existence was relative essentially to the amount of land owned and the hope of all was to share or increase one's share in this ownership. Christianne Marcilhacy's study of the diocese of Orléans, and numerous other local studies like that of Vigier, or André Armengaud's work on the overwhelmingly agricultural departments of the Ariège, Haute-Garonne, Tarn, Tarn-et-Garonne[10] all reveal this prestige of the land; even where in the Alpine region considered by Vigier the wealthiest landowners were relatively impoverished, they retained at this stage the respect of their even more impoverished small-holding fellows. As in the eighteenth century, the sign of success whether in industry, commerce or the liberal professions was the transference of much, if not most, of the wealth acquired into the form of land.

On a more general basis, but again emphasizing the importance of possession, A. J. Tudesq observes that, 'What makes a notable is above all possession, the *grand notable* has goods, has knowledge, has contacts, has a family, has a function which gives him public authority, either through delegation of power if he is a magistrate or an official, or by election; he has a name and often a title, he is notable because of what he has.'[11] Marcilhacy emphasizes possession of land, and in a society where secondary education costs money, this other element of prestige can only belong to the possessors, and so consequently must the administration.

It is safe to conclude on the basis of political representation and social prestige that at the local level the dominant social group was that which owned sufficient land to avoid manual labour. If it can tentatively be asserted from the lack of effective opposition to the regime that almost all substantial landowners were quite satisfied with the existing society. If it can be asserted that the prestige of land was such that even in an industrial city like Lyon an analysis of declarations after death shows that an individual's wealth, however made, tended to be invested more and more in real estate as it increased,[12] and similarly for Paris, although as the size of a city increased the real estate would, except for the very wealthy, take the form of urban land or buildings. This then all indicates that at a local level in rural France, as Philippe Vigier suggests, the term 'notable' might be more usefully used to describe the dominating social group than either noble or bourgeois. As our subsequent study of group ideology and its development will show more clearly, the funda-mental division in the countryside was that between wealth and poverty, both terms being used in a relative sense, between notables and people. Indeed this was recognized by the law where electoral rights were attached to wealth and where conscription could be avoided by the purchase of a replacement, and in practice by the fact that only wealth could buy the secondary education essential for social significance. At this local, rural level at any rate it was

35

the landowner, whatever his accessory label, who was dominant.

Tudesq also concludes that the dominance of notables is typical of a society in which large cities are rare, and where prominent person-alities are generally known and their various functions frequently given recognition,[13] but slowly France was industrializing, and hence it is necessary to consider to what extent the social hierarchy in large urban centres, more divorced from the countryside, was different.

In Alsace and particularly the more industrialized arrondissements of Altkirch and Colmar, the influence of a new type of notable, the industrialist was clearly evident both in the paternalistic management of enterprises, clearly evincing the subordination of the labour forces, and in the continued collaboration of the administration with the relatively small number of families, who closely interrelated, directed economic activity.[14] By contrast, in Lille the leading industrial figures seem to have renounced socio-political leadership for the more limited concerns of industrial profitability, giving far more leeway to lesser figures mainly occupied in the liberal professions.[15] Addition-ally, and this was true of almost all industrial areas with the exception of those of Alsace, outside the towns there existed regions of large-scale landholding with the result that regional political leadership went rather to the landowner than the industrialist, a further reflection of social values. Alsace, by comparison, was dominated agriculturally by smallholdings, resulting in a lack of competition for the political power of the industrial patriciate.

If the political significance of the industrial bourgeoisie was generally limited at this local level it should not be forgotten that as an employer the social significance of the capitalist was great in partly determining the conditions of existence and social activity of the urban masses.

Even so, his abstention from politics and his often relatively low standard of wealth and life as a notable in a society in which hierarchy was based upon wealth, reduced the industrialist or merchant usually to the role of campfollower of the landowner particularly where, as in the North, their material interests coincided, and the land-owner as a sugar-beet producer, demanded protective customs dues.

As for the administration at a local level it is generally true to say that it could do little or nothing without the support, or at least failure to oppose, of the local notables. Indeed coming from the same broad social group, the only social group which at this time was national in character, with shared interests and a way of life, it had little impulse to impose its views. This was only possible and desirable where the conflict of local personalities necessitated the re-imposition of a sense of direction or of stability in local politics.[16]

Lyon itself illustrates the conclusion to be made at this point concerning the dominance by landowners both of the electorate numerically, and of the social psychology. C. Aboucaya, basing himself on declarations after death, has constructed a chart of the social hierarchy in Lyon during the July Monarchy.[17] With relation to this it must be observed that of bankers' fortunes 20·05 per cent were held in real estate; of very great commercial figures 43·54 per cent; of industrialists 52·62 per cent. For these last two business premises are undoubtedly included, but land remains significant. Senior military officers and state officials additionally retained their fortunes primarily in land.

Aboucaya's definition of the Lyon social hierarchy is as follows. The figures relate to average fortunes:

Over 1,000,000 francs	Very great proprietors-rentiers
	Bankers
	Very great merchants
Between 500,000 and 1,000,000 francs	Great proprietors-rentiers
	Industrialists
100,000 and 500,000 francs	The most senior government officials
	Medium proprietor-rentiers
	Great merchants
10,000 and 100,000 francs	Liberal Professions
	Medium merchants
	Military officers
	High clergy
	Senior government officials
2,000 and 10,000 francs	Small merchants
	Small proprietors
	Artisans
	Servants
	Junior government officials
100 and 2,000 francs	Workers
	Parish priests
	Soldiers

If in defining hierachy less quantifiable factors are taken into account, the above might be changed somewhat. The general way of life would essentially be related to wealth, but various individuals with the prestige and influence of high office in the state administration, army or church or distinction in the liberal professions, or even less tangible family background might be able in practice to accede to the highest ranks of the hierarchy to which their wealth would not obviously fit them. In a country divided into a number of local societies wealth was a relative factor, at any rate on this local level. The notable of the mountain arrondissement, so-called due to the size of his land-holding and wealth compared with that of his peasant neighbours, was only the poor country cousin of the landowners engaged for instance in commercial agriculture in northern France. The relative security given by a certain degree of possession, as compared with the everyday struggle for existence of the worker and peasant, divided society into two. Security was a sign of the bourgeois, however little his wealth might be compared with that of the great financier. The attitude of bourgeois groups to political reform can be taken as a fair representation of their place within the bourgeois hierarchy, their liberalism increasing with the lowliness of their place. But common to them all was the view that only success identified by possessions and the avoidance of manual labour gave the right to play a political role. Towards the masses liberalism turned into conservatism.

In Lyon as Paris, the premier cities of France, the social hierarchy was a function of wealth[18] and in the 1840s wealth, economic power, was still mainly the product of land ownership, increasingly less so perhaps, but if the economic significance of land was declining relative to that of industry its prestige remained to an extent that made land ownership the sign of success even for the industrialist. Success meant the assimilation by the industrial and financial bourgeosie of the way of life and much of the social mentality of the landed nobility; more accurately a process of mutual assimilation occurred.

If local independence was substantially due to poor communications, if the basis of individual power and influence was local then his power was used in urban surroundings, above all in Paris. It was the manner in which this power was used that Marx sought to characterize. It might be possible to assert as he did that power was wielded in the interests of financiers and great industrialists if the influence of these can be shown to have exceeded their numerical and even economic power as a fraction of the ruling élite, if in fact there was a partial divorce between the main initial source of authority, making men ministers and deputies, namely land ownership, and the objective of most of these landowners and presumably of the men who elected them – the safeguarding and increasing of wealth of all kinds. At first glance indeed this might appear possible in a society structured on a traditional manner, but subject to increasingly rapid change.

It is necessary to concern ourselves, therefore, with the practical activity of the governing circles at a national level, and not simply with this but with the authority of government, the extent to which its decisions were accepted or rejected in the country, its power to win acceptance and as part of this the forces of opposition. This has already been dealt with substantially in emphasizing the shared interests of the wealthy at a local level.

To Marx's characterization of the use of power at a national level, certain factors give support, above all the apparent bourgeois domination of government, using this word as it was used contemporaneously to describe the non-aristocratic wealthy, men with a certain manner of life, a manner indeed above that of the penny-pinching habits of most manufacturers. De Tocqueville complained that from 1830 this group ruled to the exclusion of all others.[19] Balzac in many of his novels echoed the complaint.

The July Monarchy began with a government led by a banker, Laffitte, to be succeeded by another banker, Casimir Perier, and Louis Philippe, praised and condemned as the bourgeois monarch for his style of life, if not for his imperious desire to rule, consistantly chose ministers from among the *grande bourgeoisie* or the intellectuals accepted through their success and wealth as part of it.

Tudesq provides us with the professional structure of the Chamber of Deputies in 1840. Of a total of 459 deputies, there were 137 proprietors without other professions, although most had at one time or another had a profession, 175 functionaries, 87 members of the liberal professions, 73 men of law, 60 involved in the economic professions including 10 bankers, 19 engaged in manufacture including 7 in metallurgy and 7 in textiles, and 31 merchants, some of whom were also engaged in some form of industry.[20]

Most of these deputies were bourgeoisie, but of the landowning type. This Marx allows for. What might seem more to falsify his analysis is the large proportion of state officials and lawyers, the

39

famous elements of corruption within the Chamber providing a base for monarchical independence. The recent work of the Higonnets has however thrown some additional light on this. In the first place the social origins of officials, particularly in an age when high officials were insufficiently payed to live from this alone, at the standard which was expected from them, could only be similar to that of the remainder of the Chamber, they being essentially landed proprietors. Further, it is shown that over one-third of these senior bureaucrats were magistrates and their voting behaviour in the Chamber, although no doubt subject to government pressure, was so to a surprisingly limited extent in that it was essentially the same as that of lawyers, and reveals therefore a voting pattern according to membership of a socio-professional group rather than government corruption.

A further conclusion which emphasizes the landed character of the Chamber of 1846 is that the great majority of deputies had no contact with the business world,[21] but this gives an impression which certain conclusions reached by Tudesq correct and here it is useful to follow his analysis carefully.

First, that the Chamber of Deputies was unrepresentative even of the narrow electorate, and this was obviously possible due to the higher tax qualification essential for a candidate. The assembly was a homogeneous grouping with certain limited exceptions and this the sterility of political debate and paucity of political ideas serves to prove. Argument revolved around personalities, conflict was between 'ins' and 'outs', and the main concern of deputies was to represent the local interests of which their own personal concerns were an example. The only portion of the electorate to which they had to answer for their acts were their peers at the summit of the local social hierarchy. Often officials or lawyers resident in Paris were allowed by these dominating figures to serve as representatives of their interests, acting on the assumption that their continued closeness to the centre of power would permit a more successful serving of local interests.

The prime example of conflict of interest was that over customs duties and this was particularly revealing as it took the form not of conflict between social groups but economic interest groups, uniting for example wine producers and silk spinners on the one hand, desirous of extending external markets, against on the other, iron masters, cereal growers and stock breeders demanding a protected home market. As most deputies and peers had agricultural interests, there was thus a majority in favour of protection and this included both aristocratic and bourgeois landowners.

Legislative and administrative activity during the July Monarchy showed however a marked concern for the interests not simply of the landowners who formed the majority of the Chamber but for financial and industrial interests. Consider for example the favourable terms offered in railway financing, or the particularly blatant example described by Bertrand Gille involving the financial difficulties of the Société des Mines de la Grand Combe in 1837. This company was temporarily saved by a state loan of six million francs voted by the Chamber on the intervention of Marshal Soult and Odillon Barrot. This intervention reveals something of the mentality of the Chamber in that it was known that both these men had extensive financial interests in the company in question.[22] The regime's generally repressive reaction to the strikes and attempts at organization by industrial workers or artisans seeking to protect their interests was again indicative of a certain attitude favourable to industrial entrepreneurs.

There are signs then of the influence on government of those groups mentioned by Marx – 'bankers, stock-exchange kings, railway kings, owners of coal and iron mines and forests' seemingly not proportionate to their limited presence in the Chamber.

This fact reflects the growing importance of industry and the growing social emphasis on wealth in all its forms. The landowner was increasingly interested in industrial activity, whether he be aristocratic and bound by tradition in his socio-political ideals or bourgeois. The example of the landowner exploiting the coal and iron resources or the forests found on his land was fairly common. Tudesq has examined the composition of the boards of administration of fifteen of the largest limited companies at this time – 7 assurance, 5 railway, 1 road transport, 1 coal mining, 1 canal, in all 165 individuals of whom 37·7 per cent were bankers or great merchants, 10·3 per cent manufacturers, 24·4 per cent landed proprietors, 15·7 per cent functionaries and 10·9 per cent members of the liberal professions.[23] This reveals an involvement of landowners, officials and lawyers in the growing sphere of finance and industry and helps to explain the support for the interests of this sphere in governing circles. The world of politics, administration and economic life was in fact the preserve of a narrow circle sharing similar interests and attitudes and cooperating to develop these. The cohesiveness of the small body of men interested in and capable of increasing their wealth in all economic spheres evinced in their strenuous defence of their interests, above all of protection, made them one of the few forces in politics which when united on a specific issue, as against the proposed customs union with Belgium, forced the government to accede to their wishes.

As Marx emphasized, the great financiers benefitted much from interest on loans to the government. It is obvious that where a government as the July Monarchy often found itself with a deficit, and where continued business confidence was a vital factor in maintaining prosperity then it had to pay some attention to the providers of capital, although the extent of this was limited by the divisions amongst the bankers. And not only the government was dependent for capital on a small number of great financiers, but the whole economic world.

Stendhal considered the relations of the bankers with the regime, and their leading role in the economy generally and wrote – 'the banks are masters of the state. The bourgeois has replaced the Faubourg Saint-Germain, and the bank is the aristocracy of the bourgeois class.' This leading role is borne out by an estimate of Gille's, bearing on the participation of the Paris House of Rothschild in railway investment up to February, 1848. He warns that the figures include sums invested by the Rothschilds on behalf of clients, but even so these figures evince the role of one man, or one family in French economic life.[24]

Railway Company	Rothschild Subscription	Total
Paris–Strasbourg	7,000,000	125,000,000
Bordeaux–Cette	3,275,000	140,000,000
Paris–Lyon	5,000,000	200,000,000
Creil–Saint-Quentin	15,250,000	30,000,000
Lyon–Avignon	2,750,000	150,000,000
Avignon–Marseilles	2,000,000	20,000,000
Nord	51,349,000	200,000,000
	86,624,000	865,000,000

Effective control, that is, of 10 per cent of the total investment in these companies. This seems almost to justify Marx's description of Guizot as serving to unconsciously 'barter away piecemeal the whole of the French state and the whole of French society to the financial sharks of the Paris Bourse'.[25]

It might also seem to emphasize the subordination of the vast majority of Frenchmen involved in economic life to the few controlling figures, and as far as economic development was concerned, if international competition helped shape its essentials, the role of these financiers in determining the rate and form of investment was significant. Georges Duveau described Marx's distinction between an industrial and financial bourgeoisie as *tranchante*, given the former's resentment of the economic authority of the latter,[26] and indeed if the concentration of industrial production had not proceeded far in Paris and in France then the concentration of financial power had, and this to a certain extent provided for the co-ordination of investment through the activity of a small number of powerful men. It should, however, be remembered that if most manufacturers resented the power of the great financiers, the greatest industrialists were often deeply involved in finance and vice versa – here the examples of the Delesserts, Periers and of Schneider are significant. This in a sense increased the power of the financiers in including within their select circle the most serious competitors for markets with whom the great mass of French manufacturers had to contend. In another respect, too, Marx appears correct, in indicating the resentment felt by most manufacturers of government fiscal policy. Responses to the enquiry made by the 'Association pour la défense du travail national' in Alsace in June, 1848, and published by Mme Kahen-Rabecq indicate the feeling that taxation was too high and priced French goods out of foreign markets.

Whatever the influence at particular moments of the great financiers our attention must return at the national as at the local level to the significance of land. The very council of the Bank of France illustrates this, being composed to a large extent of men who were great landowners. Tudesq has calculated that of the 512 richest men in France assessed for taxation purposes at over 5,000 frs, 377 were exclusively landed proprietors, only 45 were bankers or merchants and 26 industrialists. The proportion of landowners, as part of the total, increased with wealth, until of those assessed at 15,000 frs, 13 were landowners, with one each of bankers and industrialists. Marx is never clear concerning where power lay in French society during the July Monarchy. If, as we have largely assumed, and as will be further emphasized later, political power was based on regional economic power then the source of power remained the land, and to this as dominantly represented in the administration and the Chamber the great financiers must bow or rather associate themselves.

43

Tudesq reveals a further vital factor in that of these dominating wealthy, of the 512 taxed at over 5,000 frs, 238 were aristocrats and 78 had pretensions to nobility. It must be assumed that a large proportion of these were Legitimists.[27]

If the latter often abstained from politics, thus strengthening the dominance of the 'bourgeoisie', their local land-based political power remained strong. Indeed their withdrawal to their estates must often have strengthened both individual economic strength and social influence in the locality. The way in which, during the Second Republic and in the Versailles Assembly of 1871, this power was to be reactivated is sufficient evidence of their continuing social influence.

It might furthermore be worth considering whether the degree of withdrawal of Legitimists from the administration, army and Chamber might not have been commonly exaggerated in the past. In all, if the open expression of Legitimist political opinions at a national level was limited, the economic and social power of Legitimists remained substantial. It must be presumed that to a large extent they were satisfied with the representation of their vital interests by the 'bourgeois' monarchy.

To associate Legitimism with large landowners and to oppose it to the Orleanism of industry and finance is to misrepresent and oversimplify. The characterization of Legitimacy is correct in highlighting its major body of support, the characterization of committed supporters of the July Monarchy is incorrect in exaggerating the sociopolitical significance of financiers and industrialists, however great individually, in an essentially agricultural society, in which for the period of the Second Republic at least, elements of continuity will continue to dominate elements of change. This fault is perhaps due to an analysis of French society based to a large extent on an analysis of Parisian society. Paris is not, and was not, France.

If the conservative reaction to the February Revolution is to be considered then it is necessary to consider the psychology of the dominant social groups before the revolution, to consider what was the position from which they reacted and additionally to consider the extent of their ideological influence outside their own closely defined circle. Involved in this is a consideration of the elements of mental outlook making for divisions within the dominant group of wealthy men and the basic elements resulting in a degree of unity.

The forms which the expression of ideas took during the July Monarchy will be considered briefly under three basic groupings.

First the official philosophy acceptable to governing circles, then that of the Legitimist opposition, that opposition which in fact was regarded as most dangerous to the survival of the regime, and finally the various forms of republican thought.

In the official view the regime defined itself in terms of liberalism – a parliamentary monarchy, the product of a revolution to end all revolutions which restored to France the gains of the early years of that first revolution begun in 1789 and in eliminating the rule of the senior Bourbon line eliminated also the last barrier to progress, replacing the rule of privilege by that of the élite.

Consider Guizot as a spokesman of the regime. In a speech justifying the existing restrictions on the franchise, made in March, 1847, he assumed that property exemplified worldly success and ability and that those with this proven ability are best suited both to govern and take part in political discussion. This outlook included the belief that those with a material interest in society could best be trusted to guard that society's interests as having most to lose from mistakes, and given their greater ability compared with most of their poorer fellows, it was in the latter's own interest to submit to the rule of the wealthy. A belief, that is, in the natural inequality of men.

The virtues of this world were those which contributed to success – practical cleverness, prudence, order, economy, and regular hard work, virtues which not only resulted in the individual's enrichment but in that of the nation as a whole and which made it fitting that in the chamber of Deputies these interests be represented.

During this period the rich *rentier* living off the profits of investment was relatively uncommon. From the heights of this society, stratified according to wealth, from the great financiers to the small-scale manufacturers involved in a daily competition for markets and existence, the basis of success was hard work. Many, especially of the manufacturers were self-made men wholly committed both materially and mentally to their enterprise. For all of these, hard work had brought tangible rewards, property which must have been valued especially highly because of the struggle its winning normally involved. Inevitable, therefore, a commitment both to private property, to hard work, to the belief that survival in the fierce, competitive struggle of an expanding industry subject to continual crises, was a sign of ability. Commitment also to a pride in family, both in respect of the total family involvement in a business so common in France, and in that at the end of one life the result of hard work

45

would not be wasted, but benefit the entrepreneurs nearest and dearest. These were, and are, the ideals of a society favouring private property, the ideals indeed of strong and able men, of whom it was hoped that additionally they 'would give themselves up to the relief of suffering', to aid those less fortunate, because less able, less virtuous than themselves, who in the ideal society 'would be resigned to the will of God and to the laws of society' and 'would seek in regular and steady work the satisfaction of their needs; in a moral and provident manner of life for the betterment of their lot; in a future promised to man elsewhere for their consolation and their hope'.[28]

This is a vital factor where the strong and able rule, namely their attitude towards the poor, regarded as the unsuccessful, which is commonly dictated by their explanation of this failure in comparison with their own success.

Poverty was explained in moral terms, as the simple absence of the virtues and abilities which had guaranteed success to so many. For pauperism 'is almost always the fault of the worker'. It was not a product of the industrial system or the level of wages but of misconduct.[29] The reply of the commission of the canton of Kayserberg (Haut-Rhin) to the Enquiry of 1848 on industry and agriculture claimed that the more workers were paid the more they took to drink and debauchery instead of saving.[30] The worker was like a child and should consequently be seen and not heard. If his working and living conditions were bad then this was not, according to the prevailing economic philosophy, the responsibility of his employer. If his costs were increased the patron would be unable to sell his goods and the worker would be unemployed, and anyway if wages were increased the results would be only worse debauchery. The response of the canton of Altkirch (Haut-Rhin) to the Enquiry of 1848 stated that in order to improve the conditions of factory workers 'it was less necessary to increase their wages than to reform their morals' to produce habits of 'order and economy'.[31] Habitually the symptoms and causes of poverty were confused.

In this basic ideology the successful businessman justified his success and the means used. Hypocritically the worker was generally regarded as incapable and unequal, yet to justify low wages he was often presented as equal to the patron and able to negotiate a fair wage, or else move elsewhere. This in a period of continued and large-scale unemployment.

The social attitude of the possessing classes and its self-interested-ness can be indicated here in relation to a number of vital questions. Consider first the state.

When legislation to protect child labour was in question, opposition was centred on a concept of the state as unable to interfere in economic life and with the free play of market forces. Yet it was regarded as the state's duty to erect a protective customs barrier around French industry and to secure the investments of great financiers in railways. The state was essentially seen as a gendarme providing the basic conditions of security necessary to individual economic planning. As such its major role was to turn a blind eye to the tacit association of entrepreneurs to further their interests whilst severely repressing any associations of workers similarly designed. Although the famous *loi Le Chapelier* and subsequent legislation prohibited all association designed to interfere with free market forces, the application of this legislation and the obvious willingness of the authorities to provide troops to act as strike breakers if necessary are significant examples of the use of the force of the state directed by members of the possessing classes to aid their fellows.

Significantly the administration rarely saw the causes of strikes as misery or the threat of misery, but blamed them on 'bad' workers or even foreign gold, and exaggerated the danger from associations of workers however insignificant their apparent purpose. Thus the *procureur général* at Rennes in March 1837, reported of an apparently harmless mutual aid society that its long term aim would be 'a universal and simultaneous attack against a social order based on the principle of private property'.[32] Thus any sign of organization by the masses was to be feared.

Two examples of legislation might seem to partially contradict this, the law on child labour of 1841, though this was mild and largely ineffective and the Education Act of 1833. The first was perhaps the product of the real sympathy of the landowners of the Chamber of Deputies, and indication even of the division of interests between the landowning bourgeoisie and those more interested in manufacture. It was little observed, but this increased in time as entrepreneurs realized that a reduction in the working day for all workers by increasing the energy of the labour force increased productivity. It seems to have been observed or not observed according to the manufacturer's definition of his personal interests. In most industrial concentrations the result was similar to that observed by the Prefect of the Nord, who in December 1842 reported that in Lille most of those in positions of responsibility were representative of industrial interests and could not be expected to act in a manner seen as counter to these interests.[33] The inefficacy of voluntary inspection and the limitations of a law which did not apply to workshops and domestic labour, where exploitation was possibly greatest, is evident. The second, although effective in reducing the number of illiterates, was 'class' legislation in the Marxian sense in spite of this. It reflected both the contempt and fear felt by the bourgeoisie for the masses, less of their organized will to resist than of a blind unreasoning violence. It reflected the felt need to civilize the savages.

Guizot, in presenting his primary education bill to the Chamber of Deputies, emphasized its moralizing intent whilst recognizing the danger inherent in the attempt to moralize – 'What is needed is that the general atmosphere of the school should be moral and religious – Take care . . . intellectual development added to moral and religious development is a fine thing, but when it is isolated or separated from moral and religious development it becomes a source of pride, indiscipline and selfishness and is, in consequence, dangerous to society.'[34] That the poor were almost inevitably excluded from secondary education anyway limited the possibility of them enjoying the fruits of education and helped ensure that if an élite ruled its ranks would be made up from the already wealthy.

Conservatives demanded the repression of all ideas which threatened the *status quo* and an attempt to mould men's minds to accept what already existed. The agents of this policy must be the government as gendarme and teacher, as guarantor of social order. In fact for its supporters the July regime represented that liberty which guaranteed order that liberty which permitted only what was compatible with the continuance of the existing social regime, that liberty which excluded both absolutism and democracy, the latter as the rule of mere numbers, the despotism of material passions. These supporters were above all, as we have observed, the landed and industrial or commercial bourgeoisie committed not to a king but to a regime, and who, if often apparently engaged in political conflict, restricted their demands to simple tinkerings with the constitutional framework.

For many of them there was another essential element of social conservatism closely linked to their desire to educate the masses in a moralizing manner, that was religion.

The opinions concerning religion of much of the non-aristocratic possessing classes seem designed almost to illustrate the Marxian concept of religion as a weapon of those interested in social conservatism. The French bourgeoisie, following a period in which Church and State had in alliance attempted to create an authoritarian and aristocratic political and social regime, was profoundly anti-clerical, though of course this is a generalization, and if not anti-religious at least indifferent in personal terms. This is the fairly general opinion of historians and contemporary observers. Consider the views of the rich merchant, Crevel, in Balzac's *Cousin Bette* who, defending himself against suggestions that he be charitable affirms that 'I am a worldly creature, I fear God, but I am even more afraid of the hell of poverty. To be penniless is that last degree of misfortune in our present social order. I am of my own time, and I honour money!'[35]

If the individual bourgeois was often personally non-religious he was, during the period of Orleanist rule, increasingly less indifferent to religion. He remained Voltairean but the aspect of Voltaire increasingly emphasized was the Voltaire who, whilst residing on his country estate, never missed mass for fear of sowing doubts in the minds of his ignorant peasants. The Church made itself acceptable when its theologians, whilst generally repudiating any right to interfere in economic matters, attacked socialist theories as subversive of social and religious order, where a relatively enlightened bishop like Monseigneur Giraud, Archbishop of Cambrai, saw work as God's punishment for the sins of Adam, and demanded that his clergy preach to the workers resignation, fidelity and temperance.[36] The good works of a Church and of religious men with such attitudes were hardly calculated to transform society.

To influence the masses by education, through the clergy and through charity, to induce them to accept their subordinate position was the aim of so much of the philanthropic activity of the period, including that involving industrial patrons, and represented a desire to dominate rather than a will to help. Most charitable works were performed by zealous Catholics and Protestants with the belief that this was the duty of the wealthy and was good for their souls, not that it was a right of the poor. Charity must be voluntary to have this spiritual effect, and the state must therefore be excluded. Again the condition of dependence and of inferiority was emphasized. There was a general lack of understanding of the new conditions of poverty due to industrial society. The old solutions to a new problem were stressed with, as an important aim, the preservation of the old social hierarchy.

49

Marx distinguishes the Legitimists from the Orleanists by their role as great landowners, a not altogether clear distinguishing feature as we have seen. He believed that 'The Legitimate Monarchy was merely the political expression of the hereditary rule of lords of the soil, as the July Monarchy was only the political expression of the usurped rule of the bourgeois parvenus. What kept the two factions apart, therefore, was not any so-called principles, it was their material conditions of existence, two different kinds of property, it was the old contrast between town and country, the rivalry between capital and landed property' but 'That at the same time old memories, personal enmities, fears and hopes, prejudices and illusions, sympathies and antipathies, convictions, articles of faith and principles bound them to one or the other royal house; who is there that denies this?'[37] He stresses the limited significance of ideological, and in his schema superstructural, elements on human behaviour. Our own view is that he underestimates the significance of these during the period of the July Monarchy. If in 1815 a war-weary nation accepted the imposition by foreign powers of a regime which favoured the noble landowners, this must have appeared as an anachronism by comparison with the immediately preceding period. Then the conflict of urban and rural bourgeoisie and noble landowners had some reality. 1830 turned the aristocratic landowners largely into a group of political 'outs'. But if these resented the loss of political power, resented the assault of the wealthy on the privileges of their caste they increasingly rallied, or ceased to oppose the Orleanist regime, from shared socio-economic interests and conceptions.

Marx stresses the significance of the Second Republic in producing this rapprochement to an excessive extent. The events of the Republic further restrained the political conflict of Orleanists and Legitimists, but to blame what remained on differing material interests was to ignore two facts.[38] One, that in this society dominated by bourgeoisie, all men of significance were landowners and even financial circles retained a pre-industrial psychology. The main evidence of conflicting material interests during the July Monarchy is the protectionist controversy which cut across political divisions and united Legitimist and Orleanist wine growers and merchants, for example, against Legitimist and Orleanist cereal growers and textile producers. To blame political conflict on differing material interests is to falsify. Material interests were significant rather in the sense that the outlook of men whose socio-economic power had traditionally been based on the land, differed from that of men whose power rested proportionately less on landownership and traditional social relationships but was relatively new and based on the acquiring of wealth in all its forms. One form of power emphasized relationships between human beings, the other was more concerned with the impersonal, more institutionalized, conditions for economic and social control. If Legitimists were aware that continued economic change in the direction of industrialization might further weaken their economic and social significance, their resistance was negligible and more commonly they assisted change by capitalizing agriculture. Political argument, between men holding differing conceptions of social control and involving 'ins' and 'outs' on a broad political plain, was between liberal conservatives and totalitarian conservatives.

Legitimist thought lacked clarity but was above all paternalistic. Society as a whole was compared with the family and a hierarchy of rights and duties adduced graded according to the presumed maturity and capacity of the elements of which the social family was composed. Balzac, through the mouth of Doctor Benassis, a man constantly involved in aiding the poor, expressed the following opinion – 'Certainly, I think I have sufficiently well proven my attachment to the poor and suffering class. I cannot be accused of wishing its misfortune; but, while still admiring the industrious life which it leads, sublime in patience and resignation, I declare it to be incapable of participating in the government. The proletarians seem to me to be the minors of a nation, and should always remain in a state of tutelage.'[39] The enlightened few chosen by God to possess material goods had in this possession not only the rights involved in its exploitation, but a positive duty towards the less fortunate, a duty involving aid to the necessitous and general leadership for society, which contrasts with the almost complete inactivity of the non-aristocratic wealthy unless they shared the religious, social and political conceptions of the Legitimists or were Protestants and members of a relatively self-contained community.

In a practical sense in the countryside this ideal often worked so that 'the chateau is to the village like a public fountain where all the inhabitants come to draw; various artisans find work there, the labourer his daily employment; the beggar, aid; the sick, a cure; the man with difficult problems, advice; the oppressed, support; the needs, the general interests of the community, an intelligent interpreter and a powerful defender, the whole population, good example.'[40]

Loyalty to a king came into this with an ideal of a monarch above all sectional interest, under whose rule only could the problems of France and particularly those of poverty be solved. The devotion to the person of Henri v is difficult to explain except in terms of family sentiment, and of the myth of the *ancien régime* which required the resumption of the line of development interrupted by the Revolution. This wish to restore aspects of the past reflected a desire to restore lost social power and a total way of life. The stubbornness of the loyalty to Henri v evinces a degree of sentimental irrationality in human conduct which resulted in the preparedness of many to sacrifice their careers and influence in 1830, and of others to indulge in a demagogy which went as far as the acceptance by the *Gazette de France* directed by the Abbé de Genoudé of universal male suffrage, in a gamble on the willingness of the masses to accept aristocratic Legitimist leadership against the politically dominant bourgeoisie. This was seen by most Legitimists as an unacceptable readiness to risk social order in the interests of an ideal. Large sections of Legitimist opinion were nevertheless prepared in one way or another to risk to varying degrees their material interests for less tangible ideals.

In their attitude to the Orleanist regime their conception of society was clear. In emphasizing regional interests and the necessity for the decentralization of the administration they emphasized the interests of those influential at a local level who would gain from an increased independence of a capital city which was moreover the centre for the distribution of socially disruptive doctrines. Legitimist strength was to be found especially in peripheral areas, and is characterized by Tudesq as being 'traditionalist in the west, reactionary or counter-revolutionary in the Midi, essentially Catholic in Flanders, especially conservative at Lyon. . . .'[41] It was based as a political force on the retained influence of aristocrats on peasants in the west, and additionally bourgeois merchants and small-scale manufacturers on their workers in the towns of the Midi.

The common factor in this influence was the significance of religion and of the Church. Legitimist thought contained a large religious element which made it a complete political and social system, considering society in moral terms. The complacency, materialism and greed of ruling circles was condemned and the importance of principles, particularly those of religion, emphasized. In failing to give a lead to the poor, in failing to express a charitable concern with their problems, the Orleanist notables were leaving room for the sowers of discord. Indeed their actions were positively harmful because in emphasizing the supremacy of individuals judged by their wealth, they emphasized the competitive element in society at the expense of the God-created hierarchy, with the result that 'The contagion thus spreads to all ranks – it is a revolt against Providence, which has given to each his place; no-one is any longer content with this.'[42]

In spite of often bitter condemnation of the regime and the notion presented that all ills would end with the accession of Henri V and the concomitant apparatus of corporation and religion, the main concern of most Legitimist writers appears to have been social conservation. If in regret for its lost authority most of the clergy also dreamed of the restoration of the pre-revolutionary regime, the main impulse behind its social thought and action seems to have been defensive.

The myth of the *ancien régime* which hid the already obvious decline in the Church's influence, and the anti-clericalism of all other political regimes except that created in 1815 threw Legitimists and the clergy together. Their ideal concepts fused this alliance. Both desired a totalitarian control of society, each was aware that only with the support of the other could its strength be really significant.

The desire to dominate comes out clearly in the respective notions of Church and Legitimists with regard to education. Here they had much in common with the developing attitude of Orleanists in the desire to subordinate mass opinion. The Orleanists, however, wished to defend the independence of secondary education from the restricting grip of religion, to defend reason from superstition, at least for their sons' sakes. For them religion was a virtue for the poor. It meant far more to the Legitimists for whom 'Christianity bids the poor to endure the rich; the rich, to soothe the miseries of the poor',[43] for the former the promise of eternal rest in Heaven in return for resignation on Earth, for the latter eternal damnation if they lacked in charity. That this was the sincere view of many cannot be doubted. Its practical significance, which was not incompatible with sincere religious beliefs, is expressed by de Falloux, who wrote that 'Kings and even popes have, as temporal sovereigns, put off necessary reforms too long; they have paid for this adjournment by revolutions. Landowners, under pain of sharing the same fate, should in our century hasten to redeem their cause by good actions.'[44] Charity from faith and from interest, but both directed at conservation even of a society whose government was headed by the House of Orleans. If on occasion the whole process of industrial concentration was attacked, and even by the Baron de Gérando, as creating an industrial feudalism, in general, social conservation rather than reaction was stressed by those more aware of the problems of the developing industrial society, who it must be stressed were relatively few in number, as indeed were those actively engaged in charity, in anything, other than a more direct repression.

The Legitimist view of poverty was essentially the same as that of the Orleanists. 'Misery . . . is an evil inherent in society, which one is able to temperate, alleviate, not suppress. . . .' In this situation the duty of government is simply to preserve order.[45] Police and charity. The poor must expect no rights, but only kindnesses.

If Legitimists and Orleanists often shared material interests, if in many respects their ideology was similar, they differed in the personal significance individuals attached to religion and to a whole tradition of life bound up with a Church and a monarchy and a rural society. To the Legitimists, all these were bound together to form a total outlook, for Orleanists landownership was simply the most important element in wealth, and religion and monarchy means to an end. The distinguishing features were essentially those of the mind rather than material interest narrowly defined.

One last identifiable body of thought supported by members of the urban bourgeoisie in particular was that favouring a republic. Crushed as an active political movement in the 1830s, the prosperity of the 1840s further undermined mass support for republican groups. The most significant of these were grouped around two newspapers, the moderate *National* and the more radical *Réforme*. Of the first group Marx said that 'The bourgeois republicans of the *National* did not represent any large faction of their class resting on economic foundations' but rather an ideal concept of bourgeois rule and personal ambition.[46] Whilst the latter, though directed by men of similar social origins, was seen by Marx as representative of the interests of the petty bourgeoisie.[47] If this analysis is correct, then presumably the demands for social change voiced by both groups were limited as both represented the owners of property in the existing society.

What is most obvious in republican writing in the 1840s is a disgust with poverty and a belief that a truly representative government could do much to end this situation, seemingly by appealing to the basic goodness of men. They desired at most a reduction in the striking inequality of men's conditions in society. Political programmes for this government rather than theories were presented and these based essentially on Robespierre's declaration to the Convention demanding an extension of the franchise and social reform. The *National* emphasized the gradual nature of this process to a greater extent than the *Réforme*. Both disliked violence and were hesitant in supporting strikes, but in the glorification of the Terror increasingly found in historical literature, individual supporters unconsciously helped create an ethos which made violence acceptable, particularly for less conservative intellectuals and more impatient workers.

The republicans had little influence on the masses and neither did the socialists and communists of whom they, as the Monarchists, were afraid, as the spectre of communism rose over Europe, at least in their combined imaginations. The language of violence was popular. Even moderate republicans used the threat of violence by the masses as a political weapon, but essentially they evinced a distrust in the masses with whom they had little contact. Charles de Rémusat seems to have been correct when in observing of these bourgeois republicans of the *National* that whilst they still wanted the republic they were unwilling to act because they were afraid the workers might demand social reforms that were in their eyes too extreme.[48] The republican rank and file as well as many of the leaders, were men with professional skills rather than material property, were young rather than old, were doctors, lawyers, journalists, schoolteachers and students. It seemed as though the less wealthy and those excluded from political power were challenging the successful. They were men who came sufficiently into contact with the working classes to know the extent of their suffering and to be disgusted by it. This was a disgust which united a hostility towards the indifferent figures close to power and a repugnance for the dirty, uneducated masses. If their aim was a fairer sharing of society's wealth and power, it was additionally to prevent any threat to their own existing way and standard of life.

The spread of republican ideas had some effect. It was tinged with a vague humanitarianism and even socialism, and this vague idealism was spread throughout society as a contrast to the official ideology and the existing state of society. It helped increase the desire for change and to prepare the way for a republican government.

The role of these groups in forming a government in February 1848 was an important factor in history. Their conception of society appeared to differ to such an extent from that of most of the notables of France, that they were considered as a threat to the very existence of society, unnecessarily it might seem, but their ideas were subversive of a regime which emphasized in a restricted franchise the privileges and the superiority of wealth. Ideas shaped their behaviour and if this might have differed only to a limited extent in respect of the maintenance of social inequality from that of conservative property owners in general, republican action and the conservative reaction to their ideas and acts was to have a significant effect.

Of these three basic forms of ideological expression Marx admits republicanism to be somehow independent of material interests. Another, that of Legitimacy, seems often to have influenced political behaviour in a manner incompatible with a narrow interpretation of material interest. The third, that of the dominant Orleanists, remains the most naked expression of the defence of material interests. Perhaps Marx generalized from this one example, and in this respect his theory of ideology reflects reality in that the dominating social group created a body of thought which reinforced its practical domination. Yet much of the threat to this dominance came from political forces which were united around certain ideals – King, Church, humanity, or else the personal ambition of the political 'outs'. It may be a function of oppositions to appeal to ideals and eschew the greater, enforced realism of those who hold power, to appeal to an ideal conception of the past or future. But whatever the reason, the appeal is made and the limited political conflict of the July Monarchy is not by any means solely explicable in terms of conflicting material interests.

Condition of the Masses

The purpose of this section of what is a review of French society at the end of the July Monarchy is to consider the conditions of existence of the elements of social instability, those social groups least satisfied with the *status quo*, which would play a revolutionary role at some time or other in the years 1848 to 1851, and after this to consider the degree of consciousness they possessed, each of its separate existence and interests.

The working life of the worker engaged in large-scale production was in general spent in almost unimaginably deplorable conditions. He, or she, spent most commonly 13–14 hours, not including breaks for meals, in a badly ventilated building overheated by a furnace, or because of the need for a humid atmosphere in textile spinning, in an atmosphere often full of small particles, especially where the preparation and cleaning of raw cotton or wool was involved, which entered the mouth and nose, and caused as time went on the worker to cough increasingly and often develop consumption. Cleanliness was uncommon. The workers were dominated by the routine of the machine, involved in uninteresting, repetitive labour which resulted in lassitude and, because as much of the length of the working day as of the physical content of the labour, exhaustion.

At the end of a long day a long journey home was sometimes necessary. The worker came out of the overheated factory into the cold exterior with further ill effects as regard his none-too-buoyant health. For five, five and a half, or six days a week, for almost all his working hours the worker existed amongst a mass of machinery and transmission belts where lack of alertness might mean a fatal accident, though these were usually caused by more conscious activity, e.g. in the attempt to clean machinery whilst it was still in motion, in order to avoid a reduction in wages paid according to piece rates. These were not the only dangers where precautions were sacrificed to costs. The effects of acids and dyes used in textiles, of chemicals more generally, particularly of phosphorous in match factories can be guessed at.

In an environment of noise and dust men, women and children worked side by side in the textile factories of Lille, Roubaix or Mulhouse with no real sense of purpose, except to earn money to live.

Even these conditions were normally better than those of the domestic workers who, to maintain similar minimum standards of life, were forced to work longer hours, often for 18 hours, in rooms which were even less well ventilated than the factories, sometimes even in cellars where the requisite conditions of humidity could more easily be maintained. Living and working in one or two rooms a family might use all its physical energy simply to exist, and for the domestic weaver the only power utilizable was that of his own body.

Pulling part of the loom against his chest time after time, he was particularly susceptible to chest diseases. The weaver was one of the most common figures engaged in domestic production, which included lace-makers, tailors, hardware manufacturers, helped by their families, all finding it increasingly difficult to compete with machine industry.

The rewards of this labour were always minimal whether wages were paid according to piece rates, which patrons usually preferred because they induced the worker to work harder, or by the day, week, etc. They were generally just sufficient to permit the worker to exist in a manner yet to be considered. The optimum condition for the working class family was to have children old enough to work, permitting then their mother also to work. Young children, unable to work – those below eight or twelve, depending on the industry – could be a tremendous strain on a family's resources, as could the process of aging. From about 40–45 as the worker's physical capacity declined, so his earnings fell.

The general feeling of the worker must have been one of insecurity. If in a prosperous year the costs of living could be just met, in a period of crisis, and ten of the eighteen years of the July Monarchy were clearly that, he must depend on a public or private charity and reduce his living standards even further. Unemployment, short time working and seasonal unemployment due to lack of motive power where water power was used as commonly in Alsace, or to a patron's concentration of total production into part of the year in order to minimize costs, were common. There could be little room for complaint against wages, conditions or even against cheating in payment of piece rates where mechanization, whilst reducing the domestic labourer to unemployment, failed to absorb all these unemployed and where even in prosperity a permanent pool of surplus labour existed ready to replace dismissed workers. Organized action by groups of workers taking the form of a strike had this to contend with as well as the hostility of the law.

Competition for employment took an organized form in many industries like mining and building where employers engaged teams of workers, *L'équipe*, employed and paid as a team and competing with other teams for this employment. Competition existed even between the factory and the domestic worker who often possessed a small-holding which enabled him to tolerate very low returns on his industrial activity. Exploitation was maximized by fines for bad quality goods, lateness, smoking, etc., by company shops and company houses. Some employers attempted to improve their workers' conditions by encouraging and contributing to mutual aid societies, cheap housing, etc., but these were relatively few and their actions limited by the need to keep costs low, to face ferocious competition, and build reserves to modernize and to survive crises. In few respects did the conditions for factory workers improve in the period up to 1848 – hours were generally longer to permit maximum utilization of the new machinery while real income remained at best stationary. Only some glimmerings of hope could be seen, and this particularly in Alsace in the department of Haut-Rhin, where half self-interested, half-philanthropic entrepreneurs began to see the need for a better educated proletariat as machines grew more complicated and to realize that productivity might increase with fewer hours of work.

This of course is and must be a generalized view to which the only exceptions were the more skilled workers who earned more than the mass of unskilled labour, but even these suffered from the feeling and reality of insecurity.

To complete this picture of the life of the worker, a view of his home life is needed. The most obvious immediate statement to be made here is of the limits to this when he worked from twelve to fourteen hours a day, and needed sleep. If the factory was a factor in the demoralization of the urban worker then it will become evident that his inability to escape an environment of misery at any point in his everyday existence must have had significant psychological effects.

Of the conditions of the Parisian workers employed as we have seen in small-scale artisan production and often enjoying living standards superior to those of the factory workers of Lille and Mulhouse, the Prefect of the Seine reported in 1846 that 'There still remain 231,000 households to which one is able quite justifiably to give the title of distressed. . . . If one multiplies this figure . . . by 2·64 which is the average number of people composing a household, one finds 610,000 distressed inhabitants. . . . It is necessary to add to this the workers living in lodgings, of whom there are at least 25,000.'[1] 65–75 per cent of the population of Paris were then living in conditions of poverty.[2]

Contemporaries agreed that living standards were worst at Lille. A report of the Lille Conseil de Salubrité for 1841 described working class accommodation in cellars or small rooms where ventilation was so bad that the air was foul, where the walls were covered with filth. If they had a bed it was composed of some dirty planks covered with rotting straw and a coarse sheet the colour and material of which were hidden under a layer of dirt. The furniture was broken and worm-eaten and covered with filth. Utensils were scattered across the room. The windows were always closed, and were fitted with paper or glass which was so dirty, so smoke-blackened as to exclude all light. The floor of the dwelling was the dirtiest part – everywhere there were heaps of rubbish, of ashes, remains of food, rotting straw, nests for animals of all sorts. The report complained that 'One is oppressed in these hovels by an insipid, nauseating odour . . . of dirtiness, of excrement, of man. . . .' The clothing of their inhabitants were rags, of flimsy materials, worn and patched and not very clean. These people were obviously physically very dirty.[3] A description of extreme conditions maybe, but revealing of human degradation, and not at all unusual, the common effects of the influx of a rural population into urban surroundings which in the early stages of industrialization were ill-prepared to receive them, and of a new civilization which they were ill-prepared to endure.

The result of the enquiry of 1848 in the Haut-Rhin did not reveal anything quite as bad, or else the enquirers lacked the requisite descriptive ability. They reveal, though, the variations in living standards between workers. The commission of enquiry of the canton of Ferrette admitted that if the conditions of workers in metallurgy were relatively good, those of the workers of textile factories were not, indeed their lodgings were hideous. The metallurgists owed their conditions to the fact that they earned about 2 francs a day and their employer furnished them with accommodation, the wood they needed, and a vegetable garden.[4] Again it was the domestic worker whose conditions were worst. The commission of the canton of Sainte-Marie-aux-Mines reported that 'The worker is generally badly lodged, badly clothed and especially badly nourished. Misery and all the evils it involves are at their worst for the weaver. His family sleeps crowded together on a straw bed, with father, mother, sons, brothers and sisters all together. Here begins demoralization then comes prostitution and finally hospital or prison.' Most weavers had only inadequate clothing and two-fifths were, it was claimed, dependent on charity for the clothes they did possess. The commission adds that other workers were 'in normal times able to live comfortably'.[5]

The basic picture is one of poverty – low wages providing for mere subsistence and this only during periods of prosperity. All workers were faced with the constant threat of declining into the conditions of misery which have been described. If the metallurgists and miners of Le Creusot, for example, lived in a small community and were comparatively well housed they remained over-worked, badly paid and consequently badly fed. Only in the Midi and paradoxically because of its economic backwardness were the urban concentrations of misery largely avoided and the links between town and country more closely guarded, improving food and health, though within limits.

André Lasserre has made the following estimate of a working family's budget at Lille during the 1840s, and this for what he regards as relatively well-off families: 51–56 per cent of income was spent on food and drink, whilst the poorer might spend 70–80 per cent. Then perhaps 6 per cent or even 10–12 per cent on rent, 13–21 per cent on clothing, 8–12 per cent for heating, lighting and furniture, and anything remaining for medical care, recreation, etc.[6] Most of the expenditure on food would have been for bread in the Nord, or potatoes in Alsace. Meat was rarely eaten more than once a week. Villermé wrote the following description of the diet of workers in Lille in 1838, Pierre Pierrard, quoting it, comments that there was little change by 1870.'[7] 'The normal food of poor workers in Lille is potatoes, some vegetables, thin soups, a little butter, cheese, milk or pork. Usually they only have one of these things with their bread. Water is the only drink during the meal, but a large number of men and women go to a bar each day to drink beer, or more often a little glass of their detestable liqueur.' The quality of this food was atrocious.[8]

These quotations reveal not simply the poverty of living conditions but also the effects. The home surroundings were hardly calculated to provide for comfort and the recourse of many workers was to drown their sorrows in strong drink, often accompanied by their whole families. From this desire to forget, to enjoy some pleasures, grew drunkenness and promiscuous sexual activity. The worker, male and female, could afford little else. Excessive patronizing of the cabaret seems to have been a major cause of the unbalancing of a family's budget. Here the poor sought companionship, cheerfulness, and warmth and in this the middle-class commentator saw the vice which he presumed was the essential cause of poverty.

The result of work, house and cabaret was general ill-health. Just consider the character of the six main illnesses, causing over 50 per cent of deaths at Lille even during the Second Empire. These were consumption 14·16 per cent, enteritis 11 per cent, pulmonary congestion 10 per cent, rachitism and syphilitic debility 6·6 per cent, meningitis 5·77 per cent, convulsions 4·85 per cent.[9] All serve to illustrate a way of life and deny perhaps any exaggeration in the quotations used above. As for infant mortality, almost half the children born to textile workers at Mulhouse died before they were two years old.[10] At Lille, if between 1842 and 1846 21·1 per cent of the children of the bougeoisie died before they were five, over 50 per cent of those of workers did so.[11] Mortality dropped sharply for subsequent age groups as if the process of natural selection was almost terminated. Even so the physical condition of the industrial worker was such that Charles Dupin in the Chamber of Deputies in 1840 complained that 50 per cent of conscripts from industrial departments were rejected as unfit compared with 20 per cent of those from agricultural.[12] In addition to the normal causes of death must be listed the epidemics, especially smallpox, cholera and typhoid which affected particularly the insalubrious working-class districts – the cholera epidemic of 1849 in Paris resulted in the death rate for that year being 45·6 per 1,000 compared with 25·4 in a more normal year, that of 1845.[13]

Significant was the difference in the rate of dying between the poor and the more prosperous. The figures on infant mortality quoted above have indicated this. Suffice it to add that in Lille in 1860 the highest death rate was in the 6th arrondissement at 38·38 per 1,000, the lowest 21·87 per 1,000 in the prosperous 5th.[14] Chevalier pertinently commented that similar statistics relating to Paris indicated through 'inequality in death the most certain measure of inequality in life.'[15]

Amongst the densely packed urban industrial population two facts were obvious – poor health and poor morals. Buret regretfully concluded that 'The lower classes are little by little rejecting the customs and laws of civilized life and returning through suffering and misery to the state of barbarism.'[16] Drunkenness has been emphasized add to it crime, concubinage, illegitimacy and prostitution, the latter especially during economic crises. Marx commented on the 'practical absence of the family among proletarians'[17] and by the mid 1840s this must have appeared to be the course of development. Where the wife worked the same long day as her husband, how could she care adequately for accommodation, food or children? Where she started work as a child herself how could she acquire the basic knowledge of domestic responsibilities? The decline of the family was evident in Lille and Mulhouse where such conditions existed. The children were ill-cared for and tended to reciprocate this lack of practical affection; where the wife did not work, as at Le Creusot or in mining areas, the family unit assumed a far greater significance, and retained this against the challenge of the bar-room.

The areas of physical and moral decline seem to have been the new industrial centres on which Marx based his hopes for revolution, and the centres of immigration. Paris, Lille and Mulhouse are the prime examples. Here those attracted by higher wages, more extensive charity or simply driven from their former occupations by unemployment, settled. The strangeness of a new life intensified the general feeling of insecurity and judging from some figures on charity presented by Louis Chevalier many were unable to respond adequately to the challenge and depended on charity to a more significant extent than more settled inhabitants.[18] This argument is supported by considering the workers of a less industrialized town like Orléans, less attractive to immigrants, where the workers were largely of local origin and more firmly based in society, were in the conventional sense far more moral. More significant for the future development of our argument is the consideration of the artisans of Paris. In the artisan areas of Paris, the Faubourgs Saint-Antoine, Saint-Jacques, and Saint-Marcel population was fairly stable. Here skilled artisans, even if not living in especially good conditions, were more commonly literate or had not forgotten their lessons because using elementary knowledge in their work. Involved in skilled labour which necessitated thought and discouraged lassitude they tended to think more generally on the problems of life and as a consequence to limit their families so as to minimize their poverty, to avoid the expense of frequent drinking and to enjoy the pleasures of a home family life given to them by relatively high wages. These were the skilled workers employed in printing, engraving, watch-making, in the luxury, artistic trades, the products of a long apprenticeship. Although subject to crises, they enjoyed a relative security.

In most of the towns and villages of France this picture was repeated. An élite of skilled artisans producing, in the large cities, luxuries, in the small towns and villages often the basic necessities of life, necessary both in and out of crisis – the smith or baker – separated from the mass of industrial and domestic workers by their relative security and comfort, education and interests. This should be borne in mind for subsequent consideration, as should the fact already emphasized that in Paris, if most of the workers in small-scale industry were less skilled and less secure they shared to some extent both these characteristics and avoided the extremes of degradation described as existing in the new industrial cities of the north and north-east. Even so, in an essay published in 1842 concerning *L'Ouvrier de Paris*, M. J. Brisset could distinguish between the skilled and unskilled. Brisset observed that 'The mechanic, the decorator, the jeweller and printing workers, for example, have few relations with labourers, quarrymen, masons and stonecutters.' Wage differences and the differing nature of their work led to a situation in which 'under the generic title, "the workers of Paris" there existed distinct classes' with the skilled distinguished by relative education and prosperity from the poor and ignorant.[19]

The most obvious things which can be said about the conditions of existence of the peasant and agricultural labourer concern the general primitiveness of techniques which in the absence of adequate application of natural and artificial fertilizers led to a rapid tiring of the land and low yields. The lack of mechanical aids made farming a tiring and ill-rewarding job performed on most smallholdings by the labour of a family, with labourers employed on the larger holdings when required – much of this labour, used during the harvest, being migratory in character. The hours of work were long and varied according to the season, perhaps from six in the morning to eight at night in spring, from four to eight or nine in summer, from five or six in the morning until five or six in the evening in autumn and winter. Again, as with the industrial worker, there was little time for repose except in winter, with a minimum of about eleven hours and a maximum of sixteen.

Peasant housing was generally rudimentary. In areas of the Midi houses were of clay or brick with one room and an earthen floor. Light was shed on this through one window usually without glass. Under the same roof and separated from the living room by a thin wooden wall was the stable. Pierre Labracherie's description of the living conditions of the Breton peasant in 1848 is similar.[20] Mme Kahan-Rabecq emphasizes the variation in standards of housing even within the area of Alsace but seems generally to agree on its low standards, although the agricultural labourer, or indeed the industrial worker living in the country, possessed a distinct advantage over his urban compatriots in the possession of a garden or field.[21] The quality of housing inevitably depended on the prosperity of agriculture, of the individual peasant or labourer, but even in the prosperous Beauce notions of hygiene and living conditions compared unfavourably with many of the less industrialized urban centres, although the absence of concentrations of misery made rural life less appalling.

As for food, Armengaud describes that of relatively rich grain growing areas as being essentially of bread and porridge made from maize, added to which were soups made from potatoes, haricots or cabbages for example. Meat was rare and wine normally too expensive. In mountain areas, diets were even more frugal, with bread giving way in the Pyrenean region to porridge and potatoes. The enquiry of 1848 in the Haut-Rhin reported for the canton of Kayserberg that 'The basic food of workers is the potato, dairy produce and cheese. In many households in the mountains bread is almost a luxury. Little meat and almost no wine is consumed.'[22] Only feasts prepared for weddings and funerals seem to have broken this monotony of diet, and indeed of life. Clothing took the form essentially of the sabot and smock, the cheapest available.

In respect of food, clothing and housing it is possible to equate the small-holder or sharecropper and the labourer. Differences occur in the extent to which crises tended to effect each of these broad categories – bad crops, seasonal unemployment or sickness would reduce the labourer and indeed if a crop were bad enough, the small-holder, to dependence on charity often gained through begging. The masses of small producers in the countryside shared with the urban workers a feeling of insecurity due to their inability, from small crops, to save sufficient in a prosperous year to tide them over a bad one and the consequent resort to borrowing. The responses of the cantonal commissions of enquiry in the Haut-Rhin in 1848 repeatedly illustrate this point.

That of the canton of Ensisheim stated that most peasants were in debt. It complained of the usurious rates of interest, of the fact that revenue from the land was often inadequate to meet the charges in the form of taxes and debt repayment which rested on it. A storm, flood or fire could ruin a peasant forcing him to borrow and ultimately often leading to the forced expropriation of his holding to pay his creditors. It claimed that of 20 inventories after death 14 recorded net debts.[23]

65

The response of the canton of Colmar blamed the land hunger of the peasant for his indebtedness. Land was expensive and the peasant could only acquire it by spreading purchase over a long period. Thus he was forced to borrow at a rate of interest of 5 per cent whereas the return on his investment would be at best only 2·5 per cent.[24]

The enquirers of the canton of Neuf-Brisach add a further ray of enlightenment where they blame parcellation for the poverty of the rural population, adding that individuals often borrowed to buy out co-heirs to a piece of land.[25]

These generalizations could be applied to the areas of France in which small-scale farming dominated. At this particular period conditions were being further worsened for peasant proprietors and labourers in all areas by the decline of domestic industry, useful to supplement the earnings of the land, in the face of intensified mechanization and by the restrictions on traditional rights in forest and on the use of common land designed to prevent the abusive over-use of both. This latter mainly affected the more isolated backward areas in which these traditions were still strong. For many peasants with insufficient land of their own, the common pasture was the only grazing available for their few beasts. For peasants and labourers the communal, state or private woods were vital sources of wood for heating and building, and further sources of grazing. Balzac in *Les Paysans* amply illustrates the tenacity of the rural poor in attempting to maintain its accustomed rights.

The poorest areas were those most adversely affected by these changes. Prosperity generally brought with it as an additional benefit of trade contacts a more general enlightenment and ambition. Those areas which could afford to maintain a larger population were also those in which the limitation of families was practised, whilst poverty was accompanied by higher birth rates which increased the pressure on the land and the tendency towards relative over-population.

In some areas the result of extreme poverty was similar to that in the industrial cities – drunkenness, and a general tendency towards demoralization, but it is more difficult to generalize about agricultural communities than about the workers engaged in say mechanized textile production. Other factors were important in determining the social psychology of rural communities. Poverty was simply one, important, but not the only element which helped to determine the reaction of sections of the rural community to specific stimuli.

One basic factor of peasant mentality seems to have been a hunger for land. This was perfectly understandable. For the relatively prosperous an increased area to cultivate presumably meant increased prosperity, for the poor peasant or landless labourer even a small piece of land meant a greater security, at least the ability to provide one's food. The prospect of permanent migration to the city was as yet a novel idea. Conditions on the land were not so unbearable by comparison with conditions in the city. Migration was primarily a means of earning money with which to return home and buy land. The old routine of peasant life had changed little by the 1840s, the individual was dominated by the communal memory, his ambition by the desire for land. On the achievement of this ambition, according to the amount of land owned, was constructed a social hierarchy even amongst the poor.

Whatever the poverty of the rural poor, significant comparisons could yet be made with the urban poor. In favour of the latter, first the more distinct possibility that they had received a rudimentary education. Children were even more useful as labour on the land than in the factory. Any possible intellectual development was stunted especially quickly. Nadaud recounted the opposition to his father's desire that he go to school: 'My mother protested with the greatest vigour saying that she had need of me in the fields.'[26] But in his favour was the better health and physical condition produced by his work in the open air and particularly, with respect to his outlook on life, the influence of his general environment. Nadaud wrote in 1850, 'We have experienced misery in all its varieties, and have been able to compare that of the countryside and that of the towns, this latter is much more dreadful; it weakens the body and spirit, kills the bodily strength and smothers the moral.'[27] Poverty was not a leveller. Existence in the more closely-knit rural community demanded the observance of certain basic standards of behaviour and thus created a barrier to extreme demoralization. The peasant belonged to his family and to his village, and this gave him additional powers of resistance to the impulses which, derived from poverty, might have resulted in new patterns of behaviour in the individual.

Now to the last element of social discontent to be discussed here, the groups lowest ranking within the hierarchy of the middle classes, called for convenience the petty bourgeoisie but as such difficult to delineate, to separate from the workers and especially the artisans below and the members of the liberal professions, officials of state and members of the economic professions above.

Marx defines the Parisian petty bourgeoisie as being the 'keepers of cafés and restaurants, *marchands de vins*, small traders, shopkeepers, handicraftsmen, etc.'[28] This class was for him essentially reactionary but it was threatened by the development of capitalism, by the large-scale producers and merchants with whom it had to compete and from whom it had to purchase its goods and by the control of credit facilities by the few great financiers.[29] The economic position of the petty bourgeoisie was threatened, and Marx in *The Communist Manifesto* foresaw its decline in numbers and socio-economic significance as its members declined into the ranks of the proletariat, and society was, through economic development, polarized into two great classes.

This process as we have seen, had not developed far in France. There were large numbers of shopkeepers and merchants, artisans and minor functionaries who were distinguished from the workers in the cities sometimes not by superior living standards, though generally these were somewhat superior, but by their functions which involved the ownership of property or at least access to credit and placed them in the bourgeois hierarchy by the smallness of their wealth. In the countryside there were again minor officials, shopkeepers, café proprietors, the richer artisans like coopers and smiths, even here some doctors and notaries more closely linked with those engaged in small commerce and industry than in the larger towns because of the smallness of the community possessing property and unattached to the land – a middle class whose small size made subdivision more difficult and emphasized its community of interest. In the larger towns their education and group exclusiveness made the members of the liberal professions more bourgeois than petty bourgeois. All generally lived not off the land or rents though perhaps possessing both.

If the small businessmen possessed something and this distinguished them from the workers and peasants, they shared the latter's insecurity. In an era of constant crisis and economic difficulty the number of business failures was particularly great. Buret used these characteristics to define the petty bourgeoisie as *populairé* by its antecedents and daily contacts, but especially by its 'uncertainty of existence, one of the traits which characterize the life of the poor'. What distinguished it from the 'true proletariat' was the fact that its members had, or had once had, some hopes of improving their social position, whereas the proletariat could be concerned only with fulfilling its immediate needs.[30]

Such a social group must, as Marx believed, be drawn in two directions – opposing the changes in society, especially economic, determined by the wealthier, if by anyone, which have adverse effects on its position and yet asserting its independence and individuality *vis à vis* the urban masses who do not share the possession of property. Buret's statement hints at the importance of social mobility. Marx's notion of the polarization of classes requires, to be correct, that upward social mobility be reduced proportionately to this developing polarization. The consciousness of a society in which the improvement of living conditions by social ascension is common, must obviously differ from that in which this is absent or becoming more difficult.

It is necessary, therefore, to consider the extent to which social mobility was present in French society, and to consider whether or not frustration existed which increased the social discontent caused by poverty and economic insecurity.

As far as Paris is concerned the conclusions of Adeline Daumard are most revealing. Of the period of the Restoration and July Monarchy Mlle Daumard claims that upward social mobility was possible without the initial benefit of inherited capital but far more likely with it, and becoming increasingly more difficult without.[31] Daumard concludes that, because of the increasingly large initial investment necessary for success in the economic professions, and because of the increasing emphasis on wealth as a pre-requisite for a significant place in the social hierarchy, social ascension was becoming more difficult. The conclusions of Guy Palmade and of Jean Lambert-Dansette, amongst others, all support this view.

If social mobility was declining this was due essentially to new economic forces, to the development of mechanization and of financial concentration, and consequent upon this the development of modified feelings of social exclusiveness amongst various sections of the population. But if mobility was declining it still continued, because economic development opened new opportunities, created a need for professional and administrative services. However, the development of inventive or business capacity required generally the investment of greater sums of capital, not only to provide equipment but to meet competition and to survive crises, whilst to benefit from other opportunities in the law or administration a secondary education was necessary which could only be bought. The Parisian bourgeoisie was largely renewed by immigration and the individuals concerned tended to be representative of the provincial bourgeoisie, rather than by social mobility within Paris. Where this occurred, and this is true also of the provinces, it tended to take a step by step form. The cases of workmen becoming millionaires were extremely rare, and here Balzac tends to give a false impression in his tendency to deal with the more successful. The workman might hope rather to become the patron of a small workshop or a shop in a working quarter whilst his son, if successful, might own a factory or a shop serving more wealthy customers. Social mobility was in all parts of the hierarchy a slow process, but nowhere must it have been as slow or as difficult as amongst the workers and peasants who possessed little or no financial resources, or education. Daumard again makes a significant point where she considers the 12th arrondissement of Paris by means of declarations after death and concludes that 66 per cent of the members of the economic professions, deceased in 1847 who made declarations, that is of shopkeepers and merchants, had begun their career with a small or medium capital. Her conclusions seem to indicate that somewhere between 20–30 per cent of this group would have been composed of former workers.[32] Louis Chevalier, whilst perhaps exaggerating the possibilities of mobility by basing his estimates on the dossiers of bankruptcy which would contain a high proportion of former workers who had begun in business with limited capital, claims that the higher figure is more likely.[33]

In Paris and in artisanal production a significant, if limited, possibility of social promotion remained for the worker. It is obvious that in the industrial towns of the provinces, the decline of domestic and artisanal production increasingly restricted these possibilities. Thus, Jean Lambert-Dansette considers the origins of the textile patrons of the Nord – most were of commercial origin, many others from the bourgeois non-economic professions, more peasants than workers or artisans.[34] By contrast, Marx in the part of *Capital* concerned with its accumulation, would seem to give a more significant role to bankers and a less to bourgeois landowners and members of the liberal professions than Lambert-Dansette's conclusions would merit.[35]

There would seem to have been little real change in the social structure until the end of the nineteenth century. The rich grew richer and the number of poor increased, those in between remained numerous. The possessors of wealth in all degrees saw their social position as rewards for hard work available to all, and around this feeling and the way of life which wealth produced grew a conscious-pleasure at being set above the poverty-stricken masses, a social segre-gation increasingly strict in its application which more than anything tion increasingly strict in its application which more than anything else produced a consciousness amongst the poor of the increasingly limited possibilities of ever escaping their poverty. Charles Kuhlmann, President of the Chamber of Commerce of Lille observed this in 1858. He concluded that if since 1848 the patrons had lost much of their influence this was in part due to the influence of new social ideas amongst the workers, but additionally because of the indiffer-ence of the patrons towards the workers, and especially that of patrons who had risen from the workshop floor and who were even more concerned than others to stress their new-found status.[36]

During the reign of Louis-Philippe this exclusiveness was most observed and condemned as a feature of the *grande bourgeoisie* which was seen to be becoming a caste to which entry was severely limited, a caste based on intermarriage which possessed to the greatest extent that attribute which made them admired, feared and followed by all other possessors of wealth. Moreover, it possessed a wealth which led to marriage alliances with members of the higher administration thus reinforcing the power of this caste.

Where the groups in between these rich men and the great mass of poor varied in terms of wealth a structure was created. Marriages and social intercourse took place between the members of families with similar wealth and way of life, were arranged often consciously with family interests in mind, or simply occurred as in all societies because of this common way of life. It was the increasing differences between ways of life which above all caused a consciousness of separate interest, a lack of mutual understanding, and even an increasing desire to live apart, not yet developed as fully as it was to be but even before Haussman seen in the move of the more prosperous from the centre of Paris or Lyon to more peripheral areas.

The main link between the men of wealth and the propertyless was represented by the numerically large group of shopkeepers and small workshop proprietors, by this petty bourgeoisie often ambitious but insecure, struggling constantly to maintain both its relative wealth and its distinctive social position, but in the absence of a strict legal definition of the limits between various bourgeois groups possessing as all these groups the hope of improvement, and real proof in everyday life of this possibility.

Most opportunities for social ascension were created by economic expansion. If this were halted then an anyway increasingly difficult position would become almost impossible, indeed retrogression would threaten many individuals. In addition a common element of the thought of bourgeois and worker, namely that hard work brought its just reward, would further decline in validity, giving way to a clearer concept of antagonistic interests. This perhaps was the significance of the economic crisis of 1846–1847.

Little is said by Marx of the attitudes of the workers before February. All historical essays have to begin and end somewhere and the decision is necessarily an arbitrary one. Yet February was the product of events occurring under the Orleanist regime, and men's reactions to events during the Second Republic were largely dictated by attitudes developed during the previous regime.

There were a number of signs of a developing social consciousness amongst the workers after 1830. The most common expression of this took the form of strikes, an obvious form of protest against the general misery of life. Unfortunately a pattern in respect of the number of strikes per year and the number of workers involved cannot be established because of the inadequacies of archive material and press reporting, but some conclusions can usefully be drawn.

First the relatively small number of workers engaged in strikes at all; secondly, the unorganized spontaneous character of most strikes which were generally immediate reactions to the threat or rumour of a reduction in wages and were shortlived. The laws against the association of workers and the general administrative practice of assuming that whenever a large number of workers left their work at one time an association existed, made organization difficult even if the will existed. Where labour surplus to demand was available, protest was usually doomed to failure and could only be the last resort of workers already living at subsistence level and as such with only limited capacity for resistance.

Some movements, however, stand out and these always of skilled craftsmen. J-P Aguet describes the existence of a strike movement amongst the tailors of La Rochelle at the end of 1837. The seizure of papers by the police revealed contacts with, and support from other tailors' associations at Nantes and Bordeaux and more frightening as far as the administration was concerned, a letter of sympathy from the association at Angers – 'No sacrifice must be too great to free ourselves from our oppressors. What! Would we see our brothers forced to bow their heads to the earth! For what purpose would our societies serve? Union and force, that is our motto'.[37] This linked a feeling of professional and even working-class solidarity with the usual professional complaints, and exemplifies the small number of instances of co-operation between workers in different towns or even on an intra-professional level more common in and around Paris and Lyon. The most important example of the latter occurred in Paris in 1840 although the co-operation was tacit rather than planned and took the form of a wave of strikes involving 20–30,000 workers, largely in the building industry.[38]

Most strikes failed because of the lack of organization, the failure to collect funds and to impose a common discipline on the workers. Organization where it existed was often based on a mutual aid society which served as a cover for the collection of funds and, because of its permanence, permitted a surveillance of the employers after a successful strike to ensure that the gains were preserved. Permanent organization enabled the printing workers of Paris to select representatives to meet those of the patrons in 1843, to draw up a tariff; organization also enabled the carpenters of the same city, on strike in 1845, to organize aid for strikers, permits to work for those employers who had acceded to their demands, and contributions from the workers employed by these to aid their fellows still on strike.[39] This denotes a degree of consciousness of common interest which was uncommon and which was with the exception of the close-knit communities of coal miners the exclusive possession of the artisans and building workers.

The industrial workers of the factory towns evinced in general little capacity for organization or resistance and seem to have been characterized by an apathetic resignation after sometimes an initial outburst of resentment involving perhaps the breaking of windows or even the smashing of machines. Aguet's conclusions were that artisans and building workers tended to strike in prosperous periods and often made gains whilst avoiding loss of the limited work available even at reduced wages during a crisis. Factory workers, particularly the majority who were textile workers, normally found it difficult to exist, which explains their often violent reactions when a crisis further reduced their wages.

In all of this there were few signs of class consciousness even

73

amongst the limited number capable of organizing a strike, and few signs of political motives or of more than a limited sympathy from republican groups. Those participating in organized strikes were the privileged, relatively well paid, skilled workers of old urban centres with a tradition of communal existence and of self defence. The strikes of factory workers indicate a lack of purpose beyond the immediate sense of protest but do reveal the tension between workers and employers.

The most common features of working-class organization were mutual aid societies designed to give aid in case of sickness. In some areas these were elements of self-help, and as such could become centres of resistance. In others they were more often dominated by the employers and this was especially true of the new industrial areas, of the department of the Nord and Alsace. Here they were designed, and often in fact served, to bind the workers to a particular establishment and to a particular employer.

A further symptom of a developing consciousness among the urban workers of themselves and of their place in society was to be found in the creation of newspapers written by workers, few in number, often ephemeral and with tiny circulations but indicative of the mentality of those workers who served or were to serve as leaders for their fellows, indicative also of the outer limits of intellectual development amongst the workers. The most significant in respect of influence and of the clarity of the ideas expressed was the Parisian *Atelier*. It was unusual also in that the thoughts expressed were those of workers who remained workers, rather than of self-proclaimed representatives of the workers or workers turned intellectuals.

The writers of the *Atelier* reveal a relatively developed consciousness. Many of their more practical claims, for example for higher wages and a shorter working day, also for the abolition of *marchandage*, of the intermediary between worker and employer in many trades who competed for a contract to supply labour, making a profit on the difference between the sum the employer offered him and the sum he paid to the workers, or even their more general desire to emphasize the human need for dignity were common to the more conscious workers, who after February would be politically significant. The demands of the *Atelier* can be compared with many of those petitions presented to the Luxembourg Commission early in 1848. These demands, therefore, bear further examination.

The *Atelier* tended to view political problems in moral terms. It emphasized the need for moral regeneration before social reconstruction could be possible. But as a means to this regeneration an improvement in the workers' material conditions was essential and to achieve this, political reform was necessary and would strike at the root of the problem. These two factors produced a critique of existing society which at times could almost be Marxist. Thus, in August 1841, 'Struggle, antagonism does not cease for a moment between master and worker; it is this struggle . . . which sometimes reveals itself to the world in the shape of interdiction, of downing-of-tools, of coalition and of gatherings, as in September 1840, and which makes itself felt continually in each workshop.'[40] An awareness of a social conflict of interests.

The state and the army were seen as serving the interests of the employers – 'Isn't it obvious that all the major laws were made with the intention of keeping the working classes in a state of perpetual dependence?'[41] Even the Church was attacked, in a manner which indicates that the avowed catholicism of the *Atelier* was rather the vague religiosity common to the urban masses, not as vague perhaps, but certainly not Catholic in its rejection of the institutional Church which 'has put religion at the service of the most corrupt power in the world, because when the Revolution broke out, it did not understand that its duty was to aid it and to sacrifice in its interest, the immense wealth which it possessed.'[42]

Moderate in politics, indeed tending to follow the moderate republican *National* except in its hesitation over the social question, the *Atelier* saw the future in terms of universal suffrage resulting in a state willing to provide minimum conditions of social well-being and financial aid to the process of association amongst workers, from resources provided by progressive taxation. This process of association, the voluntary submission of the individual to the collective, together with the latter's protection of the individual would be a process of moral regeneration for whose fulfilment the editors of the *Atelier* were prepared to wait centuries. They repeatedly stressed that to be worthwhile the liberation of the workers must be their own work.

Serious and moderate, the *Atelier* with a circulation of at most 1,500, had little attraction for most workers in its ten years of existence.[43] Cuvillier believed that most of its readers were intellectuals or inquisitive bourgeois to whom it gave perhaps a false impression of the moderation of the workers' demands, but he assumed that its indirect influence on the workers, derived from their leaders, was significant. Nadaud seems to have favoured the *Populaire* of Cabet, which probably attracted most readers of the socialist or communist press.[44]

But, to return to the *Atelier*. It is significant, if not surprising, that this and other papers written by workers derived their contributors from the same circles as those which engaged in organized strikes at this period. Of the 75 editors of the *Atelier* known to Cuvillier, 26 were employed in the printing trade, and then in order of significance came jewellers, mechanics, bookbinders, carpenters and tailors.[45]

What of the popular consciousness in general? It would be impossible to associate it with any particular, identifiable body of doctrine, or with a specific political movement. A small number as workers had been associated with the republican plots of the 1830s, and with republican secret societies, but in the 1840s few of these latter survived. What remained from the early period of the July Monarchy was the feeling of disappointment, that those who had fought on the streets to overthrow Charles X had been cheated of their just reward, and together with this presumably the feeling, even confidence, that what had happened once could recur, a feeling of the power and force of the masses.

In spite of repression and censorship a large number of critics of the regime, whether republican, socialist or communist, liberal, Legitimist or Bonapartist, were able to have their tracts printed and this contributed to the creation of a vague and commonly-felt notion that the existing society was unjust and could be improved. An organized political movement was not created but rather a collection of values, a sentiment of common suffering, a sense of *we* – the essential pre-requisite for collective action.

One contemporary observer noted of the Parisian worker that often as he worked, he listened to and participated in the reading and discussion of newspaper articles.[46] Nadaud described two other means of acquiring a form of socio-political education. One through the reading of a newspaper in a cabaret and the subsequent discussion among the workers which aided their absorption of its criticisms, and the other through the experiences of everyday life. He recalled how in 1842, working on a building in Paris, he could see opposite a school directed by the Abbé Dupanloup in which were educated the children of the wealthy. He could not help but compare the condition of these children with that of children who accompanied their brutalized mothers to bars in the immediate vicinity, in the poor streets near the rue Saint-Victor and Place Maubert.[47]

The contrasts are extreme, but so must have been many of those which greeted the eyes of the urban population every day. As long as these contrasts, the wealth and poverty which they exemplified, were felt to be inevitable they could be greeted with nothing other than resignation, but new ideas and continual criticism must erode this feeling, must widen the concept of resistance already accepted by workers defending their professional position.

Those most receptive to new ideas were obviously, in the first place, those who could read. Since 1833 literacy had greatly increased particularly in urban areas and amongst the skilled workers who in their professions utilized an elementary education. They were mainly craftsmen living in the larger cities, particularly Paris and Lyon, which possessed an intellectual atmosphere, the former especially with numbers of *déclassé* intellectuals to add to the petty bourgeoisie in daily contact with the workers. Less or more than a proletariat, these together were the 'people'. Their social consciousness was not entirely the product of the development of economic conditions. In Paris, there was an absence of the appalling factory conditions and of the extreme misery of life generally found in Lille. In Paris a mass of men of various professions but generally skilled, accepted and enjoyed the almost indefinable atmosphere of intellectual ferment of the big city. Their consciousness was the product of this tradition of involvement and of the ideas which appeared in print and were discussed at work or in the cabaret. An economic crisis intensified the extent of involvement and its intensity, in emphasizing the meaning of poverty; changing economic conditions worsened the situation of some professions. What cannot be claimed is that this new consciousness was the product of the concentration of workers in the factory. In Paris rather the reverse. The minority of factory workers accepted the dominant artisanal mentality of the quarters in which they lived. Marx, in claiming the Parisian workers for his own, in labelling them proletarians, as indiscriminately he labelled all French urban workers, gave a false impression of a social-class consciousness developing with industry. Consciousness developed in more traditional, artisanal surroundings and was singularly absent in the factory worker. Consciousness was the product of the slow development of ideas in an urban environment which permitted the contrasting of rich and poor. Consciousness developed first amongst those who had the

77

greatest opportunity as workers of social ascension and who consequently desired to increase the opportunities of sharing in property even by means of association.

The factory worker was often a former peasant, agricultural or domestic worker and in many cases still lived in the countryside and tended in his limited spare time a small field. These early generations of workers still thought as peasants, still had too much respect for property to listen to socialist propaganda, were badly educated and in their memories of the unchanging life of the countryside tended to see the universe as static.

As has been indicated, the factory worker had his moments of temper, of blind reaction to misery, sometimes leading to riots and machine breaking, but these were more akin to the peasant *jacquerie* than to organized industrial protest.

Brutalized by long hours of work and poor conditions, numbed by the noise and routine of a factory in which discipline was harsh in attempting to make tired men, women and children as efficient and regular as the machines they tended, the factory worker generally had little time, energy or capacity for thought. His reactions to misery rather took the form of crime, suicide, concubinage, drunkenness and more commonly simple apathy. They evince the inability of men in strange surroundings to adapt to these.

A sociologist has said that '... informal organization ... will develop spontaneously out of work experience only among workers who have in fact a considerable commitment to work and its associated conventions ... organized labour protest is a sign of involvement in the system; the uncommitted worker will normally behave apathetically or quit. He may on occasion engage in individual acts of protest through sabotage or in very fleeting forms of collective protest such as machine smashing.'[48] This would seem true of the major new industrial centres of France in the 1840s. If this is accepted, it was this feeling of commitment which was absent in the former peasant, and this was something that time and social immobility would alter. The period of the July Monarchy can be seen for the factory worker as one of acclimatization during which there developed, however slowly, some sort of a common attitude in the growing urban concentrations, a feeling of hostility and jealousy towards those better off which could later be harnessed by radical political groups. But first it was necessary to acquire a sense of power and force to to replace a common consciousness of inferiority.

In all this, the differences between the artisan and the factory worker are obvious – the former usually enjoyed better living and working conditions and the facilities for limited intellectual development. In a crisis both groups shared misery and always they felt insecure. This misery and insecurity was felt to an even greater extent by the large numbers of domestic workers who, isolated at work and often living in villages, lacked voth the intellectual development and the force given by concentration.

One significant factor in the attitudes of all three was the scale of production and the consequent relationship with the employer. For the craftsman working in a small workshop these were on a personal level. For the factory worker, the employer was an unknown, distant figure who could more easily be viewed as the symbol of an impersonal force labelled *they*. If the artisan might share many of the attitudes of his employer, if his aim was to become an employer himself, if he could hope for this, the factory worker lived in a world different from that of his employer, they shared nothing except a growing lack of understanding and antagonism. The artisan and his patron could still share socio-political aspirations, a common hostility to competitors and to the apparently idle rich. If the factory worker was to acquire a consciousness of his interests, then at this time it must include a hostility to those who obviously exploited him. If the domestic worker was exploited even more severely he was isolated, ignorant, and the exploiter was so distant as to be almost unidentifiable. However, compared with the artisan the conflict of interests here must have seemed more obvious if only at the level of the false measures so often used by the merchants buying the domestic worker's product.

This theory of relative hostility which was essentially true in practice and will help an understanding of worker reactions after February 1848, was however nuanced in certain areas by the paternalism of the employers. This was especially true of Alsace where employers were active in charity and in the establishment of mutual aid societies, so reducing the extremes of misery and winning a real feeling of gratitude, from a working class whose feeling of inferiority permitted it at this time to submit to what was an extremely authoritarian paternalism, and to whom, with more success than in many areas, the clergy, Protestant, Catholic, and Jewish constantly preached resignation.

Regional variation was significant in workers' attitudes. Paris, the city of artisans, possessed the most politically conscious groups. Also in many towns of the economically backward Midi advanced ideas were influential, again due to an urban environment and an absence of the extreme misery which drove men to apathy. The conclusion is that generally republican and socialist ideas were accepted more easily by urban, skilled craftsmen, suffering less from poverty, with a hope and will for improvement, while the factory workers and the miners slowly acquired a feeling of power from their spontaneous reactions, but remained outside politics.

Many artisans worked in rural villages supplying the everyday needs of the local population as coopers, smiths, etc. As such they seem usually to have shared the common mentality of their environment, sometimes including the more ideological shape given to this by the local representatives of the liberal professions, more rarely accepting radical ideas in opposition to the general attitude.

In Paris the petty bourgeoisie of shopkeepers and merchants and that of the less successful members of the liberal professions, the Bohemian element, were insecure and discontented, economically and psychologically, and played a vital part in the transference and adaptation of political and social ideas from their creators, who were often more substantial members of the community, and in the survival of the ideals of the first Jacobins, and in the adaptation of these to a changing socio-economic situation. They identified themselves with the great amorphous mass of the 'people' whose interests they defined in a vaguely humanitarian manner which reflected above all their own discontents.

In the countryside, in villages and small market towns where the members of the liberal professions with the richer artisans performed the social role of the petty bourgeoisie, they sometimes competed for influence with the landowning bourgeoisie and aristocracy, but more often were influential where these were absent – in the large villages or market towns roughly of over 1,000 souls where many of their customers were of similar social status and attitudes. Otherwise they tended, whether doctors or shopkeepers, to be dependent, to become part of the clientele of the notables on whom they depended for trade. This was particularly true of large provincial towns like Orléans or Toulouse where many artisans were Legitimists like their noble customers. Nowhere outside the larger cities did significant opposition to the July regime reveal itself.

The peasants were sharecroppers, the agricultural labourers even when possessing a smallholding, and most of those renting farms were obvious examples of dependents and could be presumed to have followed the will of the local landowner wherever he wished to enforce this. Of the more independent peasantry cultivating their land with the help of their families, hard work left little time for education or abstract thought. Apathy and resignation were common especially in the more backward regions and the most extreme exception to this was the riot which maintained the fear of *jacquerie* amongst the richer land-landowners, who generally, as befits an agricultural society, saw the peasant as the most dangerous threat to order. Besides this threat of spontaneous reaction to extremes of misery the personal influence of the local notables, their power of employment, often the influence of the clergy and the general respect for the rights of property, maintained an unquestioning acceptance of the social order.

As long as the routine of rural life remained unchanged, as long as the possibility of social transformation seemed a lie in the face of the eternal order of things, the peasant would resignedly accept his lot.

The only elements of discord were the ever-present poor, the continued if declining fear that the nobility would one day attempt to reclaim their feudal rights, the hatred of those who might threaten a peasant's ownership of his land – the usurer to whom he owed money, the tax collector who might enforce its sale. The poorer peasants and labourers hated the officials and property owners who sought to enclose the common land and protect the forests, whilst the more prosperous often favoured the former as an opportunity to increase their landholdings. Among the peasants who had acquired sufficient independence, materially and spiritually there was an erosion of respect for the traditional authorities, as they tended to see the social conservation of the Church and the noble or bourgeois landowner as merely a limit put on their opportunities for acquiring land, whilst sharing with these authorities a more general respect for property. Balzac well illustrated the views of these latter in *Les Paysans*. Only in certain circumstances would they support the very wealthy.

The advent of the Second Republic would more clearly indicate peasant attitudes to the existing society and it is better to postpone a more detailed discussion. Suffice it then to emphasize the differences apparent during the July Monarchy between areas as regards patterns of landowning and also agricultural prosperity or poverty. The economic crisis beginning in 1846 or even earlier by creating stresses resulted in a wealth of information concerning peasant mentalities, and the factors which contributed to produce these. This is the whole value of crisis and revolution to the social historian. It tends to compress into a short period a series of reactions to stimuli, increases the awareness and interest of contemporary commentators and consequently the richness of the material available to the historian.

Relatively little can be said of the political and social outlook of the French masses during the July Monarchy if only because they wrote nothing themselves. Official reports, in spite of the exaggerated suspicions, indicate that especially outside Paris disturbances were mainly spontaneous in character, that republican political groups and socialist ideas had little influence or support. All that had really happened was that industrial concentration had attained such a level as to make misery more keenly felt by those who endured it, and more repugnant or threatening to those who observed it from afar. It had created a keener interest in the social question.

Crisis of a Regime

The social crisis which preceded the February Revolution began years earlier. This crisis was provoked initially by a series of poor harvests worsened by the appearance from 1845 of the potato disease which was sweeping Europe with such devastating effect, especially in Ireland. It was, according to Labrousse, a crisis of an old type, a crisis common to the pre-mechanized industrial epoch, characterized by the predominant role of the agricultural sector, from which crisis spread to industry and commerce.[1] Labrousse illustrates again the fundamental factor for any historian of mid-nineteenth century France, namely its basically agricultural character, a factor not sufficiently dealt with by the great mass of historians who, urban dwellers themselves, exaggerate the significance of the town.

The most obvious effect of a bad crop is a shortage of food and a consequent increase in prices. Thus in the market at Caen a hectolitre of wheat costing on average 22 francs 89 centimes in 1846, reached a

peak of 46 francs 26 centimes in May 1847, and throughout that
year had an average price of 31 francs 49 centimes, which was
substantially above normal.[2] Similarly, potatoes which at Caen
normally cost from 2 to 4 francs a hectolitre, by the end of 1845 cost
5 to 6 francs, and by 1847 were 12 francs 30 centimes.[3] These are
just figurative examples which reveal an increase in the cost of living
which, if it varied in extent between areas, was yet common to all.
The fact that it was not due solely to the initial shortage but partly
to the panic hoarding with which those who could afford it greeted
a threatened food shortage, and to widespread speculation which
withheld stocks from the market in the hope of further price increases
contributed greatly to an increase in social tension.

Most of the income of the agricultural labourer or urban worker
was utilized in acquiring foodstuffs. The consequences of precipitate
rises in the prices of the two basic constituents of the worker's diet,
even if these increases were slightly alleviated by local action to
subsidize bakers or buy stocks for sale at a relatively low price, can
be imagined. The budget of the worker could often be balanced only
with difficulty in a period of prosperity. Even a small rise in the price
of his basic necessities created difficulty, but the increases prevalent
in 1846 and 1847 were more than small. A calculation of the variations
in the cost of living in an agricultural department reveals the extent
of the problem of the poor.

Taking 1843 as his base year, Georges Dupeux makes the following
calculation:[4]

1843	100	1846	112
1844	99	1847	135
1845	97	1848	90

The agricultural aspect of the crisis was however only part of the
story. As the revenue of the agricultural population declined, so
inevitably must its purchasing power, and this would affect particularly purchases of clothing, the consumer goods they required most
often, and therefore must result in a crisis in the most developed of
French industries, textiles.

Worsening this crisis in industry were factors peculiar more to the
new industrial and financial developments than to an agricultural
country. A crisis of a new type was increasingly making its appearance
in France and in what was in effect a transition economy, adding itself
to the older agriculturally caused crisis. Thus, in 1846–47 the
economic situation was worsened by industrial over-production, by

financial speculation and by a shortage of credit occurring also in England, with which France had close economic and financial connections.

The results of this crisis were underemployment and a decline in wages in most sectors of industry, at a time when substantial increases had occurred in the cost of living. At Roubaix for example, of 13,000 workers, 8,000 were unemployed at the beginning of May, 1847.[5] If only a slight decline occurred in the wages of those still employed there was a substantial decline in purchasing power. Even more adversely affected were the domestic workers. Here a decline in demand could be met simply by not supplying them with raw material. There were no overheads which had to be paid whether production continued or not, no threat of disorder from this dispersed population comparable to that presented by the unemployed urban artisans and factory workers. In many cases where domestic industry was a necessary support for the family of the peasant smallholder or agricultural labourer depression here served to further reduce an income already adversely affected by the crises in agriculture, by high prices and underemployment.

The seriousness of the industrial crisis can perhaps be gauged from the fact that in 1847 there were in France 4,672 business failures, compared with 2,618 in 1840 which in itself was not altogether prosperous.[6] It has been observed, however, that in 1847 these were almost exclusively failures of small enterprises, at least to a relatively greater extent than during the crisis of 1830, which indicates the increasingly secure position of the large-scale unit in the French economy.

Never before had the prices of the two staple elements of the diet of the poor risen to such a high level at the same time. There could be no recourse to a cheaper alternative source of food. Meat even in a normal period was too expensive. Never to such an extent had the elements of old and new crises combined with such a resultant decline in revenue of all kinds.

It is necessary, however, to avoid some of the possible conclusions which can be drawn from the assumption made by Marx that a 'general discontent' existed. Discontent might have been widespread but levels of discontent, the psychological reactions to misery varied, not simply according to the degree of misery, as some of the simplest versions of the Marxian theory might suggest.

Those most adversely affected by the high food prices were the urban population and that part of the rural population which was wage earning and not fed by its employers or which owned or farmed land but produced less than it consumed. Those who could be calculated to have generally benefitted by selling at high prices were the producers on a large scale with a substantial surplus disposable on the market. Similarly in the industrial sphere the small producers were in the weakest position, lacking the reserves possessed by their larger scale competitors and unable to compete by reducing prices for the diminishing market.

Food prices were highest in the north and north-east, that is in the major industrial centres, and especially Alsace. They declined towards the south-west, Massif Central and south. This pattern was the product of various factors involving weather, types of crop, etc., and the non-existence of a national market due to poor communications which greatly hindered the transport of food. It might be worth stressing even at this point for repetition later that the pattern of social disturbance did not follow that of high prices, rather the reverse. In Alsace, in the departments of Bas- and Haut-Rhin harvests were increasingly bad from 1844 and as early as the end of 1845 the prefects of both departments were appealing to the government to stop grain exports and meeting in response a refusal from a regime which was so reluctant to interfere with the free play of the market that it even objected to releasing its own reserves of food. Most of the urban workers and many of the rural in this region of extreme parcellation were dependent on public and private charity. The price of wheat reached a peak in May 1847 in Bas-Rhin at what was the highest national figure, over 50 francs per hectolitre,[7] but from then on conditions started to improve and especially with the good harvest of 1847, although the fact that many smallholders had eaten the reserves normally held for seeding in the previous year helped limit the extent of the recovery.

By comparison the Mediterranean department of the Var experienced far lower prices and a less significant variation. The highest rise experienced in the price of cereals was from 29 francs 30 centimes, to 34 francs from January to May 1847, at a time when prices per hectolitre at Altkirch in Haut-Rhin rose from 36 francs 30 centimes to 49 francs 50 centimes.[8] The differences are sufficient to permit a meaningful comparison between the degree of misery in the one and in the other, and were largely due to the facility of importation of foodstuffs into the Var. Both departments, however, shared one common feature – the almost total absence of disturbances.

Price levels are not clear indicators of the degree of misery of a population. Thus in the area of East Aquitain covered by the departments of Haute-Garonne, Ariège, Tarn and Tarn-et-Garonne if prices were not as high as the national average in 1847 they had been rising since 1842 and this long period of relative hardship for the poorer section of the community made it especially difficult for them to face even the limited increase in 1846–47.[9]

Variation after variation could be cited to illustrate both the difference in economic conditions and the difficulties of historical generalization. Suffice it then to consider one last example on a more limited geographical scale, namely that described by Philippe Vigier in his work on the Alpine Region.

Vigier contrasts the areas of plain in the departments of Drôme, Isère and Vaucluse where other crops partially made up for the failure of wheat, where the discontent of the labourers was thus alleviated and many proprietors remained prosperous, with the mountain regions especially in Basses- and Hautes-Alpes heavily dependent on the single crop of potatoes, where the prevalence of small property resulted in an uniform pattern of misery.[10]

As far as industrial centres were concerned conditions were fairly uniformly grim with a decline in the demand for textiles, luxury artisanal goods and the products of metallurgy, but not in some areas, for example the north, for coal. The coal miners were thus a relatively well-off group, but were as such exceptions, only joined by the dock workers of some ports engaged in the importation of food-stuffs and especially those of Marseille.

This is sufficient to indicate the varying economic condition. In all areas and sectors of production recovery was apparent from mid-1847 even though wages remained low and prices relatively high. Unemployment too was common. Revolution occurred in this period of increasing economic activity rather than at the height of the crisis, but that the Revolution could occur in February 1848 was in large part due to the social unrest and discontent caused by the economic crisis.

The intense misery of large numbers of people during 1846 and 1847 is obvious from statistics concerning mortality, for example. Thus in Paris mortality per 1,000 increased from 25·4 in 1845 to 27·1 in 1846, to 29·3 in 1847,[11] or from the number of people helped by public assistance which increased as follows:[12]

1843	854,968
1844	844,637
1845	835,175
1846	923,347
1847	1,185,632

This ignores those in receipt of private charity, those too proud to seek aid and those unable to find any because of the inadequate organization of the service, particularly in the face of a major crisis. None of these figures reveals sufficiently the extent of misery among the masses, possibly more revealing is the figure of 268,090 aided in the industrial department of the Nord, evidence of a concentration of poverty. This compares with 188,477 in the more prosperous if still depressed year of 1845[13] and reveals a substantial increase in the number of unemployed.

The symptoms of this misery were seen especially in an increase of death by natural causes, or by suicide,[14] the increased need for charity, and commonly a substantial increase in the number of crimes committed.[15] For our purposes the incidences of group rather than individual action are even more interesting. Here use can be made of Remi Gossez's map pinpointing disturbances due to the high price of foodstuffs, including attempts to stop food exports, pillaging of convoys, forced sale in markets, riots, threats, and the appearance of bands of beggars.[16] Gossez shows such incidents to have been most common in the departments of the extreme north, that is the Nord and Pas-de-Calais, and in the north-west in the Loire, Normandy amd Poitou, in such departments as Eure-er-Loir, Ille-et-Vilaine, Mayenne, Indre-et-Loire and Indre. These disturbances were prevalent in some areas of modern industry, in those of traditional textile industry, and in the agricultural departments of the north-west, but not in similar areas in Alsace and the south generally.

In the Nord the symptoms of extreme misery in the form of luddism, bands of beggars, attacks on bakeries, the pillaging of boats, waggons and markets, were all present. These were spontaneous expressions of misery most common in the rural and industrial villages of the department. Strikes were few and spontaneous and given the weakness of the workers' position, shortlived. The only manifestations of discontent which could be associated at all with politics were the seditious cries which again expressed exasperation rather than a thought-out attitude or political organization. The most striking feature was the continued resignation of the workers in industrial towns like Lille which must however, even in its apathy

D

have concealed an increasing dissatisfaction with the social and political *status quo*, with the regime exemplified in the workers' minds by the monarch.

The departments of the Nord and Pas-de-Calais exemplified a latent discontent but a lack of consciousness of class or group interests. This was even more true of the Haut-Rhin, where if some shortlived strikes and one serious riot occurred in protest against the high price of bread, the spirit of resignation remained for some time even stronger than in the Nord, at least in the industrial towns.

Some centres of more traditional textile production were also affected by unrest. In the Rouen region that most primitive form of popular action, begging, was increasingly common from the winter of 1845–46 and by the beginning of 1847 the situation was worsened from the point of view of the authorities by a large number of riots in the market places of small market towns or industrial centres in which participated primarily domestic weavers and industrial workers, with a majority of women. Again there were no signs of political motivation but an awareness of their power must have been acquired by the workers concerned, particularly as the local authorities often preferred a sympathetic inaction to repression. As in the Nord there was a natural tendency to blame misery on the regime. A song popular at Elbeuf blamed high prices on speculators who enjoyed the protection of the king and spoke of 'The monster who reigns in France'.[17]

If the misery of the domestic textile workers was probably most extreme they did not in most areas resort to violence. Thus in Bas-Rhin these dispersed workers finding little time for anything save work appeared to have been the most resigned of all. The domestic weavers of Alsace differed from those of the Rouen area in their greater geographical dispersion and the lack of a lead given by an urban population which might entrain them to disorder.

Of industrial workers generally the physical expression of unrest was most likely to occur in the departments of the Nord, Pas-de-Calais and Seine-Inferieure, and in Paris, and was far less likely in Alsace. Material conditions of existence were similar, consequently the reason for this difference in behaviour must be searched for elsewhere. At this stage the following can only be suggested – the geographical and linguistic isolation of Alsace, the successful application there of philanthropy in ameliorating the misery and reinforcing relations of dependence and the influence of religion. The older urban traditions of the towns of the Nord and Seine-Inférieure might also be a factor of some significance. Whatever our final conclusions concerning the role of non-economic factors in influencing mass behaviour, it is possible here to stress their importance.

If the spirit of resignation was marginally less strong in some industrial areas than others, the conclusion which must be drawn concerning the areas considered above, and the workers whether engaged in factory or domestic production is one which highlights their lack of political consciousness. Nevertheless they were dissatisfied and the July Monarchy could look for no support from them.

Inevitably disorder mainly occurred in agricultural regions. Here in periods of high prices the old fear of famine was quickly reborn, the customary rights in forests and on common land which had provided a limited guarantee against misery were re-affirmed. In the countryside protests were directed against the individuals easily associated with causes or symptoms of crisis – the employers, merchants, speculators, landlords or officials who had reduced their labour forces, cut wages, or who threatened by hoarding to force prices higher, or to export food, or who were associated with the assault on traditional rights. The rural disturbances of 1847 took a traditional form, indeed the forms already listed for the industrial regions, indicating again the closeness of the factory worker or domestic weaver to the peasant. The participants were vine growers, small peasant proprietors, landless or insufficiently landed labourers and rural craftsmen; primarily those who possessed insufficient land to benefit from the high prices, and were forced by the smallness of their crops to return to the market as purchasers. The targets of their aggression were the foodstuffs possessed by their wealthier neighbours. In this respect an element of tension in the relationships of rich and poor was obvious although limited by the philanthropic activities in many areas of the rich, and the general dependence both psychological and practical of the poor, the maintenance of ideas of hierarchy. The disturbances of 1847 were similar to those of the eighteenth century to those which had preceded the revolutions of 1789 and 1830.

This is the picture of rural disturbances as they occurred in the agricultural departments of the north-west. Gossez additionally suggests that these incidents were especially serious where an element of urban concentration, a number of artisanal, mining or factory workers, however small, existed in a rural area.[18] Here presumably discontent would be concentrated and mob emotions aroused.

Variations between regions were significant with a relative absence of disturbances in the south, especially, and in the north-east. The more mountainous areas of the Alpine region experienced extreme misery, to a degree which would only be revealed after February 1848, in an assault on the agents and property of the state and private owners of forests. The change of government would serve to impel the poor to act, but in 1847 they appeared outwardly to be resigned to their condition. Similar comments could be made concerning the peasants of Alsace. In these areas of extreme misery all that lacked for disturbances to occur was some sort of a spark to move the populations from their traditional apathy. In the absence of large private landowners hostility was towards the state in the Alps, and towards the Jews in Alsace.

Of the behaviour of the populations in the majority of departments in the south few explanations have been offered by historians. A number of reasons for this passivity might, however, be presented including geographical isolation, the lesser degree of industrial development and therefore of socially disruptive urban influences, the greater significance in some areas, for example, near the Pyrenees, of Legitimist notabilities with their traditional concepts of social hierarchy still acceptable to the mass of the population in an unchanging world, of the acceptance of the need for resignation preached by the Church. Significant also was the less intense nature of the crisis in, for example, coastal regions where importation was easier and food prices lower. In vine-growing areas 1847 was generally not such a bad year. Essentially economic backwardness meant the survival of a traditional society and traditional ideas and only where these were challenged, where an economically independent peasantry or petty bourgeoisie existed able to challenge the greater landowners and Church would, during the Second Republic, social unrest become more evident. But again a political spark was essential – misery combined with a felt hope of improvement would end resignation.

What needs to be observed concerning group behaviour in 1847 is the complicated set of causal factors, economic, social and ideological, and their interlinking. It would be difficult to assert the primacy of the economic; rather it can be said that revolution would occur in 1848 when misery existed due to economic depression, at a time when non-economic factors – political and psychological – though these were in part economically conditioned – served to create an impulse to act.

Variation was significant as were its causes, resignation might mean the survival of traditional society, it might be due to extreme misery and as such sooner or later change to revolt. But in 1847 whatever the nature or extent of reaction to misery two facts were evident. First the extensive discontent, whether latent or not, of the masses. Secondly their inability to present a threat to the regime even where they threatened public order. The mentality conducive to *jacquerie* could only become revolutionary when leadership in organization and ideas came from other social groups.

For revolution to occur certain preconditions were necessary: first, an army possessed of a vague ideal and purpose; second, leaders to clarify this purpose, organize the army and benefit from its victory. According to Marx the Paris proletariat and petty bourgeoisie formed the ranks of the army in February 1848, its officers and non-commissioned officers were petty bourgeois and republican bourgeois. He ascribed the success of this revolt additionally to the centralization of the French state which gave control of France to whoever controlled Paris.[19] This differs from our emphasis not so much on this aspect of centralization but in ignoring the passivity of those social groups who in the election of 1846 had recorded an overwhelming vote of support for the political regime. In February 1848, they were not prepared to exert themselves to defend it whether at the centre in Paris or in the provinces.

The main impulse to change came initially from groups relatively low in the bourgeois hierarchy, from those who enjoyed the franchise in only the largest cities, who felt that their under-representation meant the adoption of policies unfavourable to their economic position. Already in 1846 their support of opposition candidates in Paris, Lille, Marseille, Nantes and Bordeaux had permitted the success of these. In this respect the compaign for constitutional reform reflected the social divisions within the larger body of the bourgeoisie. The discontented favoured reform not revolution, but their political acitivity had significant, unexpected results which earned from the police spy Lucien de la Hodde a severe castigation – for revolution to occur, he observed, 'It is necessary that the bourgeoisie through anger, as in 1830 or inconsistency, as in 1848, stimulates insurrection.'[20]

Contributing to this sense of discord were other more emotive factors – a proud nationalism which resented a foreign policy avoiding risks, a disgust at scandals involving close associates of the government, at the obvious corruption in elections and even in the Chamber which, if resorted to by all parties, could be achieved more successfully by the government. The politically insignificant developed a contempt for the government and blamed all things on it. They could not but feel that their greater participation in politics would improve matters. Unfairly perhaps even the causes of the economic crisis were seen as political, as arising out of diplomatic complications which had occurred at the same time as Paris became aware of the economic crisis. If some individuals attacked the government for doing insufficient to protect the poor against the worst effects of unemployment and high prices, others taking a traditional view of the need to balance the budget demanded further reductions in government expenditure.

The general picture is of a loss of confidence in the government, and in the future. This decline in confidence brought latent political opposition to the fore. Prosperity had been as a protector to the regime. Even men like Thiers had little loyalty to the king as such, but rather to a system guaranteeing order and prosperity. What was new in February was not only the severity of the economic crisis but the crisis of confidence within the ruling classes, and the fact that economic events forced on various groups of the bourgeoisie an awareness of separate interests, exemplified in the ability of the large enterprises to survive, whilst so many of the smaller collapsed, above all in the financial crisis dividing those cautious men who controlled credit resources from the many who desperately required credit.

By 1848 a revolutionary situation existed, produced by mass discontent, and the inculcation of republican and revolutionary ideals in a generalized manner. A campaign of banquets involving bourgeois intellectuals and petty bourgeoisie demanded limited reform but excited opinion, and provided accidentally the occasion for a demonstration which was to lead equally accidentally, through shots fired, to revolution.

The pattern of support for revolution or unwillingness to oppose it can be seen in the reaction of the Paris National Guard on 23 February. On previous occasions the firm defender of the regime this organization was composed largely of the shopkeepers and merchants, the middle classes of Paris, those whose economic problems and political aspirations made them discontented, and who now refused to involve themselves in repression and prevented the army from doing so, particularly by undermining its morale. The exceptions to this generalization were the 1st Legion from the quarter of the Champs-Elysées, Place Vendôme and Tuileries, and part of the 10th Invalides, Faubourg-Saint-Germain, the Legions in which the wealthiest served.[21]

The involvement of the workers was assured by vague ideals, material discontent, and the influence of the intellectuals and students, on the petty bourgeoisie and on its own élite, who both used this discontent and, once it was aroused, were pushed further than many might have wished by those workers who largely acted in a spontaneous manner, beginning on February 22 as spectators at a demonstration, but who as the day passed, because of 'the excitement communicated from one to the other' and 'the sight of sabres being brought down on the heads of the crowd' were brought to believe themselves face to face with an enemy.[22]

In opposition to this force, some few National Guards and demoralized troops. Paralysed by inertia or illwill as in the case of the Legitimist aristocracy resident in Paris, the majority of the *grande bourgeoisie* seems to have submitted to a feeling of pessimism. The sentiments expressed at this time by diverse personalities like de Tocqueville, the Austrian diplomat Apponyi or Charles de Rémusat, all evince this feeling. More significantly it was shared by the king himself. Rémusat, Thiers and Guizot all agree that Louis-Philippe lost his head and was unwilling to resist once he found that the National Guard had deserted him. This is proof of the importance of the individual in history. If Louis-Philippe had done as Thiers claimed he advised, and withdrawn from Paris to gather troops, he might have succeeded in reoccupying the city as did Thiers in 1871. But he did not, and the Republic was established.

Discontent in all sections of the population, largely due to the economic situation had deprived the regime of its normal supporters and increased the number and will of those prepared to resort to revolution. But this discontent was expressed in various ideological forms, one of which, that of the republic, determined the form of the new regime. This was the ideology which the great mass of active barricade fighters accepted, and which, in the staffs of two newspapers, possessed personnel willing and able to assume the responsibility of government, to make use of the situation in which the former ruling classes had meekly resigned but which they had not themselves

93

provoked. The economic crisis had weakened not so much the economic power of the ruling group, but its will-power. It expected revolution. Apponyi wrote on February 18 that 'Europe appears to be on the eve of a general outburst' and predicted 'the war of those who have nothing against those who have something.'[23] The mounting wave of unrest and of extremist publications accepted at face value had created a fear, a belief in a possible red terror, amongst the better informed. This was an irrational, psychological impulse which produced a strange and temporary willingness to accept the inevitable. Rémusat, who was present at the Tuileries on February 24, was later to write apologetically of the spirit of himself and of his colleagues on that day – 'it is the inertia of our will which humiliates when I think of it.'[24] This was a fear which for the middle classes, the less wealthy and less informed was at this time eclipsed by the dire need to improve their political, social and economic situation.

Thus many factors combined to create a revolution – economic crisis, the discontent of the poor and of many of the possessors, the failures in the eyes of others of a government supposedly existing to preserve order, an accidental shooting of demonstrators. These factors provided a mass army, ready to accept the leadership of a small group with a conscious revolutionary purpose, and in France, as in Paris, potential opposition would fade away.

A hierarchy of causes could be constructed in which the socio-economic situation at the beginning of 1848 would come first as a cause of revolution. But entering into this situation so many different factors can be observed which made for the peculiarity of this socio-political crisis, which explain why revolution occurred when it did and not earlier as to indicate the excessive simplicity of the Marxian account.

Revolution occurred in Paris and succeeded in France. Marx explains the latter as due to political centralization. More significant was again the factor of pessimism. But shock, too, was important. The provinces do not seem to have had such a pessimistic view of the future as that prevailing in Paris. Outside a few large cities social antagonism cannot have been so obvious. Peasants and workers were rarely politically conscious. If there was therefore little active support for a king not prepared to fight for himself, there was little overt support for the newly established regime, but rather, for some, hope that vague aspirations would be satisfied and by comparison a latent fear and opposition from those who retained economic and social power.

III

February – June 1848

To the crowds who had overthrown the monarchy the obvious alternative must have seemed to have been a republic. Liberty, equality and fraternity, the ideals of the first Revolution had been preserved by the folk memory aided by journalism, had been given new content to increase their appeal to the poor. Those who stepped into the political vacuum, created by the flight of Louis-Philippe, were republicans who owed their fame largely to journalism. Republicanism was the only political faith which appealed to the masses and they selected by popular acclaim its best-known figures to govern France.

The initial period of the Republic was one of apparent harmony. Members of all social groups, of the administration, army, and Church vied with each other in their declarations of loyalty to the new regime. It seemed to many observers that a new society based on brotherly love was emerging.

The economy imposed the limits to this. The possessing classes might declare their loyalty to the Provisional Government of the Republic, but they had little confidence in their future under republican institutions. They were not prepared to risk investing their capital when the political future remained uncertain. France had been recovering from the economic crisis of earlier years, now conditions rapidly worsened, commerce and production again dried up and unemployment again increased.

In these conditions the work of the Provisional Government was difficult. Its members were, in the main, rather cautious, prepared to support political liberalization, but not far-reaching social reform. This government sought to conciliate all social classes. It sought to give confidence to the wealthy and practical aid to the poor. In many respects its measures were radical new departures, but given the seriousness of the situation they were never radical enough. The Provisional Government and moderate republicans generally took up a centre position from which they were never able to satisfy either extreme.

The elections of April 1848, the first held under universal manhood suffrage returned a Constituent Assembly with a large majority apparently committed to supporting the moderate policy introduced by the Provisional Government, but who were primarily conservatives.

In Paris unemployment and misery made much of the population receptive to the ideas of men who claimed that the Provisional Government was doing insufficient for the people. The National Workshops created by the Government and hailed originally as an institution designed to end unemployment proved to be only a means of making relief payments. Yet these symbolized on the one hand the promise of the Republic, they were the one positive measure of social reform, and on the other the threat of social revolution, a threat made to seem real by the continued demonstrations and general unrest in Paris.

In the Assembly deputies demanded an end to disorder and uncertainty concerning the future. The workers organized in the National Workshops were the ever-present threat of a new revolution. The government elected by the Constituent Assembly was composed of the same moderates as had been the Provisional Government. They feared the mobs in the streets, and feared also the political isolation which disagreement with the majority in the Assembly would mean. In deciding to close the National Workshops, they chose an armed conflict with the poor people of Paris. In this conflict they were supported not only by the property owners of Paris, but by the vast majority of the provincial population afraid of, or not understanding the 'red menace', and by the army.

The initial acceptance of the new order by former declared supporters of monarchical institutions was the product of fear and stupor. A fear based on the memories of the Terror which symbolized for them the achievements of the first Republic, a fear born of the sudden and unexpected revolution, of the seeming total nature of change to be expected in a situation where the masses held physical power, control of the streets in the major urban centres, and would have at the elections a legal right to select as members of the legislative body individuals who might promise to satisfy their every whim. To most wealthy men, to the men who had dominated society during the two previous regimes, the masses were an unknown – it was this mystery of their existence and desires which made the situation so especially ominous. A once familiar world was disorganized, men's expectations as to their future role in society, activity planned for the near future, all was thrown into doubt. The result was a dazed or stunned acceptance of what had occurred, which was allied with the desire to make the best of what must have seemed irreversible.

The evidence for this interpretation is substantial. Alexis de Tocqueville provides in his *Souvenirs* some of the most clearly expressed reflections of this period. He reveals both the essential cause of fear amongst the possessing groups and one factor which led to a rapid regaining of confidence. De Tocqueville records that on February 25 'I spent the whole afternoon walking in Paris. Two things struck me: the first was the exclusively popular character of the revolution which had occurred; the total power it had given to the people properly so-called, that is to say to the classes who work with their hands, over all the others. The second, was how little these people made the passion of hatred felt, or indeed any passion.'[1] This was to him an essential feature distinguishing 1848 from previous insurrections. This made a resigned attitude possible.

Even more revealing of the mental anguish combined with resignation common to the conservative wealthy was the individual reaction of Charles de Rémusat: 'My first concern was to call my children . . . I attempted to prepare them for their new situation. Up to the present they had been able to believe themselves to be amongst the privileged of society. . . . Their future had seemed assured; everything would be easy for them. Now, it would cease to be so. They would probably live under an indifferent or even hostile regime.'[2]

The ultramontane, conservative newspaper, the *Univers* of Louis Veuillot proclaimed on February 27 that 'God speaks by the voice of events. The revolution of 1848 is the intimation of Providence.' The Legitimist *Gazette de France* on February 27 felt that 'Who has not seen Paris this evening: Paris full of order, of harmony, of majesty, in the middle even of the sublime disorder of the barricade, will never know the great beauty of the sovereignty of the people.' Generally the old official press, the *Journal de Débats* and the *Constitutionnel* became mildly liberal, whilst the former press of the dynastic opposition and the old republican press assumed in this period an official tone. The Legitimist press, and this is symptomatic of

97

Legitimists generally, accepted the Republic in the hope of further change. All these newspapers adopted a tone of sympathy and understanding towards the masses. All reflected indeed the expressed opinions and half-felt hopes of their readers in that catering exclusively for the highly educated minority they reflected rather than formed opinion. Their attitude as that of their readers in February – March 1848, was restrained, and in the light of their subsequent conduct opportunistic.

The commissaire of the new government at Limoges wrote in a report of March 4 that 'All the Philippistes proclaim themselves republicans today. It should not be forgotten though that the rich have in general little sympathy for this new form of government . . . and it is evident to me that fear, the impossibility of resistance, the need to support the Provisional Government in the interests of order and tranquillity, have created . . . the appearance of unanimity . . .'[3]

The accuracy of this interpretation can be gauged from the opinion of the English ambassador to France, Lord Normanby, who after discussions with leading politicians of the Orleanist period observed that 'all seemed to consider that the only present hope for the country was to rally round the existing Government, and trust in its efforts to moderate the popular feeling, and re-establish order and confidence.'[4] The Genevan, William de la Rive, wrote to his wife from Paris on March 2, of the Provisional Government that 'Everyone supports it and with reason, in that it is a barrier against the complete disorganization of society.'[5]

Soon after the revolution was published a little book entitled *Le gouvernement provisoire : Histoire anecdotique et politique de ses membres* which taking as its motto 'order everywhere! Liberty for all!' attempted to increase confidence in the Provisional Government by a review of the anti-communist utterances made by its various members in the past. A government which included Lamartine, Garnier-Pagès and Marie could not be too extreme.[6] Conservatives then had a plank to grasp. The moderation of the new government and of the masses, the obvious attempts of this government to win the favour of all sections of the community through financial measures and the establishment of public works, all contributed to a rebirth of confidence and as the situation seemed to improve and they recovered from their initial shock conservatives became more critical of their new situation.

As early as March 1, an editorial in the *Constitutionnel* indicated this trend, in language having little in common with the still pre-vailing aura of social harmony. According to the writer 'The re-establishment of order is today the principal preoccupation of all honest men' and this because of the extensive disorder and extension of crime. Legitimate remarks perhaps, but given the Paris situation, exaggerated and reflecting rather the feeling remembered by the paper's proprietor Dr Véron in his memoirs. He was to write that 'The day following the February Revolution, the bourgeois of Paris trembled for his head, and, once he was sure of retaining it, he trembled for his purse.'[7] The effervescence of socialist ideas made this understandable.

It was then the Republic of moderation which conservatives supported, and only conditionally, until some more satisfying institutions could be created, and this whatever the phrases favouring harmony, and the real or pretended desire to improve the conditions of the poor. Acceptance of the Republic was combined with ill-will and this is especially obvious in judging the attitudes of provincial conservatives to the February revolution. These can be contrasted with Parisian attitudes so as to highlight the strength and inevitability of a socio-political reaction.

To provincial opinion the revolution must have seemed profoundly Parisian, sudden and political in character. This is the conclusion of Louis Chevalier in his thesis covering the Parisian region. Only in Paris did the totality of economic and political causes of the revolution coincide to create a revolutionary situation. Elsewhere the revolution must have assumed a somewhat artificial and imposed character.

Uncertainty concerning the future must have been greater away from the centre of power, and amongst the politically less sophisti-cated. Fear could be expressed more openly away from the centres of republican strength and be allowed to influence a large proportion of the population. Already on 27 February came an isolated appeal for the unity of conservatives in the Orléanist *Journal de Loir-et-Cher* which referred to the 'horrible tempest which has burst upon our unfortunate country' and called for 'all honest men' to unite to prevent 'the violation in the name of liberty' of the rights of individuals and especially that of property.[8] This clarion call was, however, unusual. Far more common in most areas where order was undis-turbed was the surprise and stupefaction observed by the *procureur général* at Aix.[9] The awakening from this initial state of shock was to produce a report of March 2, which indicated an attitude amongst the socially dominant elements of the population similar to that found amongst Parisian conservatives – 'Everywhere the new order is accepted. Everyone understands the necessity to avoid confusion and anarchy, of adhesion to the Provisional Government... but the sympathies of this backward population of the Midi are not in its favour...'[10]

If anything, the revolution of February 1848 was a great psychological shock to those who had favoured the social *status quo*, and particularly to those who had provided the ruling cadres – A. J. Tudesq's *grands notables*. Marx does not recognize this psychic factor in his account, preferring rather to describe events in terms of the relative power of particular alliances of social groups at particular periods, but to observe that one group was removed from power is not to explain why it accepted this so easily. The particular form the political conflict was to take subsequently was the result of the retention of social influence and power by the *grands notables*. The fact that this power remained undisturbed is partly explained by the apparently whole-hearted acceptance of the republic by these groups which made punitive measures against them appear unnecessary. Only the absence of resistance permitted the republic to be moderate, enabled measures involving the redeployment of socio-economic power to be avoided. The psychological reaction of the ruling groups provides the key to an understanding of this situation.

Closely connected with this latter point – the most striking fact about both the administration and the army was the effort made by senior officials and officers to retain their posts. Compared with the spate of resignations in 1830 the absence of firm convictions is obvious. These individuals shared the attitude of resignation which was the general reaction of the middle- and upper-class circles from which most of them originated.

This was not, however, altogether true of the army. It submitted. This was its traditional response. It owed loyalty to France and to the government in place rather than to a particular form of regime. Even in 1830 Legitimist officers in resigning rather than attempting to fight had recognized this. In the first months of 1848 moreover a general European war was expected and the maintenance of the military structure seemed essential. But its apparent homogeneity was no more. Raoul Giradet lists the elements of division, the rivalries and jealousies of professional men for promotion, political rivalries, differences of generation, rivalry between those officers who had served in Africa and those retained in metropolitan France, social origins – forming a gulf separating the large number of especially junior officers promoted from the ranks and those who were products of the specialized schools. This produced a crisis of morale to worsen that already caused by the expulsion of the army from Paris, and by the rapid change in governmental authority, and contributed to a relaxation in discipline which was especially frightening to conservative elements of the population taught to regard the army as an element of the Jacobin revolution.

Cohesion, it seems, was only possible for the French army in periods of political stability when a government strong enough to impose silence on the diverse interests existed. The indiscipline of early 1848 was to create within the army a reinforced desire for strong government. This, the psychological need to punish those who in Paris had so humiliated it in February, the social background of senior officers who soon regarded the word 'republic' as a synonym for anarchy, and the general *esprit de corps* – another psychological element, would ensure that the future reactions of the army would not be favourable to the more extreme republicans.

The participation of the Church in the harmonious feeling of this early period of the Second Republic has struck many historians when compared with the violent anti-clericalism of 1830. The presence of priests at public ceremonies celebrating the advent of the Republic, and the favourable messages from the bishops represented acceptance of the liberal lead given by Pius IX represented also the relief of the Church at the fall of a regime condemned as Voltairean and materialistic. The Church, for the workers in large urban centres, was an element of the opposition to the Orleanist monarchy and would help create the new era. Christ was the great socialist and the clergy if anybody represented Him. Indeed the bishops preached the duty to help the suffering, and adhered to the principles of liberty, fraternity and equality which were now described as eternal principles of Christianity. In his historical essays Marx labelled the Church as an instrument of the bourgeoisie and implicitly found the clergy as much as the class it represented guilty of hypocrisy in these early weeks. In as much as it accepted the Republic with real enthusiasm, accepting at face value its promise of freedom of education, then the Church as a whole, was concerned primarily with its own interests as a religious institution. In many areas, however, by contrast with Paris, the revolution was the signal for anti-clerical outbursts, and in this respect as in the question of social harmony generally a gulf separated Paris and the provinces, a gulf caused by differences of social structure and political awareness which renders inaccurate many of the older historical works insufficiently aware of regional variation and excessively concerned with political developments in Paris.

Incidents such as the destruction of convents at Lyon by workers who saw them as mere shelters for cheap labour revealed the limitations to the new fraternal attitude of the urban masses, and increasingly as the whole basis of the society in which the Church existed appeared to be threatened, then its reaction and particularly the statements of the bishops would be similar to those of fellow members of the middle classes in the desire for social conservation, but again this could be seen to be as much a concern for its own interests as for its supposed class loyalties.

The *grands notables* and the middle classes generally, submitted and hoped that nothing would change except the form of government. This new submissiveness would end with two things – the felt need to defend their possessions against the lower orders and the similarly felt possibility that a socio-political restoration was possible. In this early period the activity of the Government and of the masses were the factors determining a move from initial shocked resignation. The initiative of the ruling groups had been lost, their behaviour was in response to the initiatives of others.

The most obvious immediate creation of February was the Provisional Government, which according to Marx 'necessarily mirrored in its composition the different parties which had shared in the victory. It could not be anything but a compromise between the different classes which together had overturned the July throne, but whose interests were mutually antagonistic. The great majority of its members consisted of representatives of the bourgeoisie. The republican petty bourgeoisie was represented by Ledru-Rollin and Flocon, the republican bourgeoisie by the people from the *National*, the dynastic opposition by Cremieux, Dupont de L'Eure, etc. The working class had only two representatives, Louis Blanc and Albert. Finally, Lamartine in the Provisional Government, this was at first no real interest, no definite class; this was the February Revolution itself, the common uprising with its illusions, its poetry, its visionary content and its phrases. For the rest, the spokesman of the February Revolution, by his position and his views, belonged to the bourgeoisie.'[11]

The feasibility of this interpretation has been hinted at while considering the factors which caused the revolution, which produced a degree of unity in the streets amongst members of disparate social groups. From the differing initial concepts of what the republic would be, would stem conflict. It beholds us consequently to explain the differences and examine the consequences.

Take first the men of the *National*. On February 27 an editorial presented the following advice to the Government, which can be taken as representing the views of the newspaper's former editors now members of the Government – 'it must interest in the maintenance of order that considerable portion of citizens who, until now deprived of all political rights, are not perhaps aware of the means by which legitimate demands will all be satisfied.' It recommended patience to the masses or else 'These reforms ... would be compromised'. In addition to ameliorating the conditions of the masses, 'The Provisional Government must act in a manner which will confirm the good opinion that it has already given of itself to citizens who under the old order of things did not desire as radical a change, but who resigned themselves loyally to accept the *fait accompli*.' The protection of interests demands the substantial maintenance of the social *status quo*. For men like Marrast then 'The principle of the republican government is a principle of order.'

More radical were those labelled as representatives of the petty bourgeoisie, of small property owners and businessmen, whose political and social aims were represented by another newspaper the *Réforme*. On February 26, in demanding an end to machine breaking, it asserted that the enemy had not been the means of production but 'the feudal-industrial government which in order to found its empire on the servitude of the starving, debased labour and refused credit and association to the workers.' In the sovereignty of the people the writer sees hope for a better future. His appeal was to the small men, oppressed by those who controlled credit, as was further indicated by an article of March 8 desiring state credits at low interest.

The views of a social group can usually only be determined from those expressed by its representatives. In the *National* this period could be read opinions concerning society little different from those of political conservatives. In the *Réforme* on the other hand, the attack is maintained against the financial oligarchy believed to have dominated France under the July Monarchy. Change was demanded by means of easier credit, and who would this benefit other than the owners of small businesses or the yet-to-be-organized associations of workers. The notion of credit does, however, involve acceptance of property relationships, the conditions of the workers should be improved but without crippling their masters. The status of most workers as opposed to that of the patrons would remain fundamentally what it was before. Just as the *National* so the *Réforme* showed great concern for the preservation of order. Lucien de la Hodde recorded the participation at a meeting of fifty republicans in the offices of the *Réforme* on February 21. It included 11 journalists, 4 innkeepers, 1 *rentier*, 1 clerk, 1 printing worker, 2 mechanics, 1 commercial traveller, 1 grocer, 1 proprietor of a bathing establishment, 2 shopkeepers, 1 commercial agent, 4 captains in the National Guard (and thus presumably men of some financial standing), 3 employees, 1 watchmaker, 1 leather worker, 1 dentist, 1 doctor, 1 painter, 1 insurance broker and 1 student. This was representative of the Parisian petty bourgeoisie with some of the more politically conscious workers with whom they were in continual contact.[12]

The measures introduced by the Provisional Government were revealing of the character and intentions of this Government. The heterogeneous character of the government has been observed. Agreement on practical measures by such a group must obviously have been difficult. The majority of its members seem to have believed that their role was simply to maintain order and administrative continuity, keeping their acts to a minimum before the election of a Constituent Assembly. Thus a reluctance even to proclaim the Republic of their own responsibility. These moderate bourgeois republicans evinced a supreme concern for legality even in revolution. For them the Republic meant the consent of the ruled and given the lack of open opposition to its existence there seemed no good reason to resort to revolutionary measures for which they as moderates had great distaste. Proudhon was for one critical of their inaction and wrote – 'Many words and not one idea. The government, because it has no ideas, does nothing, is able to do nothing, and wants to do nothing . . .'[13] This was not wholly true. Popular pressure forced the government to act. The pattern of its action might be seen as due to its lack of ideas, but the extent of this action in the socio-economic sphere was greater than that engaged in by any previous government.

Measures such as the reduction of the working day in Paris to ten hours and in the provinces to eleven were a significant break with the *laissez-faire* social attitude of government during the July Monarchy and thus in many respects extremely radical. Given the social context it could be seen as progressive.

The first of its reforms was the decree establishing the National Workshops of February 25, which promised 'to guarantee work for all citizens.'[14] Marx brushes this aside as a cynical bourgeois trick designed to discredit Louis Blanc and socialism generally by linking what were simply measures of charity with Blanc's socialist ideas. In addition the Provisional Government according to Marx saw in the workers organized in these Workshops a mass of men which could be used as a political counterweight to the socialists.

In seeing a plot by moderate members of the government Marx grants to them a degree of perspicacity and decisiveness which his earlier characterization, both of the government and its individual members, would hardly appear to make possible. Far more likely is the view that faced with the demands of the workers for an alleviation of their condition, urged on even by a real sympathy, the government resorted to what were the age old means of relief, to the most obvious solution of the problem, taking the form of the eighteenth century charity workshops but with a title more acceptable to the developed political consciousness and to the demands of the workers. There was an element of cynicism in a decree promising something new and permanent, there was also danger in awakening hopes which most members of the government had no intention of fulfilling.

There is, however, a great deal of evidence which can be quoted to support Marx's view. Emile Thomas, director of the National Workshops, reported some of the opinions expressed by Marie, minister responsible, who was to claim with justice that 'I was not a socialist. I have never believed in the right to work.'[15] His official role was nevertheless to provide for exactly this. He felt, or so he told Thomas, that at least the experience of the National Workshops would prove to the workers the inapplicability of socialist ideas.[16] As early as March 22 Marie instructed Thomas: 'Attach the workers to yourself and do not worry about the cost. The day is not far when it will be necessary to make them take to the streets.'[17]

Lamartine too, though in retrospect, claimed that the National Workshops were intended to provide armed support for the government, but admitted that in origin they were only an expedient.[18]

Marx exaggerated in assuming that the National Workshops were created with a definite, positive, counter-revolutionary purpose in mind. They were intended to limit discontent by providing a means of livelihood and it was only after their establishment that other purposes consciously seen as counter to further revolution were ascribed to them by the directors of government, as a response to continued pressure from organized radical groups.

Similarly we can concern ourselves with the Luxembourg Commission established to enquire into means of improving working-class conditions. With reference to Louis Blanc and Albert, Marx asserts that 'In this way the representatives of the working class were banished from the seat of the Provisional Government, the bourgeois part of which retained the real state power and the reins of administration exclusively in its hands. . . . Unlike any profane state power, they had no budget, no executive authority at their disposal.'[19]

Not so much the deliberateness of this act as its effectiveness is in question. Blanc and Albert with their knowledge of working class conditions must have seemed the obvious candidates to conduct such an enquiry. But this did not exclude them from the councils of government. They participated quite as much as other ministers in its meetings.[20] What is true is that they were, as Paul Bastid said, given a function full of promises without any means of realization, and due to this their prestige must have suffered; and their potential effectiveness as political figures.

Marx bitterly condemns the Provisional Government for its concern to maintain financial stability, its willingness to assume the obligations of the monarchy. For him its essential moderation was nowhere as clearly revealed as in its attempt to restore business confidence and credit. In terms of specific measures he attacks the support given to the Bank of France which he accuses of deliberately restricting credit so as to discredit the new regime, although its conservative credit policy would, given the financial theories of the period seem to have been only what could have been expected. Marx condemns a policy devoted to the interests of the rich bourgeoisie, which in limiting savings bank withdrawals alienated the lower middle classes, and which in imposing a supplementary tax of 45 per cent to bear essentially on land was to alienate the vast mass of peasants. In sum 'By honouring the bills drawn on the State by the old bourgeois society the Provisional Government succumbed to the latter. It had become the hard-pressed debtor of bourgeois society instead of confronting it as the pressing creditor that had to collect the revolutionary debts of many years. It had to consolidate the shaky bourgeois relationships in order to fulfil obligations which are only to be fulfilled within these relationships.'[22]

Marx could have expected nothing else from these men. Few besides utopians and extreme socialist intellectuals were prepared at this moment for the overthrow of the institutions of bourgeois society which a more radical financial policy would have involved.

The measures of the government, given the context of the time, were not so unreasonable, with the possible exception of the early repayment of interest due to *rentiers* which achieved little except to weaken the government's financial position. The imposition of a supplementary tax was necessary given the abolition of the drink tax, and of the *octroi* and the salt tax promised for January 1849, and in view also of the need for increased government expenditure to finance public works, charity and the attempt to establish provincial credit institutions to facilitate industrial recovery.

Garnier-Pagès at the finance ministry was especially open to the advice of and pressure from industrialists, bankers and merchants, rather than agricultural interests, but his policy reflected the belief that agriculture, following a good crop, was in a better position to support an increased tax than industry. As evidence of his relatively advanced views there is the fact that he proposed the introduction of progressive taxation, and that this government advocated nationalization of the railways.

Whether this financial policy was politically wise is another thing. The government by its financial measures seemed to confirm the belief of the more radical that they were concerned mainly to safeguard the interests of those elements which had or were believed to have dominated the July Monarchy. At the same time the threat of progressive taxation, and later the propagandist use of the measures on savings banks and the 45 centimes tax alienated respectively middle class, lower middle class and peasantry, although this only in March and April and then reinforcing to varying extents their already obvious discontents. The policy of the Provisional Government designed essentially to restore business confidence and thus industrial and commercial prosperity and employment was ineffective largely because political conditions maintained uncertainty.

According to Marx 'the proletarians confused the finance aristocracy with the bourgeoisie in general', so that for them 'the rule of the bourgeoisie was abolished with the introduction of the republic'.[23] This was their republic, and in the absence of internal resistance and foreign intervention they were lulled into a hopeful self-confidence. The future was theirs. Their demands were limited, they 'thought they would be able to emancipate themselves side by side with the bourgeoisie'.[24] Inevitably for Marx, this moderation was interpreted as a sign of limited class consciousness due to the limited extent of economic development, but this was united with a confidence in their own power which led them to demonstrate and force the Provisional Government to make at least some concessions – the National Workshops and the Luxembourg Commission. In this respect Marx asserted of the Republic that 'Having secured it arms in hand, the proletariat impressed its stamp upon it and proclaimed it to be a social republic.'[25]

The Marxian interpretation, of course, hides the nuances, the differences of opinion amongst the Parisian masses, but it is correct in affirming that the initial attitude was essentially one which welcomed a new era of social harmony, which looked forward to a better life. Joseph Mairet, a leader of the printing workers, was to write that 'We had all the illusions of the first moment and an heroic confidence in the Provisional Government. It is necessary to have lived through these days to believe this and to understand it.'[26] The surprise of de Tocqueville at the calm which succeeded revolution echoes this. More expressive evidence perhaps are the words of a popular song written at this time by one Flavius – the *Chant de l'Atelier national* of which the second verse proclaims:

> *A new era arises,*
> *It announces better days,*
> *No more misery, no more strikes,*
> *For the working people.*[27]

Georges Duveau believed that the workers saw the Provisional Government as about to create something akin to the Icarie of Cabet,[28] and indeed the psychological climate in Paris was such as to encourage vague utopian longings.

The demands expressed to the new government by workers or their accepted representatives were however on the one hand more practical and limited, and on the other often tinged with the threat of aggression.

The great themes of 1848 were those of the first Revolution and especially various interpretations of Robespierre's *Declaration of the*

Rights of Man to which was commonly added a newer idea, that of the right to work.

The petition presented by the worker Marche to the government on February 25 demanded:

1. The organization of labour, a guaranteed right to work.
2. An assured minimum for the worker and his family in case of sickness, the worker saved from misery when he is incapable of work, by means to be chosen by the sovereign nation.[29]

Demands that is for reform of the relationship between the worker and society.

Significant confirmation of the limited nature of the workers' demands can be obtained from the petitions sent from all over France, but primarily from Paris, to the Luxembourg Commission.[30] Initially a quantitative assessment of these petitions was attempted. This proved to be valuable in indicating which were the demands most commonly made. It did not, however, seem possible to construct a genuine statistical table on the basis of petitions each of which generally contained a large number of demands varying greatly in nature where the relative significance of each demand to the petitioners was impossible to assess.[31]

The most common feature of the petitions were professional demands and especially those for higher wages or a guaranteed minimum tariff, and to a lesser extent for improved working conditions. Another large category was comprised of demands which might properly be called restrictive, which were concerned to protect the workers' livelihoods by ending competition from machines, foreign workers, labour in prisons, barracks and convents, from women, or by abuses of apprenticeships. Many were concerned to alter the relationships between employer and worker by making it easier for the latter to organize, by abolishing *marchandage*, by increasing the possibility of arbitration through the Luxembourg Commission or fairly constituted representative negotiating commissions. The desire for greater security was evident in petitions favouring National Workshops for each profession and state aid to industry.

These were the demands repeatedly made, evincing a desire for better material conditions and also the feeling that man was equal to master and should be treated as equal. Other demands were made, including the cancellation of rents for 1848 and a share in profits, but these were far less representative of what workers wanted and asked for. In these demands, there was little that could be labelled as utopian. They were what any trades union would have wanted to secure. They were not the demands of social revolutionaries.

But combined with this practicality there was a determination that some real gains would be made. This was especially evident in the thoughts of those workers most conscious of their interests and power. Thus in the *Représentant du Peuple* of 29 February, dominated at this stage by printing workers an article combined conciliation with threats – 'Oppressors reassure yourselves, we do not want your fortune, nor your family, nor your goods. The people is opposed to spoliation, but understand clearly, if you want its support, if you want it to respect your goods, your families, your persons, you must from now respect that which belongs to it. In future there must only be amongst men, workers, associates. Master, workman must disappear, the bourgeoisie must dissolve itself amongst the mass of the people, no more classes superior and inferior, no more aristocracy and proletariat, one family, humanity.' Expression of a firm desire for equality on the part of those workers who had begun to look beyond simple professional demands. This desire was associated with a great wave of organization amongst the skilled trades, and especially the printing and building workers. Rémi Gossez saw this as a sign of the consciousness of these workers of the significance of Paris within France, of their own power in Paris, and of the desire to preserve and reinforce this power.[32] In immediate practical terms it gave them the authority to pursue collective bargaining with their employers. Martin Nadaud grasped the significance of this movement. 'Never in effect', he wrote, 'have the workers taken such direct measures to bring down the existing system of wage labour.'[33] The numbers involved in this movement, and the increased scope of its pretensions gave it a real significance.

Another effect of it was undoubtedly to annoy the possessing classes. The privilege of the employer was under assault along with numerous other forms of privilege. If the instances of machine breaking were more immediately destructive, the persistent demand for equality was a more dangerous threat to society.

This demand by groups of workers was especially dangerous because reinforced by the demands of the swarm of newspapers and clubs formed after February. If the direction of these was generally not in the hands of the workers themselves but rather in the hands of middle-class journalists, professional men and shopkeepers, and generally the least successful of these professionally,[34] then these organizers appealed to the real desires of the masses of poor; shaping their demands to meet the popular need no doubt but additionally helping to determine this mood and make it more extravagant. This was the setting for demagogy, in which the limited and more practical demands of the workers themselves were lost amongst a chaos of wild promises and threats. Mass hysteria replaced calculation particularly when the ill-educated were presented with ideas conforming to their sense of power and utopian expectation. This is the explanation of the coexistence of utopian expectation and limited practical demands.

In common with many other writers, Marx overdoes his emphasis on the fraternity of February, and underestimates the significance of the Revolution itself. There were real limits to the fraternal feelings, derived from the influence of press and clubs, from a tradition of violence and from a situation in which new attitudes took root amongst the workers as a whole, whatever their respective faith in social reform or utopias. Louis Chevalier saw the revolution as speeding up the process by which ideas of social change spread, giving the workers a new consciousness of themselves and revised attitudes to other social groups, and changing in return the attitudes of these to the workers.[35] Perhaps for the first time, though on a limited scale, a real proletariat existed, at least in terms of political consciousness. It is from this self-confidence, gained in February and evinced in the move to association and in interest in social and political affairs, that an explanation can be derived of the behaviour of the Parisian workers in subsequent months in conjunction with the activity of other social groups. The most extreme and effective manifestation of this confidence was found in the press and clubs, which, if probably only participated in by a minority of workers, over a long period attracted the interest of the majority, or of sufficient numbers of forcibly idle individuals to inculcate or reinforce attitudes favourable to a new recourse to violence, and at least to give the middle classes generally the impression that this was so – and often impressions matter more than reality.

Odilon Barrot wrote with some justice that the easy victory of February had given the workers 'an exaggerated opinion of their power; an opinion which all the acts of the Provisional Government, all the addresses, all the proclamations and the prudent reserve of other citizens, carried to a drunkenness, to a delirium'. The Parisian workers were determined to gain something from this revolution and with this frame of mind 'All resistance to its will appears to it as an assault on its rights, a real insurrection against its victory.'[36] Given the heightened misery due to the economic crisis, the fact of revolution gave rise to a sense of expectation throughout France and particularly in those centres of artisanal production with a tradition of working-class organization. An awareness of new possibilities was added to a sense of dissatisfaction and in the new freedom a ferment of ideas provided expression to these desires.

Again it is necessary to emphasize that this situation was apparent even in the first halcyon days of the Republic. Marche, demanding work for the masses, represented their new will and it was this that conservatives of all shades would resist as they regained their lost confidence. In February hope of improvement restrained most workers, fear most conservatives, whilst others on both sides were prepared to accept moderation.

Evidence must be presented to support this denigration of harmony. First another song – the first verse of the popular *Marseillaise du Peuple* published in February.[37]

> *Soldiers of France at the ready,*
> *People who have twice been betrayed,*
> *Do not put down your arms,*
> *We have only chased away the kings.*
> *If the exploiter of our misery*
> *Dreams again of enslaving us,*
> *March, to victory or to death. . . .*

An expression of distrust echoed even in the pacific *Atelier* on February 25, when it warned against a repetition of 1830 when the workers had been robbed of the fruits of their victory.[38]

1830 served as a warning to the more extreme republicans, and as a social memory on the basis of which to begin their attack on a republic quickly seen as too moderate.

From February to June about 200 new newspapers appeared. Many were ephemeral, some influenced the mass consciousness. For conservatives names like *Ami du Peuple, Père Duchesne, Journal des Sans-Culottes, Le Robespierre*, inspired by the great Revolution, could create little confidence. If the revolutionary demands of extremists like Sobrier favouring social protection of the poor and needy at the cost of heavy taxes for the wealthy appeared threatening, the declarations and discussions of the clubs, 250 of which appeared in a month, were far more so, the declarations from vagueness, the discussions from their often obvious hostility.

Consider a declaration of intent made by one of the most famous clubs, that of the 'Société des Droits de l'Homme et du Citoyen' of Vilain, Lebon, Huber and Barbès, taking as its article of faith the *Declaration of the Rights of Man* of Robespierre and affirming that 'in the social revolution which begins, the Society . . . places itself . . . between the PARIAHS and the PRIVILEGED of the old society; to the first it says: remain united, but calm, there is your strength. Your number is such that it will be enough for you to demonstrate your will to obtain what you desire; it is also such that you are only able to desire what is just; your voice and your will are the voice and will of God! To the other it says: The old social form has disappeared, the reign of privilege and exploitation has passed. . . .'[39]

Above all these men desired conciliation of classes, favoured social reform rather than revolution but their tone must have been for conservatives far more threatening even than the reforms they favoured. For the provisional government the clubs represented permanent interference as they pursued what was their main aim, of surveillance of the government, to ensure that it preserved its revolutionary purity. Marc Dufraisse at the Club de la Révolution on March 21 swore that if the government were to 'violate the condition of its investiture, we would re-adopt the attitude we have always taken against those who forget their duty and the sanctity of their mission'.[40] This was a constant threat to the government and all those who stood to profit from stability.

The frightening chaos of the clubs which conservatives especially noticed was well described by Flaubert in his *Education sentimentale* – a chaos of sentiment, wild ideas, disagreement, shouts and threats, with agreement on the vague, simple, often extreme solutions to society's ills.

Contemporary observers denied that many clubs in Paris or the provinces included a majority of workers. Alphonse Lucas believed that only one Parisian club and that the most orderly and pacific, the 'Club des Compagnons des Devoirs Réunis' was composed wholly of workers.[41] Alphonse Audiganne added that these particular workers soon lost interest and the club closed, although 'there remained a certain number of workers in other assemblies mixed with various more ardent groups'. It seems to have been these latter elements who set a tone which was, as already observed, often extreme.

Audiganne defines them vaguely as those 'discontented spirits' with 'cankered hearts'.[42] Lucas includes a large number of perpetual students from the Latin Quarter and claims that the Club Blanqui, one of the largest and most important included only a minority of workers among its members.[43]

No adequate study of club membership exists. Those in provincial towns seem by general agreement to have involved the lower middle class and artisans, but mainly the café drinkers and talkers amongst these, and to have quickly driven away bored workers.[44] The same could be said of Parisian clubs except for the fact that a more developed political and social consciousness among the artisanate and even unskilled made them more receptive to the club orators. Let us conclude that if, as Nadaud asserts many workers, bored with words which did not improve their conditions deserted the clubs,[45] yet a large number must have remained. If artisans and workers of all sorts were a minority then presumably the remainder of the audience were students, small shopkeepers and manufacturers, curious bourgeoisie and the whole mass of unclassifiable people found in a large city.

Of the activity of the clubs, seemingly concerned with vague ideals and demands on the one hand, and increasingly, as the elections approached, with the minute details of voter registration and procedures on the other, Suzanne Wassermann concluded that they contributed to the development of the popular consciousness and to the maintainance of agitation but otherwise wasted their time in talk.[46] They remained isolated, their efforts dispersed, and it is in this failure to organize the discontented and aspiring masses for political action that the pattern of protest and its failure, up to and including the June rising can to a large extent be explained. This was true of France as a whole. In Paris, Lyon and Limoges, where the workers were willing to act they were never sufficiently organized. Elsewhere at this stage few were conscious even of the possibility of action, although continued unemployment maintained agitation.

For Karl Marx, '*fraternité* was the real catchword of the February Revolution' and indeed as far as public statements by government, conservatives, republicans and workers went, this was often so. But behind the display was a basic distrust and antagonism. Marx would seem to be accusing the conservatives of hypocrisy because of their fraternal declarations. In this there is much truth. He would seem to be accusing the republicans and workers of Paris of extreme naivety,[47] and again this is to an extent true, but he exaggerates it and minimizes the significance of the will of both the more radical republicans and of the masses to defend the gains and dreams of February, and to extend their scope. Blanqui on February 25 made a speech designed to restrain the desire of some groups for immediate further revolution. He claimed that 'France is not republican, the revolution which has occurred is a happy surprise, nothing more.' He demanded a few days in which to organize the people, to gain sufficient strength by this means to dominate the situation.[48] Already then, even before the government had had time to reveal its intentions by action or inaction the men of the left were moving.

In the Provinces, in large towns like Lyon, Lille and Rouen, demonstrations occurred which were clearly social, rather than political, in character, involving an attack on the property and thus rights of employers whatever the political allegiances of these latter. Admittedly the degree of class consciousness necessary for such action is limited but it is revealing of the hostility of one social group to another, a hostility which was usually unorganized and lacking in aim other than the immediate demand for employment and higher wages. However where, as in Lyon, organization existed then a movement more exclusive to workers and certainly separate from and opposed to the moderate republicans emerged during the first days of the Republic. Lyon was exceptional, perhaps because it combined both concentration of workers in one industry, in a small area, and their employment on an artisanal basis in workshops, factors conducive to consciousness of shared interests and the fermentation of ideas. Generally it could be said of the industrial workers of the provinces that any consciousness of class was embryonic.

The most common response to the news of the foundation of the republic amongst workers was to see this as a guarantee of the right to remove what was disliked. The inevitable relaxation of an unsure administration encouraged this with a resultant agitation involving machine breaking, threats against foreign workers competing on the labour market and more common professional demands.[49] The superior consciousness of common interest in Paris and Lyon, the artisanal centres, by contrast to the newer industrial areas is revealed in the far greater degree of permanent organization engaged in by workers in these two cities. In the textile centres of Lille and Rouen there was, however, consciousness of separateness from other social groups not found at this time in Paris where classes still lived and worked in fairly close contact. Lyon combined this feeling of separateness with conditions favouring its organization. The decline of the feeling of harmony, of the hope for improvement of social conditions through the cooperation of classes, would lead to a situation in Paris similar to that in Lyon.

Above all, the workers of Paris and the provinces had gained hope from the events of February, hope of both immediate and long term gain. The miners of Rive-de-Gier for a short time believed that the establishment of a republic was the promise of a 'better future'. But nothing changed, and an early euphoria was followed here and in many places by quick disappointment due to the very nature of the revolution and with this a return to political indifference.[50] To most workers what mattered was the question of the material conditions of existence.

Dissatisfaction did not always lead to apathy. On March 17 occurred the first great demonstration in Paris, intended to exert pressure on the Provisional Government to force it to act more radically, and more immediately to postpone the election of a Constituent Assembly and of officers of the National Guard, but forced by a demonstration of middle-class National Guards in the previous day, to demonstrate its support for the government instead.

Georges Duveau agreed with Marx that the demonstration on March 16 moderated the aims of those leading that of March 17,[51] and it is doubtful whether these aims were in fact anything other than moderate for those involved in the demonstration – Wassermann certainly concludes to this effect and further asserts that whatever the language of its petitions the 'Société républicaine' of Blanqui intended no more than a peaceful demonstration[52] calculated nevertheless to exert pressure on the government, to warn it that more radical measures were desired, as well as to obtain a postponement of the elections.

Blanqui's two petitions for postponement stressed the need for time to educate the masses and remove them from the influence of employers, notables and clergy.[53] The Provisional Government conceded a limited postponement which satisfied no-one, but merely discredited itself in the eyes of moderates and conservatives. The participants in this demonstration were presumably the members of clubs and those they influenced, the artisans, workers, small patrons and shopkeepers who formed the Parisian masses. Employment in the National Workshops was preferred by many workers to involvement in this.[54] Curiosity no doubt involved many. The limited political consciousness of the period is revealed by the minimal participation of workers in the election of National Guard officers on March 18.[55]

Part of the significance of March 17 was that it revealed the Parisian masses and their leaders as yet unwilling to act in a forceful manner, still hoping for concessions by the government. More significantly it increased the level of hostility within society. Together with the demonstration of the previous day it clearly defined the elements in conflict for the first time, even for contemporaries. Among the poor, underprivileged and discontented it revealed a feeling expressed by a manifesto of the relatively moderate 'Club de la Révolution' – 'We have still only the title Republic, we need more. Political reform is only the instrument of social reform. The Republic must satisfy the workers and the proletariat.'[56] Popular attitudes to the government were becoming increasingly less ambiguous, not only because of what was beginning to be seen as a betrayal by the government but because the continuation of economic depression made the need for radical government action seem more than ever necessary.

In the countryside too the already widespread unrest had reached new heights after the proclamation of the Republic. This unrest followed an age-old pattern; similar events had occurred with each previous relaxation of governmental authority, in 1789 and 1830, for example. Its immediate political effect was not evident; but peasant unrest would provide a fertile ground for ideas of social transformation and radical political groups existed which would take an interest in arousing the rural population.

In an essentially rural country, with a tradition of peasant violence, more people were concerned with the danger of social unrest in the countryside than in the towns. For the inhabitants of market towns and villages, and indeed even for the *grands notables* usually so closely linked to the land, the threat of disorder closer to hand than at Paris, the immediate threat of peasant violence, must often have assumed more significance than Parisian events relegated to a secondary position as presumed stimuli of provincial unrest. The character of rural unrest and the pains taken to suppress it support this.

The basic forms of its expression were attempts to regain customary rights of usage in state and private forests and on alienated common land. According to Albert Soboul this was the last period of violent resistance by the traditional peasant community to the encroachment of capitalist agriculture, of the small-scale producer against the large, of those who needed to supplement the produce of their small-holdings with that of the common or forest in order to maintain their families, against those who wished to produce on a larger scale and more rationally for the market.[57] The *procureur général* at Toulouse wrote in June 1848 of the events of preceding months – 'The rural population in this area are imbued with the idea that they have been unjustly deprived of property rights, which from time immemorial belonged to them in the woods.'[58]

An earlier report of this same official highlighted the character of this aspect of unrest and its real causes – referring to the administration of the forests during the July Monarchy – 'the legislation on forests and especially its application in mountainous areas, fails to recognize the first needs of the population, who living in the middle of the forests have been deprived of the wood for heating and construction. The situation of the places, the difficulties of transport, the poverty of most of this mountain population does not make it possible for them to import wood purchased elsewhere. To protect themselves against the rigours of winter, the old and children were obliged to remain in bed for days. To cook their food some people burnt wood from the framework of their houses and old furniture.

On receiving news of . . . the Revolution, the mountain people believed that the forest administration would be abolished. With cries of long live Liberty, long live the Republic, they invaded the forests and chased away the guards. . . .'[59]

A later correspondent of the Minister of Justice, the deputy for the department of Bas-Rhin, Goldenberg, also explained the misery caused by the forest legislation – 'Through the loss of pasture . . . in the forests, the inhabitants have been obliged to give up stock-raising almost entirely, and a village which 25 years ago had 150 to 200 cows and 300 to 400 pigs, no longer has more than 60 to 80 cows and 5 to 6 pigs.'[60] The strong feelings of the rural population with regard to the forests are thus easily understood.

The form of their action was attacks on the officials of the forest administration and particularly the forest guards, and additionally on private owners of forests. The assaults on the authority of the state also took the form of burning tax registers, that on the rights of private property-owners involved disputes over one-time common land as well as forests, strikes by agricultural labourers, machine breaking and threats or attacks on wealthier members of particular communities especially those accused of usury. All this revealed a contempt for the authority of the state, and in many areas where anticlericalism revealed itself, similarly for that of the Church, and more significantly a hostility towards the rich, a basic social division.[61]

These, however, are generalizations which do not apply to the whole of France but assume a prominence in specific areas for special reasons. In large part this unrest was a continuation of that which we have already observed as occurring during 1846–47, with the same basic causes, but amplified by the collapse of the Orleanist regime and the opportunity for improvement which the masses saw in this situation, given their vague ideal of the republic.

There was considerable diversity in the behaviour of the rural masses as between regions. Most incidents in these early months of 1848 occurred in the Pyrenean Region and the East with less numerous incidents, though they remained significant in the Massif Central, and isolated occurrences throughout the Parisian Region, Mediterranean, West and North. Compared with the troubles of 1846–47, the centre of gravity had shifted from the Parisian Region and area to the north-west, south-west and west of it to the East and Pyrenees. As regards the character of the incidents, spontaneous reactions to hunger causing attacks on grain shipments or market riots had decreased with the improved economic situation and the troubles were now the product of more long-term interests. It is probably true to say that these movements of complaint were more conscious, more political in character and took the form often of a challenge to the socio-economic power of the rich, of the richer landowners and the usurers, or to the authority of the state as tax collector and forest guard. This consciousness was embryonic in form and yet significant in expressing an increasing hostility of the poor towards the rich as a group rather than towards individual rich men, thus continuing a trend evident at least from the days of the great revolution and reinforced with each economic crisis, with each open declaration of conflicting interests.

In all areas forest incidents took pride of place indicating the strength of feeling against the forest legislation. The frequency of these incidents was to decline from about May as the state's authority was reasserted, although as late as 1850 some occurred. The East was exceptional not only in its anti-semitism due to the identification of Jews with commercial and usurious harshness and dominance, but also in the continuance of trouble concerning food exports.

E

Although there are signs that the economic crisis and more especially the problem of food had been alleviated, the reactions of peasantry throughout France and particularly in the regions noted above were indicative of a situation which remained serious. This pattern of events remained true throughout the first half of 1848, although from April there were signs that they would soon be replaced by another concern, the collection of the additional tax introduced by the Provisional Government.

The regional variations in peasant behaviour can be explained essentially by varying social and economic conditions.

Soboul's division of France into two regions separated by a mixed zone,[62] although obviously a simplification, has some validity. According to him in the North, the region of most advanced agriculture, collective rights and the traditional rural community had already to a large extent disappeared under the pressure of production for the market. However, the surplus agricultural population was readily absorbed by the growing urban industrial centres and the countryside at least found the numbers of its discontented reduced, its poor presented with migration as an alternative to rioting, even if in 1848 migration might result more often in acquiring charity than work.

The social structure in the northern countryside was dominated by large-scale landowners or farmers with a sizeable number of agricultural labourers, whilst the number of small-holders declined numerically and in cohesiveness. Once the food crisis had been relieved the North remained largely quiescent, social unrest occurred now primarily in areas of small farming and sharecropping where poor communications permitted the existence of an essentially subsistence agriculture and of the traditional rural community.

The February Revolution in those areas most severely effected by the poor harvests of preceding years intensified the struggle for economic and social survival. It seemed to present an opportunity for the redress of grievances. Peasant hatred was directed at whoever seemed to threaten their survival – the usurer threatening foreclosure in the East, the owner of former common land, or of forests in most regions. In the Alpine mountains hostility was directed at the state and not at local notables simply because it was the state as owner of the local forests which directly applied legislation limiting their use by the local population. Similarly, where the relatively prosperous small vineyard proprietors were agitated their hostility was directed against the state and its collectors of the drink tax. Coquerelle notes that where a particular type of production was dominant in an area, for example, viniculture or forestry, or else a specific mode of exploitation, small-holdings or sharecropping, then a movement of protest tended to involve or engage the passive support of the whole population, which experienced a basic uniformity of conditions and problems of existence.[63] Louis Chevalier in his thesis, whilst recognizing the influence of Parisian ideas, spread by seasonal workers and the constructors of the new railways, affirmed that the demands of the countryside generally took an old form – 'it is a question of a great settlement of accounts, in which they had not ceased to believe, of an agrarian revolution involving violence against the nobles and the priests.'[64] But this was true only of those areas where old traditions had survived, that is, those which were economically backward in terms of communications and not the more advanced or the areas such as the west where tradition was less hostile to the rich landowners.

The point is that the peasantry as a homogeneous class conscious of its own interests did not exist. Marx realized that. What he did not realise was the extreme complexity of the causes of action or inaction by the peasantry. His division of them into conservative and revolutionary groups is, therefore, facile. If he implicitly links poverty with revolutionary activity it will become increasingly evident that the aims of his revolutionary peasants were to turn the clock back to a pre-capitalist, non-feudal society, whilst his conservative peasants, if including the poor subsistence farmers, who were too isolated and submissive to act, also included those who had sufficient initiative to adapt to market agriculture or else to realise their inability to survive in the rural community, and thus to move to the town.

A Revolution had occurred in Paris, one result of which was a widespread intensification of urban and rural unrest. To complete this analysis of the effects of the February Revolution it is necessary to consider the change, or lack of change, in the institutional power structure of France, the degree to which the new political leaders imposed their ideals, to which they manifested their will. In effect the strengths and weaknesses of the republican movement will be considered.

Most characteristic of the Revolution was its restraint. The monarchy was overthrown but most of its former servants and the institutions in which they served remained in place. This was true of the army and of the central and provincial administration.

The effects of the Revolution were limited in Paris and even more so in the provinces, even in that sphere of the popular consciousness in which the most significant effects of the revolution can perhaps be observed. The surprise of the provinces and the total unpreparedness of the republicans there to assume power has already been commented upon, but it would be wrong to assume as many historians in the past that provincial events in this period can almost be ignored. Regional studies such as those by Louis Chevalier and Philippe Vigier demand a re-interpretation in order to balance an excessive concern with Paris.

Chevalier describes a municipal revolution widespread in the Parisian region, occurring to the benefit of the lower middle classes in the towns and larger villages, in which they existed in sufficient number and with a degree of socio-economic independence of the upper classes, whilst these *grands notables* were willing to efface themselves. This was a change in administrative personnel with few practical consequences, occurring almost entirely in the administrative centres of departments and arrondissements, and lacking any firm basis as long as the *grands notables* with their economic strength and social influence remained in the background awaiting a suitable opportunity to re-assert themselves and to re-introduce their nominees.[65] Generally there was no independent political action by the masses, those who gained were the small merchants and entrepreneurs and the members of the liberal professions, whose similarity of outlook imposed a basic national uniformity on such events, and ensured moderation. The significance of this Revolution lies mainly in the experience, confidence and intensified will to acquire socio-political authority which it conferred on the lower middle classes, and these involving the masses in their rivalries necessarily increased the political consciousness of even wider circles.

The most radical political developments occurred in a number of industrial cities – Lyon, Limoges, Reims, Rouen, where there existed an embryonic class consciousness created by the harshness of economic conditions. Here workers tended to support republicans associated with the politics of *La Réforme* and even press for the inclusion of their own representatives in the new municipalities. In Lyon in particular the artisan-workers of the silk industry maintained their independent organization which the new moderate middle class republican municipality found threatening.[66]

Where municipal revolution occurred it generally replaced the old council by a republican lower middle class and liberal profession grouping, or simply added to the old some new members. Over a large part of the country not even this limited change occurred. In all areas it was property owners who still held power. The Revolution had occurred throughout France rather than simply in Paris, but its form was that of a struggle for power between various factions of the property-owning classes.

From mid-March the former ruling groups began to regain the political and social initiative. The basic strength of conservatism should be obvious from our earlier consideration of the social structure of France. Revolution had occurred because of a combination of circumstances stimulating some groups to action, others to inaction. Reaction would occur when various social groups felt a need to defend vital interests, and had some confidence in their ability to do so. Its strength must depend on the number and social power of those groups which felt threatened.

A vital factor in any explanation of the failure of the moderate republic to gain lasting support from the majority of Frenchmen was this continuation, even worsening, of the economic crisis after the February Revolution. Economic recovery had been well under way before the Revolution, the quickly perceived effect of which was to cause a worsening of the economic situation due primarily, historians agree, to the lack of confidence in the future amongst those possessing capital resources.

The extent of this renewed depression, in financial terms, can be measured by the fact that on the Bourse, the 5 per cent rentes which had stood at 116·60 on February 18 had fallen to 69 by March 17, and to their lowest point of 50 francs on April 6. Thereafter came the beginning of a renewed confidence associated to a small extent with government financial measures and more with the election campaign and its results. On the announcement of these results the 5 per cent reached 70.[67] This pattern was true of other shares and securities, and most symptomatic, of the normally stable shares of the Bank of France, which stood at 3195 on February 18, fell to 1300 on March 17 and reached lows at such points as the postponement of the elections after the demonstration of March 17 and the government proposal on April 4 to nationalize the railways to Orléans and the Centre. The Bank's gold reserves fell from 226 million francs on the eve of the Revolution to 59 million by March 15, and it certainly needed the government support which Marx condemned, and which was to some degree effective, as was the 45 per cent supplementary tax which did to a limited extent increase business confidence, if the movement in the value of the Bank's shares are anything to go by.[68]

The immediate loss of confidence in Paris had spread rapidly through the provinces. The result of this must be the drying up of credit, of sales, and of production. This affected different social groups in varying ways. Obviously for financiers, industrialists, merchants, farmers producing for the market, and small shopkeepers, for all those involved in industry and commerce, this was unwelcome and must have adverse effects on their business activities.

At the same time large agricultural areas were subject, after the relatively good crop of 1847, to a significant decline in the price of foodstuffs. With the exception of the small-owning peasants involved in subsistence farming all rural groups were adversely affected by this: large and small producers for the market, by declining revenue; tenant farmers by the additional difficulty of finding the means to pay their rent; labourers by the inability of many employers to pay the wages of as much labour as usual once the harvest was over. Most sectors of agricultural production were faced with this decline of prices, from wheat to vine cultivation. The effect on the latter in the department of Loir-et-Cher was calculated by Georges Dupeux. According to his index of the purchasing power of vine growers, this dropped from 106 in 1847 to 80 in 1848.[69]

Many of the rural population who had borrowed money in the crisis years of 1846–47, or more commonly in the more prosperous preceding period would in the succeeding period of low prices find it extremely difficult to repay their loans.

Essentially this is a picture of widespread discontent due to a politically inspired loss of confidence, and declining agricultural prices. The effects of the latter in terms of the declining purchasing power of the rural population, would further affect industry and commerce. As usual, those who suffered most in the countryside were the smaller producers, not producing in sufficient quantity to gain from increased sales. Those who gained were those industrial workers still in employment for whom food became cheap.

The effects of this renewed depression on group psychology varied. Louis Chevalier observed with reason that whereas for Parisians a political explanation of economic crisis was developed before the Revolution and to the detriment of the July Monarchy, for much of the provincial population such a political explanation developed more slowly and to the detriment of the Revolution, and of the Republic.[70] Businessmen, conscious of their lack of confidence in the future blamed this on events in Paris, whether these were in the streets, or were government measures. Tudesq sees the dominant feeling after the initial shock of revolution had worn off as being a fear, not for personal security, but for economic security among those who possessed.[71] One businessman of the period in Lyon noted on March 8 that 'Work does not recommence, the workers are always parading and all peaceful men begin to grow alarmed. Everyone hides his money . . .'[72] Increasingly, economic interests pushed men to demand order in the streets and a government they could trust.

As far as the less politically conscious were concerned, for workers and especially peasants, the republic existed as a broken promise. It brought with it not a better life but increased misery. They tended to judge it in terms of the economic conditions accompanying it.

These conditions thus had the effect of alienating or further alienating from the republic those social groups which required economic security, those who were involved in production or distribution, from the great financier to the village artisan, the peasant, and the shopkeeper, and this especially in the provinces, more ignorant of and unconcerned for political matters.

In relation to this economic influence on group psychology there were two other closely connected factors – government action directed at improving the situation and the political action of the more radical groups, both of which affected the pace and direction of reaction.

Of government measures the most significant in terms of its consequences was that imposing an additional tax of 45 per cent. The very fact of its imposition greatly increased hostility to the already established National Workshops for which it was presumed to be paying. Hostility to the workers and their demands was increased when other social groups had to meet the cost. The measure limiting withdrawals from the savings banks in so far as it had political effects had them primarily in this same manner. For all those social groups which were not part of the urban working class, which nevertheless had severe problems due to the economic crisis, especially the small merchants and manufacturers and the peasants, the government must have appeared to have been unfairly pandering to the workers.

Ménard wrote that 'For the peasants, generally indifferent to political questions, the Republic was the 45 centimes tax.'[73] Odilon Barrot commented that 'This measure prevented the horrors of a bankruptcy, but it would kill the Republic: for it brought on it the hatred of the countryside without giving it the love of the towns.'[74] More strikingly Louis Chevalier shows that even in communes in the Paris region news of the revolution was not received until about March 2, and that the first real awareness of change was the news of the 45 centimes.[75] This must have been even more true of areas further afield. Thus for many the Republic was a threat from its beginnings.

But our conclusions should be subtler. The government provided for the relief of the poor from liability but left the choice of who was to pay to the arbitrary decision of mayor and tax-collector. Even so, the effect was ameliorated.

Peasant reaction to the tax began in March, especially in those regions least able to pay,[76] for due to the severity of the economic crisis and the shortage of money many were simply unable to pay; but reaction was limited by the vital fact that no effort was made to collect the tax until after the elections to the Constituent Assembly. The existence of the tax was, however, a conservative weapon in the election campaign, indeed one delegate of the Club of Clubs in the Lot wrote on April 5 that 'The great lever which alarmists use is the 45 centimes tax.'[77]

Other measures of social reform besides the establishment of the National Workshops included the reduction of the working day which again appeared as pandering to the workers, to those who employed them and those who would not benefit from such protection. The *Constitutionnel* of March 12 attacked this interference with the immutable laws of economics.

Amongst administrative measures a circular from the Minister of the Interior, Ledru-Rollin, to the government's commissaires in the provinces advocating the use of revolutionary measures is presumed to have increased the fears of those concerned about the possibility of the repetition of the Terror of 1793. It had little effect on the behaviour of these officials who, in terms of social origins, were largely similar to the Prefects they had replaced, and behaved with moderation, but nonetheless contributed to the creation of a psychologically unfavourable reaction, especially when taken in conjunction with the postponement of the elections after the mass demonstration of

March 17. For many the Provisional Government seemed to be preparing a social revolution.

On March 16 already there had appeared an obvious symptom of discontent amongst the middle classes, in a demonstration protesting against aspects of the democratization of the Paris National Guard. Barrot wrote that 'this was the first symptom of the reawakening of the bourgeoisie, its transition from the state of observation to that of action . . . from this moment it would not stop.'[78]

Some of the causes of reaction have been examined; now, in relation to others its progress will be considered. According to Marx, there was a process of realignment occurring in social groups.[79] For Tudesq 'The economic and financial crisis and the incompetence of their adversaries had . . . contributed towards reintegrating the notables in the majority; the social majority in favour of individual property would prepare the way for a political majority in favour of a moderate republic, more moderate than republican.'[80]

There are two vital factors to be noted, first the attitude of the *grands notables* who remained extremely influential, and second the failure of the Provisional Government to pursue policies which might have countered or threatened this influence.

The socially dominant groups accepted the February Revolution from fear and lack of an alternative. For both these reasons they echoed the humanitarianism of its early days, with a sincerity limited by the desire to preserve vested interests.

In this latter respect the apparently 'socialist' leanings of the Provisional Government gave little confidence. Society was changing. Continual mass demonstrations, meetings, public discussions, the mass of hawkers selling newspapers – the streets had changed in character, the unknown masses had taken possession of them and threatened openly, if some Club spokesmen were to be accepted at their word, to take possession of much more. And in April these same masses were, through the untried process of universal suffrage, to elect a Constituent Assembly.

As early as the first day of March the *Constitutionnel* was placing at the head of its list of priorities for government action, the need for order in the streets and in society, and by mid-March the conservative press as a whole echoed these sentiments.

Observers generally seem to agree that as far as the beginning of active opposition to the new regime can be given a date this should be, in Paris, March 16–17, under the dual effect of the middle class demonstrations of the first day and that organized by the clubs on the second, and in the provinces, only partly as an effect of this, generally in the middle weeks of March. Furthermore the strength of this opposition to social reform was to increase with every incident from these dates, especially with the demonstration of April 16, not quite innocent in purpose but magnified by conservatives and members of the government into a socialist plot.

The desire to resist change had obviously existed earlier, but by mid-March conservatives were finding the courage to act. Those whom Tudesq called notables had retained their economic and social power and once the initial shock of revolution had passed were normally able to reassert their local influence even to the extent of reversing many of the municipal revolutions which had occurred.

Odilon Barrot wrote that 'Other revolutions, before that of 24 February 1848, had modified more or less profoundly the forms and conditions of governments, but none of them had put as directly in question the principles of the family and of property. . . .'[81] This was less violent but more frightening. Because it was less violent the notables had little immediate fear for their lives, but did feel that their property was threatened. This was the basis of their society and once they realized that they enjoyed at least personal security then property became the cause and symbol of their defence of the existing society. Flaubert perfectly illustrates this – 'Now Property was raised to the level of Religion and became indistinguishable from God. The attacks being made on it took on the appearance of sacrilege, almost of cannibalism. In spite of the most humanitarian legislation ever passed in France, the spectre of '93 reappeared, and the sound of the guillotine made itself heard in every syllable of the word 'Republic' – although this did not prevent people from despising it for its weakness. Conscious of no longer having a master, France began to cry out in terror, like a blind man without a stick, or a child who has lost its nurse.'[82]

A foreign observer, the Austrian diplomat Apponyi, noted on March 16 in reflecting on the middle class demonstration of that day that 'Paris finds itself divided into two camps: one is for the maintainance of order at all costs, even that of the overthrow of the Provisional Government and of the Republic; the other wishes, on the contrary, not only to maintain what exists, but to push the machine to extremes, labelling as aristocrats all those who will not accept disorder . . . and the people so impressionable, passes from one side to

the other, with the same ease with which it changes its meeting place
. . .'[83] An aristocratic contempt for the masses, the description also of
a polarization of opinion in Paris, between those who possessed
property and those who did not.

Alexis de Tocqueville described the situation in April, agreeing with
Apponyi – 'I saw society cut in two: those who possessed nothing,
united in a common greed; those who possessed something, in a
common fear. No more links, no more sympathy between these two
classes, everywhere the idea of an inevitable and close struggle. . . .'[84]
Again recognition of the increasing unity of view between all those
with property – those middle class social groups which had welcomed
political change in February now began to be afraid of its wider
consequences. This is true of all elements of the middle classes
and is seen, for example, in the attitude of the republican from Lyon,
Joseph Bergier. He wrote on March 24 – 'in spite of all the patience,
all the kindness the authorities have shown towards the workers, it
will be necessary, I believe, to take rigorous measures, and without
doubt to fight. The workers abuse their position to secure arbitrary
legislation and everyone is tired of always giving in to them.'[85] The
National, particularly from the beginning of April, was more than
ever concerned with the need to establish social order before social
reform was attempted.

That a broad conservative alliance had become possible, reflected
the failure of the government to make the effort essential to win over
the lower middle classes and the peasantry. Even the workers
essentially wished to share in property, not to destroy it. A policy in
favour of small property might have preserved the democratic
republic but property was indivisible, and its free use an element of
the democratic beliefs of the majority of the Provisional Government
and most certainly of its servants.

The lower middle class and peasantry able therefore to expect
nothing from the government and feeling threatened by the urban
workers had no obvious alternative to following the lead of the more
traditional rulers of society. No one else appealed to their interests.

The degree of fear present in society has been well presented by
Lamartine – the general opinion was that 'with property' socialism
'would abolish society, the family, man . . .'[86] To accede to the demands of socialist theoreticians and of the ignorant masses would,
according to the conservative press and opinion, result in a universal
levelling down of standards of life and civilization.

It is generally agreed by historians that the response of the notables to the threat to their social position was an alliance in defence of basic interests. In support of this view some of the most useful evidence is contained in the letters of the delegates of the Club of Clubs sent into the provinces to conduct electoral propaganda.[87] These letters have to be used with care given their one-sided character but taken into consideration against a background of conservative activity and checked against this some are of great value.

A delegate writing from Rennes on April 12 observed that 'the priest, Legitimist and Philippist parties appear to have fused in a reactionary manner.'[88] In the Charente according to another delegate 'bourgeois, nobles, men of money, yesterday separated into several opposed parties today united to pervert the spirit of the revolution and stop the torrent of reforms.'[89] Even earlier, from Poitiers this same delegate had described the opposition as being composed of 'several elements in appearance heterogeneous; but united by circumstances namely: the nobles, the high clergy, the bar, the bourgeois and bankers, and some poor dupes. . .'[90]

In most areas of France alliances are described including Legitimists, Orleanists, aristocrats and bourgeoisie – the *grands notables*. On the social question there was no difference between the Catholic and the Voltairean bourgeois, relatively little between the Monarchist and moderate republican – many of whom saw the accomplishments of February, for them the maximum of republican evolution, as threatened – little again where supporters of the two Monarchist houses felt themselves threatened. It was a similar way of life which was under assault and which needed defending. The press of the various conservative factions all made the same plea for social order.

The conservative alliance came into existence most easily where the threat was most obvious, in Paris, and in the more industrialized departments of the North and North-East, where social tensions had been especially aggravated by the economic crisis, and socialist ideas appeared to have more relevance. Elsewhere in the Midi, West and Centre a vaguer fear of the *partageux* existed but combined action was more difficult to arrange. In areas of the west, Legitimist and Orleanist rivalry continued where Legitimist social dominance made social revolution unlikely.

The higher ranks of the administration, Church and army behaved as one would expect from the social origins of the personnel involved; the lower ranks mainly obeyed. With regard to the army whose role was to be of such vital importance throughout the Second Republic, conservatives had doubts concerning its loyalty and radicals' hopes that it would, in the Jacobin tradition, act as a revolutionary force. But with its officers, in spite of their rivalries, united to defend social order and to maintain intact the tradition of military discipline, and exerting themselves to restore this through the isolation of troops from contacts with the civilian population and from radical propaganda, the army as a whole was increasingly becoming a reliable element of social conservation.

The notables in society were relatively few in number and by themselves would have been impotent. Their success depended on their acquiring or retaining a mass following.

An editorial in *Le Constitutionnel* of April 18 indicated the basis for this latter. Following an attack on socialist and communist theories, and on the demonstration of April 16, the writer concluded that 'The communists should have realized that if property will ever be abolished, France is the last country in the world where this will occur. The reason is simple: there is no country where fortunes are as divided. . . . If property is theft, as one adept of communism has claimed, the thieves include the vast majority of Frenchmen . . .'

From Paris by means of provincial subscribers to Parisian newspapers or through the provincial press reprinting articles taken from the Parisian press, through personal experiences, or the letters of friends, spread a will for conservation reinforced by provincial disorders. Anxiety concerning the future pushed to action. The social prestige granted to property, the conditions of dependence linking conservative notables to the urban and rural middle classes, peasants and workers made the work of propaganda easy. If the republic had been greeted as a symbol of a better future 'when they heard speak of the disorder which reigned in Paris, of new taxes . . ., of the general war which was feared, when they saw commerce at a standstill and money disappear . . . and especially when they learned that the principle of property was under attack, they realized that it had been a question of more than Louis-Philippe. Fear, which had at first been limited to the heights of society, descended then amongst the popular class, and a universal terror spread throughout the country . . .'[91] The myth of the *partageux* was reborn. Even in Paris, on April 16 the demonstration by the clubs was greeted with shouts of *A bas les communistes*! from a National Guard which included many workers.

A delegate of the Club of Clubs in the department of the Loire wrote on April 6 that conservatives, including republicans, were attempting to discredit radical propagandists by denouncing them as 'communist terrorists demanding the division of property.'[92]

France seems to have developed a socio-political pattern similar to that described by Marx, with little islands of radical republican strength in the larger artisanal manufacturing towns amongst workers and the lower middle class. This is confirmed by, for example, a letter of one Mourot from Luneville to the Club of Clubs dated April 4 – 'there are two separate camps, one composed of bourgeoisie such as notaries, lawyers, solicitors and manufacturers of all sorts, the other of the petty bourgeoisie and workers.'[93]

The Club's delegate to the Charente, Marcelino Prat, sheds further light on this pattern in a letter of April 13 in which he complained that 'The further I move from large towns the more I find memories of the past and a lack of understanding of the situation . . . In Paris, amongst that people so great and comprehending which overthrew the government of privilege, they understand that social inequality is ended and hope for the future promised by the man of Nazareth. In the main towns of departments, one finds again generous and devoted hearts, spirits who have some idea of the destiny which the coming of the Republic makes possible for us. In the localities of the third degree everything is different: their citizens are the prey of egoism, of narrow ideas, and of deplorable prejudices.'[94]

What else could be expected when 'in all the Communes nothing has changed so that the country people believe that as in 1830 the government has only changed its name.'[95] Exaggerated but essentially true – not only had nothing changed, but the economic crisis had worsened and the peasant and petty bourgeois had been told by those whose judgment he had so long valued or upon whom he depended for his livelihood, that property, the family and religion were under attack.

It was because this great mass of people tended to accept these alarming ideas, that according to Marx they 'had to vote under the leadership of a bourgeoisie spoiling for a fight and of big landowners frantic for restoration.'[96] The election campaign and its results were extremely revealing of the state of mind of various social groups at this time.

The campaign reflected the lack of experience of universal suffrage. All manner of opinions were expressed by a large number of candidates and the electoral committees which selected and/or supported them. The same candidate often appeared on a number of lists, but generally a division between advanced and moderate republicans and conservative notables is evident. It must be noted, however, that even the latter accepted the title of 'republican' and that, indicating their continued lack of self-confidence the electoral lists supported by conservatives usually contained more moderate republicans than overt monarchists. Take, for example, the Loir-et-Cher. As in other areas the campaign had a local rather than Parisian impulsion, the candidates being essentially local men. In this particular case the twenty significant candidates were mainly bourgeois manufacturers, landowners and especially members of the liberal professions. There were no artisans or shopkeepers, but three landowners working their own land, one teacher and one foreman. Most candidates were prominent local notables who would have been enfranchised even under the July Monarchy.[97]

A. J. Tudesq emphasizes the great diversity in the actions of the aristocratic and upper bourgeois notables between regions, departments, arrondissements and even cantons, but concludes that there was a political effacement of the notables except in those industrial areas where the threat from the lower classes was thought to be more serious and a more assertive policy appeared necessary, or those areas such as much of the Parisian region and the West and South-west where their socio-economic dominance appeared unchallengeable. But, as Tudesq further concludes, notables whether as members of election committees, through the clergy, press, and their positions as employers or landowners exercised a great influence on the selection of candidates and voting behaviour.[98] Social power remained with the former ruling classes, and because of this, their political effacement could only be temporary.

The conservative propaganda campaign demanded support for those who favoured the defence of order, the family and religion. On a more mundane level it attacked the weakness of the Provisional Government and particular features of its policy, notably the 45 centimes tax. A constant feature of this campaign was the demand to be free of the tyranny of Paris. Similarly to former avowed Monarchists, moderate, socially conservative republicans emphasized 'the legitimate rights of society, the sacred rights of the family ... of property and labour.'[99] They were a little more ready to recognize their duty to abolish social abuses. All sections of opinion affirmed their loyalty to the Republic, and even criticism of the government was restrained in many areas by fear of mob action against the offending presses. This propaganda, whether in newspaper or brochure or in the statements of election candidates was essentially vague and non-committal and limited in its influence. It merely reflected the opinions of the better educated, whilst the masses were influenced in more traditional ways.

In terms of ideological expression, Tudesq, in his great study, sees a process by which 'former liberals became counter-revolutionaries and former traditionalists rallied to a conservative liberalism.'[100] As part of the process of increasing conservative unity, it is evident that the principles of most conservatives were being amended to facilitate combined action in defence of social order.

This electoral campaign is also revealing of the nature of conservative power and pressures. The mass of workers and peasants were ignorant of the significance of universal suffrage and frightened by the words of agitators, the prediction of a new Terror and talk of the *partageux*. They both blamed the new government for the economic crisis and often retained some hope that in spite of the supplementary tax this government would do something to improve their position. Ignorance and fear persuaded them to turn to their traditional leaders. Even in Paris the workers retained a feeling of personal inferiority in respect of the educated and rich. At this stage ideas of radical social transformation remained alien to most of these politically uneducated.

Given that the size of this new electorate made electoral control difficult, if not impossible, when the techniques of mass persuasion were undeveloped, it was an influence freely accepted which was most efficacious. A circular from the Ministry of the Interior ordered the government commissaires administering the departments to act as the representatives of a revolutionary power, but this was disowned by the Provisional Government which ordered its commissaires not to influence the election.[101] Cobban's studies on this election see them as the freest of the nineteenth century but in which the absence of government intervention meant that the socially dominant notables were opposed only by some of the more radical republicans[102] – a weak opposition.

Falloux wrote of this first experience of universal suffrage, that 'Each elector at first directed his attention and made his combinations in the strict limits of his own surroundings.'[103] Candidates selected themselves or were selected by small groups. The electorate was presented with names few of whom had any meaning outside their own immediate locales. Men voted for those whose names they knew, or who were recommended to them. They turned for advice to those whom they respected and the canons according to which respect was granted were primarily wealth, especially the possession of property, and superior knowledge, especially religious. More obvious pressures rarely had to be exerted, but obviously could be and were by landlords, employers, etc. Generally, peasant and worker acted as though in recognition of their inferior status.

The reports of the delegates of the Club of Clubs reveal the weakness of republicanism, and especially of its more radical adherents. Most of the real commitment to republican institutions it appears came from urban workers, whilst middle-class support where it existed was often condemned as too moderate.

Reports from urban centres, particularly the smaller complained of the ignorance of the workers, of the pressure from the richer, landowning bourgeoisie on the lower middle class and workers – thus a report from Napoléon Vendée of April 12 – 'the frightened bourgeoisie has made it known to various entrepreneurs that if they continue to frequent the clubs it will not give them any work. The entrepreneurs obey and in their turn threaten their workers who retire little by little, the small number remaining being subject to continual threats.'[104] Such pressures were more common because more necessary in urban surroundings.

More characteristic and illustrative is a report from an already quoted delegate of the Club of Clubs to the Charente of April 21, – 'The people has not the instruction necessary to use its rights. It obeys old prejudices and narrow interests, it doesn't understand the great task it will accomplish tomorrow, it will allow itself to be led by the bourgeoisie. The result will be that the bourgeoisie alone will make these elections. The workers and the peasants still tremble in front of their old seigneurs and masters.'[105]

The same delegate in a post-mortem on the election written on May 7 affirmed that 'If they had understood the aims of the revolution, they would have been animated by an excellent spirit, because they have the democratic instinct. But they are totally deprived of instruction and are easily led astray. In the recent elections for example, they voted like a flock. Because of their ignorance the bourgeois, the nobles and the priests have conserved a great influence over them. Several years of republican life will be necessary for them before they open their eyes. Accustomed to obey and to serve, they distrust promises not immediately made effective, and when one says to them that the rule of abuse and privilege is going to completely disappear, they reply, shaking their heads: "That is how things have always been, and always will be." '

The role of the nobles and bourgeois in this has already been considered but additionally the extremely significant role of the clergy must be recognized. This varied; by no means all clergy supported conservative candidates, but in general where the clergy did express an interest it was in support, as one would expect, of conservative interests, with varying effect according to the religiosity of the population, but most of this still remained susceptible to the influence of the Church. Thus if the relatively restrained Bishop of Blois advised his clergy against excessive participation in the electoral campaign, and forbade them to make propaganda he did permit them to give advice and emphasized that this should be in support of social order.[106] Other bishops often drew up lists of candidates for the parish clergy to recommend to their parishioners. A circular of the Bishop of Rennes to his parish clergy can be taken as fairly typical:

> We charge you . . . to invite . . . your faithful parishioners to accomplish with fidelity the sacred duty of electors which is imposed on them.
>
> We know, dear Cooperator, the legitimate confidence which you enjoy with them. Help them then with wise counsel in this important circumstance; teach them how to conduct themselves both in choosing a candidate, and in the exercise of their electoral rights, destroy their objections, dissipate their fears.
>
> Take care to make them understand that in the face of the great interests they have to defend, all party spirit must disappear; they must only concern themselves with one thing, that is to choose as representatives men of recognized probity, clearly decided to found in France a republic, which will respect the sacred rights of religion, of liberty, of property, of the family. . . .
>
> . . . Finally, dear Cooperator, set a good example to your parishioners, go to the elections at the head of your flock. . . .[107]

The delegates of the Club of Clubs combated the results of such exhortations and their complaints about clerical activity are revealing both of the precise nature of this and of the society in which it occurred.

With regard to the effect of the above circular of the Bishop of Rennes, one Deceau wrote on April 10 from St Malo that 'the clergy has a great influence, the Bishop of Rennes holds in his hand 1,100 priests who are able to dispose of 20 votes each.'[108] From Mayenne the complaint that, 'the village priests are threatening not to give citizens Absolution if they do not vote in favour of the names they spread everywhere.'[109]

From the Isère priests were accused of 'attaching to themselves the mothers of families knowing the influence these have on their families'.[110]

For Marx universal suffrage 'possessed the incomparably higher merit of unchaining the class struggle.'[111] The electoral campaign of March–April 1848, is certainly revealing of growing social hostility. The weakness of Republicanism has been observed at a number of points. In some villages and small market towns of the provinces it seems to have been consciously accepted by 'minor officials, vine growers, peasant proprietors in conflict with their priests',[112] by those groups possessing some small degree of economic and social independence, mainly in regions where in addition, for whatever reason, there was hostility to the 'natural' leaders of society.

With regard to the workers, the delegates of the Club of Clubs constantly complained about their ignorance and apathy, or else about their divisions. Citizen Dahubert in an undated letter, probably written in early April, wrote of Rouen that 'The workers divide themselves into two classes, those of the factories and those of the various trades'. The second are 'very democratic and understand liberty in the true sense of the word'. These were a minority.

'The first, on the contrary, takes liberty for licence and is capable of committing disorder to revenge itself for the suffering its employers had made it endure, and capable then of compromising our cause'.[113] As elsewhere the prime source of republican support was the urban artisan.

Even in Paris where general political consciousness was at a relatively high level, there were two levels of activity. Skilled artisans were attempting to organize unions and cooperative groups and even created a central organization to coordinate this activity – the 'central Committee of the Workers of the Department of the Seine'. But this in effect involved relatively few workers belonging to some of the highly skilled artisanal trades.

On the practical political level the indifference or limited political

consciousness of most workers is revealed by their failure to participate in the important election of National Guard officers on March 18,
and by the reiterated appeals to them to register as voters. Their
slowness in this respect must have made the radical republican
demand for postponement of the elections seem of crucial importance.

The demonstration of April 16 was designed to secure this and to
remind the Government of the power of the masses. It only revealed
the divisions and personal animosities between republicans.
Lamartine, Ledru-Rollin and Barbès united in horror of Blanqui, of
his person and revolutionary ideals, and the workers themselves
divided. A police report of April 16 described a crowd shouting
*Vive la République! À bas les communistes!, à bas Cabet!, à bas
Blanqui!* added that 'The blouses . . . numerous in the ranks of
the National Guard, did not pronounce themselves with less energy
than those who are called today the Rich'.[114] The Guard of the most
proletarian arrondissement of Paris, the Twelfth, had answered the
government's call to arms. Moderate republicans opposed any social
reform but the most gradual, the more radical of the character of
Ledru-Rollin, recognized social divisions, but were inhibited by a
terror of the Parisian mob. For the first time moderate and democratic
republicans united against a threat from the workers.

In the electoral campaign some provincial republicans combined the
old ideals of Jacobinism and the new socialism, in some vague idealistic
whole. However, there were obvious limits to this support for and
awareness of the possibility of social change. Official propaganda activity was extremely limited. It is true that, for the first time the school-
teachers were organized by commissaires and education officials as a
counterbalance to clerical activity, but the many threats of disciplinary
action against those failing to obey indicates the reluctance of teachers to
enter politics or their opposition to the Republic, in spite of the impulsion to action given by poor conditions and clerical interference with
their teaching. Often anyway the influence of a school teacher was extremely limited, peasants in this period were likely to be contemptuous
of them as men who did no work and owned no property. Because of
these limits to government and private activity the central organization of the Parisian clubs, the Club of Clubs, sent forth its delegates.
One estimate claims that 251 delegates were sent to 85 departments
and a further 37 to the army.[115]

Their reports emphasize the fact that republican strength was
based on lower middle class and artisan support but the main

impression gained is one of the lack of success which greeted their activity, the hostility or indifference with which they were received by all sections of the population and particularly by the government's commissaires. Like the clubs and republican press they lacked a clear analysis of the situation, they were unable to make real promises and lacked social prestige. With little to offer, and no overall plan of campaign, they failed to organize much support.

The lists of electoral candidates which emerged from this activity often included individuals of varying opinions, but a general picture remains. As one element of this, the extreme reluctance of workers and peasants to accept the candidature of anyone but those regarded as socially and educationally superior. In Paris the skilled workers involved with the Luxembourg Commission, the 'Central Committee of Workers' and the newspaper *L'Atelier* included on their lists members of the Provisional Government – the last all its members, the other two only Ledru-Rollin, Blanc, Albert and Flocon – socialist idealogues, and club spokesmen, with workers in inferior positions on the lists. It is significant that even the skilled and more politically conscious workers were unable to reach agreement on a single list. In the provinces moreover it was especially difficult to find sufficiently well-known candidates.[116]

In terms of actual voting there was very little intimidation or violence. The Government and its commissaires recommended certain condidates, the latter especially themselves. Mayors and school-teachers handed out completed ballot papers and clubs attempted to organize a mass march to the voting place to impose unanimity.[117] They enjoyed little success as compared with the efforts of local notables. The very principles of 1848 precluded extensive government interference; lack of experience of electoral manipulation, the divisions and small number of convinced republicans, all contributed to a situation in which, given the failure to materialize of the promise of the Republic, nothing could challenge the existing moral authority of the established local notables.

Marx wrote of the Constituent National Assembly which met on May 4 that in it 'the *bourgeois republicaines*, the republicans of the *National*, had the upper hand. Even Legitimists and Orleanists at first dared to show themselves only under the mask of bourgeois republicanism.' His opinion of the political character of the Assembly can be further indicated by his claim that it intended to pursue 'The fight against the proletariat'.[118]

The election results seem to bear him out. Only in the south, in the twenty-three departments south of the line Ain-Gironde did a significant and democratic renewal of the deputies of the July Monarchy take place. In extremely general terms Legitimists tended to be elected in Brittany, the Vendée and the poor departments of the Massif Central. Orleanists in the north and Normandy, moderate republicans in the east and centre and democrats and socialists only in the big towns and in the south.

In terms of the political antecedents of members of the Assembly historians' conclusions vary. Charles Seignebos estimated that there were about 500 moderate republicans, less than 100 radical republicans, less than 200 Orleanists and about 100 Legitimists.[119] Other historians have tended to accept this, but in a recent article an American historian maintains that in terms of voting behaviour only 270–280 deputies could be clearly distinguished from the radical and Monarchist groups, whilst the moderate republican caucus established in late May never attracted more than 256 deputies. Similarly he reduces the number of radicals and socialists from about 100 to 70–80.[120] This accords with Lamartine's description of the Assembly as 'non-republican or little republican'.[121] The moderate republican strength seemed greater than it was because men with more conservative political leanings tended often to accept a moderate republican label at this time.

Whatever this may be, the conservatism of the Assembly and the failure of the radical and especially socialist candidates is established – even in Paris, where the seven first elected were moderate republican members of the Provisional Government, with its radical members Ledru-Rollin and Louis Blanc, coming respectively 24th and 27th, and more clearly working class leaders like Blanqui and Raspail failing completely.

Marx's point concerning the social attitude of the great majority of the Assembly can perhaps be more clearly illustrated by considering the social origins of its members.

A. J. Tudesq concluded that this was an Assembly differing more politically than socially from those of the July Monarchy.[122] Confirming this impression Alexis de Tocqueville maintained that it included more great landowners and gentlemen and more priests than the Orleanist Chamber.[123]

More precisely, and again, according to Tudesq the bourgeois professional groups dominated with 176 lawyers, 53 doctors and intellectuals, 100 officers and former officers, 67 public officials, mainly magistrates, besides 67 former commissaires of the Provisional Government. The economic professions were he claims, better represented than formerly by mainly petty and middle bourgeoisie. There were 100 landed proprietors, great and small, but less than 30 workers, and these mostly rather conservative.[124] Whatever the shortcomings of this classification, one conclusion common to historians is that this was a bourgeois assembly, and moreover an assembly of relatively wealthy men. One estimate concludes that 691 of its members paid more than 500 francs per annum in direct taxation and would have been eligible for election to the Orleanist Chamber[125] and Tudesq calculates that about half had been once either elected by the limited suffrage or were closely related to such figures.[126]

Most of these 880 deputies were politically inexperienced, most were members of the middle and lower middle class elected as local notables but there was a large group of former deputies, experienced parliamentarians, formerly of the dynastic left and centre left, who would assume a role out of all proportion to their number.

Lord Normanby, the British Ambassador, effectively summed up the meaning of this Assembly – 'My own impression is that it is more social than political in its signification; that it is principally to be considered as a protest on behalf of the owner of every variety of property, which is extremely subdivided here, against the dangerous doctrines which have been held by the most prominent amongst the ultra-revolutionists. . . . In the provinces the most predominant feeling was a determination that Paris should not dictate to them.'[127]

Its members were mainly provincial with little knowledge of or liking for Paris and a minimum of sympathy for her problems. Monarchists joined with the majority of republicans in desiring stability above all else. Thiers told Nassau Senior that the Assembly 'was sincerely republican not as believing a republic suitable to France but as seeing that despotism or anarchy were the only alternatives'.[128]

These elections were initially seen as a triumph for moderate republicans, and were well received by all those who had been afraid of a democratic or socialist victory. The *Gazette de France* would affirm of the Assembly that 'it has been sent to oppose the demagogic movement'.

Until the elections the moderate republican majority in the Provisional Government had been dominated by the Parisian masses. This election result increased the confidence of both government and conservatives generally. Continued demonstrations and threats would maintain fear but the massive conservative vote of the working classes, and especially the peasantry, was encouraging. 'The notables had feared the worst, the worst had been avoided. The danger of a violent transformation of society having passed, they would tend to minimize this danger, to regret their effacement and to become embittered against the men behind whom they had sheltered, beginning with the members of the Provincial Government.'[129] Reaction seemed more than ever possible and even moderate republicans would soon appear as too radical.

The reaction of the more radical republicans to this Assembly obviously differed. The lack of confidence in the results of universal suffrage of many of these has been observed, but the size of the defeat was still a shock. The division of republicans into moderates and radicals in the Assembly was quickly evident and necessarily as a result of this the slim chance of social reform.

If in a number of places the announcement of election results unfavourable to the extreme left had led to riots,[130] the election revealed that generally the urban workers were apathetic and uninterested in politics. In Rouen, the scene of the most serious riots, only about one third of the workers had voted, and radical political leaders were bitterly aware of the weakness of support for them.[131]

An editorial in the *Réforme* on April 30, regretted that 'The reaction has succeeded in its aims. It has separated the nation into two camps....' It saw the results as anti-republican. The *Vraie République* represented better the feelings of a large number of Parisian workers, and the way these feelings would develop in the weeks ahead, as expectations of a better life were finally shattered by this conservative assembly. On April 30 it lamented that a coalition of the privileged had triumphed over the People. It saw the future role of the extreme republicans it represented as not that of a parliamentary opposition, but of combatants willing to fight to create the *République sociale*. The threat was obvious, and conservatives, their confidence restored, were willing and would be increasingly anxious for an opportunity to meet the threat and vanquish it.

One commentator wrote of the National Assembly soon after it met that it is 'perhaps moderate in its great majority, but fear will prevail over moderation....'[132] This Assembly signified for most people the hope of a return to calm and order, to some kind of normality. But this was not to be.

The conservative character of the Assembly was quickly emphasized by the exclusion of the human symbols of social change, namely
Blanc and Albert, from the Executive Commission it elected.
Lamartine, previously regarded as the saviour of France lost much
of his influence in appearing to pander to the more radical republicans
by supporting Ledru-Rollin's inclusion. The conservative wish to
exclude Ledru-Rollin symbolized a desire to reject not only major concessions to the workers, but also the less drastic proposals of Ledru-
Rollin's associates, of reforms to aid the small property owners.

The attitudes of the new assembly, patently hostile to the substantial reforms desired by the workers, together with the brutal
dispersal of demonstrating workers in Rouen, inevitably made the
Parisian workers feel that their hopes for a new society would be
betrayed. They increasingly saw a bourgeois plot.

In Rouen workers had demonstrated against the election results
unfavourable to the more radical list, and 59 workers had been killed
whilst the troops and the National Guard, from which workers had
successfully been excluded, had no serious casualties, indicating
that the workers had been unarmed.[133]

Blanqui saw Rouen as a manifestation of counter-revolution,[134] and
on this the extreme left tended to be united. Even the more pacific
Club des Amis du Peuple of Raspail concluded that 'this horrible
event at Rouen coincides with the abortive attempt of April 16 in
Paris, which indicates a plot organized throughout France against the
public liberties'.[135]

More revealing of mass emotion as reflected in the clubs, a police
report dated May 2 claimed that 'It is generally felt . . . that this
unrest will translate itself soon into gunfire, the extremist leaders
make no secret of this.' But for the moment the leaders in the clubs
felt that they had insufficient mass support for an armed rising.
Another report of the following day predicted that they would in the
immediate future attempt to overawe the Assembly and at the same
time hope for a provoking clash with the National Guard.[136] Thus
the events of May 15 are presaged, and are even more explicable when
the popular view of this Assembly is considered; not simply the
disappointment at its attitudes, but the view of its function, expressed
for example by a speaker at the *Société Centrale Republicaine* on May
9. Referring to the deputies he maintained that 'these faithless men
forget too soon from where they came, and misfortune to them if they
believe themselves already . . . strong enough to crush the people,

their sovereign master. The Constituent Assembly is nothing more than a *national workshop*. The group of workers charged by the people to work for its benefit. Once these workers fail to perform their duty towards their masters, these are able to chase them from the workshop and replace them by more faithful servants.'[137] Already at this early date, both police reports and club speeches see some sort of a clash in the near future as inevitable.

In contrast to the interpretation of events at Rouen by club spokesmen and workers the conservative press and government officials blamed events there on agitators.[138] The moderate republican *National* which perhaps best represented the opinion of the Executive Commission and its ministers maintained that where universal suffrage existed then violent protest was unnecessary and anti-democratic.[139] A formalistic assertion of the faith of middle-class republicans which reveals what their reaction must be to any threat to order.

The continuation of the economic crisis and consequently of unrest amongst both workers and peasants meant a condition of anxiety for those social groups against whom the unrest seemed to be directed, and this prevented a restoration of business confidence.

The unemployed urban workers were provided for by simple charity, or the more or less disguised charity of public works. This did not wholly ease their discontent. Emile Thomas, the director of the most important system of public works, the Parisian National Workshops, complained of his inability to employ workers at their own skills, rather than as simple labourers.[140] On April 11 he reported to the Minister of Public Works that each day he was only able to employ one worker in 4, and this only by giving useless tasks to twice as many men as were needed to perform them. He was frightened by growing unrest amongst the workers, by the demoralization produced by idleness, by the consequent threat of disorder.[141]

The election campaign in which conservatives had attacked all hints of socialism and of increased taxes which they related to the former, had focused attention on the National Workshops as the symbol of the new regime.

In this post-election period, with the exception of those in Paris, workers tended to be less and less active politically, being discouraged with the republic and slowly able to return to work. They acted when misery forced them to express their discontent, and for no other reason.

In the countryside unrest remained widespread and if changing in character, retained its spontaneous nature. The isolation of Paris in France was increasingly obvious.

Resistance to the tax collectors had been evident since the beginning of the Republic, mainly from those unable to pay. But the election campaign had included much propaganda against the new supplementary tax, the collection of which was subsequently faced with a great deal of resistance. Take as a significant and typical example of this propaganda, an article in the *Courrier du Cantal* linking the tax with the National Workshops – 'it cannot be doubted that these workshops are an excellent thing for . . . one knows not who; but the provinces would be more satisfied if they knew why the results of their energy should serve to pay . . . for they know not what. Thus they begin to grow tired of nourishing men whom they believe to be by their nature hardly industrious, lazy men who for the most part, make a trade of avoiding work.'[142]

Protests occurred in those areas worst affected by the crisis of declining prices, and in those recently affected by a series of natural calamities; by, for example, bad weather adversely affecting the crops in parts of east and north-east, or by the Loire floods of 1846. In this latter respect Gossez differentiates between the vinegrowers of the south-east, not affected, and those of the south-west. Incidents occurred most commonly in the south-western departments in the Charentes, Creuse, Lot-et-Garonne, Lot, Tarn-et-Garonne, Tarn, Lozère, Gard, Hérault and others. It was most dangerous where large numbers of people experienced relatively uniform conditions of existence and problems, and significantly also where migrant workers had brought home ideas of organization, as in the Creuse.[143]

The peasant population was in general disillusioned with the Republic, with the Government and Assembly which maintained the new tax, and with the workers of Paris for whose benefit it was supposedly being collected. Their agitation was divorced from and often hostile to that of the workers, but occurring simultaneously worried the authorities, and with reason it seems, if the following reports are taken to be not too exaggerated – that of a lieutenant of gendarmerie at Mirande dated 11 June 1848, who observed that 'resistance organizes itself on a grand scale, more than 100 communes belonging to the department of the Gers, and to those of the Hautes- and Basses-Pyrénées, are at this moment allied . . . emissaries circulate continually so as to recruit supporters, and it appears that this recruitment is easy, whilst those who will not freely engage them-selves are threatened with death or burning. . . . Infantry and cannon are needed . . . they talk of marching on Paris, this is hardly serious, but does at least demonstrate their excitement.'[144] And more typically a report concerning events at Laloubère in the Hautes-Pyrénées in August – 'The inhabitants, in considerable numbers, armed them-selves with axes, guns and other instruments, the alarm-bell was sounded and the officials of the financial administration only escaped violence . . . with difficulty.'[145] Such demonstrations were common.

The general anxiety was intensified by the events of May 15, when the 'proletariat . . . pushed its way into the National Assembly, sought in vain to recapture its revolutionary influence and only delivered its energetic leaders to the jailers of the bourgeoisie.'[146]

Conservative opinion saw the motives of the demonstrators of May 15 as being more extreme, the rapporteur of the commission of enquiry into the events of May and June was to tell the Assembly that the main aim of the demonstration was to dissolve it and create in its place a Committee of Public Safety. And in support of this he could present papers seized at the home of the revolutionary Sobrier.[147] The conservative press tended to see a plot by the clubs involving also, it was implied, radical leaders like Ledru-Rollin, with the apparent reason for the demonstration, the demand for aid to Poland against Russian oppression, as a mere pretext. This might well have been true of some club spokesmen, men like Sobrier and Huber. Certainly a police report exists, dated May 14, which com-plained that agitators were using all manner of pretexts but especially the cause of Polish freedom to excite the masses, and another of 11 a.m. on May 15 reports of groups gathering on the Place de la Bastille that at the moment they were not very numerous but com-posed of extremists attempting to organize a demonstration by claiming that 'the government has done nothing and does not wish to do anything for the people.'[148]

It is likely that there was a minority of activists prepared to attempt a coup, but of most club leaders and other participants it can safely be maintained that at most they wished to overawe the assembly and that Poland was more than a pretext, but a sympathetic reaction due to the continued influence of the Jacobin concept of the duty of France to free the European peoples.[149]

Thus there was a division amongst the demonstrators which pre-vented united action when an opportunity for a coup presented itself. This division can be seen in the reluctance of Blanqui to involve himself in a demonstration which might lead by accident to conflict. The usually well-informed correspondent of the *Liberté* of Rouen reported that in the days preceding May 15 Blanqui, generally seen as the great proponent of revolutionary violence had been attempting to impose moderation on his supporters in case precipitant action would lead to repression before the clubs were strong enough to oppose this. But pressure from other club members forced Blanqui to participate. There was a general feeling of contempt for the Assembly and widespread support for a demonstration of this, but not for anything more drastic.

By chance not the few bearers of a petition but a large number of demonstrators entered the Assembly, seemingly because the local military commander was unwilling to act firmly from fear of compromising himself, at a time when the government might change again, because also as commonly occurs in a demonstration, those at the rear of the column simply pushed forward those at the front.

Events in the Assembly really serve to illustrate the points already made. Huber indeed was to declare the Assembly dissolved, but an unorganized mob could not be utilized for an effective seizure of power, and many of its number were opposed to this. Blanqui spoke demanding that the Assembly provide for an improvement in the condition of the workers, and also that an ultimatum be delivered to Russia demanding the reconstitution of Poland and threatening war if this not be agreed.[150] This was threatening, frightening, an unacceptable pressure on a sovereign Assembly but not immediately revolutionary.

Alexis de Tocqueville, sitting in the Assembly noticed that some of the crowd who had invaded it were armed, but regarded them as more curious in attitude than hostile and felt certain that they were an unorganized mob without leadership. He believed that May 15 was designed to frighten rather than destroy the Assembly,[151] and is supported in this by the views of another deputy present at these events, Charles de Rémusat,[152] and additionally by Odilon Barrot.[153] Proudhon wrote that if the cause of Poland could have been imposed on the Assembly then it would have been captured for the cause of reform more generally.[154] War would radicalize the government as in 1792. Its declaration would signify the capitulation of the Assembly to the extreme left. Even so participants on May 15, interrogated after the June insurrection, generally registered that they were shocked when, on that day, demands not connected with the Polish question were made.[155]

It is difficult, if not impossible, to judge who were the participants in this demonstration. The significant fact politically was that for the first time a large number of the workers in the National Workshops had taken part in a demonstration. Emile Thomas estimated their number at about 14,000 of the 100,000 enrolled.[156] Previously the government had hoped to use this body as a counter-revolutionary force, but now its own desire to dissolve it would be combined with the pressure from all those who saw the Workshops as a threat to social order.

The most authoritative leaders of the left, including Blanqui, Raspail, Huber, Barbès, and Albert were arrested, and radicals like Ledru-Rollin further discredited, the National Guard purged, and a generally repressive, inevitably counter-revolutionary policy began to be implemented against the clubs. Even more significant were the effects on conservative attitudes. The demand grew that 'This situation must end.'[157] Groups in the Assembly and in society as a whole began more than ever to consciously long for a final struggle, for something to provoke the workers of Paris into revolt.

The reaction throughout France to the news of May 15 was decisive. The *Courrier du Gard* of Nîmes reflected on May 26 that 'the reaction of which no-one thought during the first days is dreamed of now by many men of order as the only means to put an end to the crisis, to save us from anarchy, to protect our civilization'.[158] Significantly the moderate republican newspaper the *National* expressed horror at this assault on the nation's representatives and demanded order and strong government.[159] The more radical *Réforme* recognized the justice of the people's complaints but deplored any pressure on deputies other than that of public opinion.[160]

This all denoted a definite intensification of the isolation of the Parisian masses and the alienation from them of all property-owning groups. It denoted additionally a definitive separation between revolutionary republicans and both moderates and the more radical associates of Ledru-Rollin.

As well as discrediting the more radical republicans, May 15 discredited the Executive Commission and government, convicted of incompetence; it increased the confidence of conservatives because of the apparent ease of its suppression and generally strengthened the support for repression, in part because of this underestimation of the strength and tenacity of the Parisian workers. For many middle class republicans the republic appeared to be threatened from the left.

In spite of this victory for order, unrestrained disorder continued. The economic and social situation was much the same as before May 15 except that now the force for repression had been strengthened in number and will. Balzac wrote plaintively on May 20 'It's like the end of the world. Debtors do not pay; creditors do not prosecute; governments do not govern; soldiers are disarmed; magistrates do not prosecute any more, the legs lead the head!'[161] Paris was alarmed by the continual presence of large groups of workers on the streets – by mid-June 700–800 of these were arrested each evening,[162] for nothing more serious than blocking the highway, but they were frightening. Daumier's cartoons of this period include a series *Alarmistes et Alarmés* – one shows a terrified bourgeois peeping through his curtains. His wife has taken up an attitude of prayer and asks 'A fire?' He answers, with obvious relief 'No, three lanterns in the window of a neighbour!' Another shows a frightened bourgeois couple rushing for safety, whilst a group of children playing at soldiers, led by a drummer, march along the street. They ask themselves 'Where can that group of armed men be going?' More soberly an editorial in the *Constitutionnel* of June 13 complained of the continual disorder in the streets which seemed to herald a state of anarchy. Social relations had deteriorated to such an extent that at the great parade of the 'festival of Harmony' of May 21, most deputies attended with hidden arms[163] whilst in the provinces 'tempers rose against Paris and for the first time in sixty years, they dared face the idea of resisting it; they armed themselves and prepared to come to the aid of the Assembly; thousands of addresses were sent to it to congratulate it on its victory of May 15. The ruin of commerce, the universal war, the fear of socialism made the Republic more and more detested.'[164]

All this served to strengthen the conservative alliance in process of formation. Tudesq sees this as partly revealed by the growing ideological rapprochement of Legitimists and Orleanists, the former increasingly emphasizing the defence of property, and accepting political and economic liberalism, the latter formerly liberals stressing order even more than previously.[165]

The attitudes of moderate republicans can be gauged from the correspondence between two bourgeois of Lyon, one of them temporarily resident in Paris, and especially from a letter sent from Lyon, dated May 27 – 'Since the terrorists failed (on May 15) we begin . . . to regain courage: please God that this will be permanent and that strong and virtuous men will create a well-conducted Republic, abstraction made of all utopian ideas and supporting themselves on the real people and not on the plebs. . . .'[166] A great mass of propaganda blamed the economic crisis on social disorder. This and their economic difficulties threw property owners, all those involved in commerce and industry behind the *grands notables* in their campaign to restore order. The Roubaix Chamber of Commerce represented their fears and demands in a petition of early June. It demanded that agitators 'no longer excite the worker against his chiefs . . . no longer present him as the victim of exploitation, especially when the facts prove that the paternalism of these chiefs has never been more active than in these last years'.[167]

In the Assembly political divisions remained obvious in the growing dissatisfaction of conservative deputies with the Government, increasing as the former politically dominant groups left a growing popular desire for reaction to be supporting them. The actual timing of the June insurrection and much of the subsequent course of the history of the Second Republic is only explicable when this continued hostility due to differing political rather than social conceptions is understood. Complaints were constant concerning the weakness of the Government. A police report of May 29 revealed the discouragement amongst elements of the Parisian National Guard due to the failure to take energetic measures against disorder.[168] In the Assembly itself criticism was continuous and pressure exerted in favour of sterner measures.

For some time early in June, however, both the Executive Commission and its Government, as if in reaction against this pressure, reaffirmed their republicanism, promising financial reforms, cheap credit facilities for the peasants, a modification of the salt tax, a purge of reactionary groups in the administration and even the nationalization of railway and assurance companies, the former to provide employment for the National Workshops.

The effect of this was to precipitate the reaction inside and outside the Assembly, in the face of which the Executive Commission, perhaps afraid of the political isolation consequent upon alienating the conservatives, whilst having few sympathies with revolutionary groups, capitulated and returned to a decision tentatively taken on

May 23 to dissolve the National Workshops; that is, accepted a reactionary rather than a reformist alignment.

The proposed nationalizations especially had awakened bitter and revealing opposition. The *Journal des Débats* complained that 'The role of the State is not to make itself manufacturer or merchant . . . it is to place society in the moral and political conditions which are favourable to capital formation by private industry'.[169] In the Assembly Montalembert, affirming his lack of financial interest, claimed to find 'the project an assault on the rights of property'.[170]

According to Tudesq the language of the republic was united with that favouring the interests of the notables. Legitimists and Catholics no longer attacked the use of property made by the bourgeoisie but defended the ideas of the liberal economists.

The Executive Commission had been concerned to dissolve the National Workshops at least since May 13, and had resolved to do so on May 23, but seemed reluctant to take the risk of an immediate dissolution before a substantial recovery of the economy could provide employment.

Increasing criticism in the Assembly combined with other factors to force action upon them. The supplementary elections of June 4 revealed a polarization of opinion and a consequent decline of the middle party, the moderate republicans. Especially threatening to order were the signs of increasing unity and organization amongst the workers in Paris designed with some success to secure the election of candidates who had previously failed like Caussidière, Leroux and Proudhon. Conservative opinion was extremely frightened by the election of notorious figures of the left in spite of the great conservative success in these elections, and demanded action from the government.

If the middle classes as a whole tended to desire an end to the threat of revolution there remained a desire amongst their less wealthy components for social reform. This was clearly expressed even at this time of social danger. In part it merged with more extreme revolutionary demands, even commonly shared these demands if not the methods proposed for achievement. It was significant as representing the growth of a political movement vitally important throughout the Second Republic whatever the weakness and divisions of the radical left in the Assembly, even if, as Ménard suggests, its deputies were isolating themselves from the people,[171] they were encouraging activists outside the Assembly with

F

their statements of principle, their demands for social reform, and attacks on the growing power of money, on financiers who were turning the country into a 'Jewish France'. Their demands that 'the salariat must disappear', to be replaced by state-aided associations of small proprietors, of agricultural and industrial workers, their affirmation that 'society owes to the individual and must guarantee him: liberty, education, justice, security, property, protection',[172] both developed and reflected the desires of the mass of Parisian and French small property owners and the propertyless and indicated the continued feeling for and possibility of an alliance of these social groups against the socially dominant force. These ideas appealed not only to the consciousness of the petty bourgeoisie, but also that of the workers.

However, in terms of the proposed means to attain these ends, other influences were becoming more effective. Among the '20,000 bandits, mainly escaped from the hulks or prisons and the 80,000 workers payed by the State to learn revolt in the idleness of the bar' as one paper described the poor of Paris,[173] demoralization due to idleness was indeed increasing,[174] making the workers increasingly susceptible to extremist propaganda. Men employed in the National Workshops were disappointed at the failure of the hoped-for social transformation to occur, were enraged at the attacks on them for an idleness they could not help and did not much enjoy, at the demands for the dissolution of these Workshops which were the only security they possessed, the only gains made by the revolution which their action had brought about.

Nadaud complained of the activity of Bonapartist agitators amongst the workers.[175] This is an element of the pre-insurrection period which Marx ignores – the obvious popularity of Louis-Napoléon Bonaparte amongst the workers. After the election of Bonaparte to the Presidency of the Republic Marx will explain working-class support for him as expressing a protest against the bourgeois republic which had crushed the movement of June. But this support pre-dated June, and existed for more positive reasons.

Police reports throughout the early weeks of June are full of descriptions of workers' expressions of Bonapartist sentiments, including a petition from the workers of La Vilette requiring Louis-Napoléon to be declared consul,[176] and one from the 7th Legion of the National Guard demanding his appointment as their colonel in place of the imprisoned Barbès.[177] The significance of these is exemplified by the common shouting of 'Vive Barbès! Vive Napoléon!'[178] Bonaparte held out a particular promise to the workers. According to the *Gazette des Tribunaux* many of those arrested in the early days of June for demonstrating in favour of Louis-Napoléon had been involved in the events of May 15, or more recently found amongst groups demonstrating in favour of Barbès. It stressed the apparent contradiction found where members of 'ultra-republican' clubs shouted 'Vive l'Empéreur'! in the streets.[179] Bonapartist propaganda was partly directed at the workers and promised social reform.[180] It was less the means of securing reform which seems to have mattered to these desperately poor men, than the reforms themselves. Thus at this stage in the evolution of the political consciousness of the Parisian workers, some form of popular Caesarism might have appeared attractive, especially as the conservative Assembly in its hostility to the newly elected Louis Bonaparte identified him sympathetically for the masses.

In the absence of the most influential revolutionary leaders, arrested after May 15, leadership tended to devolve on men of lesser ability and renown, particularly on the workers elected as representatives to the Luxembourg Commission which, though officially dissolved, remained as a political centre for workers[181] already organized in units of the National Guard and of the National Workshops, already agitated by the clubs, press and Bonapartists. Alphonse Audiganne claimed that these men were drawn from the most highly skilled trades, were the better educated who could grasp the more attractive elements of socialist propaganda whilst, he added with disdain, lacking the degree of education necessary to indicate the impracticality of those ideas.[182]

As the threat to the existence of the National Workshops grew so did the support for extreme action among its workers. As early as May 27–28 two police reports indicated a growing readiness to defend the existence of the Workshops by force.[183] The Club de la Révolution published an address to Barbès on June 9 – 'Liberty, equality, fraternity are threatened, and . . . a deplorable struggle is likely to occur. . . . A new social crisis approaches: the responsibility will rest on those who have provoked it. Because of the stupidity of some, and the bad wishes of others . . . this victory of February which should have been . . . the glorious complement of the work of our fathers will perhaps leave in history no other memory than that of a puff of wind between two tempests.'[184]

153

The tentative proposals to dissolve the National Workshops had alarmed the masses and increased the appeal of extremist agitators for them. This had thrown the government into increased dependence on the Assembly as insurrection appeared to be threatening, and thus increased its determination to close the National Workshops.

IV

The June Insurrection

The June days clearly revealed how far men's attitudes had changed since the first relatively harmonious days of the Republic. They indicated the insufficiency of political reform, even that granting universal male suffrage, as a means of giving satisfaction to the poor. They indicated the desperation with which those who had a vested interest under the *status quo* would defend this. Above all they indicated the shape of things to come by revealing this basic split in society and convincing many that differences between social groups could only be resolved by conflict. French society and its politics were for long to bear the mark of the hatreds generated by this insurrection of June 1848, and its brutal suppression.

Events in Paris

As early as 23 May a secret decision had been taken by the government to end enrolment in the National Workshops and force its unmarried workers either to enlist in the army or accept dismissal. The government was either genuinely reluctant or too weak to implement this policy, but came under increasing pressure from a large section of public opinion to do so.

This opinion was expressed most clearly by the Constituent Assembly, in which the Comte de Falloux, chairman of the special committee which finally demanded dissolution, was warmly applauded

155

for a speech asserting that the National Workshops were not only very expensive but a dangerous centre of political agitation.[1] Lacordaire, who became rapidly more conservative after 15 May opposed the 'right to work' which the National Workshops symbolized because it gave 'to the duty of Christian charity an obligatory character, which threatened to deny all merit to the benefactor and all gratitude from the grateful.'[2]

In the government Trélat, now Minister of Public Works, represented this hostility to the most obvious social reform of February. He saw the Workshops as a temporary organization, as disguised charity for the execution of useless projects, as a means by which the government provided relief to workers in dispute with their employers as well as to the genuinely unemployed. To Emile Thomas he declared that the Workshops were 'a permanent centre for insurrection; it is necessary to dissolve them as soon as possible'.[3] Revealing of his attitude was his suppression of the report of a commission of enquiry he had established on May 17. This rapidly prepared and inadequate report was in favour of dissolution but angered the minister by advising that this be slow and gradual, to accompany economic recovery.[4]

Gradualism was simply not what conservatives, including moderate republicans, wanted. The National Workshops symbolized disorder, and disorder had to end. Incessant street demonstrations seemed to require drastic action in response. 'Every day new alarms put on foot the National Guard and the army. . . . Everyone ardently desired to avoid the necessity of a conflict and all felt vaguely that this necessity was becoming each moment more inevitable. . . .'[5] The promise of a better future had hastily been made to the workers and they were determined that it should be kept. Continued economic crisis and unemployment made the National Workshops appear to them to be necessary. Equally determined was the feeling that such concessions were impossible.

Nassau Senior recorded on May 24 the belief of Michel Chevalier that a bloody struggle was near in which middle-class National Guards – 'so disgusted with the loss of time and money occasioned by the present state of agitation and security . . . will show no mercy.'[6] Police reports support this view. One of May 29 reported of the National Guard that 'It is ready to act energetically; for all the citizens who have some interest in industry, or a shop, will prefer a violent crisis to a state of languor which will undermine them more surely still.'[7]

The feeling that conflict was inevitable, was widespread. Men do not seek to avoid the inevitable but tend rather to hasten its outcome, especially if it promises to be favourable to them. The Executive Commission, constantly criticized for its weakness, submitted to the logic of events, and to the political pressure which threatened otherwise to isolate it, although aware of the probable consequences of any move towards dissolution.[8]

The manner in which dissolution was decreed was revealing both of the government's incompetence and also of the general desire of conservatives to end an uncertain situation. The *Constitutionnel*, whilst welcoming the dissolution, complained that it should have been announced after more preparation and with more prudence.

'It is obvious that the assistance given to the worker will only cease when he is unable to find other resources . . . the Government has no doubt new measures to propose. It should have made them known. . . . We regret that it did not take such precautions to prevent disquiet amongst the workers. . . . The decision could not have been introduced in a more unfortunate manner. . . .'[9] The government by its action had accepted the Assembly's demands for haste. Symptomatic of its willingness to accept any possible end to the continued crisis was the uncompromising attitude of the member of the Executive commission who met a delegation of workers on the morning of June 22. Marie responded to their complaints by telling them – 'Obey the orders of the Government; the workers do not wish to go to the provinces, we will compel them by force . . . by force, do you understand!'[10]

On June 21 a decree had appeared which, in addition to the growing restriction on entry into the National Workshops and the plans for public works in the provinces, primarily draining marshes in the Sologne, ordered the expulsion of all unmarried workers or their enrolment in the army. 'The workers were left no choice; they had to starve or let fly.'[11] Whether this was the real alternative was another matter, but the workers believed it was, and saw this as the end of all their hopes developing from February. Disillusionment was obvious, and this was one motive for insurrection.

The report of the official enquiry into the events of May 15 and June saw, with true police suspicion, an organized socialist revolt as having taken place. More revealing although no less dangerous to use as evidence are the statements of those arrested for participation in the insurrection. Most claim to have been forced to take part. The

Liberté of Rouen with some justice claimed that this was true of two-thirds of those interrogated. Typical of these was the following response of a wine-merchant called Haury, 'When I saw a barricade beginning to be constructed about 20 metres from my home, I approached it to try to prevent its completion; but I was the object of threats and of violence, and was even forced to place paving stones on the barricade.'[12]

Even more typical of the confused responses made was that of one Brichet, a labourer on the railway to the north, and a National Guard, who affirmed that 'While awaiting the call to arms, I went out with my rifle. They made me drink and led me to a barricade. . . . There, they asked me: "Can you see, will you fire?" Dam' at what? I replied. "Will you fire?" they repeated, "if you won't we will disarm you," and they took my gun. The following day they made me take the gun of someone wounded. . . . I only fired two shots.' Asked why he fired at all he responded – 'I was led astray like many others. Those who would not march, were called faint-hearted, and badly treated. . . . They excited us; and gave us drink.' Furthermore the prisoner explained that 'Someone like me, who has come from the countryside, who has never heard of anything, never seen anything, who does not know how to read or write is easy to lead astray.'[13] Most prisoners took the unheroic line of ignorance in their defence, they sought to deny personal responsibility. Men claimed to have been threatened,[14] persuaded by neighbours,[15] or even their women-folk,[16] obeyed the orders of officers commanding their National Guard Companies[17], were present simply out of curiosity,[18] or to defend order and property,[19] or after being misled into believing that they were defending the Republic against the plots of the various pretenders.[20] These were in many cases no doubt the real reasons for involvement, a combination of circumstances which seemed to demand some sort of action, the excited atmosphere of a crowd producing an almost hysterical response from the individual.

Out of the great mass of confused ideas and denials some basic facts stand out. First consider police reports concerning the outbreak of the insurrection.

At 11 o'clock on June 22 a crowd was reported on the Place de l'Hôtel de Ville – 'The men who compose it say that they will not leave for the Sologne, they would prefer to die here. They add that they will take up arms against the National Assembly and that they will be supported by the Mobile Guard.'

At midday amongst these demonstrators 'They are talking of the Sologne, they say that the area is unhealthy, that the workers must refuse to leave, and that the Government has only introduced this measure to rid itself of them. They are consumed with anger against citizens Lamartine and Marie, and say that the rich are thieves. . . .'

At 3 p.m. 'they concern themselves with the question of the National Workshops.'

By 7 p.m. four to five thousand people from the workers' quarters of Saint-Jacques, Saint-Marcel and Saint-Antoine were reported as marching in columns behind the flags of the National Workshops shouting 'Work! Work! Bread! We will not leave!'[21] The immediate concern of the workers was then the proposed running down of the National Workshops, the fear of being unable to provide for their own needs, and for those of their families, the desire not to be sent to the reputedly unhealthy Sologne. Lamartine riding through the streets attempting to persuade insurgents to return home, or else to encourage the soldiers and National Guards was told by insurgents 'of their griefs against the Assembly, of their sadness at seeing the revolution stain itself with blood . . . of their misery, of their hunger, of the destitution of their children and of their wives.'[22] The fact that a large proportion of those arrested were married men, who would normally be reluctant to risk involvement which might deprive their families of a breadwinner, indicates the feeling of desperation, and lends support to a point made by Louis Blanc to the effect that 'The worker will not arm himself in the name of personal suffering; he will arm himself because he feels the suffering of his old father, of his wife, of his children, of his comrades. He will protest against the continuation of misery, not only because it tortures the body, but because it oppresses the soul.'[23] To relate the insurrection simply to hunger is to grossly simplify. Flaubert wrote that the alternative to unemployment offered, 'infuriated the young men of Paris, who were convinced that it was an attempt to destroy the Republic. Life away from the capital struck them as an exile; they saw themselves dying of fever in desolate regions. Many of them, too, were accustomed to skilled work and regarded farming as a degrading occupation; in short, this was a trap, an insult, an outright refutation of all the promises which had been made to them. If they resisted, force would be used against them; they had no doubts on this score and got ready to forestall it.'[24]

Louis Bosquet, a hatter, replying to his interrogator's demand to know why he had been involved in constructing a barricade, replied that 'It had been started when we arrived there; we worked there because they wanted to send the workers from Paris; we did not have bad intentions, we thought that it was like in February.'[25] This is significant. Those involved felt this to be a just insurrection, as that of February had been, and even more so because it intended only to preserve the promise of February.

This tends to be borne out by some of the few scraps of information available concerning the attitudes of workers, rather than intellectuals in the days immediately preceding the insurrection. Consider as representative a description of conversations between groups of workers, by a professor at the Ecole Centrale, for the Commission of Enquiry – 'They spoke of the misery of the workers of the Faubourg St Antoine, of their contempt for the Executive Commission, and a little of the need to rally to Prince Louis-Napoléon.

But the question constantly approached was that of an armed struggle to overthrow the Assembly. One man . . . spoke of socialism. A worker, he exercised some authority over the various groups. "The mistake of the people in February, and against which it is necessary we guard ourselves this time," he said "was not to have named our deputies on the barricades themselves, it is there that they should be named, because there we see them at work. Yes, it's necessary to finish with the Aristo. Lamartine is an Aristo . . ."

. . . Speaking of industry and commerce "He thought that to advance money to the chiefs of the great industries would be more profitable for the workers, than charity, even earned at the National Workshops. He repeated this . . . and it was greatly appreciated . . . ."

The workers felt assured that the *Garde mobile* would support them, they all claimed to have guns and ammunition and felt that the bourgeois National Guards would be too frightened to fight, and that the army had had enough in February.

A common aspiration seems to have been to have Louis-Napoléon as President of the Republic – 'he's good, that one. He will make everything work, commerce and industry. He is rich'.

'. . . The workers always ended thus, "They have been rich for too long, they possess everything, and have no heart; they make fun of us, it is necessary to end our great misery."

Several gave assurances that they did not eat every day, that they had numerous children. They traced sinister pictures of their homes . . .'

These workers apparently spoke little of the Luxembourg Commission or of Louis Blanc whilst 'The equality of wages seemed impossible to them.'[26]

This is revealing of the confused character of the socio-political images possessed by the workers. There are few signs of the influence of socialist theories but rather the old hatred of the rich reinforced by the disappointments which had followed February and the vague aspirations for a better life which must have been influenced by socialist thought. There is only a partial rejection of the existing social structure. A poster signed by the brigadiers of the National Workshops, is evidence of this. Whilst seeing the National Workshops as the possible basis in the future of a vast network of associations for production, they demanded the aid of the existing state and additionally saw these associations as reservoirs providing labour for private industry.[27] An officer of the National Guard reported his conversation with an insurgent leader – 'he gave me for motive of the revolt that they wished the democratic and social republic ... I demanded an explanation of social, he replied ... the right accorded to the workers to unite together according to their skills to compete for public and private contracts.' The insurgents had most strenuously denied any desire to interfere with existing rights of property.[28]

Occasionally, more precise concepts of a social republic were presented but always with limited aims, not of social revolution but of social reforms which would bring increased material comfort and equally important to many, dignity to the worker. An engineering worker declared himself to have been fighting for *la République sociale* by which he claimed to mean 'a republic with social reforms: universal suffrage has been decreed, but the people has not profited from this, it is an instrument which it does not know how to use; I want free and obligatory education for all, the organization of labour by association, which would ensure for the worker all the product of his work, of which today a part is taken from him by those who possess capital. Then, there would be no misery, and no revolution to fear. If this had been done, instead of wasting enormous sums on the National Workshops, the June insurrection would not have taken place. The workers ... would have preferred to work at their trades than to be paid for doing nothing....'[29] These ideas of a worker with a relatively developed political consciousness are symptomatic of the limited development of this consciousness in Paris as a whole, of the hasty, feverish attraction to vague and great plans of social reform and particularly to the notion of association between workers to eliminate exploitation by and subordination to employers and commercial middlemen. This could occur gradually within the framework of the existing society. The overall hope was summed up by the journal of the former workers' delegates to the defunct Luxembourg Commission – 'Our aim, brothers, is the emancipation of the proletariat, the conquest of our social rights.'[30] This served as a 'generalized belief', a simple slogan providing the degree of unity necessary for even the minimum of organized action.

The National Workshops in themselves were indeed not a reason for insurrection but they symbolized hopes, however vague in character. They were the only gain of February which remained to the masses and they were determined to defend them – all the more determined as feelings of social hostility developed in the preceding period. The insurrection grew out of this accumulation of hatred, fear and lack of understanding. The threat of the dissolution of the National Workshops was the occasion. This presaged not only unemployment but a future without hope. Charles de Rémusat blamed the June rising on the ease with which the victory of February had been won, and the confidence which this gave to its victors, on the hopes which arose from this and the promises which were made, as well as on the discrediting of established political figures, the economic crisis and the agitation of a mass of clubs and newspapers. In sum, this was an event 'presaged by twenty different causes. . . .'[31]

The participants in this insurrection have been described throughout as 'workers' but the question of participation has still to be examined. This is not as simple as Marx and Engels seem to indicate. The insurrection tends to assume, on closer examination, the character of a rising of the poor against the rich, with a far wider definition given to the former than that conveyed by the term 'proletarian'.

According to Marx it was 'the workers' who 'with unexampled bravery and ingenuity, without leaders, without a common plan, without means and for the most part lacking weapons held in check the army, the Mobile Guard, the Paris National Guard, and the National Guard that streamed in from the provinces.'[32] Engels in the *Neue Rheinische Zeitung* had been even more explicit in claiming that 'The insurrection is purely working class.'[33] This was powerful support for a historico-political theory which both predicted and wished for the seizure and use of power by the workers.

To compare with Marx's account of participation in the June

insurrection we have a register containing the names, occupations, ages, etc., of 11,727 individuals arrested. It is suggested that this is a sufficiently large sample to permit general conclusions concerning participation to be made.

Some comments need to be made on the methods used and on the shortcomings of the material available.

The notation of profession was not constant, sometimes actual profession was recorded – as, for example, locksmith working on buildings, sometimes employment in a particular industry, as for example, the building industry. As far as possible the terminology used by the contemporaries was noted and by a long process of trial and error a method of collation developed which satisfied two basic criteria – one, it brought together in broad groups those professions which bore a marked similarity to each other, in which the workers would have had similar working and living conditions and would enjoy daily contact one with the other, and largely common attitudes; secondly, the broad groupings would permit some comparison with census conclusions so as to permit a judgement of the likelihood of workers employed in a particular profession to participate in the insurrection.

Confidence in the efficacy of this method was increased by an article written by Adeline Daumard which sought to evolve methodological guides for the process of classification of population structure. Following the *Institut National de la statistique et des Études Économiques* she advised that classification should 'involve choosing certain professions as typical examples of a category and including in the same categories the professions which resemble those regarded as typical examples'.[34] In this way is minimized what Daumard calls 'the paradox of history'[35] created by the historian's need of initial classification to permit work, which involves risk of prejudicing the result.

In spite of the great care taken, absolute statistical accuracy was impossible to achieve. Especially important is the inability to always distinguish patrons from workers, from the information given in the register, a difficulty increased by the fact that in contemporary usage the term *ouvrier* continued to be applied to patrons as well as employees. Nevertheless an impression of occupational involvement is gained.

In the same manner it was not possible to distinguish between workers involved in artisanal production and those working in factories, and we have to fall back on the information concerning

particular occupational groups provided by the Parisian census of
1847–48 which reveals the essentially small-scale nature of Parisian
industry in which the average industrial establishment employed
5·28 workers.[36] The census includes unskilled workers as part of the
occupational groups amongst whom they worked. The register of
arrests tends often to describe them simply as labourers. Some of the
categories of the census, especially that of building workers, are thus
inflated by comparison with the numbers arrested so that the likelihood of building workers to participate in insurrection is under-
estimated.

In terms of numbers arrested, and it is presumed involved,
building workers were most significant, followed by metalworkers and
mechanics of all sorts, followed by those employed in shoe and
clothing production and repair, followed by labourers, then furniture
workers, and with no other professional group of nearly such significance. The presence of metal workers is significant because it
involved the participation of factory workers. These cannot be
statistically separated from the workers involved in more traditional
metal industries, but their presence can be presumed because of the
participation in the insurrection of groups from the nearer suburbs of
Paris, from Belleville, Neuilly and Passy, for example, where the new
developing industries were grouped,[39] and by the involvement of
a large number of workers from the engineering workshops of
Jean-François Cail at La Chapelle and of railway workshop employees
at Chapelle St Denis to the north of Paris and Ivry to the south.[40]
These metal workers were skilled and tended to enjoy the same standard of life and share the attitudes of the skilled artisans of the
traditional industries amongst whom they lived.

The quite large numbers of members of the liberal professions,
clerical workers and commercial professions, mainly small shop- or
tavern-keepers are worth noting. Not including workshop patrons,
but including proprietors and *rentiers*, clerks, and members of the
liberal, artistic and commercial professions, 9·71 per cent of those
arrested (1,215) were clearly members of the lower middle classes,
and this figure of one in ten would be far higher if the number of
patrons could be estimated. This anyway is not an inconsiderable
figure, representing the effects of economic crisis, and even of
inclusion in the National Workshops on these men. By comparison
with previous Parisian insurrections the number of students involved
was very small, a fact which is perhaps symptomatic of the social,

rather than political character of the insurrection, but lower middle class participation remained significant enough to make a description of the rising consisting wholly of workers inaccurate. To describe it as 'proletarian' was even more inaccurate. This was a revolt of the poorer elements of the Parisian population, of the 'people', the small

Table I[37]

PARTICIPATION IN THE INSURRECTION OF JUNE, 1848: PROFESSIONS OF THOSE ARRESTED

Profession	No. arrested	% of total arrested	Approx. % of workers engaged in profession arrested	Approx. % of men engaged in profession arrested
Building	1,725	14·82	3·96	4·11
Food and drink[38]	438	3·76	4·04	5·31
Furniture	1,004	8·62	2·65	3·32
Clothing and shoes	1,225	10·52	1·31	3·86
Textiles	351	3·01	0·93	3·09
Skin and leather	157	1·35	3·32	3·58
Coach building, saddlery and military equipment	223	1·92	1·62	2·11
Chemicals and ceramics	116	1·00	1·14	1·69
Metal, engineering and metal products	1,312	11·27	4·25	4·79
Precious metals and jewellery	231	1·98	1·31	2·03
Coopers and basket-makers	68	0·58	1·20	1·62
Printing workers	433	3·72	2·48	3·8
Labourers and navvies	1,093	9·39		
Cultivators, gardeners and herdsmen	141	1·21		
Transport workers	522	4·48		
Concièrges, servants, cooks and waiters	282	2·42		
Proprietors, rentiers	47	0·40	Calculation would be too inaccurate because of vagueness of categories used in both the census of 1847–1848 and in the list of prisoners	
Clerical workers	438	3·76		
Liberal professions	208	1·79		
Artistic professions	72	0·62		
Commercial professions (incl. shopkeepers)	450	3·77		
Students	39	0·33		
Garde mobile	163	1·40		
Police and soldiers	216	1·86		
Lumpenproletariat	297	2·55		
Others	297	2·56		
Occupation not specified	94	0·81	Error 29 below official figure	
	11,642	99·9		

shopkeepers, tavernkeepers and patrons of workshops as well as the artisans, labourers and, given the structure of Parisian industry, of only a relatively small number of factory workers. According to Ernest Labrousse in this period 'one finds a sort of economic proximity, a proximity of level, between the state of a wage earning worker and that of an artisan or small-scale merchant'.[41] Given that the average number of workers employed per industrial or commercial establishment at this time was 5·28, that only 7,117 establishments employed more than 10 workers whilst 57,699 employed fewer than ten,[42] then the validity of Labrousse's conclusion seems guaranteed.

As far as it was possible to calculate the percentage of workers engaged in a particular profession who were arrested, then this, it is believed, is an accurate portrayal of the likelihood of workers in a professional group to participate. This has only been attempted where the calculation did not threaten to be too inaccurate due to the vagueness of and lack of concordance between the categories used in the Parisian census of 1847–48 and those of the list of prisoners. It must however, for similar reasons, remain suspect and the only figures which can be with reasonable certainty accepted as accurate are those of the first two columns of Table 1.

At any rate, the results seem to indicate that likelihood to participate, and perhaps therefore political consciousness was greatest among the men of the food and drink industries, followed by metal workers and then building workers, and was lowest among those employed in producing barrels, basketwork, precious metals and jewellery, saddlery, coaches and military equipment. The relatively high proportion of workers in food and drink industries arrested is surprising because they suffered least from unemployment, but the numerical figure for participation is low and perhaps too much significance should not be attached to this. The category of *lumpenproletariat* follows both Marx's definition by profession[43] and those of other contemporary writers and includes mainly rag-pickers, knife grinders and tinkers. These and few other *lumpenproletarian* occupations are identified in the register of arrested. 2·43 per cent of those arrested were nonetheless so categorized and if brothel keepers, swindlers, literati, etc., could have been identified, this proportion would have been greatly increased. Marx is thus wrong to identify these demi-world figures with the forces of reaction. The fact is inescapable that the world of the impoverished urban workers shaded indefinably into that of the criminal, and both tend to act in a similar manner, though the motives of the latter in an insurrection might be less than wholly honest.

One letter of evidence to the Commission of Enquiry described 'the poor class which has often great virtues, but also ... the bad class, filthy, without fixed abode, living off shameful and guilty expedients, living side by side.'[44] The number of these paupers was estimated in 1836 as about 64,000 individuals.[45] Moreover such social groups play an important part in mobilizing crowds for action, because, relatively free from inhibitions themselves, they take a stimulating lead, encouraging others to act. In a situation of potential social conflict particularly in a society with a large semi-criminal population 'To the workers without work join themselves the freed convicts, and, with them, the frivolous characters who take pleasure in the carnage.'[46]

The table below indicates some concordance between arrests, participation, and the level of unemployment within a particular profession, with the notable exception again of the food industry.

Another significant concordance is revealed by a comparison of the

Table 2

Occupation	Unemployed workers	As a % of total normally employed	No. employed in National Workshops
Food and drink	2,024	19·02	1,320
Building	26,791	64·39	24,440
Furniture	26,352	73·03	14,619
Clothing and Shoes	46,013 (max. of 28,748 males)	51·09	6,309
Textiles	19,452 (max. of 11,253 males)	53·02	3,424
Skin and leather	1,819	39·78	724
Coach building, saddlery and military equipment	6,586	47·88	1,143
Chemicals and ceramics	4,525	46·78	252
Metal, engineering and metal products	14,486	58·19	8,024
Precious metals and jewellery	9,656	57·46	2,758
Coopers and basket makers	2,500	46·31	
Articles de Paris	18,446	51·70	Impossible to judge
Printing workers	7,755	46·42	2,943

proportion of unemployed in a particular occupational group organized in the National Workshops and the proportion of its members arrested. For the first time food production tends to fit into a pattern, in the sense that a large proportion of its unemployed (65·22 per cent) were so organized. This was even more true of building (91·23 per cent of its unemployed), and was even true of the metal industries (55·4 per cent) by comparison with, for example, precious metals and jewellery, and chemicals and ceramics. Again, however, a divergence occurs where the case of the men employed in the clothing industry is concerned, and to some extent those employed in printing, although in the latter case organization in the National Workshops would not have been as necessary to heighten the political consciousness of an already politically involved profession.

In general, therefore, it can be assumed that organization in the National Workshops was an important factor in determining the involvement of particular professional groups in the insurrection, together with the existing level of organization and consciousness of the professions concerned. On the other hand, a large number of workers not employed in the National Workshops took part in the rising. Cavaignac, on July 3, estimated the insurgents as being at most 50,000 and he probably had little desire to minimize his, and the army's, achievement. 105,000 workers had been engaged in the National Workshops, so that even if all 50,000 had been included only a minority of its workers had been prepared to risk a conflict. Large numbers of workers had been refused admission to the Workshops. On June 20 Faucher estimated that 50–60,000 of these remained in Paris.[48] It seems likely that many of these, the most deprived and impoverished of workers, being probably relative newcomers from the provinces, feeling insecure in their new environment would have been likely to resort to violence.

There exists an important respect in which the figures of those arrested might falsify the impression we gain of participation in the insurrection. A reading of police reports and of the conservative press, or even of novels indicates a value judgement by the upper and middle classes according to which certain professional groups were seen as more likely to participate in insurrection or criminal activities than others.

As can be seen from this chart there was a tendency whilst making arrests to exaggerate the participation of some professions more than others. This was true especially of building workers, of those engaged in producing furniture, clothing and shoes, that is, the traditional Parisian trades, and also as one would expect the category we have labelled *lumpenproletariat*. A smaller proportion of workers in chemicals and ceramics, and in metal work were released after arrest. These were the developing industries less identified in the public mind with the Parisian masses and these arrests were less likely to be

Table 3

CRIMINAL CLASSES

Profession	Percentage of those arrested	Percentage of those sentenced	
Building	14·12	12·47	—
Food and drink	3·62	4·64	+
Furniture	8·86	8·23	—
Clothing and shoes	10·02	8·7	—
Textiles	2·95	3·8	+
Skin and leather	1·30	1·34	+
Coachbuilding, saddlery, and military equipment	1·70	1·82	+
Chemicals and ceramics	0·95	1·61	+
Metal, engineering and metal products	10·73	12·99	+
Precious metals and jewellery	1·89	1·72	—
Coopers and basketmakers	0·56	0·47	—
Printing workers	3·39	3·55	+
Labourers	8·95	10·09	+
Cultivators, gardeners and herdsmen	1·17	0·54	—
Transport	4·29	4·03	—
Concièrges, servants, cooks and waiters	2·32	4·90	+
Proprietors, *rentiers*	0·39	0·47	+
Clerks	3·59	2·71	—
Liberal professions	1·70	1·08	—
Artistic professions	0·60	0·66	+
Commercial professions	3·70	3·54	—
Students	0·33	0·19	—
Police, soldiers, *garde mobile*	1·55	3·18	+
Lumpenproletariat	2·43	2·12	—
Without profession	2·35	4·62	+
Occupation not specified	0·78	0·71	—

mistakes. This was also true of the food and drink industries and commerce, possibly because including as it must, bakers and inn-keepers, it must similarly be less identified with the populus, of textiles, skin and leather processing, coachbuilding, saddlery and military equipment, industries employing relatively few workers, less true also of printing workers always heavily involved in political activity, of labourers most seriously effected by unemployment, and of police or soldiers most likely to meet with severity.

Of the members of the liberal professions and even students arrested a number were doctors or medical students arrested whilst aiding the wounded and quickly released.

It can at this point be safely concluded that those professions most likely to participate in insurrection included some of those in which industrial concentration and technical development was most advanced such as metallurgy, but most participants worked in the traditional industries of Paris, and the ethos of the insurrection reflected the role of the latter.

Most of those involved were relative newcomers to Paris from the provinces who had come to obtain a professional training, to which purpose the economic crisis had provided a setback. The same reason must have involved many workshop patrons and small shopkeepers.

The insurrection had three main centres, the third, fourth and sixth arrondissements; the seventh, eight and ninth; and the left bank, the Latin Quarter and the eleventh and twelfth arrondissements. Each of these main centres was dominated by a distinct trade – the carters of La Villette, the coal heavers and dockers along the Saint-Martin Canal, the bronze workers of the Boulevard du Temple, the joiners and cabinet makers of the Faubourg Saint-Antoine. In the northern banlieu insurrection occurred where a mixture of artisans, industrial workers and members of the lower middle classes lived and social conditions thus were similar to those of the city. The grievances of these individuals were expressed less against individual patrons with whom relations seem on the whole to have been rather good, particularly in the small and thence more intimate workshops, but against an economic system and a society which could permit unemployment and misery. The agents of this system were variously identified as shopkeepers who refused credit, landlords, moneylenders, and on a wider plain, against the rich generally. The small workshop owner rarely appeared as the representative of wealth and was himself subject to exploitation by commercial middlemen. As a harbinger of things to come, however, the strikes of workers in the larger new industrial plants, of engineering and railway workshop men after February, had evinced the hostility of the factory worker against the rich, unseen employer – of the true proletarian against the bourgeoisie. Significant, also, in this respect was the action of railwaymen at Chapelle Saint-Denis and Ivry in blocking the railway lines bringing troop reinforcements. Unlike most insurgents, concerned only with the defence of their own quarters, these men seem to have had the sense of a wider solidarity, particularly as well qualified, well paid and not unemployed, they were not rising from despair.[50]

Labour relations were also bad where the domestic system of production was employed and exploitation maximized to permit competition with mechanized producers – workers in, for example, the clothing industry might really have been involved out of despair.

De Tocqueville wrote that 'this terrible insurrection was not the work of a small group of conspirators, but the uprising of one part of the population against another.' For him the participation of women was particularly significant. 'It can be said that these women brought to the struggle the passions of housewives; they depended on victory so as to be able to give some comfort to their husbands and to be able to bring up their children . . .'[51] This picture is of a mass rising from despair, and those who were despairing were the unemployed workers or small businessmen reduced to pauperism by an economic crisis, joined by the perpetual down-and-outs. This was not and could not be, given the economic conditions of the period and place, the rising of a homogeneous proletariat, and in this respect Marx, whether deliberately or by careless use of words, gives a false impression.

It is worth stressing that this insurrection was the work of a minority of workers. Proudhon, walking in the Faubourg Saint-Antoine on June 23, questioned insurgents as to their numbers. The general response was that 'we are very few – most are not socialists'.[52] The National Workshops continued to function and pay, a fact which must have dissuaded many workers living on a day-to-day basis, from participating. Nevertheless the figure of arrests is large enough to give at least credibility to a contemporary figure of 40,000–50,000 insurgents, participating to a greater or lesser extent.[53]

Our picture of the insurgents can further be enlarged by considering first the living conditions of workers. It is probably more than a coincidence that those professions most commonly found in the worst kind of lodgings – building workers, labourers, clothing and shoe workers, bakers[54] were all amongst the professions most heavily involved in the insurrection.

Secondly, the ages of those arrested:

Table 4[55]

AGES OF THOSE ARRESTED

Age	Number arrested	% of total
10–14	61	0·52
15–19	993	8·47
20–24	1,725	14·71
25–29	2,042	17·41
30–34	1,897	16·17
35–39	1,564	13·33
40–44	1,317	11·23
45–49	997	8·50
50–54	584	4·98
55–59	275	2·34
60–64	119	1·01
65–69	46	0·39
70–74	13	0·11
75–79	6	0·05
80–84	1	0·009
Unknown	69	0·58
Total	11,709	99·80
	Error: 18	

Over 70 per cent of those arrested were aged between 20 and 44, which is hardly surprising. The most significant single age group, was that between 25 and 29, with that between 30 and 34 close behind and significant differences on either side of 25 and 34. Revolutionary consciousness could be said to reach a peak in this period of life when men had gained experience of life and retained vigour. The extent of migration created a population with a relatively large proportion of young men and a large number of newcomers and temporary migrants not wholly at ease in the city.

Significant variation is revealed when the place of birth of those arrested is considered. This does seem to indicate that the place of origin was of some importance in determining susceptibility to insurrection. This is a factor of some complication and reveals the limitations of a simple Marxian picture of class conflict. Paris was a market and a source of employment, much of which was migratory. Louis Chevalier conceives of a situation of interdependence in terms of socio-political ideas between Paris and the provinces,[57] with the social structure of various regions influencing receptivity to new ideas. Until mid-nineteenth century most migrants originated from the north and east, from urban areas with traditions of active municipal

Table 5[56]

PLACE OF BIRTH OF THOSE ARRESTED

Place of birth	No. arrested	Component per 1,000 of those arrested	Component per 1,000 of total no. originating in department, (approx.)
Ain	41	3·5	15·0
Allier	46	3·9	2·0
Aisne	271	23·0	20·6
Alpes (Basses)	14	1·2	2·0
Alpes (Hautes)	7	0·69	12·0
Ardèche	23	2·0	14·0
Ardennes	154	13·1	15·4
Ariège	21	1·8	25·5
Aube	74	6·8	5·0
Aude	17	1·5	12·0
Aveyron	57	4·6	16·4
Bouches du Rhône	18	1·6	6·6
Calvados	198	16·8	10·9
Cantal	149	12·7	10·2
Charente	21	1·8	6·7
Charente Inf.	37	3·0	7·1
Cher	32	2·7	9·8
Corrèze	33	2·8	25·3
Corse	9	6·7	13·1
Côte-d'Or	177	15·0	7·4
Côtes-du-Nord	41	3·5	19·0
Creuse	279	23·7	28·0
Dordogne	25	2·1	9·4
Doubs	75	6·4	8·5
Drôme	23	2·0	13·0
Eure	132	11·1	7·8
Eure-et-Loire	150	12·8	10·4
Finistère	30	2·5	8·0
Gard	25	2·1	8·9
Haute Garonne	49	4·2	18·8
Gers	15	1·2	9·0
Gironde (Haute)	58	4·9	8·6
Hérault	15	1·2	6·0
Ille-et-Vilaine	71	6·1	9·5
Indre	41	3·5	10·8
Indre-et-Loire	54	4·6	8·5
Isère	76	6·5	10·6
Jura	84	7·1	13·4
Landes	14	1·2	27·5
Loir-et-Cher	77	6·6	17·8
Loire	70	6·0	21·4
Haute-Loire	48	4·1	16·3
Loire Inf.	46	3·9	9·6
Loiret	153	12·9	10·8

Place of birth	No. arrested	Component per 1,000 of those arrested	Component per 1,000 of total no. originating in department, (approx.)
Lot	34	3·9	10·8
Lot-et-Garonne	20	1·7	10·0
Lozère	12	1·0	10·7
Maine-et-Loire	49	4·5	8·5
Manche	86	8·3	4·8
Marne	135	11·5	8·5
Haut-Marne	80	6·8	5·4
Mayenne	80	6·8	14·0
Meurthe	53	4·5	3·5
Meuse	187	15·9	11·6
Morbihan	49	4·2	23·1
Moselle	445	37·8	20·0
Nièvre	74	6·3	12·5
Nord	108	9·2	4·3
Oise	g239	20·3	13·5
Orne	209	16·9	10·4
Pas-de-Calais	84	7·1	5·7
Puy-de-Dôme	79	6·7	7·7
Pyrénées (Basses)	22	1·9	10·4
Pyrénées (Hautes)	32	2·7	48·8
Pyrénées (Orientales)	6	0·5	7·5
Rhin (Haut)	69	5·9	9·5
Rhin (Bas)	121	10·2	16·7
Rhône	108	9·2	9·5
Saône (Haute)	173	14·7	12·3
Saône-et-Loire	93	7·9	14·2
Sarthe	144	12·2	14·4
Seine	520	44·2	1·1
Seine-Inf.	237	20·2	9·4
Seine-et-Marne	397	33·8	8·9
Seine-et-Oise	637	54·2	7·3
Sèvres (Deux)	7	0·6	7·5
Somme	276	23·4	10·9
Tarn	12	1·0	15·0
Tarn-et-Garonne	15	1·2	6·9
Var	14	1·2	7·5
Vaucluse	15	1·2	11·2
Vendée	17	1·5	10·5
Vienne	23	2·0	10·2
Vienne (Haute)	74	6·3	18·8
Vosges	89	7·5	12·3
Yonne	108	9·2	3·7
French Colonies	2	0·2	1·9
Paris	3,257	276·8	2·6
Foreigners	833	70·8	10·8
Unknown	30	2·5	

life. Poor communications limited migration essentially to the region bounded by the Yonne, Côte d'Or, Haute-Saône and, exceptionally, Loiret and Cantal.[58]

In terms of Paris itself migrants from various regions tended to congregate together in particular quarters and thus their traditional ideas were more resistant to change although gradually Paris swallowed all. Migration was above all to the developing industrial suburbs, although Chevalier judges that most migrants to Paris were seeking non-industrial employment.[59]

Contemporaries attached great significance to the role of these migrants, as can be seen from a report in the Rouen *La Liberté* which advocated stricter control of the standards of furnished accommodation – 'It is there, in effect, that this floating population of more than 20,000 men, carries itself, and where are recruited the malefactors and instruments of all disorders'. In terms of numerical participation Chevalier's strictures concerning migration are, as would be expected from the pattern of communications, true. In terms of likelihood to participate expressed as a component per 1,000 of the migrants from a particular department living in Paris,[60] the picture is far more complicated, reflecting the complexity of social conditions. Besides native born Parisians those most likely to have participated (more than 15 per 1,000) originated in the departments of the north and north-east like the Ardennes, Moselle, Bas-Rhin, but also from the Breton departments of Côtes-du-Nord, and Morbihan. The natives of the Parisian Basin, with the exception of Loir-et-Cher and Aisne were particularly inactive, whilst those of Limousin, the Massif Central proper – of Creuse and Corrèze, and of the Jura, from Ain, Loire and Haute-Loire, and even from the Pyrénées and part of Aquitain were far more likely to have participated in this insurrection.

Chevalier is not wholly correct in emphasizing the revolutionary role of those originating from the north. Numerically they did predominate, but less zealously than groups from other regions. Tendencies towards political radicalism it appears can be to some extent associated with the more mountainous regions rather than simply those with an urban tradition. It is perhaps significant that these regions tended to be areas where small-scale peasant farming predominated, and where in the absence of a socially dominant land-owner independence of mind might develop.

Another important figure is that given for the participation of foreigners, many of whom, as in the case of Poles, were political refugees, most of whom, as in the case of the Germans, were crafts-men gaining practical experience in Paris and susceptible to the ideas of the milieu in which they mixed. Of the former an official report maintained that 'The Polish refugees are signalled as having partici-pated in a direct manner in all the action which has prepared and facilitated the insurrection.'[61]

The official enquiry into the insurrection concluded that it had been organized as a deliberate assault on the institutions of govern-ment and society – 'the incitement by certain clubs engendered the civil war. . . . The misery of many insurgents no doubt served to feed the revolt but . . . the determinant cause . . . is to be found in per-fidious theories and in disturbing and savage ambitions'.[62] Proof of this was seen in the participation of relatively highly paid and not unemployed railway mechanics and in the strength of resistance which military advisers maintained must have been well organized.[63] The rapporteur of the commission maintained on this basis that 'the rising was not instantaneous, it was not caused by hunger, but was organized, with its regulations, its leaders, its meeting places, with numerous ramifications in the departments'.[64] Thus from June the myth grew for conservatives of a socialist plot to destroy society. Marx on the other hand maintained that this insurrection had been spon-taneous and developed another myth of 'how the workers, with unexampled bravery and ingenuity, without leaders, without a common plan, without means and, for the most part, lacking weapons held in check for five days', the mass of troops and National Guards.[65] This is exaggerated but nearer the truth.

Some elements of organization and even of leadership obviously existed. If most of the leading figures of the extreme left had been arrested following May 15 those of secondary importance remained. But even the more influential leaders had been unable to agree and impose some unity on the mass involved in clubs, or simply dis-contented, and these lesser figures were even less likely to do so. Insufficient time had passed to permit the emergence of new, known and respected leaders. It seems probable, however, that preparations were under way for a struggle. The fatalistic attitude prevalent amongst the politically conscious of all shades of opinion is a strong hint at this.

More concretely it is known that the workers' delegates to the Luxembourg Commission, suppressed after May 15, continued to meet and established contacts with the elected delegates of the workers of the National Workshops, whom the new director of the Workshops, Lalanne, had forbidden to meet together.[66] Militants in the National Workshops, in the increasingly well-organized crafts and in the clubs shared a vague ideology, examplified by the slogan *la République démocratique et sociale*, which served as a common ground for organization. On June 21 representatives of the National Workshops, clubs and former delegates of the Luxembourg Commission did in fact meet to organize a protest against the threatened dissolution of the Workshops.

A recent paper using the minutes of the Society of the Rights of Man affirms that these revealed an increasing stress on the military character of this club in the period preceding the insurrection.[67] Historians generally assume that the clubs were preparing for the eventuality of a new revolution which was more and more felt to be likely.[68]

If the middle-class club leaders and journalists were prepared to use the language of revolution and even to prepare for the event, if they in so doing encouraged their followers to believe it would occur, they were themselves hesitant. When the rising did occur, it is noteworthy that the usual middle-class political leaders of the Parisian masses were largely absent, the most prominent in prison, others unwilling to act because they regarded the rising as either unnecessary or futile. To a significant degree then this was a spontaneous uprising but it was given a certain degree of unity by the shared ideals, the slogans accepted by the participants, and by a grassroots leadership which in this moment of stress had emerged, and also by some elements of organization. Homogeneity developed as emotions grew more intense.

Lamartine believed that the insurrection was organized in the National Workshops,[69] and it is true that amongst the leaders who emerged were the brigadiers of the National Workshops. Before June Emile Thomas had given a warning to the Minister of Public Works – 'I must not hide from you the fears which such an organization must inspire . . . for it is not very different in its form from the organization . . . by sections of secret societies.'[70] These fears were confirmed, for as the correspondent of *La Liberté* of Rouen reported concerning the organization of the insurgents – 'The organization by sections and brigades was already complete for it corresponded to that of the National Workshops: there were lieutenants, brigadiers, squadron leaders, and one can understand how easily projects could be prepared and orders transmitted between men placed thus in day-to-day relations.'

This was one basis for organization but others existed. Not all the insurrectionaries had been workers in the National Workshops. Of vital importance was the democratization of the National Guard after the February Revolution. This provided both arms and an additional basis for organization during the insurrection. A representative of the military commission of enquiry wrote to the *procureur général* at Paris on August 22 that 'Belleville you know has been one of the principal centres of insurrection, the struggle there has been most bitter. Of 7,000 National Guards, at least 3,000 took part in the insurrection.'[71] A correspondent of the Rouen *Liberté* was more explicit – of the legions of the National Guard 'the 12th was entirely against us, as were the greatest part of the 6th, the 5th, the 7th and of the 9th legion; the 8th was behind the barricades just as the 12th. Two legions of the suburbs acted similarly or would not march. . . .'[72]

The insurrection was mainly localized, insurgents barricaded their own quarters and attempted to defend them, and for this the National Guard, uniting in a definite organization a whole group of neighbours, was ideal and was probably the most important form of organization.

Peter Amann points out the involvement as coherent units of the members of some clubs of the northern and eastern suburbs, and the coordinating activity of notably the Club des Antonins of the Faubourg Saint-Antoine. He correctly emphasizes however the fact that clubs organized for talking and electioneering would have been unsuitable as bases for fighting organizations, even if their lower middle class leaders had not generally been opposed to the insurrection.[73]

Is it possible to determine who the anonymous leaders of this rising were? From the register of arrests the professions of those sentenced to five years imprisonment or more can be gauged. It can be assumed that those subject to such long sentences were at least suspected of playing a more than ordinary role in the insurrection. The problem is that this would include not only those who took a leadership role but also those guilty of crimes such as murder or looting. Additionally this sample is numerically small. Nevertheless we will attempt to draw some general conclusions (see page 179).

The police and soldiers can be discounted as likely to receive especially severe sentences for their breaches of discipline.

Table 6[74]

INDIVIDUALS RECEIVING MORE THAN FIVE YEAR SENTENCES

Building	10 = 7·87%	*of all those sentenced to over 5*
Food and drink	6 = 4·72%	*years imprisonment.*
Furniture	10 = 7·87%	
Clothing and shoes	8 = 6·3%	
Textiles	2 = 1·57%	
Skin and Leather	4 = 3·15%	
Coach, saddlery and military equipment	0	
Chemicals and ceramics	5 = 3·94%	
Metal workers	12 = 9·45%	
Jewellery	3 = 2·36%	
Cooper and basketmakers	1 = 0·79%	
Printing	4 = 3·15%	
Labourers	6 = 4.72%	
Agricultural workers	0	
Transport workers	7 = 5·51%	
Servants	0	
Proprietors	2 = 1·57%	
Clerical workers	5 = 3·94%	
Liberal professions	4 = 3·15%	
Artistic professions	0	
Commercial and manufacturing professions	10 = 7·87%	
Students	1 = 0·79%	
Police and soldiers	13 = 10·24%	
Lumpenproletariat	2 = 1·57%	
Others	2 = 1·57%	
Not specified	2 = 1·57%	
Cited only as National Guard Officers	8 = 6·3%	
Total	**127**	

Otherwise professions which might be assumed to have played a leading role include the building workers, the furniture makers, the metal workers and the lower middle class members of the manufacturing and commercial professions all of whom were quite definitely patrons. This confirms what we know the pattern of militancy amongst Parisian trades. The eight individuals cited only as National Guard Officers were most probably also the owners of small businesses and added to the others of the various middle class professions they serve to emphasize the significance of lower middle class participation and leadership in the June insurrection, making up 22·83 per cent of those receiving these relatively long sentences of imprisonment. These were men who had been influential because they lived and worked in the poorer quarters and were themselves relatively poor, but were assured prominence by some small property or function, rather than by political activity although this might reinforce their influence.

The hostility of the *grands notables* to such a rising could be taken for granted. The *Constitutionnel* of June 29 maintained in its editorial that the struggle was between 'on one side, order, liberty, civilization, the honest Republic, France; on the other, barbarians, convicts emerging from their lairs to massacre and pillage, members of odious sects with savage doctrines in which the family is only a name and property theft'.

The bulk of the participants in the armed struggle were however the holders of a more lowly position in the bourgeois hierarchy. Rémi Gossez concluded that the National Guard taking part in the repression of the insurrection were formed of five great categories, 'proprietors', shopkeepers, clerks, members of the liberal professions or intellectuals and workers.[75] In the main these were the guards of the 1st, 2nd, 3rd and 10th Legions, the more middle class a quarter was, then the more National Guards who answered the call to arms. The lower middle class Guards of the centre of Paris significantly tended to stay at home as though reflecting their position between bourgeoisie and workers, both geographically and psychologically but the lower middle class as a whole was drawn more towards the rest of the middle class than towards the workers. Everywhere though there was a great reluctance to be involved in this struggle.

Proprietors believed themselves to be fighting in defence of the property which gave them status in society, all of which they now believed was threatened. The owners of property in Paris were especially anxious as already in many cases they had since February met with the refusal of tenants to pay rent,[76] and the relationships of the less wealthy owners or chief-tenants of tenements were rarely good with the tenants or sub-tenants they exploited, often out of the felt necessity to maintain their own standards of living.[77] Many were also *rentiers*, suffering from the decline in values caused by the crisis.

Often small property owners and shopkeepers resented the permanent political crisis and the economic crisis blamed on social unrest. To some extent it can be assumed that they tended to behave as their clientele. As we have indicated a significant number joined the insurrection, but more, in the quarters of the east, assumed a position of neutrality, anxious to protect their shops and often also alienated from the masses whom they in their small way tended to exploit with adulterated wares. Contemporary opinion gave exaggerated expression to the place of the shopkeepers in the ranks of order, but it must have been important. A hymn of praise written at the time, entitled *Order reigns in Paris* made this point. Its first verse respectfully (or satirically)[78] advised:

> *Bourgeois heroes, return to your shops,*
> *You deserve well of your country,*
> *By crushing the political soldiers*
> *Always branded, decried and hated.*
> *All ceded in the face of your menace,*
> *Thanks to your watchfulness the Montagnards are taken,*
> *Go in peace to sell your molasses:*
> > *Order reigns in Paris.*[79]

The German observer Lorenz von Stein wrote that 'The communist-socialist segments of the movement of the proletariat had, almost without exception, taken a stand against private property. Thus the proletariat had taken, in the eyes of the public, a position which differed from what its great part really stood for. Rather than being the champion of those opposed to the rule of capital, it appeared as the opponent of all kinds of property; it thereby united the whole mass of owners and forced the small owners to make common cause with the big owners, who, within the system of industrial competition, were natural enemies. Thus it was not capital and labour, but property owners and propertyless who were in opposition to each other'.[80]

In fact many patrons of small workshops refused to involve themselves. Often they enjoyed good relations with their fellow workers, additionally they seem to have been far more interested in protecting their shops or workshops against the forces of order or the insurgents. Most of them lived in the quarters of the east, and would have anyway been neutralized. Their common inaction was revealing of the nature of social conflict in Paris at this time. It tended not to be between employer and employee, but between, as we have already suggested, the poor and those whom they felt were exploiting them. The proprietor of a small workshop was neither sufficiently wealthy, nor so apart from his workers that upward social mobility was not possible for them. Thus they were not as hostile to him as they might be to landlords and shopkeepers, to factory owners, or in response to the snobbery of clerks.

The role of white-collar workers, of office workers employed by the state and private enterprise, the latter including for example commercial travellers and bank clerks, was important. They too resented the economic crisis which threatened their livelihoods, the pandering to the workers which the National Workshops represented, the pretensions of the workers which threatened their sense of social status. The whole aura of disorder conflicted with the ordered mental attitudes which their social functions imposed on them. Their attitudes reflected the major social gulf between those who worked with their hands and those who did not.[81]

Gossez stresses the role of intellectuals. He characterizes the 11th Legion of the National Guard as that of the intellectuals and reflects upon the relative zeal this formation showed.[82] We have observed that in contrast with past Parisian uprisings the insurrectional role of intellectuals including students in June 1848, was severely limited. The social character of this insurrection is clearly revealed by the conservative action of the politically conscious and usually radical intellectuals. 1848 seems to have brought for them a great crisis of conscience, to have begun a decline in their idealism and faith in progress. Renan wrote that 'The crisis of 1848 moved us profoundly – it was for young and active spirits, like the fall of a curtain which would conceal the horizon.'[83]

The fifth category listed by Gossez was that of workers. He emphasizes that even in the middle-class-dominated quarters of Western Paris where normally workers formed about one third of the National Guard, in June they formed only one fifth and were thus far more reluctant to fight for social order than any other social group.[84] This is what one would expect. Nevertheless, contemporary observers did tend to notice a large proportion of workers amongst the ranks of the National Guard involved in repression. It is probably true that many workers saw the rising as a threat to the Republic inspired possibly by Monarchist pretenders and were impelled to fight in its defence. Others might have remained at home, or even fought on the side of the insurrection until it became obvious that it was doomed to failure and then joined the National Guard companies so as to avoid possible penalties. It remained true, however, that where workers had fought this had been largely in support of the insurrection.

The lines of conflict established in June cut across political divisions. This is especially revealed by the action of various republican groups.

The moderate republican *National* saw the workers of Paris as being led astray by agitators, using the National Workshops as their excuse.[85] Its agonized editorial of June 25 reflects the lack of understanding with which these socially conservative republicans greeted the insurrection.

> With universal suffrage, liberty of the press, and the right of association, an insurrection is absurd, an attack on the popular sovereignty, a social crime. It does not rest with a minority to translate its griefs, if it has them, into gunshots . . . what purpose will this battle serve . . . ? The condition of the proletarians could not be changed in a day.
>
> . . . Deceived by appearances, seduced by lying promises, how many . . . brave men have already paid for their cruel error with their lives! . . . how many also are dead . . . who have consecrated their whole lives to the defence of these workers, who today strike them. In the fatal and forever to be deplored battle which is engaged in, republicans fall on both sides.
>
> We have tears, regrets for them; but we have only hatred and contempt for the artisans of disorder . . . for these conspirators who finance sedition with foreign gold. Order will be re-established, because a society cannot abandon itself to the will of a minority, and to live is at the same time its duty and its right.

A theory of conspiracy was more psychologically satisfying than an admittance of the seriousness of the social problem.

The more radical republicans, represented in the Constituent Assembly by Ledru-Rollin seem to have been frightened of the Paris mob, to have accepted to a significant degree the common view of it as a barbarous force. These Montagnards were consequently rather passive. Charles de Rémusat reported that 'The Mountain had clearly an embarrassed air. It would not approve, it would not affect a great horror for the revolt, but it contained itself. . . .'[86] It desired social reform but was not anxious for a recourse to violence in which its ability to restrain the masses would be doubtful. The *Réforme*, by comparison with the *National* showed more understanding of the causes of insurrection, of the disappointed hopes of the masses but affirmed that social reform must be slow and studied and must be a compromise between existing interests and those of the workers, rather than the total change which as Von Stein claimed, public opinion felt the workers desired. If the people had great and legitimate

G

183

grievances, the government had on its side 'the principle of the Republic' and whatever its faults it had not violated popular sovereignty and thus revolt was not justified.[87] A great fear of the unknown masses united all those who felt that they had something to lose.

Even the most prominent of those newspapers written by workers themselves, the *Atelier*, condemned the uprising, basing itself upon its republican principles.[88] The clear Marxian picture of class conflict is rendered increasingly complicated. Here political loyalties cut across class.

As for the army's part in the suppression of the insurrection after June it could be said that the army increasingly controlled the destiny of the regime. In June it evinced a certain lassitude and lack of enthusiasm for the struggle. Yet few soldiers joined the insurgents, and in suppressing the revolt it preserved the regime.

In general, political ideologies lost their sharpness in an army trained to obey the existing political authority. During previous regimes republican insurgents had been the enemy and revolutionary ideology had lost whatever influence it might once have had.

Soldiers felt the humiliation of their exclusion from Paris in February.[81] Mainly peasants by origin they were shocked by the disorders following the revolution. Relatively well fed, regularly paid and appreciating this in such a period of unemployment and misery, there was amongst the ranks a conservative impulse which permitted a rapid disciplining of nonconformist elements. This spirit had been reinforced by frequent changes of garrison, long periods of service and inadequate transport facilities limiting contacts with a civilian milieu, and with the ideological currents prevalent at any time. To some extent, therefore, the rank and file of the army were a *déclassé* element willing to be used by those who paid them, united by a loyalty to the flag and to comrades which provided for the psychological need to belong.

The officers on the other hand, in spite of the jealous conflicts which occurred after the February Revolution, were far more in touch with the social milieu from which they originated. Extensive leaves of absence provided for this. The officer corps was middle class and aristocratic. Even officers emerging from the ranks were generally lower middle class sons of artisans or shopkeepers and in the more senior positions the products of the military schools predominated, all from secure, wealthy upper class backgrounds because of the long and costly years of education needed before entry to the military schools, even if a few received grants when in them.

The officer with his background, his particular concept of honour and duty, his fear often of political democracy as threatening military discipline must then essentially be conservative, and, destined himself to command, favour authoritarian or at least strong government.[90]

In the absence of a reliable force to keep order after February the government had decided to recruit a *Garde mobile* from amongst young and unemployed workers aged between 16 and 30, although many recruits were in fact younger and the bulk of the force according to the British ambassador, Lord Normanby, were 'boys from 15 to 17 years of age . . . of the genus *Gamin de Paris*.'[91] It was hoped that the discipline of barrack life would turn these into a reliable force.

According to Audiganne the creation of this force of over 15,000 men permitted the government 'to master the most nomadic and disorderly part of the Parisian population . . . the lists containing especially the names of men gathered from the pavements of the city.'[92] This certainly seems in part to have been the governments intention.[93]

Gossez maintains that many *gardes mobiles* were recruited from unemployed workers, many of whom were recent immigrants, from young men who were insecure, and restless, and had played a leading role in February. Possessing only a limited loyalty to their families where relationships had been given little chance to develop because of the necessity to send children to work as soon as possible, they welcomed the pay and comradeship of the Guard. Their inbred feeling of social inferiority helped them respect and obey and even elect their middle class officers.[94] They owed their new lives to the Republic and in the face of an insurrection fomented, or so they were told by counter-revolutionaries, they fought in its defence with a fury inflamed by the struggle itself. They were thus as much workers as any generation at their age had ever been, and were even in June in many cases acting from the same motives as other workers – the defence of the Republic. Before the event they were regarded with great distrust by conservatives. Archival sources indicate that there was real cause for this suspicion.[95] The whole tends to show that in terms of social composition the *Garde mobile* could not be clearly distinguished from the Parisian lower classes. An undated report, obviously written early in 1849, was to claim that many members of the *Garde mobile* would not re-enlist because of the recommending of work in the workshops'.[96]

The very course of the struggle in the streets of Paris was symptomatic of the extent to which social relations had been embittered. Already before its outbreak the government had been making military preparations and had, according to Lamartine, decided to meet a rising by the concentration of troops rather than their division into small units.[97] The process of concentration, when insurrection occurred, meant that there was no attempt to prevent the initial construction of barricades. The authorities were not interested in minimizing the conflict it seemed but were more concerned to utterly crush the threat to society. Hugo described the consequences of this decision:

> The Saint-Antoine barricade was tremendous; it was three stories high and seven hundred feet wide. It barred the vast opening of the Faubourg, that is to say, three streets from angle to angle, ravined, jagged, cut up, divided, crenellated, with an immense rent, buttressed with piles that were bastions in themselves, throwing out capes here and there, powerfully backed up by two great promontories of houses of the Faubourg . . . Nineteen barricades were ranged one behind the other, in the depths of the streets behind this principal barricade. . . . Of what was that barricade made? Of the ruins of three six-storey houses demolished expressly, said some. . . . It was the collaboration of the pavement, the block of stone, the beam, the bar of iron, the rag, the scrap, the broken pane, the unseated chair, the cabbage-stalk, the tatter, the rag, and the malediction.
>
> Overturned carts broke the uniformity of the slope; an immense dray was spread out there crossways, its axle pointing heavenward . . . an omnibus hoisted gayly, by main force, to the very summit of the heap. . . .[98]

In squares and narrow streets a struggle occurred which became more and more ferocious as it progressed. The zeal of those National Guard units which did participate reveals social hostility, the eagerness of most deputies to grant power to Cavaignac indicates their concern with social conservation. They were willing to accept the dictatorship of a general before that of Louis-Napoléon.

The conflict was at its most brutal where the *gardes mobiles* and insurgents clashed. Their similar social origins intensified their mutual hostility. The young *gardes mobiles* believed the rumours of atrocity, as indeed did many other conservatives. Castellane confided to his diary on June 25 that 'General Bréa has been taken prisoner with his aide ... it appears that the insurgents have massacred him; they have torn out his eyes and cut off both his legs before he was dead.'[99] Guards fought with desperation.[100]

The attitude of the army was fundamental in determining the nature of this conflict, and its nature was significant in determining the bitterness of social relations subsequently. Cavaignac addressed some deputies who demanded the early engagement of the army with the words 'Do you believe that I am here to defend the Parisians, and their National Guard? Let it defend its town and its shops itself! I do not wish to scatter my troops. I remember 1830, I remember February. If one of my companies is disarmed I will blow out my brains, I will not survive this dishonour.'[101] Not only Cavaignac's honour but that of the whole army was at stake. It seems as we have observed to have been determined to revenge its humiliation of February. This more than a lack of confidence in the national or mobile guards determined its tactics. De Tocqueville reported a conversation with General Lamoricière, who also refused to scatter his troops through the narrow streets of the city, preferring instead to allow the insurgents to concentrate – then they could be totally destroyed by concentrated military power.[102]

The insurgents, lacking leadership, were content to remain on the defensive with a fierceness impelled almost by the nature of street-fighting. The ordinary soldiers fought with little enthusiasm, but joined with the other cadres of the forces of order in a ferocious repression. At eleven on the morning of June 25 the Prefect of Police reported to the Minister of the Interior that on the square in front of the Hôtel-de-Ville prisoners were being shot.[103] Marx wrote with justice that 'the bourgeoisie compensated itself for the mortal anguish it suffered by unheard-of brutality.'[104] If it is not possible to estimate the casualties incurred by the insurgents the substantial number of arrests is a further hint at the degree to which social animosity had been intensified.

For Marx in June was fought 'the first great battle ... between the two classes that split modern society'. 'It ended all the illusions concerning the nature of bourgeois society and revealed that radical social reform within this social form was impossible.'[105]

This statement is both true and false. It is false in the sense that in terms of actual participation in the insurrection, this was neither a movement of factory proletarians nor even solely of unemployed

187

workers, but was a far more heterogeneous movement of the Parisian lower classes, including in this many members of the social groups Marx refers to as petty bourgeois and *lumpenproletariat*. The importance of their participation makes Marx's characterization of the struggle overly simple.

Many historians have too easily accepted the Marxian analysis but there are significant elements of truth in it. Rémusat confirmed that in the view of contemporaries 'The class war was declared. . . .'[106] If this does not accurately reflect the reality of events as revealed by statistics it does reflect the contemporary consciousness of things.

These were in terms of the development of social consciousness vitally important events, events which reflected a growing polarization of opinion and which especially further stimulated this process. In the contemporary consciousness the actual activity of social groups was analysed and a simplified picture produced.

The June conflict presented to the workers of Paris and only Paris an image of a society in which they were isolated. They included with themselves many elements no doubt properly defined as lower middle class, but the image was still one of the workers, of the people, crushed and oppressed by the bourgeoisie. Out of the actual struggle and out of this feeling of isolation developed a consciousness of class and a practical belief in the efficacy of organization, which would slowly come to fruition. Charles de Rémusat felt that from then on there would exist 'between the classes of the same society a lasting resentment and need for vengeance.'[107] The dominant conservative feeling remained one of pessimism even after victory. This would be seen in a new reliance on the power of the state, and a reversal of the old distrust of military power.

According to Jean Lhomme, modern French society dates from June 1848.[108] The threat to the existing society came, it appeared, from the workers, and if their social and political consciousness had developed, then so additionally had the consciousness of other social groups; from this point tending to develop in relation to that of the workers, in relation to the threat which they were presumed to present.

The alliance of the middle classes and the dominance of its more wealthy and influential groups was reasserted. In face of a common threat, an alliance of those who were threatened or made to feel threatened came into existence in which leadership went to those most competent, experienced and interested in political activity – the

social power of the *grands notables* was restored. Less politically conscious, less well organized social groups were in the future to have to
define their attitudes in relation also to this group as having like the
workers a *relatively* clear sense of purpose and the ability to organize,
something which the other groups – the lower middle classes and
peasantry lacked because of their more heterogeneous group structure.

In terms of immediate political consequences the alliance of
moderate republicans with other social conservatives had fatally
weakened the Republic at what had been formerly its prime source of
strength – at Paris. It had divided the moderate republicans, the only
republicans most of France could accept in positions of power, and
that only reluctantly, from the workers, who were the most devoted
supporters of republican institutions. It forced these republicans to
rely on non- or even anti-republican social groups for the preservation
of the Republic. The only alternative for radicals was to appeal to
the peasant masses with promises of social reform which did not
threaten their property. This some republicans would proceed to
do.

The Provinces in June

One other important feature of this conflict observed by Marx was
the way in which 'the National Guard . . . streamed in from the
provinces.'[1] He makes no further comment on this. The Marxist
historian Dautry claims that only reactionary provinces rushed to the
aid of the National Assembly,[2] which is emotive but credible. If
detachments in fact came from 53 departments[3] and in addition others
further away from Paris and with poor communications were so
prevented from sending contingents, this simply reflected the
'reactionary' character of most of France.

The National Guards from the provinces to some extent were a
cross-section of provincial communities including agricultural
workers, peasants, artisans and factory workers, although with a
relatively high proportion of proprietors and members of the liberal
professions, given the expense of going to Paris in terms of lost work,

and the fact that in most areas only members of the old Orleanist Guard were fully equipped.[4]

There were a number of reasons for the overwhelming provincial response in favour of repression in Paris. For one, the traditional hatred of Paris, a hatred reinforced by the accounts of agitation in Paris which was resented by all those with a taste for an ordered existence, who lacked the will for radical social change. Large sections of the population were afraid of the intentions of the Parisian poor and conservative propaganda made effective use of this, the press spreading rumours of atrocity, portraying the rising as an assault on property, on society, on the republic and on the national sovereignty incarnated in the Constituent Assembly. The insurgents were portrayed as the scum of the population, interested primarily in pillage and anarchy. Often an unlikely triumvirate of Caussidière, Ledru-Rollin and Lamartine was portrayed as directing the insurrection, an idea which reflects the hostility to the Provisional Government, or else the insurrection was blamed on a foreign plot or on the various Monarchist pretenders.[5] Given the prevailing mood, even radical newspapers did not dare defend the insurgents.

The effect of this propaganda and of rumour was not only to send National Guards hurrying to Paris but to cause a number of panics similar to the Great Fear of 1789. The government itself was partly to blame for this. Cavaignac on June 26 informed the military and civil authorities in the provinces by telegraph that 'The insurrection is completely defeated. All the insurgents have laid down their arms or are in flight across the countryside.'[6] In many areas rumours developed that bands of insurgents had escaped from Paris and were pillaging the countryside. The slightest cause led to the sounding of the tocsin and the assumption of defensive positions in towns and villages. An official in the Orne reported that a large group of people gathered for a sale, that 'people seeing and hearing them from afar believed this was a group of insurgents escaping from Paris, and terror spread rapidly through the neighbouring communes. Soon it had developed to such a degree that each village believed itself threatened with pillage and burning.'[7] The general commanding in the department of the Marne reported on June 29 that 'The town of Châlons was yesterday greatly agitated. False news announced that Épernay was in flames . . . that it had been given up to pillage . . . the villages armed themselves with forks, picks, with everything that might serve for their defence. They were saying at Châlons that

Épernay had been sacked, and the same thing at Reims of Châlons.'[8]
Again this was symptomatic of the feeling of hostility which existed
in the provinces towards insurgents from Paris.

Conservative notables in effect used June to strengthen the already
developing alliance for social order. The process by which the effacement of local notables which had followed the February revolution
in many areas, was reversed, was hastened by this crisis. In the
sacred union against anarchy these notables tended to take a leading
part, increasing their prestige and influence. The *procureur-général* at
Caen reported on July 5, that monarchist notables had been extremely
willing to engage as National Guards to fight in Paris – 'However,
they carefully explained that they did this not for the Republic which
did not have their sympathy, but uniquely for the conservation and
the maintainance of order.'[9]

This apparent willingness to defend a republican regime was then
something else. The 'Mémorial Bordelais' of July 18 affirmed its
belief that the existing government was committed to the defence of
order and added that 'It is because we know the existing government
to be animated with this intention that we defend it against its
adversaries.' Although victorious in this struggle in June 'a second
struggle is possible, it is even probable and it is because we believe
in this probability, that we regard it as a duty to support energetically
the military triumvirate which now governs us.'[10] The subordination
of Monarchist principles in this time of crisis to those of the self-
preservation of a social group was evident. The reactions of more
humble sections of the population indicated that they too shared this
fear and will to oppose social change. This is evidence of the continued
social dominance of the wealthy.

If the overwhelming response of the provinces was to mobilize in
defence of social order, there were some exceptions to the contrary.
Most of these were limited in character indicating through action a
sympathy with the Parisian insurgents but also a refusal to act in a
similar manner. Near Corbeil (Seine) barricades were constructed
in an attempt to delay troop reinforcements moving to Paris, and in
the Paris region more generally railway employees attempted to delay
National Guards, going as far at Orléans as a strike which was
ended by threats.[11] At Le Mans the divisions of the National Guard
prevented its departure and regular troops were called to maintain
order.[12] At Luçon a poster appeared appealing to National Guards
to 'remain in your homes and do not go to make war against your

own kind, for you are all workers. Uphold your rights and not those of the rich and of the aristocracy. . . .'[13] A population tired of agitation, desiring above all work did not normally respond to such appeals.

At Lyon, where action by the silk workers might have been expected, a large concentration of troops and news of the failure of the Paris insurrection overawed the workers to such a degree that the authorities were able to disarm them quite easily and restore their control of the city for the first time since February. An event which reveals the limits to the development of both ideological consciousness, organization and consequently the will to act amongst these workers.

The most important action outside Paris occurred at Marseille. Here events proceeded in a similar manner to those at Paris, with, prior to June, increasing unrest caused by sympathy with Italian nationalism, unemployment and misery and the struggle to maintain the official concession of a ten-hour working day; the failure of negotiations concerning the latter was the immediate cause of the construction of barricades.[14]

This was a revolt of workers engaged in traditional artisanal production and labour at the port, whilst workers in modern heavy industry better paid, less subject to unemployment and enjoying the ten-hour day did not involve themselves. Notions of solidarity were apparently little developed. An official list of the accused bears this out and also indicates a significant lower middle class participation. Among those accused of playing leading roles were an innkeeper, merchant, manufacturer, some shopkeepers, a clerk, a pharmacist and a health officer.[15]

If little actual conflict had occurred in the provinces at the time of the insurrection in Paris, if indeed, to the contrary, the authorities had received widespread support, these authorities remained extremely worried. The act of accusation prepared by the *procureur général* at Aix, in relation to the events at Marseilles, presented his suspicions that the Marseilles insurrection had been carefully planned to occur at the same time as that of Paris. As seen before officials subscribed to theories of conspiracy. From Reims[16] and Bordeaux and elsewhere came reports to the effect that 'the Parisian insurrection, if it had triumphed, would have found in the clubs ardent men, ready to execute its orders, whatever they were'.[17] If conservatives felt that they had triumphed in June it seemed that this triumph had done very little to quell their fears of imminent social revolution.

V

The Victory of Reaction

June 1848 - May 1849

The Constituent Assembly's gratitude to Cavaignac, victor of June
was such that it decided to retain this stern Republican general as
head of government. France as a whole was grateful but the gratitude
of political opponents tends to be short-lived. The local elections of
July, August and September revealed in most areas the continued
social eminence of those relatively wealthy figures who had been
socially and politically dominant under the Monarchy. Significantly
though, in some areas, and above all in the south-east, there were
signs in the results of a revolt by the peasants and artisans against
this dominance, signs of the development of a more independent
political consciousness amongst these groups.

   In the Assembly a Constitution was produced which reflected the
intensified conservatism of this post-June period. Lip service was
paid to Republican ideals by almost all deputies afraid of the consequences to social order of political agitation, but dissatisfaction
tended to increase with a government which occasionally tried hard
to be republican and at the very least seemed unprepared to engage
in repression sufficient to satisfy most conservatives.

   The Constitution provided for the election of a President and head
of the executive, and of an Assembly, both by universal male suffrage.
Deputies presumed that Cavaignac would be elected. He was a virtuous
man. The mass electorate, however, succumbed to the advances of a
chameleon-like character, the descendant of that Bonaparte enshrined
by tradition as both the heir to the Revolution and the strong man
who gave social stability to France. Conservative leaders, the socially
eminent throughout France, this time did not lead, they followed
mass opinion, unwilling to be isolated, confident in the possibility
of using the apparently insignificant Louis-Napoléon Bonaparte.

193

This man was elected. Conservative politicians saw in this their victory. As head of his first government Bonaparte selected the last minister of Louis-Philippe, namely Odilon Barrot. The role of this government was it seems to finally secure the political restoration of the social élite, of the monarchists, both Legitimist and Orléanist of the Party of Order. In this respect a purge of Republican personnel was necessary, the Constituent Assembly, too moderate during this conservative reaction was bullied into retirement. In May 1849, general elections confirmed the strength of conservative influence and authority. Moderate republicanism was crushed between the two extremes, the large majority of monarchists, and the minority of radical republicans – the Montagne. The election of the latter revealed a further development of the political consciousness of the masses in central and south-east France. In many respects it revealed what was to be a permanent regional allegiance to the left, a factor in politics during the Third Republic and even today, an increasingly important factor for the remaining years of the Second Republic.

The Republic of Republicans

'The history of the Constituent National Assembly since the June days is the history of the domination and the disintegration of the Republican faction of the bourgeoisie.'[1] The weakness of this faction was soon evident, as amongst conservatives a desire was increasingly and openly expressed not now simply for conservation, but, with the confidence gained by crushing the June insurgents, for reaction. From this moment scepticism of republican and even liberal ideas was expressed ever more openly. There was even a return to ideas previously believed to be discredited, 'the differences between Legitimists and pure conservatives declined. The taste for tradition became fashionable. It seemed to be a protest against the pretensions of democracy.'[2]

In the conservative press this protest took the form of the desire expressed for moral order. For a writer in the *Gazette de France* of

July 29 '. . . in a well ordered society . . . only religion is able to calm . . . agitation . . . because only it offers to infinite desire the pursuit of an equivalent good.' Montalembert was more brutally frank – 'I only know of one means . . . of making believe in property those who are not property owners, that is to make them believe in God, and not the vague God of the eclectics . . . but in the God of the catechism . . .'[3] A plan for future conservative action was being outlined. The Church and Catholics, frightened by their experience of the Republic in France and towards the end of the year by the overthrow of the Papal regime in Rome, were increasingly willing to lend themselves to conservative action, particularly if in the process they gained the great prize of a more significant role in education. Even those Catholics aware of the problem of poverty tended to regret that the republic 'pretended to have discovered something better than charity.' A pretension which was nothing less than 'an effort of human pride to dispense with God and His works.'[4]

In spite of their heightened confidence, conservatives remained afraid. The press continually called for order and for the unity of all those who wished to defend existing institutions. The Comité de la Rue de Poitiers was used to coordinate the parliamentary activity of conservatives of all allegiances, and additionally their propagandist efforts. In September a congress of delegates of the conservative provincial press met at Tours in an attempt to develop a common policy. For the meantime the conservatives held to the Republic. They had little or no confidence in its future, and no gratitude for the role of the republican government in June. 'In all the theatres allusions against the Republic (and they are not lacking in the new pieces) are received with enthusiasm,'[5] but as de Tocqueville realised 'what France wants is not this or that form of government, it is a firm and regular government.'[6] At this time no credible alternative to the Republic presented itself.

Conservatives were concerned to maintain their social power, and were organizing themselves to do so, were criticizing all apparent threats to their position. The government was not only insufficiently vigorous in suppressing the more radical republican and socialist groups but annoyingly persisted in its wish to introduce certain reforms designed to increase social equality in respect of military conscription and education.

The municipal and departmental elections of July and August were symptomatic of the growing will to act of conservatives and the reality of their social power at a local level. In a period of weak central government when the administration lacked effective direction, then the local notables were able more effectively than ever to dominate those who respectfully looked to them for advice and those who through links of dependence had no choice but to follow their advice.

In most areas, as compared with the April elections to the Constituent Assembly, a clear move to the right was evident. As significant was the extremely low poll, with often as much as two-thirds of those eligible to vote abstaining, indicating both a lack of interest in the elections and a readiness to leave affairs to the notables. In terms of the type of personnel elected little change occurred. Even where, as in the Midi, a large number of new representatives were elected, they had the same social background as those they replaced. In municipal government, previously often left by the notables to the lower middle classes a rebirth of interest on their part was evident. The notables were in effect using these elections to reaffirm their authority, not as Orleanists or Legitimists but simply as notables. Often men of different political persuasions collaborated to exclude the less wealthy, less conservative middle-class groups.

One other significant aspect of these elections was the political polarization evident in the results mainly of some larger towns. A citizen of Lyon criticized the moderate republicans as offering nothing but 'phrases and as otherwise being guilty of a complete absence of energy, except on one point, that of an absolute repulsion from democrats who are found to be too advanced.'[7] Discouraged by events, in a situation in which extreme solutions appeared attractive the moderate republicans were already being squeezed out of existence.

In September supplementary elections for the Constituent Assembly occurred, the results of which further served to emphasize the move of opinion to the right. Fifteen Monarchists were among the seventeen elected. What most struck contemporaries about this election was the success of Louis-Napoléon Bonaparte. The more thoughtful found their doubts as to the stability of the Republic increased by this particular result of universal suffrage. De Tocqueville wrote that the election 'shows the degree of horror with which the Republic is seen and the ardour with which all that was not it would be adopted no matter what . . .'[8] The Marquis de Gramont confided to Rudolphe Apponyi his contempt of an election which had resulted in Paris, in the success 'on the one hand of a socialist, on the other of Louis Bonaparte as symbol of all the discontented; and in favour of order and the existing government, who? a Jew!'[9]

Confidence had not then been anywhere near restored. The rentes indicated this, the 5 per cent rose after the June insurrection from 68 francs on June 21 to 79 francs 25 centimes on July 7, but fell again by mid-July to 71 francs. All the elected in Paris represented opinion opposed to the existing moderate republican government. Whatever it had achieved men were dissatisfied. 'Misery increases every day, the financial crisis does not diminish; the Assembly votes useless expenditure, without concerning itself with the means of paying for this. . . .'[10] At Lyon in the first week of July, 'It is said that there has been discovered the plan of a conspiracy which involved the taking-over first of the gas works, to deprive the town . . . of its lighting, then the beating of the call to arms in the various quarters of the town and the killing of the National Guards as they proceeded individually to their assembly points. Then the most important posts would be taken and the quarters inhabited above all by the rich would be burnt; but the plot was divulged and this led to searches which revealed stores of torches which would have served for the incendiaries, brand-new guillotines which would have been in constant use and a mass of other instruments of destruction.'[11] On September 24 the Austrian, Apponyi, reported to his diary after dining with the Pozzo family that 'Today they were extremely disturbed in Paris: the Pozzo family were dying of fear . . . a conflict between the different parties appears imminent, they only spoke of civil war and street fighting . . .'[12] Previous events and the continued unrest amongst the lower orders combined to maintain feelings of personal and group insecurity, a psychology of fear which the longer it lasted, the more insistently would demand to be assuaged by some more reassuring guarantee of order.

One effect of this lack of confidence in the future was to limit industrial and commercial activity, which anyway would have been experiencing difficulty. This maintained the discontent amongst the lower middle class elements like shopkeepers, small wholesalers and workshop owners. The *Réforme* indeed welcomed this discontent. Referring to a petition by shopkeepers that the cost of leases be reduced, one of its correspondents hopefully wrote that whereas after the Revolution of 1830 small businessmen had been hoodwinked into supporting repression directed against republicans, now they might be aware of their community of interest.[13]

In previous years an agricultural crisis had developed because of poor crops, but from 1847 a crisis arose due to the overproduction of most major products and particularly of wheat and wine. The result of this was of course a decline in prices and difficulty in selling even at low prices. An index constructed on the basis of statistics from the department of Loir-et-Cher shows how farm income declined after 1847:[14]

1845 — 89	1848 — 97
1846 — 108	1849 — 79
1847 — 171	1850 — 75
(1843 — 1854 = 100)	

This was the general picture throughout France and was made more serious by the fact that the supply of foodstuffs on the international market also exceeded demand.

The effects of this crisis on other sectors of the economy were, as would be expected in a predominantly agricultural country, serious. If there was an undoubted improvement in the commercial and industrial situation, caused primarily by the need for individuals and enterprises to buy certain basic necessities whose purchase had already been postponed by the crisis of 1846–47, the continued restriction of rural purchasing power, and the lack of confidence caused by the political situation severely limited the extent of this recovery.

The consequences of this economic crisis varied as between social groups. In the countryside those most adversely affected were the small-scale producers involved in production for the market who were now unable to earn sufficient money to buy the artisanal or industrial goods they needed or to pay taxes or rent or debts and buy the foodstuffs they did not produce. According to the *Indépendant* of Toulouse of 10 September 1848, 'The straitened circumstances, even more, the distress in the countryside is at its height. The cultivator is not able to sell his products, or is . . . forced to sell them at low price. There is no money. How then could he give to the tax collectors what he does not possess?'[15] In response to the enquiry ordered by the Constituent Assembly one report from Alsace dated January 1849, read that 'The stockbreeders prosper. The husbandman and the vine grower are often in need due to the usurious expenses they must pay to demanding and inhuman creditors. . . .'[16]

This illustrates the point that some sectors of production were relatively sheltered, including pastoral farmers in some areas, and more significantly those engaged in subsistence agriculture, providing however that they could pay taxes and debts in which case they lived in far more comfort than previously now that the problem of food shortage had ended.

Generally, however, the rural population with the exception of the large-scale high-yield producers selling enough to compensate for the low price suffered from a declining income. Labourers were unemployed because farmers could not afford to employ them; farmers were unable to pay their rents and because of the difficulty in replacing them were often allowed to retain their farms by converting the lease to that of a sharecropper. If a large number of expropriations was symptomatic of indebtedness, often peasants were allowed to retain land which had little attractiveness to the moneylender as the form of repayment of his loan and whose sale would not raise much in a depressed market. Resistance to the government's tax-collectors was extremely common from a population often simply unable to pay.[17] In the French countryside misery and discontent was widespread as economic crisis, whatever its causes, was prolonged. From the summer and autumn of 1848 the problems of rural poverty came to impress themselves more and more on public opinion and to become themselves of great importance in determining political behaviour. This continued with economic crisis throughout the Second Republic.

The situation of the urban workers was improved by a reduction in unemployment and in food prices, the former from about October 1848 and occurring particularly in textiles and to a lesser extent in metallurgy and building. A report from the Paris Prefect of Police of October 7, insists that 'most workshops and factories have recommenced operations, and some of them are as active as in the most prosperous years'.[18] De Castellane presented a gloomier picture which tends to accord more with what we know of the economic situation, where he recorded on 14 July 1848, that 'Misery is excessive, the number of shops shut in Paris . . . is considerable.'[19] Nothing else could be expected where purchasing power was so severely restricted and the normal business overheads so difficult to meet. If the condition of the urban factory worker tended to improve, that of the worker employed in the more technically advanced and competitive establishments did so most. Those employed in workshops and in producing luxury goods, and additionally the large number of village artisans suffered badly, as did the owners of these small workshops, and those of small shops. The building industry too continued to be extremely depressed.

The picture remains one of a society in difficulty and demographic figures perhaps best exemplify this. In 1848 and 1849 the death rate remained above normal and in 1849 above that for the year of food shortage in 1847. The higher rates of marriages for 1848 indicated a regaining of confidence whilst a decrease in 1849 and especially 1850–52 was a sign that marriages were again being deferred. This period of the Second Republic has in fact been noted as that in which change occurred from a period of rapid population increase to one of relative stagnation,[20] presumably as straitened circumstances persuaded more and more of the rural population to accept the practice of birth control. Permanent migration from the countryside was also to assume larger proportions in succeeding years.

Rates of deaths and marriages per 1,000 inhabitants in the Loir-et-Cher[21]

Year	Deaths	Marriages
1846	230	84
1847	252	72
1848	245	108
1849	261	92
1850	223	85

Opinion at the time tended to associate economic crises with political events, and to an important extent these in affecting business confidence did influence the level of economic activity. The increase in prices both of foodstuffs and of the rents after the election of Louis-Napoléon as President of the Republic is indicative of this. All the same Marx would seem to have been correct in emphasizing, at this time, the essentially secondary effect of political factors on economic conditions. De Castellane noted, in March 1849, the limited effects and artificiality of the upturn of the economy 'Commerce does not recover ... but the rents rise in an extraordinary manner.'[22]

From the economic situation in this period preceding the election of the Legislative Assembly significant things can be observed, namely the massive discontent of the rural population and of the urban lower middle class elements which had in June played a rather conservative social role whilst at the same time slow industrial recovery, low food prices and the crushing of the June insurrection resulted in far less intense political interest amongst the urban workers.

One immediate result of the repression which followed the June insurrection was to drive much of the radical movement once more underground. The resurrected secret societies were never as powerful as opinion, in all social groups, thought, but symbolized to them either the will to resist reaction or else the threat to social order. In the latter respect a circular from the Minister of Justice informed the *procureurs généraux* at the end of July of the widespread organization of secret societies.[23] The *procureurs* in response were not slow to confirm the fears of the Minister whether on the basis of an objective analysis of information or from their normal conception of the respect due to a Minister.[24]

More significant politically as has been observed was the polarization of political forces which was occurring. Moderate republicans were discouraged. They felt betrayed by the masses who had been led astray by demagogues, who were too impatient and too demanding. They either lost enthusiasm for politics, were concerned primarily for the preservation of order, as seen in the policy of a Republican government designed essentially to conciliate conservatives, or else, if rejecting this as a betrayal of principle, tended to align themselves with the more radical republicans associated with Ledru-Rollin.

This group which had on April 16 opposed the demonstration of the clubs, and which similarly had rejected the recourse to violence in June now served as a rallying point for all those who favoured some social reform, because of its vigorous opposition inside and outside the Assembly to the repressive policy favoured by conservatives. Repression in practice forced an alliance between these democrats and more socialistically inclined groups formerly opposed to them. The first manifestation of this occurred when, for a supplementary election in September 1848, the Jacobin-democrat Montagne and its supporters cooperated with socialists to secure the election of Raspail.

Electoral support needed to be garnered amongst the masses and consequently a clear appeal to their interests had to be made. To a contemporary like Alexis de Tocqueville the change in tone of the propaganda of the radical left was clear as democrats moved to a point of agreement.[25] This point for Pierre de la Gorce was socialist, but no longer dogmatic – the various ideological sects declined as 'towards the end of 1848, the party, by a clever transformation, enlarged its cadres and in changing its tactics created for itself an army. They renounced the presentation of incomprehensible or contradictory theories. They undertook to speculate no longer on the intelligence, but on the instincts. To books succeeded brochures, little leaflets, almanacs especially, of which the pedlars distributed an infinite number. Instead of addressing themselves to the workers who had become sceptical of promises, they turned towards the country population, less hardened against sophisms. They seduced them, not by vague predictions, but by the crude appeal to interests: above all exciting their greed, the dominant passion of the French peasantry.'[26]

Robespierre's declaration of human rights of 1793 was modernized by men like Delescluze, the future Communard, to promise social reform to accompany the strengthening of democracy.[27]

A persistent thread of the propaganda of the left in this period was the continued denial of any intention to deny the rights so ardently defended by conservatives, to property and a family life. Tied with the promise to guarantee the right to work of the urban worker, was a promise to preserve the rights of the small property owner from the encroachment and exploitation of the large.[28] The promise had been made before, but never as insistently as in this period when the vital need to win peasant support had been realized. To the peasant and small shopkeeper Ledru-Rollin affirmed that 'Property is liberty . . . we will therefore respect property, but on condition that it will be infinitely multiplied . . . we do not want it for some; we want it for all . . .'[29] Felix Pyat promised that the state would provide the cheap credit necessary to maximize the extension of property ownership essential for human dignity and independence.[30] Socialism was thus clearly combined with an appeal to the sacred values of the existing society.

In organizational terms this outlook took the form from November 1848 of a group called *Solidarité républicaine* directed by a council including Ledru-Rollin, Delescluze, Pyat, Martin Bernard and Agricole Perdiguier.

For its adherents the Republic was 'the only and true means of arriving at the reformation of existing institutions where they outrage the dignity of man and threaten the existence of the most numerous class. They demand the right to work, as they want the right of property'.[31] It was intended to organize republicans on a cantonal, arrondissement and departmental basis, these to supply information to a central committee which would impose direction on the movement. By the beginning of 1849 its spread was obviously causing concern to the administration.[32]

The organizing cadres of this movement were defined by Pierre de la Gorce in hostile tones as 'all those who in their daily occupations mix with the masses and who believe themselves superior to the common destiny',[33] typically then the lower middle classes of the market towns and administrative centres, the doctors, health officers, notaries, justices, tax-collectors, road-surveyors, pharmacists, school-teachers, an intellectual élite, singled out by this and their relative wealth compared to the masses, whose daily contacts gave them influence. By word of mouth, by encouraging the distribution of political literature, they spread radical ideas. They were dissatisfied with the failure of their social status to improve after the revolution, and often also faced economic difficulties. A more mundane and very common reason for their choice of political allegiance was rivalry at the local level with some other members of the same social groups. These were local notables struggling for power.

The impulse to act came primarily from Paris, but was willingly accepted by lower middle class republicans in the provinces. In Paris working class organizations which had before June exerted substantial pressure and influence on lower middle class radicals, had been suppressed leaving those middle class elements in unchallenged control of the political movement which favoured some social reform. With the threat from the workers for them seemingly ended the lower middle classes could again direct their discontent at the upper middle-class groups who remained their economic and political competitors.

As far as the mechanics of the transmission of ideas and spread of organization went, all large urban centres acted as the centres for transmission to a greater or lesser extent, usually receiving ideas from Paris and retransmitting them to smaller towns and from these to the countryside, with overall receptivity depending upon such factors as the degree of development of the means of communication, social structure and the extent of discontent prevailing. The strength of the so-called *démocrate-socialiste* movement depended essentially upon winning a significant urban following and then, using this following to win over the countryside.

Lower middle-class professional men supplied leadership in the locality whilst artisans, shop and innkeepers tended to conduct propaganda amongst the peasants. These and particularly the artisans were men who were often literate and had travelled, who had acquired knowledge of a wider world and for whom the local society with its traditional authorities had lost meaning. Amongst these were many normally migrant workers, forced to remain at home because of the economic crisis, politically relatively knowledgeable and discontented.[34]

The basic fact of course was the continued economic crisis causing widespread discontent. The rural population faced with demands for debt repayments, for rents, and for taxes was in many areas in a state making it susceptible to political propaganda. The peasants reacted primarily to economic stimuli. From June resistance to the collection of the supplementary tax imposed by the Provisional Government had significantly increased.[35] Peasant revolt expressed hostility to the Republican government which had imposed the tax and hostility to the middle-class moneylenders and landowners who exacted payment often by seizure of the land which represented the peasants claim to social estimation. It represented a basic feeling of being a peasant and an hostility to the urban bourgeoisie who exploited him. It meant inevitably a heightened group and even political consciousness in those areas in which revolt occurred which, if hostile to the republic at this stage could be and was being utilized by the more radical of republicans prepared to promise social change.

Resistance to the collection of the 45 centimes tax occurred mainly in the South and in some departments in the East. Rémi Gossez has produced a map showing the percentage of the tax collected in each department by 13 July 1848 which reveals that south of a line stretching from the Vendée to the Jura, far less than half of the tax had been collected, whilst to the north generally far more than one half had been collected. Significantly in many parts of this same area of resistance to tax collectors, in the municipal elections peasants and artisans had resisted the social power of conservative local notables and elected new men.

This new consciousness was restricted in scope, both in terms of the numbers who evinced it and of the areas in which it occurred, but it seems evident that in the region most adversely effected by the past and continuing economic crisis – the Midi, and especially the southeast, discontent in the countryside had reached a pitch at which it could be exploited for political purposes.

The Provisional Government formed in February had been

succeeded first by an Executive Commission, a more conservative body reflecting the innate conservatism of the Constituent Assembly which had elected it, and this in its turn by a government at whose head was the victor of June, General Cavaignac, which reflected the increased conservatism of the Assembly following the June insurrection, which excluded the more radical republicans and in particular Ledru-Rollin from government.

It might seem from the results of the April election that this was a republican Assembly but in practice non-republican groups were exerting an increasing influence. Additionally, these deputies were coming under increasing pressure from press and public opinion determined to make them see themselves as unrepresentative of the feeling of the nation. Politically inexperienced as many of these 'republicans' were, lacking confidence, they tended to easily accept this as true.[37]

Their inexperience was revealed in their susceptibility to the practiced oratory of men like Thiers. Through the Réunion de la Rue de Poitiers the conservative leaders were able to coordinate the activity in the Assembly of some three hundred deputies mainly monarchist, and including most of the experienced parliamentarians. Coordination made up for numerical inferiority. As early as July 1, it had resulted in a situation in which twelve of the fifteen presidents of committees of the Assembly were former deputies of the July Monarchy.

Cavaignac desired to conciliate these conservatives, even to the extent of admitting their representatives, the former Orleanist ministers, Dufaure and Vivien, to participation in his government, but conservatives were increasingly determined to abandon their policy of support for the republic as the least evil and to openly defend their own ideas and interests. In the Assembly they were able to effectively oppose all projects of reform. Concerning the taxation policy favoured by this Assembly the *Réforme* of September 8 complained that 'The Bankers and the Jews have already reconquered under the Republic the unfortunate influence they exercised on the Monarchy.'

The policy of the moderate republican government involved the repression of organizations and of the ideological expression of advanced ideas, of clubs and the press. In addition projected reforms such as the nationalization of the railways and the introduction of progressive taxation were dropped, and the established limitation on the hours of labour reversed. These were measures designed to restore upper middle class confidence.

In this they only partly succeeded. Cavaignac, if anti-socialist, remained firmly attached to a republican regime. Once he realized the strength of the reaction against republican institutions, then he attempted, however feebly, to defend them. Early in September, for example, he favoured sending representatives into the provinces to revive republican faith. He was, however, in a false position. Every new demonstration of radical, republican or socialist activity drew his administration into repressive activity, but never into repression severe enough to satisfy the mass of conservatives in the country. These were dissatisfied with both government and Assembly. De Castellane exemplified a common contempt for this latter institution. He wrote on July 25 'At the National Assembly, half the session was lost in discussing the pronunciation of the word club: some said *cleubbe*, others *club* as *plut*; it was decided that it would be pronounced *club*.'[38] He wanted action not talk. The government was too weak and, however conservative, yet not conservative enough. The finance minister, Goudchaux, actually proposed a tax on the revenue gained from stocks and shares.[39]

This is part of the background to the presidential election of December. One other important and revealing factor was the constitutional provision for this election and indeed the constitution as a whole as representative of moderate republican consciousness and weakness. The legislature was given in theory absolute power, including the authority to remove the President of the Republic for unconstitutional action, whereas the President, as head of the executive was responsible for government and controlled the entire administrative and military machine. Given additionally that the President was to assume the moral authority gained through election by universal suffrage, then his position would be extremely strong. For de Tocqueville centralized control of a mass of officials in a country which was still by habit monarchist would make of 'a president elected by the people . . . a pretender to the throne. . . .'[40]

The majority of deputies wanted a strong executive and as republicans or from fear of a strong popular reaction were unable to allow the selection of the head of this executive to occur other than through universal suffrage. It was initially presumed anyway by moderate republicans that their candidate Cavaignac, the victor of June, would be elected and as an additional guarantee of this it was decided that a successful candidate for the presidency must receive a minimum of two million votes, otherwise the Assembly – republican, or at least pro-Cavaignac in its majority – would elect. The possibility of conflict between the two basic powers of government was not therefore envisaged by the majority of deputies.

Declining moderate republican confidence was revealed by the provision that constitutional revision must be supported by three-quarters of the votes cast, as though these republicans already saw themselves as a minority and prepared to defend their constitution from this position. The growing conservatism of this Assembly was evident. A comparison of the first draft of the constitution prepared by the Assembly's committee before the June insurrection with a subsequent draft is revealing of a changed outlook. The first was indeed moderate but clearly democratic, the second submitted on August 30, did little more than maintain the democratic phraseology of the first, whilst omitting the few provisions of social reform contained in the early version – such for example, as its recognition of the right to work.

The dominant ethos of the Assembly by this time was not democratic but was represented by Thiers and other conservative leaders. The former, at a meeting of the committee discussing the constitution on September 11, rejected a guaranteed right to work as encouraging idleness. The right to work he saw as the first step on the road to the horrors of communism.[41]

Concerning progressive taxation, L'herbette in a debate in the Assembly on September 25 claimed that this if introduced would recognize not 'the just and moralizing equality of rights' but 'equality between the capable and the incapable . . . between vice and virtue, this equality which desires similar advantages for different dues, this equality which brutalizes and demoralizes.'[42]

The earlier proposal to make all citizens equally liable to military service and end the practice whereby those who could afford to, when conscripted, purchased a replacement, was rejected by de Tocqueville as potentially destructive of a liberal education.[43]

Essentially this constitution was 'a work of terminology' in which 'The royalist labels were torn off the mechanism of the old monarchy and republican labels stuck on' but with one vital difference – by maintaining universal suffrage it gave political power to the 'classes whose social slavery the constitution is to perpetuate, proletariat, peasantry, petty bourgeoisie . . .

It forces the political role of the bourgeoisie into democratic conditions, which at every moment . . . jeopardize the very foundations of bourgeois society.'[44]

The Rise of the Masses: The Presidential Election of 10 December 1848

December saw the election by universal suffrage to the supreme political post in France of a man who had been the previous February virtually unknown. By the end of May and beginning of June as discontent increased amongst workers in Paris it had become evident that a small group of Bonapartist sympathizers were attempting to make political use of the folk-memory, still strong, of the Napoleonic period. The sympathy of the Parisian masses with oppressed Poland could especially be used, the pacific foreign policy of the republic compared with the glorious campaigns of Napoleon, partly designed, at least according to legend, to free the enslaved Poles.

In the Spring of 1848 a large number of Bonapartist journals had appeared directed at all shades of opinion – the *Constitution* at conservatives, the *Napoléonien* at moderate republicans, the *Napoléon républicain*, far more radical. This represented less a conscious plan than the fact that those desiring political change could use various aspects of the policy and legend of the Emperor to encourage support for their designs.

On 4 June 1848, Louis-Napoléon Bonaparte made an appearance on the political stage through his election in four departments including the Seine, in spite of being proposed, in his absence, only a short time before the election, and being supported by a minimal propaganda effort. The power of his name was revealed and also, in spite of the reaction of the press, which ridiculed his past, it was evident that his attempted coups were not simply futile exercises. They had identified the man with the legend of his uncle. It was significant that most of Louis-Napoléon's support in Paris and its suburbs came from working-class areas – Belleville, Buttes-Chaumont, Batignolles, Saint-Denis,[1] and elsewhere from the peasantry. The obvious hostility of the Executive Commission and of the conservative press to the new Bonaparte increased sympathy for him amongst the urban workers, particularly after the suppression of the June insurrection, during which a great deal of latent popular Bonapartism was revealed in the linking of cries of 'Vive Napoléon!' and 'Vive la République démocratique et sociale!'[2] This was support for the Louis-Napoléon who had written a work on *L'Extinction du Paupérisme*. The attempted coups at Strasbourg and Boulogne were presented by Bonapartist propagandists as attempts to deliver the workers from the misery of the reign of Louis-Philippe.

By conservatives Louis-Napoléon was thus seen, at this time, as the elect of socialists and revolutionaries,[3] but after his resignation of his seat in the Assembly they soon forgot him. Then, on September 17–18, he was again elected, in five departments and in the Seine with over 110,000 votes compared with the 25,000 of June. This was an election less spontaneous in character, involving a better organized campaign with more moderate propaganda directed at the middle classes but still due essentially to worker and peasant support, the character of which is partly revealed by the fact that in the Seine workers tended to vote for Louis-Napoléon and Raspail – 'In naming Bonaparte, we have cried: Hatred to the butchers of June! In voting for Raspail: Vive la Sociale!'[4]

Yet again conservatives were disturbed, the *Gazette du Midi* of Marseille of September 23, referred to 'Louis Bonaparte, the pretender half-militarist, half-Jacobin, the friend and protégé of Louis Blanc.'[5] It was, however, hoped that the prominence of this Bonaparte would be short-lived, that the wave of popular enthusiasm would quickly decline. Few saw that massive discontent in all classes was giving increasing relevance to the Bonaparte legend.

The legend had been maintained by a wealth of books and pamphlets and, more important as far as the masses were concerned, by songs and engravings, by a popular oral tradition, and by the memories of the large numbers who had lived during the Imperial epoch and even fought in its wars. Balzac described the isolated region which was the setting for his *The Country Doctor* – 'No political event, no revolution had ever taken place in this inaccessible region, completely outside the social movement. The name of Napoléon alone had penetrated here; it is here a religion, thanks to two or three soldiers of the county returned to their firesides, and who, in the long evenings relate to these simple people fabulous adventures of this man and his armies.'[6]

On Saint Helena the Emperor had started the work of creating a legend, his companions, his nephew and less involved historians had continued this, but none so effectively as the humble old soldier. Glory was contrasted with the poverty and boredom of everyday existence. The suffering of war was soon forgotten. More significantly in this period of economic crisis the period of the Empire was remembered, especially by the peasants, as one of rising prices, of relative prosperity.

Journals of all tendencies tended to ignore or ridicule Louis-Napoléon until the September election made it obvious that a new and serious contender had appeared for the presidential election. By the end of October it was generally felt that Louis-Napoléon might succeed. De Tocqueville commented on the strange procedure by which 'In the degree to which the popular movement pronounces itself in favour of Louis-Napoléon, it drags along the parliamentary leaders ... Thiers began by being violently opposed, then violently in favour. The Legitimists will hesitate until the last. Most will finish by giving way to the torrent; the tail of society definitely leads the head.'[7] De Tocqueville explained this by the fact that above all France desired strong government whatever its constitutional form. The Napoleonic traditions seemed to conservative notables to promise this, and as Louis-Napoléon's success anyway seemed inevitable however they voted, they were impelled to jump on the bandwagon.[8] Gustave de Beaumont writing to de Tocqueville on October 29 partly ascribed this feeling to the fatalism of men in a period of massive change in which their wills appeared insignificant.[9] Charles de Rémusat saw a more conscious decision being made. If at this time conservatives favoured Cavaignac it was above all necessary that the candidate they supported succeed. 'They would not wish after all if he failed to be too compromised by him.' This would put them in opposition to the National will and the president elected in opposition to them.[10]

Similar thoughts must have influenced the decisions of more prominent conservative politicians. It seems to be generally accepted that Molé persuaded Thiers that there was no practical alternative to supporting Louis-Napoléon. Thiers reported Molé as saying that 'Louis-Napoléon hates the Republic; he will pave the way to a restoration which Cavaignac would strive to prevent; the opposition of the left will force him to rely on the right, to take its ministers and to adopt its principles; in short he will be our instrument, whereas

Cavaignac would be our master.'[11] The correctness of this prediction depended upon the correctness of his assessment of Louis-Napoléon's character and abilities, whose seemingly ridiculous attempted coups personal life and short parliamentary career contributed to an image of him as a libertine and fool. Men who were used to judging others by their capacity for speechmaking were not impressed by his efforts in the Assembly.

The conservative politicians organized behind the Comité de la rue de Poitiers were experiencing difficulties in selecting a candidate for the presidential election. Orleanists and Legitimists in particular disagreed. Increasingly, as popular support for Louis-Napoléon became evident, it was obvious that any third candidate they might agree on would have very little chance of success. Castellane wrote in his diary on October 17 that the company at a dinner given by Thiers regarded Bonaparte's success as certain.[12] The choice was therefore between Cavaignac and Bonaparte. The former promised a *status quo* with which few were satisfied, the latter existed, it seemed, to be used for the purpose of reaction. Thiers contemptuously asserted that 'We will give him women and we will lead him.'[13] He saw Bonaparte's election as a guarantee of power for himself and his friends.

Louis-Napoléon cultivated this opinion, carefully flattering Thiers, promising everything required of him. On November 5 the conservative deputies came to their meeting place in the Rue de Poitiers, and followed Thiers in deciding, at least implicitly, to support Bonaparte, as it determined to oppose all other candidates.[14] The English Ambassador, Normanby, wrote that 'History affords no parallel to this spectacle of all the eminent men of all former political parties uniting in support of a man whom no one of them would personally have selected. They, in fact, follow whilst they assume to direct, a popular impulse which they could not resist.'[15]

Those who possessed social power adopted then a pragmatic attitude. With reluctance conservative notables followed the impulse from below. The process of conversion was gradual, many minds were made up finally in the days immediately preceding the election. This process is revealed in the changing attitudes of the conservative press reflecting the new attitudes of its readers. Support of Bonaparte was justified by a variety of reasons which tended to make of this a positive virtue. Unquiet spirits need to be consoled.

In the period immediately succeeding the announcement of his candidature few newspapers beyond the ephemeral Bonapartist press lent support to Louis-Napoléon. The tacit adhesion of such conservative leaders as Molé, Thiers, Barrot and Bugeaud did much to sway editors – to such a point that in Paris only the *Journal de. Débats* of the old conservative papers remained hostile to Bonaparte and this saw Cavaignac as an even more unattractive prospect.

The *Gazette de France* which on November 4 had favoured abstention from voting, on November 5 reported the meeting at the Rue de Poitiers of conservative deputies and concluded that 'there was almost unanimity in declaring that the candidature which they would prefer . . . is that of Louis Bonaparte, and that what would be most dangerous would be the prolongation of a *status quo* which wastes all the resources of France'. This was the great positive attraction of Louis-Napoléon Bonaparte, he promised for conservatives the end of a situation in which they still felt insecure. Conservation was not what they wanted by this time. They felt strong enough to support reaction. With Louis-Napoléon they looked forward to restoring the unchallenged rule of privilege, to defeating the threat to civilization from the masses, and that to their political and administrative authority from the lower middle classes. According to the *Gazette de France* this was a candidate of whom 'the name is a living protest against tendencies to anarchy and disorder.'[16] Louis-Napoléon's election manifesto promised order for conservatives, decentralization of government for Legitimists, freedom of education for Catholics.

Lord Normanby wrote on December 12 that 'The memory of the Emperor is no doubt for something in this impulse, but the hatred of the Republic gives another signification to the name of Bonaparte.'[17] Hostility to this regime was far more intense among the Monarchists than to a far-off Imperial government around which a golden legend had been constructed. They remembered too that the path of history had previously been from Republic to Bonapartism to monarchy.[18]

Catholic support was important both because of the influence of the clergy and the existing national organization of committees organized by Montalembert under the previous regime to struggle for the freedom of the Church to expand its educational facilities. Louis-Napoléon appealed best to the conservative instincts of a Church for which change had seemed to herald dissolution and moreover he was prepared to make specific promises on education and support for the Pope faced with revolution in his temporal kingdom.

Cavaignac supported free, compulsory and state-controlled education, and was less willing to support Papal interests. Of the bishops of France only one supported Cavaignac, Fayet of Orléans, and one other, Mgr Sibour of Paris, gave his clergy freedom of conscience.[19]

Thus was Louis-Napoléon provided not only with mass support, but financial and organizational resources, and press support with which to guarantee his victory, and provide for a more distant future by more clearly impressing his image on the minds of all social groups.

Bonapartist propaganda largely took the traditional form of brochures, pictures, poems and songs, which awakened a ready response. Bonapartist propagandists with a political purpose were able to build upon a mass of sentiment. Nassau William Senior was walking near the spa of Eaux Bonnes in August 1849. He met and questioned an agricultural labourer. 'I asked if the Republic was popular. "Oh, yes", he said "we all voted for Louis-Napoléon, partly because of his uncle who was the greatest man that ever lived . . . and his nephew is the richest man in the world; he supports all the poor in Paris. He offered to supply the Treasury with all the money of which Ledru-Rollin robbed it." He would certainly be king or emperor for life, which would not much signify, as, if, they disliked him, they should turn him out, as they did his predecessors. They knew nothing of Guizot or Odilon Barrot, or Cavaignac in his country, the only names they knew were Lamartine, Ledru-Rollin, and Louis-Napoléon. As for Lamartine he was quarrelsome, a *taquineur*. Ledru-Rollin was a thief. There were 40,000 people in Paris who paid him forty sous a day apiece. He intended to make himself king. It was the money which he had carried away which made the Republic poor.'[20]

This is symptomatic of the fact that political conflict as evinced by propaganda tends to be simplified and to take the form of images particularly where, as in so much of rural France in the middle of the nineteenth century, most of the population was illiterate or semi-literate, where propaganda was communicated by word of mouth or by simply-written brochures. This could have appeal only if directed at the simple everyday life experiences of the recipient. It appealed to an understanding which at least in relation to political and economic matters was underdeveloped but not wholly irrational. In Alsace the rural population remembered that 'we had no forest laws under the Empire, we enjoyed then concessions which will be restored to us.'[21] A past experience on which to base present calculations.

The peasant Senior talked to was attracted by the glorious Napoleonic tradition, had accepted the promises of Bonapartist agents that taxes and particularly the hated 45 centimes tax would be abolished or reduced, had associated the republican regime with financial waste, economic crisis and selfish political squabbling.[22] His vote would mean 'No more taxes, down with the rich, down with the Republic, long live the emperor!'[23] He explained his political behaviour in the language of his daily life, the only language he could use to explain his motivation. Daniel Stern understood this and wrote with great indignation of Les masses populaires, – 'incapable of understanding abstract ideas, neither the whole, nor the relation and the succession of things; they personify in a single name . . . the multiple forces which combine to make social progress, and they endow these personifications with a supernatural power and an enduring legend'.[24]

This analysis was also significantly true of the urban workers and lower middle class, though it might be worth bearing in mind that 'With universal suffrage the future fate of this country is in the hands of the peasants.'[25]

Workers and shopkeepers in the small country towns and villages were mainly submerged in the feeling of the surrounding countryside, Bonapartist in most areas. Even in the politically more important larger towns and cities the ideological factor was noticeably less apparent in determining loyalties than it had been even in April. The ambiguous symbolism of Louis-Napoléon's name thus tended to blur the political spectrum.[26]

If for the majority of Frenchmen, peasants included, Bonapartism symbolized social order, for many of the urban lower classes Louis-Napoléon, as was his uncle, was the heir of the Revolution. According to Felix Pyat in Louis-Napoléon they saw 'The insurgent of Strasbourg. . . . The socialist author . . . the nephew of the Emperor. The people especially hoped that the nephew would continue the work of his uncle, that is to say the Revolution. . . .' The Empire had preserved the principle of equality. 'The Emperor himself was a parvenu, everyone was as able as the leader to affirm his worth, to attain a position according to his merit, to achieve the rank to which he had right.'[27] This was the former insurgent, the man who in his manifesto demanded a political amnesty,[28] the man who had been persecuted by the established republican regime, just as had been the insurgents of June. Normanby especially stresses this as contributing to his popularity amongst Parisians.[29] By contrast Cavaignac was the murderer of June.

Louis-Napoléon appeared to be above party squabbles, to be the saviour so ardently desired in this period of crisis and misery. Thus support for him from amongst workers in Paris and Lyon, for example, was not solely, or even primarily, negative and anti-Cavaignac in design, but represented the willingness of the masses to accept the dictatorship of a great man, where that of a social class was becoming intolerable. The existing authorities, proven to be socially conservative, had shown their hostility to Louis-Napoléon. Moreover he was reputed to favour social reform and even possess the wealth to personally guarantee this.[30] He seemed to promise reform, and the greater equality which the more politically conscious workers so ardently desired; if not liberty. If the workers' newspaper, the *Atelier*, opposed Bonaparte as the candidate of monarchist reaction,[31] it did not reflect the general opinion which would, according to the *Réforme*, result on December 10 in 'the great suicide'.[32] To the lower middle classes Louis-Napoléon could undoubtedly make an appeal similar to that made to the peasants; their economic problems were similar.

At any rate 'Thus it happened . . . that the most simple-minded man in France acquired the most multifarious significance. Just because he was nothing, he could signify everything save himself.'[33] Ignore for the moment the assault on the personality of Bonaparte. It remains true that his name stood for a multiplicity of purposes and designs 'awakening in each consciousness differing individual reactions; according to class, generation, temperament or religion, the Napoleonic representation changed meaning'.[34]

One Bonapartist electoral manifesto appealed to suffering France where:

> The unfortunate die of hunger;
> The worker is without work;
> The cultivator is no longer able to dispose of his crops;
> The merchant sells nothing;
> The proprietor no longer receives his revenue;
> The capitalist no longer dares to invest, lacking security.

and promised that 'The nephew of the great man, with his magic name, will give us security, and save us from misery.'[35]

Whatever the vagueness of this propaganda, whatever weakness of character they ascribed to Louis-Napoléon, by early December

H

republicans were complaining that 'Our coasts, our villages ring with the cry of *Vive Napoléon!* It is a vertigo, a frenzy, they regard him as a providential being. It is he, they say, who must save France.'[36]

Against this increasingly irresistible political force struggled primarily the supporters of the other main candidate, General Cavaignac, the personification for Marx of the bourgeois republic.

In most departments Cavaignac certainly seems to have been viewed by contemporaries as the candidate of the moderate republican and conservative bourgeoisie.[37] His appeal for these groups was due to a number of factors. He had given proof of his desire to preserve social order, whereas Louis-Napoléon was an essentially unknown figure, even tainted with socialism. To those middle class groups excluded from politics under the monarchies, Cavaignac appeared as a far more likely defender of republican political institutions than the Imperial pretender, behind whom moreover the Monarchist factions were obviously active. Moreover, restoration of any of the pretenders seemed to promise further revolutionary activity by republican extremists and the masses. Cavaignac appears to have been particularly popular among the commercial bourgeoisie of ports such as Marseilles for whom the Napoleonic tradition of war and glory meant declining trade and economic disaster. The Prefect of the Meuse would report that 'All those who belonged to the enlightened part of the population, to industry and commerce were for General Cavaignac.'[38] On November 28 a typical member of this commercial bourgeoisie wrote 'According to me, Cavaignac, who is I believe an honest man, summarizes in himself all our hopes: with him no shocks, no commercial or financial crises. . . . I see in him a friend of order. He has proved it.'[39] The character of the local electoral committees supporting Cavaignac as revealed by the occupations of their members lends support to the Marxian view,[40] as does the press campaign in support of the Republican general.

In the *National* the Napoleonic tradition was presented as one of war, and suffering, the threat to the Republic which Louis-Napoléon represented was a threat not only to order but to the whole path of historical development which was moving towards greater liberty.[41] It was a mere pretension that 'the imperial name is a symbol of order and security; of order through despotism, it is possible; but it is not that sort of order that the French Republic wants. Security? How? by war, without doubt, for if this name recalls anything, it is . . . war, glorious war, it is true, but even so, up to the present it is not . . .

from war that one has demanded security'.[42] The *National* further questioned the efficacy and stability of a government produced by the diverse elements uniting in support of Louis-Napoléon, whose diversity must soon again reveal itself.[43]

One significant feature of this propaganda was its negative attitude. Beyond promising social order it made few or no promises of wide appeal. From early in the campaign these moderate republicans seem to have adopted a pessimistic attitude to the possibility of their success. The most they hoped for was that Louis-Napoléon would not obtain the necessary absolute majority, and that then the Constituent Assembly would elect its most favoured candidate – almost inevitably Cavaignac. Pessimism made many middle class republicans half-hearted in their support of Cavaignac; disappointment with the Republic he had helped create, because of its lack of sympathy towards the masses, alienated others, whilst more again were attracted by the Napoleonic legend or by the promise of order which was one aspect of it, this especially in Normandy and the north-west. Much of the initial support for Cavaignac was lost before the election took place, either to the growing flood of enthusiasm for Louis-Napoléon or as a result of the inept publication of a list of pensioners of the state which included the families of individuals executed for the attempted assassination of Louis-Philippe, which offended public morality and provided an excuse to desert a sinking ship. In terms of press support particularly in the east, south-east and south, Cavaignac had significant aid, but this was from journals with fewer readers than the great conservative newspapers, and given that the press reflected rather than moulded opinion, would make few converts.

Only limited support came from other conservative social groups. The whole Napoleonic tradition had little appeal to the mainly Legitimist aristocracy and some aristocrats supported Cavaignac, and more significantly their long hostility to Bonaparte meant that its popular appeal was less apparent in areas particularly of the west and Provence, which provided then a more fertile ground for pro-Cavaignac propaganda. Other Legitimists in departments like the Vendée and the Charentes were so conservative as to see Cavaignac as the first step to communism. Legitimists often supported Louis-Napoléon from hostility to middle class commercial groups who were both liberal and Protestant.

This religious factor was an added complication. Tudesq signals the fact that in the Midi and east Protestants supported Cavaignac, as did in the same areas and in the west anticlericals.[44] But in Bas-Rhin Protestants tended to vote against Cavaignac because Roman Catholic clergy supported him after his offer of help to the Pope and elsewhere some of the declining number of liberal Catholics supported Cavaignac where Legitimists advocated Louis-Napoléon.

Some eminent liberal Orleanists, including de Tocqueville and indeed a minority of those conservatives meeting in the Rue de Poitiers felt sympathy for a man they believed had given sufficient guarantees to order and who threatened neither demagogy nor dictatorship.

These facts do not, however, alter a basic picture according to which amongst the possessing classes Cavaignac was the chosen of the middle middle classes, of the commercial and industrial groups. A political base simply not large enough to guarantee success given the still-dominant influence of local notables, who secured this influence primarily through ownership of land in an essentially agricultural country.

There were, however, certain alternatives open to Cavaignac as means of exerting influence and pressure upon the mass electorate. But he refused to resort to demagogy and even to making deliberate use of the administration, the traditional and future means of electoral control. This was to resign authority to the notables, except in a number of areas where republican officials tended from self-interest to continue to assert their authority. Whatever influence the administration did exert was in the interest of Cavaignac, a fact which diminished the image of republican purity he sought to project. But although this administrative action had some effect, Barrot saw fit to comment that such activity 'only profits governments which have a future',[45] as that of Cavaignac could hardly appear to have. Officials would not therefore be overzealous in their support.

Similarly in the other important element of the state structure – the army, the influence exerted by its officers tended to favour Cavaignac. Bonapartist propaganda was prohibited in military establishments, that of supporters of General Cavaignac was often tolerated. The general was a successful military leader who in June had restored the prestige of the army whilst, except for his name, Bonaparte was unknown, and his agents, propagandizing amongst the troops in clubs and taverns, were elements of indiscipline at a time when this had not entirely been restored to its pre-February standard. In this respect professional considerations dictated the political reactions of officers. The rank and file were more politically committed with loyalties varying, as the subsequent vote would show, according to the technical skills of particular arms of the army – engineers and artillery requiring more skilled, better educated, more largely urban recruits, less likely to be attracted by the Napoleonic legend than the mass of peasants who dominated numerically both infantry and cavalry.[46]

Cavaignac besides the middle urban bourgeoisie attracted support from the lower middle class of shopkeepers, in Paris, for example, where 'General Cavaignac will obtain the votes of all the cloth merchants of the Rue de Sentier'.[47] These were numerically a major component of his support in provincial towns in addition. Nationally an overall impression was gained by contemporaries that 'the middle classes alone remain in general with Cavaignac',[48] although voting behaviour would indicate defection by many of these. It is significant that those workers who supported Cavaignac tended to be from the skilled élite which had most imbued middle-class ideals including those of legality and democratic process, and consequently who saw the need for a tactical alliance with Cavaignac against Bonaparte who seemed to be a threat to the Republic.[49]

For the majority of workers, however, Cavaignac was the butcher of June, a fact which did not give him an appealing image. Republican political groups favouring social reform were, at least in the cities, where the election was to some extent about politics as well as personalities, as hostile to Cavaignac as to Louis-Napoléon. The *Réforme* complained of the two main candidates 'What does it matter to the people, to the worker and proletarians? One will repress the Republic and choke it in a vice! The other will kill it'.[50] It made little difference.

Two alternative candidates were presented, the former member of the Provisional Government Ledru-Rollin by 'Republicans, more ardent, but with an entirely good faith,' and Raspail by 'the communists and the muddle-headed' as one supporter of Cavaignac described them,[51] by lower middle class elements including members of the liberal professions, and the more politically committed workers, with the latter more prominent amongst Raspail's supporters.[52] These could not compare with the two major candidates, particularly in terms of personal fame, but their supporters contributed to the denigration of Cavaignac.

The election itself revealed more clearly the degree to which each candidate had voter appeal. The actual electoral process passed off quite smoothly with few reports of any violence and many signs that the political consciousness of the mass of the population remained relatively undeveloped. The Bonapartist General d'Hautpoul reported of December 10, 'It was a curious spectacle to see ... the peasants of entire villages going to the election with the name of Louis Bonaparte on their hats, and marching, with the priest at their head, to the sound of a drum. As for me ... I arrived at Castelnaudary, where the election for the arrondissement was held escorted by nearly 5,000 electors who voted as a single man.'[53] What enthusiasm there was, was for Louis-Napoléon. In Paris youths from the top of the column in the Place Vendôme distributed thousands of voting slips carrying the name of Louis-Napoléon.[54] At Grandvilliers (Oise) three workers introduced a bust of the Emperor Napoleon into the voting room and caused a disorder – 'the sight of the bust of the great man aroused in the crowd the greatest enthusiasm – the nephew of the Emperor and the benefactor of the worker, would restore the days of work and of abundance – the other candidates could only in our eyes perpetuate the times of frightful misery in which we live'.[55] In Brittany there marched to vote 'honest and free workers idolizing a name'.[56]

The result of the vote was a victory for Louis-Napoléon more over-whelming than even his most optimistic supporters could have expected, with 5,434,226 voters declaring for him; 1,448,107 for Cavaignac; 370,119 for Ledru-Rollin; 36,920 for Raspail, with 17,910 for Lamartine and 4,790 for Changarnier, the last two candidates in spite of themselves. In percentage terms this meant that 74·2 per cent of the voters had supported Louis-Napoléon (though only 55·6 per cent of those enrolled to vote), 19·5 per cent of voters had supported Cavaignac, and 6 per cent voted for all the others.

In terms of regional voting behaviour the main support for Louis-Napoléon was in the centre and centre-west, from Charente-Inférieure to Puy-de-Dôme, from the Dordogne to the Indre-et-Loire, from the north of the Paris Basin to its south-west. In most of these departments Louis-Napoléon gained over 80 per cent of the votes.

Marx labels this election as, 'The day of the peasant insurrection'[57] and as one would expect from the size of the vote and the rural character of France, Louis-Napoléon was favoured especially by the rural populations. Only one of the eight largest cities of France – Rouen, gave Bonaparte more than the national average vote for him. A comparison of the degree of support in each of these cities with that of the department as a whole is revealing of this divergence between town and country.

Percentage votes for Louis-Napoléon:[58]

In city		In whole department	
	%		%
Marseilles	14.7	Bouches-du-Rhône	20
Lille	25	Nord	50
Nantes	40.7	Loire-Inférieure	54
Paris	55	Seine	58
Toulouse	56.8	Haute Garonne	80
Bordeaux	59.4	Gironde	76
Lyon	62	Rhône	74
Rouen	79	Seine-Inférieure	84

Whatever this divergence it is significant that even in most of the major cities Louis-Napoléon was able to gain a sufficiently high proportion of the votes caste to have attracted wide support from all social classes.

Louis-Napoléon gained those departments which had voted for moderate republicans in April 1848, most of those which had shown Legitimist or Orleanist leanings and additionally those which had elected radical republicans, including the Seine. His greatest majorities were precisely in those departments in which socialist propaganda had been most successful – in Saône-et-Loire, Creuse, Haute-Vienne and Drôme.

The popular appeal of the Bonapartist heir was especially evident in Paris. A comparison of the vote for Raspail at this time with the number of votes he had gained in the supplementary election of September against Louis-Napoléon and of the vote for the latter with the combined totals for Raspail and Ledru-Rollin reveals the success of the Bonapartist appeal, and additionally the aversion for the moderate republican candidate, Cavaignac, amongst radicals. To some extent also the desertion of Raspail must indicate the feeling that, in a polarized conflict, a vote for him would have been wasted.

DECEMBER 1848 – PRESIDENTIAL ELECTION RESULTS IN PARIS[59]

Arrondissement	Votes for Louis-Napoléon	Votes for Cavaignac	Votes for Ledru-Rollin	Votes for[60] Raspail	
1	16,989	6,015	1,118	719	(3,115)
2	12,508	7,708	1,968	1,055	(4,610)
3	6,106	5,921	1,415	825	(3,230)
4	4,605	3,571	1,257	1,181	(3,491)
5	10,619	5,614	2,755	1,395	(6,608)
6	10,625	7,509	3,155	1,405	(5,948)
7	7,097	5,109	1,920	1,023	(4,912)
8	12,755	5,318	2,841	1,344	(6,258)
9	7,526	4,296	1,035	870	(2,825)
10	22,326	11,217	1,597	870	(3,318)
11	8,447	5,840	1,532	888	(3,472)
12	10,934	4,616	1,656	1,344	(5,364)
Banlieu	49,227	15,115	2,918	2,262	

The highest percentage support for Louis-Napoléon was precisely in the most popular quarters, although it is worth noting that the 10th arrondissement containing the Faubourg Saint-Germain, the most Legitimist area, also gave Bonaparte a higher percentage than the Parisian average, as if Legitimists in Paris were protesting against the pretensions of Republican government, and more especially its personnel. On the other hand its 30 per cent vote for Cavaignac was also substantially above the national average of 19·5 per cent.

In the provinces, regional support for Louis-Napoléon was least where the Legitimists had conserved greatest influence – in Brittany, Provence and Bas-Languedoc. Cavaignac won only four departments, in three of which – Bouches-du-Rhône, Morbihan and Finistère – Legitimist influence was dominant, and where in the other, the Var, it was strong. In other departments where he did relatively well – in Vaucluse (29 per cent of vote), Gard (36 per cent), Lozère (36 per cent), Hérault (25 per cent), Loire-Inférieure (38 per cent), Ille-et-Vilaine (33 per cent) and Côtes-du-Nord (32 per cent), Legitimist influence was also strong. This could represent a reaction against Legitimist notables who supported Louis-Napoléon but given the character of the society in these areas in which the rural population tended willingly to accept the lead of the notables this was unlikely. The survival of Legitimist authority in these areas had limited the appeal of the Napoleonic legend. Many Legitimist notables favoured Cavaignac as a proven guarantor of social order, and against a candidate behind whom stood former Orleanists, notably Thiers.

In general, Cavaignac was more successful in towns especially the larger, than in the country, that is in the urban areas where lived those social groups less influenced by the great notables, amongst the lower and middle middle classes. This can be seen in the 36 per cent support of the 3rd arrondissement of Paris, the 51 per cent of Le Havre, the 42 per cent gained in the Nord.[61] Usually however Cavaignac failed to win the support of the most socially influential figures, and given the existing structure and limited political experience of French society this doomed him to failure.

This was true of the other two candidates, Ledru-Rollin and Raspail. The latter had never been a nationally known figure and thus had little or no political importance outside Paris and Lyon, where a socialist appeal could be made to workers. In Lyon Raspail gained 8,695 votes compared with the 1,592 of Ledru-Rollin and the 43,573 of Bonaparte[62] who obviously was the most attractive candidate to the workers.

Ledru-Rollin was characterized by Marx as the candidate of the 'democratic petty bourgeoisie'[63] and given his radical position vis-à-vis the two principal candidates this might appear so. But it was Ledru-Rollin rather than the unknown Raspail who attracted the votes of politically conscious workers in most regions – at Nantes, in Toulouse, and generally in the Midi, in the Nord – the votes primarily of workers in artisanal production.

Ledru-Rollin was seen by most voters as the candidate of the extreme left. The total vote for him was of limited significance given the apparent promise of Louis-Napoléon and the feeling that in a polarized contest a vote for Ledru-Rollin was a wasted vote. In the expensive propaganda campaign, Ledru-Rollin could figure for very little. Yet the vote for him was a sign that a radical republican appeal could be made to diverse social groups. The rural vote was heavily in favour of Bonaparte, but in some areas with better communications, propaganda supporting Ledru-Rollin, appealing to the peasants' material interest had some effect. Certainly a vote for Ledru-Rollin indicated a higher degree of political consciousness in a worker or peasant than one for Louis-Napoléon.

Perhaps more significant than votes for Ledru-Rollin were the votes given to Louis-Napoléon in some regions, against the advice of the local notables, indicating a strong desire amongst rural populations to protest about the economic hardship they were enduring, a protest which could and would be expressed in other political forms. Thus rejection of the existing social hierarchy clearly occurred in the Alps, the south of the Paris Basin, and in departments of the centre such as Creuse and Puy-de-Dôme. Proudhon grasped this particular significance. He wrote of the peasant vote in relation to the Napoleonic tradition – 'This name, the peasant has known for a long time, it is almost a cult for him. Napoléon will be his saviour. Napoléon will free him from all the charges which weigh on him. . . . Then away with the priest! away with the notary! away with the seigneur! away with the master! away with the usurer! away with the rich! It can be said that today they are born to political life. Henceforward it is necessary to concern oneself with their condition, it is necessary to take them into account.'[64] In this respect then December 10 was 'the day of the peasant insurrection', or at least that of a minority of peasants.

For conservatives, including the majority of peasants in most areas, Louis-Napoléon's victory was seen as a rejection of the men of February. According to the *Journal des Débats*, '. . . what made the astounding success of M. Bonaparte, is the need for order and calm for which France today thirsts . . . it is the terror of France frightened by the men of February 24'.[65] Conservative political leaders had at least in Paris, the political centre, tended to unite against Cavaignac; the value of this alliance seemed proved not so much in the election of the individual Louis-Napoléon, but in the size of the majority for him, for the conservative principles which most men of wealth saw him as representing; a view confirmed by his dependence on the old political leaders seen in the selection of Odilon Barrot as President of the Council.

Economic conditions had anyway been improving but this election further increased business confidence and would be associated in future with the economic upturn.

Louis-Napoléon appeared as the elect of the whole nation, rather than of a party, indeed according to Proudhon 'France has named Louis Bonaparte President of the Republic because she is tired of parties. . . .'[66] This impression made it extremely difficult for Monarchists who had seen him as a means of transition to monarchy to return to their old conflicts. It would have seemed at least politically inept to have abandoned an apparently useful tool for social conservation. Thus according to Charles de Rémusat 'The spirit of the time, the force of opinion . . . does not leave to most of the men who today involve themselves in government more than the liberty to follow the current.'[67]

Apponyi warned concerning Louis Bonaparte 'if they believe themselves able to do anything with him and to dominate him, they are badly mistaken'.[68] For Rémusat, too, a man with some ability had been placed in a situation ideal for the use of this ability. Conservative political and social leadership had been partly resigned in return for the promise of social order contained in the election of a man who they were warned would be 'whether you wish it or not, king in opinion first, and later in reality. The logic of facts leads there. In a review some regiments will cry: *Vive l'Empéreur!* The suburbs will reply to them, and all will be said; we will be just like Spanish America, subordinate to the pleasures of the multitude and the soldiery. A glorious and fortunate destiny.'[69]

The Downfall of the Bourgeois Republic

'The period from 20 December 1848 until the dissolution of the Constituent Assembly, in May 1849, comprises the history of the downfall of the bourgeois republicans.'[1] It began with the republicans in the Assembly determined to defend republican institutions against a president who was himself a pretender to the throne of France and his government, composed almost entirely of men who supported the pretensions of two other pretenders. The majority of deputies and even of the republicans quickly and abjectly resigned their authority.

The life of the Assembly reflected changing social relationships in France. The election of Louis-Napoléon Bonaparte represented primarily the conservative urge of the vast majority of the population. In selecting the personnel necessary to form a government Bonaparte showed his awareness of this by turning to conservative leaders for advice, just as he had in the period of his election campaign. It was reported that still convinced of his insignificance men turned to Molé, and Thiers, in search of governmental appointments.[2] These leading conservative figures were too clearly identified with the past

225

to assume ministerial position themselves and persuaded Odilon Barrot to form Louis-Napoléon's first ministry.[3]

This ministry was a coalition of Orleanists and Legitimists, mainly the former, with a single moderate republican, and according to one of its members, the Vicomte de Falloux 'order was still, after, even as before the 10th December, its sole preoccupation'.[4]

Here was a combination of men drawn from a narrow social circle, of long personal acquaintance, well able to work together and present a united front against any attempts by Louis-Napoléon to interfere with the direction of policy. Their contempt for him was apparently too obvious, and in the first week of the government's existence he attempted to assert himself by demanding to see all despatches immediately they were received. His dependence on conservative politicians forced him to apologize for his temerity, but this was a hint of future conflict, as the President would increasingly evince his desire to assume personal control of government. In the meantime, whilst hoping to gradually strengthen his political position, Louis-Napoléon acceded to the government's policy of reaction and repression, partly escaping identification with this by pardoning individuals convicted of insurrection in June 1848, but accepting the government's refusal of a general amnesty.

Most republicans in the Constituent Assembly shared the government's desire for social order, but resented its hostility towards the ideals and personnel of the republic, and particularly its wholesale purge of the officials at all levels appointed since February 1848. The vote of December 10 indicated to republican deputies that they were out of touch with the feelings of most Frenchmen, and heralded a wholesale change of deputies through the legislative elections, whenever they might be. Relations between government and Assembly, the one representing the pre-revolutionary regime, the other the post-revolutionary could not therefore be easy. The policy of the government in alliance with the President would be to escape from the control of the Assembly.

This was regarded as especially important by the government because of the desire to ensure that the organic laws which would permit legal implementation of the provisions of the constitution were discussed and voted by an even more conservative Assembly. Conservative politicians therefore organized a campaign in the press and Assembly and through petitions which succeeded in further sapping the confidence of deputies to such an extent that by the end of January the Assembly was prepared to vote in favour of holding the election of a legislative assembly on May 19, thus setting a date for its own dissolution.

In the days immediately preceding this vote the Assembly had come under especially intense pressure. A government move for the urgent discussion of a measure designed to suppress the political clubs had been rejected, but instead of the resignation of the ministry which their interpretation of the constitution led them to expect, the President announced that it retained his confidence, ignoring the Assembly's vote.[5] Bonaparte was using this opportunity to make a declaration of ministerial responsibility to the President, to himself rather than to the Assembly, an important step in the move to personal government.

Faced with a government which neither asked for nor seemed to need its confidence the majority in the Assembly felt impotent. On January 29, deputies arriving at the Assembly to discuss the proposition that the date for the legislative elections be fixed found the building surrounded by troops. Changarnier, commanding in Paris, maintained that he had acted to protect the Assembly against an insurrection planned by the socialists and by members of the *Guard mobile* disaffected by the reduction of their privileges *vis-à-vis* the regular army – the attempt to discipline or else disband them. Conservatives certainly seem to have accepted the truth of this explanation[6] and discontent within the Guard was at fever pitch,[7] but whatever the reasons for Changarnier's actions,[8] the result was to frighten the republican deputies. They proceeded to vote in favour of the quick dissolution of their assembly.

The shipwreck of the moderate republican politicians was due to a mood of reaction against the results of the February Revolution evident both inside and outside the Assembly, with as part of this the increased assertiveness of the traditional socio-economic leaders. Their political authority had been tolerated, now tolerance was at an end.

The success of Louis-Napoléon in December had been greeted as a great conservative victory; confidence had been to some extent restored. In Paris and the provinces the old struggle for administrative positions, for power and influence, between competing groups of notables began again, a sure sign that the fear of revolution had declined, that unity was felt to be less necessary. Society was being restored. Apponyi could write of receptions at the Elysée that 'The salons of the prince at the last two concerts were so well composed, socially speaking, that the other day someone said in my ear, "I'll give you 100 francs for each republican you can show me in this room".'[9]

Yet a feeling of malaise remained. There was still fear of revolution. The exaggerations of electoral propaganda would heighten and spread this fear.

Pressures were then still felt which demanded unity amongst social conservatives, but the success with which the demands from national leaders for unity were met should not be exaggerated. The solidarity which the so-called party of order maintained was far greater than that attained by republicans yet the increased confidence of Legitimists gained from the restoration of their local social and thus national political significance in this period of crisis, when conservative peasants and workers looked to leadership from traditional authorities, resulted in some regions of the south and south-west in an exclusiveness directed at non-Legitimist conservatives as well as socialists.[10] In the department of Tarn-et-Garonne, for example, both Legitimists and Orleanists demanded three of the five candidatures in the election and when a compromise list was presented by the Committee of the Rue de Poiters, including only one Legitimist, these presented a separate list, with disastrous consequences in electoral terms.[11]

However in some vital respects conservatives seemed willing to accept Legitimist claims. More than ever liberal Orleanist principles were sacrificed by men who, feeling threatened, assumed some of the principles of that social group, the old landed aristocracy, whose traditions were most in contrast with the demands of the masses. This process of assimilation had long been under way and was increasingly more evident in conservative propaganda as this period of insecurity, the Second Republic, continued.

In terms of electoral organization, the usual loose structure of local committees, with some co-ordination by the Committee of the Rue de Poitiers in Paris, came into existence for the election of a legislative assembly. The strength of this organization lay not in its formal structure but in the support of those social groups most influential in society, possessing the most prestige and material resources, and supported by the vast mass of people who were frightened by change, who could not visualize society in terms other than those they already knew.

Conservative notables, dominating the electoral committees, thus selected candidates from among their own numbers, choosing men who were often relatively new figures, or had retained their prestige and sometimes leading their lists of candidates with a republican indicating both the continued popularity of this regime for some, or else the inability to agree on any alternative, or unwillingness to risk the disorder any attempt to impose an alternative might involve. Rémusat wrote that 'Many of us did not do with a good heart that which they did from reason. This republic which they upheld, they could not speak of other than in mocking tones. . . .'[12]

Superior financial resources permitted the diffusion of large numbers of pamphlets designed for the masses or else for the educated middle classes. Most of these were mediocre and had little effect, the mood was anyway for reaction. Almost all affirmed their loyalty to the Republic, the exceptions being some extreme Legitimists concerned to illustrate the path of human decline since 1789 by reference to a whole series of economic and political crises and present a solution based on Christianity and monarchy, on moral order which disciplined the human pride which unsettled social relationships.[13]

Generally though the work of the Provisional Government and Constituent Assembly was condemned. They were blamed for the social agitation, the economic crisis, the 45 centimes tax, the June insurrection. This propaganda was determined to paint radicals and socialists as immoral anarchists to create an image of them to frighten the population. It warned the masses against the false promises of radical propaganda. 'Socialism is Famine' was the title of one pamphlet.[14]

The existing form of society was presented as God-given. In it wealth was simply a reward for ability and hard work. It was often asserted that the wealthy should adopt a paternalistic attitude towards the less fortunate or less able members of the community but even where individual men of wealth lacked this social conscience they still by their demand for the products of labour, even by their caprices, provided employment for the poor.

Fear was also expressed, fear of radical republican political organization and propaganda amongst the lower middle classes, peasantry and workers.[15] The antidotes to this were the Church and army, indeed who would question 'the close relationship which exists between these two religions, sisters through sacrifice, of the cross and the flag? between the priest and the soldier, between the barracks and the convent, between the camp and the monastery'.[16]

In this campaign the Bonapartists were 'not a serious faction'.[17] Only in the Seine-et-Oise, Seine-et-Marne, and Eure-et-Loire did Bonapartists actively oppose the local leaders of the Party of Order by appealing to the rural masses. Bonapartist propagandists occasionally attacked the chaos of squabbling parties,[18] but generally all conservatives were able to associate themselves with the President of the Republic, to identify themselves with the person and his prestige.[19]

Pressures of various sorts were as usual exerted on voters. In Calvados a newspaper complained of the weavers that 'in the elections they do as their masters command, and as their vote is the same as any other vote, universal suffrage becomes a lie.'[20] Complaints were common of the distribution of voting papers in workshops, and pressure from foremen. The economic power of the dominant social groups obviously gave them enormous power through influence or else, and more rarely, overt pressures.

The agents of the government were also active. In addition to the continued purge of republican officials, and of municipalities, radical and socialist propaganda and organization were constantly hindered. As early as January 29 *Solidarité républicaine* was banned, whereas groups whose avowed aim was the overthrow of the republic in favour of Henri v or Louis-Napoléon were tolerated.[21]

The Ministry of the Interior did not openly back candidates in spite of the fact that Prefects pestered it to do so, but did recommend that these Prefects advise local voters, as the latter would indeed expect them to, especially in the choice of candidates,[22] and through minor officials on a more mundane level. A circular from the Prefect of the Rhône to mayors of 10 May 1849 recommended the support of those candidates who were opposed to 'doctrines destructive of society' and promised that if this were done then order would be re-established and prosperity return. It further warned that if the Assembly found itself composed 'of those ardent men who dream of the return of the regime of 1793 and proclaim doctrines contrary to property, to the family and to religion, agitation and disorder will reappear, commerce and industry will be paralyzed … agriculture suffer, and the people borne down by new taxes, will languish in misery'.[23]

There is little that is ambiguous in this. In terms of effectiveness, it was in the more isolated and backward areas that pressure and influence of all sorts would enjoy most success.

Associated with this conservative propaganda for social order, and indeed present on some of the conservative lists of electoral candidates were some moderate republicans. At their most adventurous in these months moderate republican declarations opposed excessive repression, illustrated by a decree restricting the right of association, but then equivocated about the means to oppose such measures, concluding that only strictly legal opposition was justified.[24]

The election of Louis-Napoléon had been a great shock to moderate republicans. They had lost all sense of initiative, were clearly conscious of their own decline. They could at this time appeal only to the fears of a monarchist restoration on the one hand, and of revolutionary violence on the other, could only offer a policy of the lesser evil which in an atmosphere of excited political declamation had little appeal.

The struggle was then essentially between the two extremes, with the majority of moderates assuming a conservative position.

The creation of a radical-socialist alliance has already been observed, as has been the new orientation of the propaganda of the left towards the countryside. This electoral campaign early in 1849 resulted in an intensification of these existing trends. The passions and conflicts which the campaign provoked resulted in a ferment of ideas and in an important awakening of the socio-political consciousness of significant social groups.

Socialist and radical republicans were able to agree on basic elements of policy, such as the need for a guaranteed right to work, free and obligatory education, and an appeal to the peasantry, and moreover government repression and increased conservative assertiveness made collaboration seem necessary. A banquet in Paris on 24 February 1849 celebrated the first anniversary of the revolution with the confirmation by its participants of a working alliance, and subsequently declared support for six propositions presented by a *Comité démocrate-socialiste de Paris*, acceptance of which should be necessary for election candidates to enjoy its support.[25] Agreement on the left was made easier by the absence of extremists like Blanqui, imprisoned after May and June.

At this stage in the political development of France a tightly-organized mass political party seemed technically impossible, but local and departmental committees were created for electoral purposes and these tended to follow the lead given by the Parisian committee and seek its aid in securing propaganda material. Other large cities performed similar functions. In Lyon, also, radical republicans and socialists negotiated in February a common programme.[26]

The pattern followed at the departmental level tended to a greater or lesser extent, to follow that described by Georges Dupeux for the Loir-et-Cher, with an organizing committee in the main town Blois composed mainly of members of the liberal professions, and in close contact with Paris. This produced a newspaper, selected election candidates and organized the electoral campaign. In the countryside it enjoyed the support of some of the local notables – doctors, lawyers and justices of the peace and in the villages that of shopkeepers and artisans and most significantly of innkeepers. The directing cadres at this level were then essentially members of the liberal professions, with other lower middle class elements playing an important subsidiary role.

The lists of candidates created by these middle class committees varied between departments, according to the strength of the various shades of opinion which the committees represented. In Haute-Garonne, for example, the list included, almost exclusively, declared supporters of Ledru-Rollin, and his radical brand of republicanism, with one socialist, and no moderate republican – similarly in the Ariège.

In Tarn-et-Garonne, by contrast, moderate republicans were included.[27]

Other elements in this organizational pattern were the clubs and secret societies, the latter according to the reports of the administration were spreading like wildfire across France as repression forced political clubs underground.[28] According to the Prefect of the Rhône – 'The leaders are in Paris. The affiliates at Lyon receive their instructions from the capital and must hold themselves ready to act at the first signal . . .'[29] The leaders in many cases being deputies in the Constituent Assembly, ideally suited to link Paris with the localities which elected them. Even allowing for the usual exaggerations by officials, this was certainly a period of intense organizational acitivity.

In the urban sphere *démocrate-socialiste* propaganda promised essentially two things, free, obligatory, secular education, and 'the right to work . . . the first of all rights . . . the right to live' in attacking 'the harshest of tyrannies . . . that of capital',[30] and connected with this, legislation limiting working hours, nationalizing railways, canals, mines, insurance companies and banks, and imposing progressive taxation. One element of this appeal was to the lower middle classes, the small producers and shopkeepers, even those living off the proceeds of small investments, against the monopoly of those 'who render dangerous and difficult the ownership of small capital', against 'financial feudalism' and especially 'the great banks of Paris'.[31] In sum, then, this was an appeal to the small against the big. Proudhon phrased the *démocrate-socialiste* promise as being '. . . Family, work, property, without usury and without abuse, in other words, free credit, identity of the worker and the capitalist, inheritance of rights, not privileges',[32] reflecting the widespread desire to spread the ownership of small property as a means to individual freedom. According to Marx, to create and maintain this alliance 'From the social demands of the proletariat the revolutionary point was broken off and a democratic turn given to them; from the democratic claims of the petty bourgeoisie the purely political form was stripped off and their socialist point thrust forward.'[33]

In the towns in spite of continual administrative and police repression and obstruction, radical newspapers, brochures, leaflets and lithographs were spread and as Alphonse Audiganne reported of Lille – 'In general, politics had the tavern for its theatre; the masters of opinion were the tavern keepers. They chose their newspaper and commented on it as they wished. Although the workers of the town almost all knew how to read, they read polemic rarely and are content with the commentary that is made for them. The newspapers read in taverns almost all were of the radical opinion.'[34]

In the countryside also repression did not prevent a vast increase in *démocrate-socialiste* propaganda, indeed the two combined to maintain a continual agitation and numerous incidents, permitting a heightening of political consciousness. Particularly in the regions of most economic distress (and in this period economic crisis was making itself felt in the countryside rather than the towns) an appeal which promised reductions of taxes, and cheap credit, promises which if kept would ease some of the major problems of the small holding peasant might enjoy some substantial success. In the struggle to make the most appealing promises these radical republicans and socialists were often driven to relatively extreme lengths in order to create a more attractive image for themselves than conservatives, who often made similar promises. In some areas *démocrate-socialistes* acting independently even encouraged resistance to tax-collectors, especially those collecting the supplementary tax of 45 centimes. This was a sure method of associating themselves with the peasant.[35]

It was in this period, according to Marx, that 'A considerable part of the peasants and of the provinces was revolutionized. Not only were they disappointed in Napoléon, but the Red party offered them, instead of the name, the content, instead of the illusory freedom from taxation, repayment of the milliard paid to the Legitimists, the adjustment of mortgages and the abolition of usury.'[36] This to a large extent was true, but one needs to be aware of the character of this revolutionizing.

First, as the election results would reveal, it had limited geographical appeal. Secondly, the revolutionary content of the appeal was also limited. The agents of the radical republican and socialist alliance in the provinces were essentially members of the lower middle class or professional men, or else migrant workers with experience of the life and ideas of the major cities. These were only interested, by and large, in limited social reform. They possessed some sort of a vested interest in the existing society, whether this be due to some official position, the ownership of a small business, or in the case of many migrant workers, the desire to own eventually a small piece of land. 'There was a fundamental desire, in a rural society to acquire land as the only means of acquiring status and economic security.'[37] Their political aim was to secure their economic and social position; the ambitions of the voters they appealed to tended to be similar. Consequently even the most extreme socialist propagandists carefully denied any desire to threaten basic elements of the existing society. Property was simply to be made more easy to attain.

Propaganda directed at the army was also intensified, with the electoral campaign providing the excuse and opportunity for an effort regarded as essential if the power of the ruling social groups was to be broken. An appeal was made to the interests of the soldiers, with promises of shorter terms of service, abolition of the right to purchase replacements, easier promotion from the ranks and better pensions for retired soldiers. An attempt was made to prove to the soldiers that their officers were simply using them as instruments for their own ends. The soldier was a child of the people, and should serve to liberate them, and not permit himself to be used as part of a police force.[38]

The *procureur général* at Nancy complained that 'the men of disorder and anarchy at this moment devote all their efforts to attacking the army.'[39] According to Castellane 'They throw pamphlets and newspapers into the barracks, they distribute them in the taverns . . . frequented by soldiers.'[40]

This activity, together with the continued effects of the period immediately succeeding the February Revolution made the complete restoration of discipline difficult. At Le Havre soldiers of the Sixty-Ninth Infantry Regiment attempted to provoke a riot to free some of their comrades arrested for distributing socialist propaganda.[41] Castellane, usually well informed, constantly complained of such incidences of indiscipline, and on May 6 plaintively wrote concerning the soldiers of the French army – 'Three-quarters vote without knowing why, obtaining ballot papers from taverns or the hands of non-commissioned officers. The officers do not interfere; if they tried to, the soldiers to show their independence, would vote contrary to their indications. It will no longer be possible to have an army, if it continues to vote; it will debate, and a debating army is no longer one. . . .'[42]

A prediction of triumph made in the *Peuple* of March 4, seemed justified. With glee conservatives were told that 'The army escapes you, you feel it slipping between your hands . . .'

There is some difficulty in accurately determining the results of the election given the lack of party structure, although compared with the first election under universal suffrage there were far more clearly differentiated shades of opinion in the lists of candidates. Often, however, moderate republicans in particular appeared as candidates on more than one list.

It seems to be generally agreed that in the new Assembly sat 75–80 moderate republicans, about 500 other conservatives, including approximately 200 Legitimists, and about 180 radical republicans and socialists, with a more committed core of about 130.

Left wing republicans gained 2,357,900 votes, 23·7 per cent of those eligible to vote, but 34·8 per cent of votes cast; the size of the abstention indicating an increasing lack of interest in political argument, the moderate republicans only about 800,000, a figure which taken with their strength in the Assembly reveals the scale of their decline. Ledru-Rollin who personified radical republicanism himself gained 720,430 votes in multiple elections. Marx correctly emphasizes this decline of the centre, of moderate republican strength, and the polarization of the parliamentary scene which had occurred. His estimate of 'more than two hundred' *démocrate-socialiste* deputies is that of contemporary conservative opinion, and historians agree that over two hundred deputies accepted this label for electoral purposes, with the far smaller number quoted above including only those clearly revealed by their voting behaviour in the Assembly as belonging to the 'Montagne'.[43]

More revealing was the social composition of the Assembly, it too indicated a polarization. The number of *grands notables* in the Assembly was greatly increased, whilst the middle middle class elements typical of moderate republicanism were greatly reduced. This reflected a situation described by Georges Dupeux as occurring in the Loir-et-Cher but more generally true, in which the further from the left one moves the wealthier become the deputies.[44] The election of so many figures representative of the traditional social hierarchy revealed their continued influence on the masses, but it remained true that more than ever before, political ideas had assumed an importance in the electoral campaign at the expense of personal significance. For the future the social polarization of the Assembly with its minority of petty bourgeois and majority of *grands notables* would mean the likelihood of a continued conflict of interests.

Of the 211 deputies initially accepting the *démocrate-socialiste* label 76 were members of the legal professions, 25 were doctors, 13 journalists, 13 teachers or writers, 19 were involved in agriculture, 19 in commerce and industry, 11 were workers, 11 soldiers or retired soldiers, 9 officials, and 7 mayors.[45] These were largely local personalities of the lower and middle middle classes. Men with close contacts with the masses, who claimed to understand and even share their problems and who, as local personalities, had earned their respect.

The conservative majority was socially far more cohesive, consisting almost entirely of *grands notables*. The north, and Normandy had elected men of commerce and industry, the west, south-west, the Comtat and Languedoc essentially Legitimist nobles and Catholic clergy. If Champagne, the south-west of the Paris Basin and the Charentes had elected some Bonapartists most, though not all of these, also belonged socially with the mass of conservatives.

This reaffirmation of the social power of the *grands notables* occurred because most of the population of France was either politically ignorant and willing to follow the lead set by leading local personalities, or by government officials, or else was consciously voting for the *status quo*.

This support had to a significant extent a regional basis in a large number of departments which seemed scarcely touched by democratic ideas – those of the north, north-east and west.

A. J. Tudesq has revealed the following pattern. In the ten departments of the north and Normandy, with the exception of six *démo-*

crate-socialistes in the department of the Nord, conservatives declaring their support for the Party of Order won all the seats (122). In this area the conservative ability to adapt to the needs of universal suffrage by creating an effective political alliance was particularly noticeable.

In the west, that is the five Breton departments plus Mayenne, Maine-et-Loire and Vendée, the eighty-six deputies were all supported by the Party of Order. Above all the resurgence of Legitimist and Catholic dominance was evident. Universal suffrage had merely served to reinforce the influence of traditional authority.

Further south, in the eight departments stretching from the Indre-et-Loire to the Gironde 58 of the 68 deputies elected were adherents of the Party of Order.

These were the most clearly conservative areas. In the south of the Paris Basin and the middle valley of the Loire Tudesq emphasizes the failure of conservatives to achieve a stable political alliance. This same weakening factor was evident also in the Midi, and in this area the Party of Order tended where successful to be represented exclusively by Legitimists or candidates supported by them – in Tarn-et-Garonne, Var, Vaucluse, Bouches-du-Rhône, and Gard, for example. In the rest of France, save for isolated instances like Basses-Pyrénées where a conservative alliance was created, and similarly in Gers, social dominance appeared lost to the notables.[46]

In general the areas where agriculture was more prosperous, the France of wheat cultivation and of relatively large-scale agriculture, seems to have voted conservative. Thus the north and the Paris Basin, the latter in spite of, or rather partly because of its proximity to Paris and the threat to property which Paris had appeared to present in 1848. Prosperous large-scale farmers, and hard-headed peasant proprietors dominated the social scene.

Conservative additionally were those areas which geographical isolation excluded from economic change and new ideas, where the existing social hierarchy and respect for the Church were preserved.

Elsewhere religious factors were significant where large Protestant communities existed, and had appeared as a continual challenge to Catholicism. In Nîmes Catholic workers voted conservative against Protestant employers, who were to some extent politically radical out of opposition to the views of the Catholic hierarchy. Everywhere however former moderate republicans moved to the right.

In spite of obvious elements of congruity it is not possible to establish a narrow relation between the political power of the notables and economic structure. The example of Nîmes indicates this, the rejection of conservative authority in departments like the Cher and Dordogne reinforces the point. However the generalizations made have some suggestive value, and have a lesser degree of finality than those made by Marx. He in particular fails to recognize the continued divisions of conservatives especially important at a local level in permitting the development of the *démocrate-socialiste* movement.

Only 70-75 moderate republicans were elected and most of them owed this to inclusion on the electoral list of a coalition of opinions, usually, as in the Jura, or Pyrénées-Orientales, that dominated by the *démocrate-socialistes* but elsewhere as in the Midi or north on more conservative lists, in the Var and Aveyron, for example, the lists dominated by Legitimists. Their candidates thus had varying significance depending upon the character of the list on which they appeared. Generally, however, with its 'half-and-half nature'[47] moderate republicanism was too democratic for the socially conservative and too moderate for those who wanted change. In a situation where political conflict tended to be between extremes it gained little support. Now that the threat to property appeared reduced the lower middle class was again more concerned with social reform than social order. The reluctance of the largely lower middle class National Guards in Paris to perform their duties was symptomatic of this.[48]

The shock result of the election was the degree of success of the *démocrate-socialiste* alliance. A 'red France' was revealed. In three areas the *démocrate-socialistes* gained over 40 per cent of the votes, with 154 seats of 196. These were the centre, the west and north of the Massif Central; the valleys of the Saône and Rhône and neighbouring areas, and the departments of Alsace. Whilst in the departments bordering the Mediterranean, in the Midi, Aquitain and the Pyrénées, and in the department of the Nord, between 30-40 per cent of the votes were gained with 41 of 170 seats.

The radical republican and socialist alliance especially benefitted from the urban vote and it seems that in general the more concentrated the population then the more likely that this support would exist. In Paris the result of the election was a confused mixture of socialist, democratic and conservative deputies. In the department of the Seine 106,466 votes were for *démocrates-socialistes*, 106,800 for candidates of the Party of Order and 42,300 for moderate republicans, Paris alone giving 79,700 votes for the extreme left. These votes were cast primarily in the arrondissements of the east. Only the eighth, the Faubourg Saint-Antoine, gave over 50 per cent of its votes to the left, but the fifth, sixth, seventh, ninth and twelfth have between 45 and 50 per cent, far above the national average, and compared with the 20–25 per cent of the first arrondissement, that of the Champs-Elysées. In fact as Jacques Bouillon's map of voting behaviour indicates, support for the *démocrate-socialiste* list fades out from east to west, from the quarters of the workers, artisans and lower middle classes to those more middle and upper middle class in character.

The second city of France, Lyon, gave 68·1 per cent of its vote to *démocrate-socialiste* candidates, but in its working class quarters support was substantially greater – at La Croix-Rousse 81·7 per cent, at la Guillotière 80·5 per cent.

In the Nord there appeared a striking constrast between a conservative countryside and the urban areas, Lille for example giving 63·2 per cent of its votes for a list headed by Ledru-Rollin. At Rouen the workers' Faubourgs of Graville and Sotteville gave majorities to the left, whilst the town as a whole only about one-third of its votes.[49]

The significance of the size of a town or village in partly determining its vote can be seen particularly where smaller provincial conglomerations are concerned. A certain size of population was required to give a village and its lower middle class in particular some independence of the authority or traditions of the countryside, and also to permit some sort of an intellectual life, a concern with ideas and the outside world.

This concern was especially evident where doctors, notaries, teachers, proprietors, inn-keepers etc., formed a small circle of republicans, and, given their local prominence, were able to exert a considerable influence on the urban and rural masses. The workers, artisans and small shopkeepers of the market towns and villages had often been part of the migratory labour force, often met travellers, and were relatively receptive to ideas promising a better society. Thus in the Aude most of the *démocrate-socialiste* vote was concentrated in the four largest towns – Carcassone, Limoux, Castelnaudary and Narbonne, and secondarily in smaller textile towns. The activity of lower middle class groups appears to have been particularly intense because of their continued political insignificance and economic problems, and the failure of moderate republicanism to improve their situation.

Again, however, there is a need to be aware of the limits to generalizations. To simply quote two examples. In the metallurgical and mining centres in the Gard, near Alès, geographical isolation was partly counteracted by the influx of workers influenced by life in major centres, this the case of metalworkers, whereas nearby mining communities with workers recruited from the locality, remained as conservative as the surrounding countryside.[50] At Nîmes, as has been observed, religious and social differences resulted in workers voting conservative. Most towns and villages, intimately linked to rural life continued on the conservative course to which there still appeared to be no real alternative. The vital radicalizing factor seems to have been this existence of lower middle class elements, themselves discontented with their social status, familiar with politics, locally respected, able and willing to act from personal ambition and human sympathy.

In the countryside at this time the economy had not recovered to the extent that it had in the towns. A large crop had resulted in a market glut and extremely low prices. The rural population was thus in large part discontented. In the Alpine region, as one example, the first quarter of 1849 was that of the highest number of expropriations of small landowners unable to pay their debts and taxes, in the period 1840–1856.[51] That which the peasant valued most, his land, was threatened.

The credibility of this view can be seen when it is compared with that expressed by the deputy of Bas-Rhin, Goldenberg, explaining the election result – 'in the election of the President of the Republic, these poor people voted as a single man for Napoléon because they hoped from him the re-establishment of the rights and usages in the forests, which they had enjoyed under the Emperor. Their hopes deceived in this respect, together with the promises made by the candidates of the opposed party to restore to them their rights in the forests, were the principle cause of the failure in the last election of the friends of the President'.[52]

It appears that the regions giving highest support to the *démocrate-socialistes* were likely to be some of those with poor soils and a relatively poor life aggravated by the continuing economic crisis. Here if the peasants were still in many respects indifferent to political questions, economic pressures impelled action. These were the areas where resistance to the collection of the 45 centimes and drink taxes had been most extensive. This in itself had resulted in a heightened feeling of collective interest, often expressed by a hostility towards the rich; misery and *démocrate-socialiste* propaganda had intensified the traditional hatred of the 'Jacques' against the 'Gros', and was serving to establish a definite challenge to the existing social hierarchy.

Démocrate-socialiste propaganda following essentially a line laid down at Paris promised reduced taxes, and cheap credit, in effect the safeguarding of existing possessions against expropriation, and an increased chance of buying land.[53] There were constant complaints in these first months of 1849 of a vast volume of propaganda being spread through the country. The propaganda process was revealed most clearly in activity based on Lyon, closer than Paris to the regions likely to be attracted by radical promises. The *procureur général* at Lyon blamed the *démocrate-socialiste* election successes in the Rhône, Ain and Loire on the influence of the press and secret societies of Lyon.[54] His colleague at Grenoble similarly explained the result in the Drôme.[55]

Other cities, and especially Marseille played similar functions in this process of the diffusion of ideas. Smaller urban centres like Bédarieux, Lodève and Béziers in the Hérault and Carcassonne in Gard served in a secondary position, linked to larger population centres and directly and effectively to the surrounding countryside. In many agricultural areas the influence of the population of small industrial towns was of great political significance.[56] The process was not quite so simple because a major population centre diffused not only radical, but also conservative ideas.[57] It remains true, however, that in certain areas the former had most appeal, and that the strength of the *démocrate-socialiste* appeal to the countryside depended in part on the degree of its success in local and regional urban centres.

The word was spread, we have seen, through books, brochures, pamphlets and newspapers and above all by word of mouth, by the influence of adepts, often men of some local prestige – the village petty bourgeoisie – challenging the local dominance of aristocrats and other bourgeois groups, also by the reading aloud of newpapers in cafés and bars, the barkeeper, adversely effected by the drink tax, being an extremely important figure in the *démocrate-socialiste* movement.[58]

The poor central and southern agricultural regions which composed in the main the areas of *démocrate-socialiste* strength were characterized by a number of other features. They were mainly regions with a high proportion of small plots of land, often cultivating the vine or olive. This gave the peasant a certain social independence, reinforced by the structure of the village, far less dispersed than in parts of the north and permitting easier social intercourse and awareness of common interest and new ideas. The existence of small plots additionally increased the hope of landless labourers that they might become owners. Where a large proportion of the land was held in the form of large estates, then the strength of resistance to the traditional social leaders was weakened, both numerically and because of the greater dispersal of smallowners, in terms of consciousness – thus in the plain of the Aude, or in most of the plains of the Alpine region, and northern France.

Besides the pattern of landholding, another significant factor in determining the success of the radical appeal must obviously have been the relative ease of communication. Ideas spread along normal communication routes and were accepted where poverty impressed the desire for change, where relatively high literacy increased awareness, where a general social structure encouraged receptivity. Thus not all areas of small property succumbed to the radical appeal. Neither were all geographically isolated areas immune. The seasonal character of much industrial and agricultural activity, particularly in the south contributed to the radicalizing of ideas in such areas as the Alps or the department of the Creuse. The *sous-préfect* at Bourganeuf reported in February 1849, that agitators were found especially amongst 'the migratory workers who bring from the big towns their subversive and badly understood doctrines'.[59] All in all there are so many variables involved in examining the question of receptivity to new ideas that even a hint of determinism is likely to be dangerously restrictive.

The *démocrate-socialiste* deputies although clearly in a minority in the new Assembly were enthusiastic about their success and probably exaggerated its significance. At any rate it was believed that important support had been gained from the army and the rural population,[60] and that conservative success was due to a large degree to ignorance and corruption which the developing process of the political education of the masses would reverse. In *L'Émancipation* of Haute-Garonne this feeling was clear – 'The Friends of Order miserably beaten in the main town, in the intelligent localities and in the military vote, succeeded thanks to the countryside. Misery, ignorance and credulity permitted the priests . . . the great proprietors, and the usurers . . . to rove again the justice of the phrase: "make the sheep electors, and hey will elect the butchers".'[61]

As the *démocrate-socialiste* reaction was optimistic in spite of everything, so the conservative reaction was pessimistic. Contemporaries were not surprised at the relative success of order, but the size of the *démocrate-socialiste* vote was a shock. The red spectre reappeared. De Tocqueville who had been in Germany noted 'I learnt of the elections and the unexpected success of the Reds. I returned in all haste. . . . Aspect of the country: exaggerated terror succeeding to an exaggerated confidence'.[62]

The political situation seemed suddenly less than promising. The election result was 'The brutal revelation of the extraordinary progress realized in some weeks by democratic ideas'.[63] Given that almost one-third of the electorate had abstained, conservative candidates had gained only a relative majority of potential voters, which compared unfavourably with Bonaparte's success and illustrated the growing attraction of *démocrate-socialiste* propaganda especially in the countryside, which augured ill for the next elections.

The localization of the *démocrate-socialiste* vote was additionally frightening, it revealed the existence of this 'red France'. Values on the Bourse fell. 'The panic is especially great in those of the provinces in which the Reds have been elected. Many instructions to sell have arrived; these contributed to the fall of 6 francs which took place today'.[64]

The vote of the army, or at least its supposed vote, especially struck contemporaries. Soldiers voted for the lists presented in their departments of origin and tended it appears to vote as their class of origin within this department and generally then conservative. But the military votes of Paris and Lyon were declared first, and these of course were more radical. Equally striking was the fact that in these cities three *démocrate-socialiste* non-commissioned officers could obtain more military votes than famous generals, like Cavaignac, Lamoricière and Bugeaud.

If Castellane, with his intimate knowledge of the army, could confidently conclude that however they voted soldiers would obey orders,[65] this was not representative of conservative feeling. Even normally well-informed official opinion shared the fear. The police chief at Lyon, Galerne, reported that 'The Army has succumbed. A few more days and the entire society will be no more than a mass of débris and ruins.'[66]

Terror was indeed universal amongst conservatives. Gustave de Beaumont believed that France was entering 'into a new period of violence and revolutionary attempts'.[67] Louis Veuillot maintained that 'No Parisian is able to say that he will not be this evening on or under the barricades.'[68]

Terror reinforced the desire for security and increased the price many were prepared to pay for this. The future key figure in Louis-Napoléon's coup, Morny, wrote on May 16 'It seems that the elections will not be as good as was expected. Socialism has made the most alarming strides. . . .' Only half in jest he suggested that soon 'there will be nothing left to do but to pack our things, get up a civil war and ask the Cossacks to come and help us!' and added that 'if you were to come into contact with the socialists you would infinitely prefer the Cossacks. There must be limits to one's patriotism!' In a more serious vein he claimed that 'The Empire is the only thing that can save the situation. Some of the principal politicians have been nibbling at the idea. . . .'[69]

More immediately though conservatives were to demand constitutional revision, including some sort of restriction of the suffrage,[70] and more simply unity in defence of society, which meant the defence of existing republican institutions, rather than the presentation of divisive monarchist claims.[71]

For Marx this election clarified the social and political situation by producing two orientations, one conservative and more than ever prepared to accept extreme solutions, the other democratic and socialist. This was the opinion of contemporaries like Barrot.[72] According to a modern historian, Paul Bastid, two extremes were in conflict without an intermediary, with their political differences reinforced by social antagonism.[73] The men of the centre, the moderates, had failed to satisfy either extreme or to break down the exaggerated picture each had of the other's aims. With the centre almost eliminated the effects of a basic lack of contact and understanding between social groups would become increasingly evident. The geographical concentration and relative clarity of purpose of the Legitimist conservatives which gave them an influence out of proportion with their numerical strength was an essential element in this.

An extremely important result of this election, and indeed of the whole period of the Republic up to this point was the development of the political consciousness of all social groups which constant propaganda implied. Universal suffrage demanded that this propaganda felt at all levels of society. The process is described by Marx – 'In this vortex of the movement, in this torment of historical unrest, in this dramatic ebb and flow of revolutionary passions, hopes and disappointments, the different classes of French society had to count their epochs of development in weeks where they had previously counted them in half centuries.'[74] He gives an exaggerated impression of the extent of this influence both in terms of the numbers effected and the clarity of consciousness achieved, but in many areas substantial numbers of poorer people were influenced by *démocrate-socialiste* propaganda and as later voting patterns indicate, were throughout the century to retain this radical affiliation.

Relative clarity of consciousness was evident primarily in urban areas, but in some rural areas also it was evident that the political opinions as well as the personalities and social prestige of candidates were increasing importance. In this respect, in, for example, the Alpine region a remarkable advance had been made in the year since the first elections held under universal suffrage. 'Who would have dared predict, only a month ago, the spectacle in which we have assisted? What a happy and unexpected change!' someone wrote in *La Constitution de* 1848 of Valence[75] just before the election day. The success of this radical propaganda revealed something of the extent of discontent in society, of the degree to which this was involving large numbers of people in protest action. This new consciousness of the masses, with the organization which contributed to its creation constituted a threat to conservatives. From their position of strength they could meet the threat by repression. Thus the conflict was further intensified.

VI

Towards its Demise

The Republic, May 1849 - December 1851

This was a period of continuous crisis. Although there was a limited recovery of industry and commerce, agriculture and the great mass of people dependent upon it remained in a bad condition.

On the political front the radical republicans in the Assembly, over-confident after the election, committed by their exaggerated speeches, were forced in June 1849, into a demonstration of protest against a breach of the Constitution. Its suppression heralded a more intense wave of anti-republican acts by the various ministries of Louis-Napoléon, including not only police and administrative repression but legislative measures designed to increase the role of the Church in education and thus cementing the renewed alliance of church and State, and also to restrict the suffrage.

Economic crisis maintained discontent and made possible in many areas the continued organization of *démocrate-socialiste* support. This preserved the conservative fear of social revolution. Whatever the divisions amongst conservative political leaders, whatever the strains, an alliance of convenience continued to exist. But unable to solve the problems of France themselves the members of this alliance were increasingly drawn towards acceptance of a Bonapartist solution. Honour made it difficult for them to desert old allegiances to the royal houses, but in practice they were less and less inclined to resist Louis-Napoléon's ambitions.

As soon as the newly elected Legislative Assembly sat it was evident that relations within it between conservatives and the *démocrate-socialiste* Montagne were tenuous; 'one breathed already the air of civil war. The speeches were brief, the gestures violent, the words excessive and the injuries outrageous and direct'.[1]

A precipitant of conflict already existed in the military expedition

246

which had been despatched to Italy in April with the blessings of the Constituent Assembly with the overt purpose of heading off Austrian intervention in the Papal States. Even Cavaignac had offered the Pope, exiled from a newly republican Rome, French protection.

Doubtless the declared motive of the expedition was partly the truth,[2] but towards the end of its life the Constituent Assembly had suspected that additionally it was intended to restore the illiberal papal regime, and voted that it be recalled to its original purpose. This vote was ignored by Louis-Napoléon anxious to create a favourable image in Catholic eyes. The Austrian Apponyi gained the impression in speaking to Falloux that the declared purpose of the expedition had become only a guise.[3] Given conservative notions of an international socialist conspiracy which meant that 'the defence of Rome is organized in Paris. . . . Oudinot will find again there those amnestied after June . . . and May 15'[4] then there was for them an especially strong case for military action at Rome.

Marx described the final assault on Rome as 'bait' thrown to the *démocrate-socialistes* to encourage them to take to the streets, which would permit their repression as a political and revolutionary threat.[5] He probably exaggerates the deliberateness with which the bait was offered. Nonetheless conservatives seemed anything but anxious to avoid conflict when it became possible. In the Assembly 'Ledru . . . told the majority that they belonged to the Party of Cossacks; they replied to him that he belonged to the party of pillagers and incendiaries'.[6]

Conservative opinion in contradiction to Marx would tend to see the events of June 13 as evidence of a widespread socialist plot, well organized and simply awaiting the excuse which the attack on Rome provided.[7] According to Falloux the Montagne 'thought this was a favourable opportunity for re-awakening the passions of Paris'.[8] Their democratic susceptibilities were offended by this French action, clearly unconstitutional, as de Tocqueville later admitted,[9] against a sister republic. Typically Victor Considérant would condemn 'This impious war of the mother Republic against the noble Roman Republic', adding that 'it is the democratic cause betrayed, the Revolution surrendered to the kings; it is a sacrilegious coalition, cemented with the blood of our brave soldiers, with the Austrians and the Cossacks, with the aristocrats, and the kings, against the Peoples'.[10]

Clearly some kind of action was demanded. Every statement ever made by the Montagne on international affairs, was a commitment.[11] Its particular interpretation of the election results, and of the growing indiscipline of the Parisian National Guard convinced it, as the *Révolution démocratique et sociale* of June 12 indicated that in Paris, in the Midi, and in the east, in the National Guard and army, it would enjoy considerable support for whatever action it decided upon.

An attempt to impeach the government failed on June 12, and Ledru-Rollin threatened to resort to force to defend the constitution, though 'hesitatingly and with visible repugnance'.[12] De Tocqueville observed the reluctance with which these Montagnard politicians, great boasters though they were, actually organized a demonstration. 'After having half drawn the sword, they appeared to want to sheath it but it was too late, the signal had been seen by their friends outside, and henceforward, they would not lead, they were led.'[13] The indecisive were forced to act and on June 13 a manifesto appeared signed by 120 deputies, although later to be disavowed by many of them.

A call to arms was issued and a peaceful, legal demonstration organized, further evidence of indecision and more so of an unwillingness to use violence. Considérant described the action of the left as 'pacific, constitutional and legal'.[14] For a contemptuous Marx it was typical of petty bourgeois half-heartedness.[15]

Whatever Ledru-Rollin and his supporters might hope, this was doomed to failure. Proudhon recognized the legality of the demonstration but condemned it as 'inopportune, politically inept, badly led'.[16]

Historians generally agree with Marx that this was 'the insurrection of the democratic petty bourgeoisie'.[17] But even their participation was disappointing to the demonstration's organizers.

As for the Parisian workers, their spirits remained crushed by the failure of the armed insurrection of the previous year. The printing worker, Bosson, remembered Ledru-Rollin's boasts concerning his role in the repression of the previous June.[18] In addition there was cholera, its effects most severely felt in the working class districts. These factors which Marx presents lend little support to his additional remark 'the proletariat maintained . . . (a) . . . sceptically watchful attitude, and awaited a seriously engaged irrevocable *mêlée* between the democratic National Guards and the army, in order then to lunge into the fight and push the revolution forward beyond the petty-bourgeois aim set for it.'[19] Marx here seems to have been engaged in wishful thinking. A closer observer, the worker and deputy Martin Nadaud, more honestly it seems, ascribed indifference to the people.[20]

The Montagne had hoped for mass desertions from the army following its presumed voting behaviour in May, but it showed no reluctance in obeying orders to disperse the demonstrators. The normal *esprit de corps* of the troops was presumably reinforced by the fact that these civilians were protesting against the action of comrades in front of Rome.[21]

Montagnard optimism was rapidly and shatteringly disabused. Scathingly, de Tocqueville commented that 'In June 1848, the leaders failed the army; in June 1849 the army the leaders'.[22] Compared with Marx's estimate of 30,000 demonstrators there seem in reality to have been between six thousand and eight thousand.[23] Seven deaths ensued indicating the brutality utilized in the dispersal of a peaceful demonstration. To the last the leaders of the movement maintained their half-heartedness and incompetence. Considérant describing the closing moments of the day's events at the Conservatoire des Arts at Métiers used as headquarters by the demonstration's organizers – 'The minutes went by. Nothing was done. There were discussions . . . comings and goings; not one decision, not one resolution taken in common . . . they continued to wait, and the National Guards . . . did not come.'[24]

In a large number of towns minor demonstrations occurred, which were seized upon by the authorities as conclusive proof of the widespread nature of socialist organization. Only at Lyon did violence erupt.

There eight barricades were constructed, 25 soldiers and 25 insurgents were killed, and large numbers arrested.[25] This rising and the demonstrations elsewhere,[26] when compared with the lesser degree of provincial support for the insurgents of June 1848 was indicative of the growing appeal of *démocrate-socialiste* propaganda.

The demonstrations of June 1849 were crushed and were followed by a new wave of repression, including a law directed against the clubs which succeeded essentially in exasperating republicans of all shades of opinion and in driving more of the opposition underground. More than ever the political situation was polarized. Those moderate republicans who had not already deserted the cause for that of social order were drawn towards their more extreme fellows in defence of the political institutions of the Republic.

In spite of the divisions and conflict of personalities amongst republicans and the initial discouragement produced by June 1849, organization was further developed, encouraged by the prevalence of mass discontent. This organization was both clandestine and open; the clandestine element based on cafés and bars, professional groupings, mutual aid societies and masonic lodges, the legal on banquets, the press and electoral campaigns, and additionally on various local phenomena such as in the Seine-et-Oise the traditional singing societies which the authorities did not dare forbid. Attention was especially paid to attempts to introduce links between local organizations and between them and Paris, where the most eminent *démocrate-socialiste* personalities remained the parliamentary deputies. This latter aspect especially frightened the authorities, whose reports are full of alarmist accounts of the spread of radical republican organizations like *Solidarité républicaine* and of preparations for insurrection. This is especially true of reports from the Midi and the east, and if the factual accuracy of these reports is often questionable they do give an idea of where the *démocrate-socialiste* appeal was greatest.[27]

In terms of local organization, leadership was still derived from the local notables. The importance of this personal influence in a society of limited education and political awareness must be stressed, as must the precarious character of organization dependent on a limited number of individuals. The press of the left began to build up a network of local correspondents, both to report local news and to distribute publications, which would be useful for later electoral purposes, and which increased the influence, already great in the movement, of journalists.

In organizational terms the *démocrate-socialistes* remained throughout the period of the Second Republic pivoted on the towns, with a major city as a central place from which influence spread to smaller centres, and these 'The small towns, the multitude of market towns scattered in the middle of the countryside became the ardent centres from which spread democratic ideas. In these small centres of population amongst people, half-urbanized, half-peasant, the democratic party had found its warmest supporters'.[28] With every election or insurrection the need to appeal to the rural population became more obvious and the effort to do so more intense.

Whatever the differences, personal and ideological within the republican and *démocrate-socialiste* movement, these had little effect at the local level to which a simple dualist appeal was made. The utopian socialism which had suffered a severe blow through the violence of the June days had not been replaced by a Marxian notion of class conflict, but by a return, if ever the discontented section of the rural population had left it, to the age-old conflict between the *Petits* and *Gros*, to simple ideas of greater equality.

Whilst the remaining moderate republicans assumed an ideological position once occupied by Ledru-Rollin, and demanded unity against 'The aristocracy of money',[29] the *démocrate-socialistes* now more deliberately appealed to the *Petits*, more clearly attacked the *status quo*.

Usury was condemned, tax reductions and cheap credit promised. The *Song of the Vine-growers* written for the campaign preceding the supplementary elections of March 10, 1850 went as follows:

> *Good villagers, vote for the Montagne,*
> *There is the hope of poor vine-growers,*
> *For with it, good countrymen*
> *Will disappear the taxes on drinks.*
> *In the hamlets, agricultural banks*
> *Will be expecially for you, good peasants,*
> *Without charge also you will have schools*
> *And money at most at three per cent.*[30]

In the supplementary elections of March 10, designed to replace deputies arrested after June 13 twenty-one republicans were elected in thirty-one contests, in spite of intense government activity against them. Especially frightening for conservatives was the election in Paris of three republicans – Flotte implicated in the rising of June 1848, Vidal, an associate of Louis Blanc, and Carnot, a moderate, but still too republican, quite clearly with the support of the arrondissements of the centre and east, those inhabited primarily by workers, artisans and members of the lower middle classes. The selection of these three symbolized for Marx and other contemporaries the new alliance in defence of the republic; the moderate republicans of the Loir-et-Cher declaring themselves for a *démocrate-socialiste* election candidate, announced an alliance with all other republicans against 'the Jesuitical union of nobles, Philippists and reactionary priests'.[31] For some at least of the more prosperous members of the middle classes, political considerations outweighed at this moment those of social stability. They united with socialists against monarchy, clericalism and excessive repression.

The main explanation of the development of the *démocrate-socialiste* position in 1849–1851 rests as Marx suggests in the economic conditions of the period.

Industrial and commercial activity in the towns increased and unemployed workers were to some extent protected by the activity of municipal authorities. The towns benefitted also from cheap agricultural products symptomatic of the crisis of low prices affecting the countryside after good crops.

The general picture is of a persistence of depression felt less severely in the towns, although even here some groups such as building and metallurgical workers were still adversely affected, the former by a lack of capital for construction and the latter by the very slow upturn of investment in railway construction.

In the countryside, however, most social groups and most regions suffered. The building workers and artisans of the small towns and villages were faced with the continued low purchasing power of those dependent on the profits of agriculture. They were consequently interested in the promises of *démocrate-socialiste* representatives and helped spread its ideas through the surrounding countryside, with some success, where the regional social structure favoured this.

The level of discontent in many areas certainly favoured a radical politics. Continued devastation of forests was one sign of unrest.[32] According to the Prefect of the Drôme, writing in August 1849, in the past 'all the small proprietors have wanted to buy [land]'; and as a result 'I do not believe to exaggerate in saying that of 10 proprietors, 7 are in debt'.[33] Again many farmers found it impossible to pay their rents and converted to sharecropping, many small owners to pay the interest on loans. Usurious rates reached new heights, varying in the Alpine region according to Vigier, between 5 per cent and 50 per cent according to the need and degree of security provided by the borrower. In the same region the number of seizures for non-payment of debts was higher than ever before in 1849 and remained high in 1850.[34]

The rural population reacted against this economic pressure and against those who seemed to be benefitting from their misery. Ferlay, the Prefect of the Drôme, in December 1849, commented on this discontent and the political use made of it. 'The bourgeoisie having sold land and become the creditor of the peasants, the demolishers have made the bourgeois suspect to the peasants, because they tell these latter that the bourgeois is opposed to the peasant freeing himself [from debt] so as to be able to hold him in some sort of serfdom'.[35] Thus social hostilities were intensified. The general commanding the tenth Military Division reported on the large number of fires deliberately caused in his area – 'It should be noticed that such offences are multiplying in the countryside and almost always to the prejudice of rich and prosperous people'.[36]

For Marx 'March 10 was a revolution'. This because it clearly revealed the continued activity of the left and because of the fright it gave to conservatives, a fright which led to an intensification of repression, to the 'legislative dictatorship of the united royalists'.[37] Not only had the conservative majority in the Assembly allowed the thirty-four deputies most clearly implicated in the demonstration of June 13 to be arrested but by a new law on clubs permitted their closure, and restricted public meetings generally; by an extension of existing press legislation made it a crime to express disrespect of the law, to incite soldiers to disobedience, to print false news; and licensed pedlars of printed materials, books and engravings. The government in a circular made even the cry of *Vive la République sociale!'* seditious, and by the summary closure of republican newspapers, expressed its will to crush all opposition.

Even these measures were regarded as inadequate by many conservatives both inside and outside the Assembly. The forcibly retired Général de Castellane bitterly complained of the weakness of the Government – 'It is not with speeches that one contains a country in revolution.'[38] The demand for strong government was being reasserted.

The major legislative achievement of this Assembly, was a law on education finally introduced in March 1850, normally known as the *loi Falloux* after one of its original movers, described rather bitterly by Marx as a law 'by which the party of Order proclaimed the unconsciousness and the forcible stupefaction of France as the condition of its life under the regime of universal suffrage'.[39]

An extra-parliamentary committee met as early as January 1849, presided over by Falloux as the then Minister of Public Instruction, and by Thiers in his absence, the latter undoubtedly the most energetic proponent of the new legislation.[40]

Thiers had written on 2 May 1848, 'Today when all social ideas are perverted, and when we appoint in each village a schoolteacher who will be a Phalansterian, I regard the priest as an indispensable rectification for the ideas of the people; he will teach them at least in the

253

name of Christ, that suffering is necessary in all estates, that it is the condition of life, and that, when the poor have a fever, it is not the rich who have sent it to them.'[41]

Conservatives were afraid of education as creator of social unrest. Montalembert, referred to the lay schoolteachers as 'The demoralizing and anarchic army'.[42] De Castellane believed that of 60,000 lay teachers two-thirds were socialists, 'They are given too much education for what they have to teach; thus they become discontented, finding themselves in a position beneath that which they deserve and are always in rivalry with the priest'.[43]

The basic intent of any legislation as M. Michel, a member of the committee, favourably quoted by Falloux, put it, was 'To aspire to train a child to the yoke of discipline and obedience, to create in him a principle of energy which will enable him to resist his passions, accept of his own free will the law of labour and duty and contract habits of order and regularity. . . .'[44] What was required from the poor was deference and the disciplined labour so essential in the emerging factory economy.

This was however the design solely for the system of primary education which served the masses. 'Whereas the masses have need of imposed truths and faith must be their only philosophy' claimed Thiers, the ruling classes 'wishing, as a right, free philosophical discussion', were 'sufficiently protected by their education against the bad passions'.[45] The Church in this sphere was to be permitted to extend its activities but examinations were to be controlled by the state, and the existing liberal and classical education preserved.

The people 'has more need of morality than knowledge. To read, to write, to count, that is what it is necessary to learn; as for the rest, that is superfluous'.[46] The essential need according to Victor Cousin was 'That the priest supervises all parts of education, and not only the teaching of the catechism, for in teaching them to read one is able to give bad doctrines to the children. . . . The school master must learn to bend and submit to the priest . . . [and] . . . to the mayor, who must be the two great authorities appointed to supervise the school'.[47]

Where the law proposed previously by the moderate republican Minister Carnot, and withdrawn by Falloux, had favoured free and obligatory education to the age of 14, better salaries, promotion prospects and the introduction of pensions for schoolteachers and would have required certificates of aptitude providing a guarantee of competence from teachers in private schools, including priests,[48] this law proceeded on the premise put by Thiers that 'The school is a luxury', that it is 'a beginning of affluence and . . . affluence is not reserved for all'.[49] It did however do something to improve the economic position of schoolteachers, if only to reduce their discontent.[50] Otherwise it provided for the continued surveillance of the lay schoolteacher by local, arrondissement and departmental committees, in which the clergy was to play a significant role, as it was from now, in the Council of the Université which remained as the central body of the French educational system. The parish clergy was to perform the function of watchdog for the prefect. Veuillot commented that what Thiers wanted was 'a corps of gendarmes in cassocks'.[51] The Church was to be encouraged to extend its own network of schools by a relaxation of the rules on requisite qualifications for teachers.

Charles Seignebos described this law as a 'political measure for the defence of society against revolution'.[52] The accuracy of this is confirmed by the whole tenor of the discussion of the law's proposals. Falloux wrote that 'the members of the Committee came to an immediate agreement upon the two essential points, the existence of social peril and the urgent need of opposing some remedy to it'.[53]

The support for this measure was indicative of its purpose. Ozanam sarcastically commented that 'there is today no Voltairean afflicted with some thousand pounds of income who does not want to send everyone to mass, on condition of not having to set foot there himself'.[54] In this respect Thiers denied all charges of apostasy by claiming to be simply defending the values of society and government he had always maintained.[55] Apponyi recorded a conversation in which an acquaintance told him that amongst Orleanists imbued with rationalist and Voltairean ideas there was occurring 'a real return to religious ideas'.[56] Personal reassurance was perhaps required as well as social order in this period when all values seemed to be under assault. The religiously more committed, including most Legitimists, believed in this law not only as a means of social preservation but as a means for the teaching of truth and many resented the restrictions on the Church's freedom of activity which remained.

Republicans could unite in opposition to this repressive design. Hugo in moderate terms, favouring religious education, warned that conservative and clerical domination of education would hinder the progress of mankind.[57] An editorial in the *Réforme* saw the clericalism

255

which the law implied as 'Radically incompatible with free consciousness, free thought, it implies the absolute obedience of the spirit, in
enchaining . . . all the intellectual and moral powers, and with them,
if possible, all real action of the faculties which characterize the
human being, it makes slavery descend even to the depths of the
soul'.[58] The more extreme, like Proudhon, saw the creation of an
oppressive trinity of Capital, State and Church, and the more
practical a dangerous restriction on their action to awaken the political
consciousness of the masses.[59]

The whole concept of this law was based on a number of miscon-
ceptions which are as revealing of French society as the ideas brought
forward in support of the law were revealing of the attitudes of
particular groups within this society.

First, that educative action by the clergy on the masses would be
efficacious. The clergy, however, simply did not understand the
changes occurring in society, was ignorant of problems consequent
upon structural change and with regard to itself was imbued with a
fatal inability to engage in self-criticism. This resulted in a growing
lack of understanding of and insufficient sympathy towards the urban
and rural masses. These were judged and perhaps condemned on the
basis of their attitudes towards the Church. The first duty of the
priest seems to have been seen as sheltering his flock from con-
tamination. This was conducive to the creation of a ghetto mentality
rather than missionary zeal. The education which intending priests
generally received contributed to this. One manual on the education
of intending priests advised that above all they needed to be taught
faith, to be led to believe in the insignificance of man, and of life in
this world as compared with eternity. They should be aware of the
justice of God, and the punishments this involved for sinners in this
world and the next.[60] This morality was indeed the conservative ideal
the propagation of which the *loi Falloux* demanded, but a moral
outlook which led the clergy to maintain that 'we must reject this
stupid and violent equality dreamt of by evil or insane levellers:
God does not hate the society He has made, with its ranks, its
hierarchy, its precedences',[61] could gain them little sympathy from
those at the foot of the hierarchical ladder, especially as new ideas
spread. Alphonse Audiganne reporting on the contempt of the
workers at Lyon for the clergy claimed this existed because they felt
that 'the teaching given from the pulpit has no other aim than to
render them more docile under the yoke'.[62]

Whatever this may be the clergy at all levels largely pursued a conservative policy. Of the Drôme it was reported that only three of five hundred Catholic priests could be identified as socialists,[63] and this represents a fair assessment of the Church's sympathies more generally. Social change it was felt, with the experience of the first revolution in mind, boded ill for the Church.

As far as their educational activity went this appeared to flourish in the succeeding years. By 1863 one quarter, as compared with one fifth in 1850, of boys were taught by the clergy.[64] Municipalities were able to choose whether to employ lay or clerical teachers – the latter were cheaper – and it is significant that centres with large populations of workers generally chose clerics. Compared with the national average, in 1860 88 per cent of pupils at Roubaix, 85 per cent at Elbeuf and 63 per cent at Lyon were so taught. Most girls at schools even before the act had received their education from nuns and by 1860 this was true of about 75 per cent.[65] It must be observed that many workers were sympathetic towards the clerical teachers who so willingly devoted themselves to their pupils, the exceptions being primarily those workers who had not come into contact with them.[66]

This was understandable, because if the competence of clerical teachers was often not high, neither was that of lay teachers and the clerics could at least be respected for their ideal of service and faith. A school inspector in the Nord reported of lay teachers that workers did not see any merit in their function, shopkeepers had contempt for their poverty, those with higher education thought them ill-educated, and those in authority suspected them of socialism.[67] This would change with the rising level and importance of education, but at this time the materially miserable *instituteur* was usually little esteemed.

Yet conservatives feared him, feared the greater receptivity to new ideas which his profession produced. Conservatives exaggerated the radicalism of schoolteachers. An inspector's report for the Loir-et-Cher of July 1849 claimed that only 27 of 278 teachers were compromised by radical sympathies.[68] Conservatives were perhaps therefore afraid of education as such. The regime engaged in repressive activity which in itself in the long run served to radicalize the teaching profession. From early 1850 over 1,200 teachers were revoked or suspended without payment, often for the flimsiest reasons.[69] In the short run this ensured the quiescence of those who remained.

257

In spite of repression, conservative electoral candidates had not done as well as had been expected in the supplementary elections of March 10, 1850. In Paris again on April 28 Eugene Sue, the democratic novelist, was elected in a contest with one of the heroes of the repression of June 1848.

Of the first result, an editorial in the *Constitutionnel* observed that it was not entirely black.[70] After the second, it was rather more concerned and demanded a strengthening of the powers of the President and an extension of his term of office, it having been demonstrated to its satisfaction that 'neither the parliamentary power, nor the Legitimist party, nor the Orleanist party, nor the revolutionary party possess the necessary and urgent solution; none of them is capable of ending the crisis and of governing the country. . . .' In these tones of panic it asserted additionally that 'Society is dying of universal suffrage'.[71]

Throughout France, as usual, great significance had been seen in the election results in the capital. At Bordeaux, for example, the rentes fell, such was the shock.[72] Conservatives gave exaggerated importance to the army vote. Soldiers as usual tended to vote according to their class and religion, and consequently those from Paris for the more radical candidates proposed there. Changarnier, commanding in Paris, was certain that whatever their vote the troops would obey but recognized the dangerous effect on public opinion of the adverse impression gained.[73] No-one seems then to have noticed the constant decline in the military vote for the left from May 1849, a product of both repression and increasing indifference.

From these results conservatives seem generally to have concluded that universal suffrage which they had begun to favour at the time of the Presidential election was an element of instability, that they were at the mercy of the fickle masses. An alarming notion was presented – 'in two years, you will have legally, constitutionally, a socialist majority'.[74] The nightmare prospect of 1852 with its elections of a new President and Assembly developed; and the desperate search for alternatives commenced.

The obvious first choice was more intense repression, and this was introduced in the form of the ever-stricter restriction of the various rights and methods of association and of the communication of ideas. Even the cry of *Vive la République!* came to be regarded with suspicion in this strange Republic.[75] Closer collaboration with the President was also envisaged by conservative leaders.

The first, and only, product of this collaboration was the new electoral law taking effect from 31 May 1850.

This law introduced a three year residential period to replace six months as a pre-requisite for acquiring the right to vote, with inscription on the roll of personal tax as the principal means to prove residence, along with parental or employer affirmation.

Whether because of insufficiently long residence, indifference, or ignorance of the legal process of inscription large numbers were excluded, primarily workers who were often unable, or unwilling, to work in one place for long.

An estimated 2,809,000 voters were excluded, that is 29 per cent of the electorate, but in certain centres the proportion was much higher – 62 per cent in Paris, 51 per cent in the Nord, 43 per cent on the Loire and Seine-Inférieure, 40 per cent in the Rhône, all relatively industrialized – or lower, only 11 per cent in the Meuse.[76] The purpose of the law was, it appeared, achieved. The *Constitutionnel* gleefully reported that 'The real effect of the law, is to strike revolutionary Paris. . . . Paris delivered from the oppression exercized by a nomadic and immoral population . . . that will be in two years the true and most real effect of the law. . . .'[77] 196,600 of the 328,000 Parisian voters were disenfranchised. Thiers, dynamic again in defence of repression, made the same point in debate in the Assembly.[78] Some observers doubted the efficacy of the law,[79] some of the more demagogic Legitimists resented the disenfranchisement of their clientele, but most conservatives were satisfied. The 5 per cent rente rose almost 5 francs in as many days.

In the Assembly conservatives had attempted half-heartedly to present the law as not unconstitutional. Pierre de la Gorce was later to represent their point of view – 'Their intentions were correct. Far from wishing, as they were accused, to diminish . . . the public liberties, they had rather the desire to affirm and to safeguard them. Their experience clearly showed them that universal suffrage, without rule, without limitation, is nothing more than the blind law of number, that is to say the most propitious instrument of despotism. . . .'[80] The immoral and those whose poverty and ignorance limited their freedom of choice were to be excluded.[81]

Montalembert eschewed hypocrisy by asserting that 'when it is necessary to choose between the Constitution and society . . . it is only fools and rogues who can hesitate'.[82]

Marx surprisingly does not repeat the belief of many leading political figures that one purpose of the law was to drive the masses in Paris into revolt and then crush them. Rémusat complained 'there is amongst the friends of order, a strongly rooted idea which reappears in moments of unrest, that a day of repressed disorder is a remedy for any evil. . . .'[83] Barrot observed the anxiety of the deputies of the left to impress on the population the need to avoid giving the authorities an excuse for further repression. He appreciated the paradox by which roles were inverted, 'moderation passing to the side of the left, whereas violence went to the right'.[84]

With anxiety Barrot noticed the silence of the government. In spite of agreeing to support this bill, ministers left debate to members of the majority, responsibility for the new law in the eyes of the public tended consequently to rest on them.[85] In the final vote the more prominent Bonapartists either voted against the bill or abstained. There appears to have been a conscious purpose behind this by which Louis-Napoléon avoided alienating conservatives desiring repression, was able to discredit the Assembly in the eyes of the masses, and yet was himself not sufficiently identified with the law to share in this discredit.[86]

The relationship between Louis-Napoléon and the Assembly up to this point had been complicated and troubled by conflict. The Legislative Assembly was dominated by former Orleanists but with a sufficient number of Legitimists and of the more radical republicans to make its meetings stormy. Conservatives seemed primarily interested in obtaining places, and their local rivalries were especially evident in the struggle for administrative posts for protégés,[87] but their ideological differences continued to divide them, especially in the period following the summer recess of 1849 during which pilgrimages had been made to consult the two exiled pretenders. The Barrot government, still attempting to conciliate moderate republicans, quickly lost favour. Its repressive action was felt to be inadequate, particularly as it failed to entirely purge republicans from the administration to make way for monarchists felt by the majority in the Assembly to be more deserving.[88]

As well as having to contend with a generally unsympathetic Assembly the Barrot government had to tolerate the continuous intrigues of conservative leaders against each other, against the government which they desired to control without sharing in its responsibility and both against and with Louis-Napoléon. The Assembly and its leaders however continued to maintain the ministry in existence as long as no alternative could be agreed upon.[89]

Amongst conservatives in the country, and even in the Assembly, there were signs of a weariness with the constant parliamentary verbal battles, reinforced by the desire for strong government. Apparently indecisive and weak, the institutions of parliamentary government were becoming isolated in a sea of conservative contempt, which desired nothing less than social order, and increasingly looked to the President of the Republic for this. Rémusat saw in the Assembly a majority of 'frightened conservatives, disorientated Orleanists, of old functionaries used to seeing all government authority in the executive'.[90] The executive was to be guarantor of order, was already the source of patronage, another powerful element of attraction. Berryer, a Legitimist leader, quickly adopted a somewhat fatalistic attitude towards any attempt by Louis-Napoléon to seize power.[91]

Initially Bonaparte had appeared to subordinate himself to the Barrot ministry and to the Assembly. The incident of the Ney telegram in August 1849, had signified Louis-Napoléon's desire to break away from this tutelage. It 'with studied indiscretion, raised the curtain of his cabinet, in order to expose himself to the eyes of the gallery as a benevolent genius who was, however, misunderstood and shackled in his own house'.[92] This was how his ministers understood it. Falloux, whilst claiming to agree with the President's criticism of illiberal features of the Papal government of Rome, resigned in protest against the publication of this telegram, which to Barrot took the form of a personal manifesto, without consultation of the government.[93] Subsequently Barrot was placed in an almost impossible position when criticized by Louis-Napoléon for failing to defend his message to Ney in the Assembly.

This was simply the prelude to the dismissal of a ministry Louis-Napoléon felt was too independent of him. On October 31, 1849 Barrot received a letter demanding his resignation which declared that 'I believe that it is absolutely necessary that I dominate all parties, in taking ministers who represent none. . . .'[94] This was expanded upon in a message to the Assembly in which the Prince-President maintained that 'The danger in the streets had hardly passed when we saw the old parties raise again their flags. . . . In the middle of this confusion, France is worried because it cannot see any leadership, it searches for the hand, the will of the elect of December

10. This will can only be felt if there is a community of ideas, of views, of convictions, between the President and his ministers. . . .'[95] The squabbling Assembly, its majority anyway feeling the Barrot ministry to be too liberal, and aware of a growing sentiment in the country in favour of Louis-Napoléon did not act in support of a ministry which had been at least its own. For de Tocqueville this was as much an attack on it as upon the ministry, especially once the names of the new ministers were revealed and they were seen to be men selected according to their probable readiness to obey Louis-Napoléon.[96] Dr Véron, owner of the *Constitutionnel*, commented that 'This message and the composition of the new cabinet were regarded almost as a *coup d'état*'.[97] Marx agrees with de Tocqueville in writing that 'The Barrot-Falloux ministry was the ministry of the royalist coalition, the d'Hautpoul ministry was the ministry of Bonaparte, the organ of the President as against the Legislative Assembly, the *ministry of the clerks*'.[98]

Louis-Napoléon followed this drastic act with a conciliatory policy – increased repression, including to the delight of conservatives a more thorough purge of the last remaining republicans from the administration. This repression reached a height following the elections of March and April 1850, which frightened both Assembly and President into an apparently close alliance, the results and limits of which, we have already observed.

In this period up to the law of 31 May 1850 Louis-Napoléon, according to Barrot, sought to appear to submit to the Assembly whilst awaiting an opportunity to compromise it.[99] The defeated often seek to exaggerate the ability and conscious designs of their rivals so as not to appear too insignificant themselves, but Barrot was close to the truth. The whole policy of reaction, the inclusion of Fould in the ministry apparently to conciliate the financial world, was the element of conciliation. In contrast there was a determination to maintain an independent image.

In the latter respect provincial tours carefully covered by teams of journalists presaged some of the future techniques of mass publicity. A policy of amnesty for the prisoners of June 1848, the suppression of the 45 centimes tax early in 1850, increased pay for military non-commissioned officers, all sought to increase the President's popularity amongst the masses. In the process of this campaign Louis-Napoléon 'voluntarily ceded to parliament everything that might wound popular sentiment; he maintained for himself the brilliant displays, the feasts, the speeches full of promises and flattery, the distribution of rewards, of crosses of honour etc., in fact everything that would attach to him more and more the masses'.[100]

By early 1850 Falloux already felt that the main danger to conservative rule came from 'Caesarism' not from the *démocrate-socialistes*,[101] and from October 1849 conservative leaders of all shades had begun to meet regularly in an effort to organize their forces partly in opposition to the growing pretensions of the President.[102] But in January 1850, Louis-Napoléon already felt sufficiently strong to affirm in a note to the press that the Ministry was responsible to him and not to the Assembly whose votes it could ignore – according to Castellane 'a new declaration of war on the Assembly'.[103] So begins the last period of the Republic, with the apparent sealing of an alliance between all conservatives.

The *démocrate-socialiste* leaders in the Assembly had refused to be drawn by the electoral law of May 1850 into an insurrection against a prepared enemy and in this provincial organizations had followed their lead. They believed, and in this had been encouraged by the election results of 1850, that a legal course would bring them success in the elections of 1852, or at least that this would be a more propitious time for a rising.

The movement was however divided in this matter of a response to what was described as an unconstitutional act by the government. As a supposedly revolutionary political force the *démocrate-socialistes* had previously utilized the language of revolution. Even the still quite moderate *National* had asserted that in the case of an attempt to limit the suffrage 'Citizens worthy of the name would have to do no more than look at the Constitution to see if there was not a means of defending and of saving liberty'.[104] This might have appeared as an appeal to that article of the constitution which presaged the defence of its provisions by force if necessary. But on June 1 the *National* excused itself – and congratulated the people on the way in which it had refused to be provoked to hasty action.

Critics of these tactics quickly made themselves heard, although their criticism was weakened by the fact that many of these critics were already in exile. Nevertheless twenty-four Montagnard deputies formed a dissenting 'New Mountain', supported by such illustrious exiles as Ledru-Rollin, Louis Blanc and Delescluze, which favoured organization for insurrection. In an article directed at the deputies of the Montagne appearing in *Le Proscrit* of 5 July 1850, Delescluze, from London wrote, 'Enough lies! Stop playing at political cleverness, stop speaking of 1852, because you believe in it less than anyone'.[105] For him, in looking towards the forthcoming general elections, these men were finding an excuse to escape responsibility. Eighty-four Montagnard deputies had signed a manifesto favouring moderation and legality which reveals the nature of the divisions and the weakness of the *démocrate-socialiste* group in the Assembly.

In conditions fairly propitious for political action and supported by the minority of deputies and many exiles a more intense move towards the organization and especially co-ordination of secret societies began.

1850 had been a year of relative industrial and commercial prosperity, 1851 saw the early onset of a mild depression and throughout the period of the republic an economic malaise continued to effect the countryside.

Marx exaggerates the prosperity of 1850 – 'one of the most splendid years of industrial and commercial prosperity'[106] in order to explain the indifference of Parisian workers to the restriction of the suffrage. Martin Nadaud observed this same indifference in Paris, and explicitly drew a contrast between this and the growing political consciousness and enthusiasm of the masses of the provinces.[107]

If the towns were more prosperous than the countryside, there remained in them substantial pockets of misery. Castellane, now commanding at Lyon wrote in April 1850 that, 'There is much misery in Lyon, the leaders profit from this to increase discontent. Work lacks also more and more at Saint-Etienne. The socialist cafés are almost all full. The leaders announce the coming end of the sufferings of the people'.[108] Marseille also experienced severe difficulties which clearly worsened in 1851.[109]

Agricultural prices seem to have reached their lowest point around October 1851. Some sectors of agriculture were protected but the major crops, cereals and wine, and livestock were depressed.

The rural population reacted primarily, as ever, to economic pressures, but was increasingly aware of simple political considerations, evincing an interest in *démocrate-socialiste* promises which frightened the authorities. The left promised to protect the poor at the expense of the rich – 'only the rich will pay taxes'.[110] The poor in certain areas longed for the day on which their interests would count, thus the great popularity from 1850 of the song by Paul Dupont:

1852
It is in two years, barely two years
That the Gallic cock will crow;
Hold your ear towards the ground
Listen to what he will say to you.
He says to the children of the earth
Who are laid out under their burden
Here is the end of misery,
Eaters of black bread, drinkers of water![111]

A simple faith, the misery which called forth this, and the belief in a near solution to all ills – the components of a religious-like fervour: these were the factors aiding political organization.

The most significant element of organization in the summer and autumn of 1850 was the co-ordinating activity of the 'New Mountain'. The secret societies were to be organized it seemed with defensive-offensive purposes in mind – the defence of the constitution and subsequently in 1852 the organization of the disenfranchised to demand their right to vote by force if necessary.[112] The main areas of activity were the Rhône region and the south-east, partly because of the prevailing level of discontent and organization here, partly because of the enthusiasm of some local leaders and especially the former deputy to the Constituent Assembly, Alphonse Gent.

This effort was relatively short-lived, and was broken by a series of arrests in October. Some of the links it created however remained in being and it gave an impression of power to those involved and a belief in a vast organization covering France, which encouraged further activity.

It is in fact difficult to distinguish reality from invention in examining this organization. The official account described preparation for a mass rising in 1852 or earlier if the President and conservatives were to quarrel. This rising would begin in the small towns and villages of the south-east – in the Rhône, Saône-et-Loire, Ain and Jura, and throughout the Midi, with columns marching on Toulon, Marseille and Lyon, joined by exiles of all nationalities from Geneva and Savoy. Once these targets were attained, then the rest of France would rise and be aided by the successful revolutionaries from the south.[113] Given the government's need to frighten conservatives much of this can be treated with scepticism, but there is no doubt that an organization had been in process of creation in

265

fifteen departments in the south-east with insurrection as its probable aim. The whole mass of official reports might give an exaggerated picture but cannot entirely be discounted.

The effect of this repression must however have discouraged even the more ardent spirits. De Castellane reported that 'Democracy in the Midi, one moment over-excited by the plans for insurrection of Gent and his supporters, has returned to its normal state. It conspires always – that is its life – but it no longer speaks of an immediate recourse to arms'.[114] The more restrained figures amongst local leaders, those to whom in 1852 the 'Millennium' would begin, regained influence lost after the failure to react immediately to the destruction of universal suffrage. To them there seemed now to be no alternative but to wait for 1852.

Faced with ever more intense repression local leaders showed little interest in taking risks. Castellane described a visit to Valence where 'The anarchist leaders . . . left the town at seven in the morning, in fear of being forced by their followers to make demonstrations on my arrival'.[115] Propaganda continued, as did organization and even preparation for insurrection in 1852, but more than ever this activity was underground. Administrative reports reveal few important incidents, most prosecutions were of small groups of individuals especially for singing seditious songs, like that in anticipation of triumph over Legitimist nobles, written by Victor Pothier and entitled *Failure*:

> *The whites, the whites,*
> *A short time ago overbearing,*
> *Are mute, trembling,*
> *Those poor whites!*[116]

or else for shouts of *Vive la République sociale*, or 'down with the priests', or even for the wearing of red bonnets.[117] It has been suggested that the pattern of such prosecutions was similar to that in more normal periods, increasing in periods of the year when work was slack and men had time to drink and talk,[118] but it was significant than even the drunks were more politically aware.

Depending upon who delivered it and at whom it was directed propaganda took various forms in these months of 1850 and 1851. The right to work was still claimed for the urban worker, cheap credit was promised to the peasants.[119] Pamphlets, newspapers and songs were still distributed, or even in Lyon prayers – one basing

266

itself on the Catechism which was familiar to almost all: 'I believe in God, the father of the people, creator of the republic, and in Jesus Christ, the first republican, who . . . was betrayed by his generals . . .',[120] is revealing of the vague religiosity even of the urban workers, another is more earthly – 'Our father who is at the Tuileries, let your name be effaced, let your reign cease, let your will be without effect on this earth as in all others. Forgive us our victories . . . and never let us succumb under the weight of your vengeance, but deliver us from your presence'.[121] A profanation of the Lord's Prayer hardly calculated to ease the fears of Catholics.

Even if the authorities were less anxious about the loyalties of the army[122] there were constant complaints about the ease with which the more extreme *démocrate-socialistes* could buy or be presented with balls and powder by soldiers, as well as reports indicating the manufacture and storing of munitions.[123]

On an organizational level co-ordination and especially closer links with Paris were continually in process of being developed, then, partially destroyed by police action. If the local administrations seem to have been unable to provide the government with much concrete evidence to support their belief that an insurrection was being prepared, their reports continuously revealed the great ferment in society, and in giving the government what it wanted, exaggerated to a degree difficult to estimate, the strength and organized character of this unrest.

Officials certainly appear to have believed in the existence of a great plot: 'France is divided by the secret societies into circles of seven to ten departments directed by a committee with which the central committee in Paris corresponds.'[124] This was quite probably the pattern, but the solidarity of the organization was certainly not as great as it was thought. In this respect too much attention was paid by officials to the reports of spies, and to the self-delusion of those involved in conspiracy. One spy reported the speech of a local secret society leader who affirmed that his society was part of a nation-wide network – 'at a signal which we await we will rise as a single man and in a quarter of an hour, the revolution will be made. . . .'[125]

The links between societies were in fact tenuous due to local and personal rivalries, the links between regions even more tenuous because added to those were even greater problems of communication. There was a suspicion in many quarters of the zeal of Parisian leaders after the failure of actions to follow words on previous occasions, and

267

in the face of police repression and spies a natural suspicion of contacts.[126]

As 1852 approached *démocrate-socialiste* leaders became more and more anxious to avoid premature action as they and their followers became more and more excited about the prospects the new year would bring. Enthusiasm knew no bounds – 'Marvellous and irrisistible power of ideas! In spite of the prefects, the *procureurs*, the policemen and the spies; in spite of the oppressive legislation, the trials, the state of siege and the bayonets, in spite of all, democracy is in full spate like one of those great floods furnished by the hand of God, of which no human will is able to halt the course. . . .'[127]

Some were concerned that the conservatives would attempt pre-emptive action but more generally there was confidence. Delescluze felt that Louis-Napoléon could not attempt a coup because of the unreliability of an army whose soldiers had been influenced by socialist and republican ideas.[128]

The authorities could not but notice this rising wave of enthusiasm,[129] could not but be frightened when men were arrested for asserting in public that 'on a given day, which is close, we must secure the priests, seize the churches, and sound the alarm bell, at which signal, the affiliates in the countryside must go to the notaries and burn the records of debt and from there pillage and burn the property of Aristocrats.'[130]

1852 promised so much – 'Truth and Justice will reign in 1852'[131] – to large sections of the urban and rural population. Their misery would end, whether through the election of a popular President and Assembly or, if the right of universal suffrage was still denied, by force of arms. On 11–12 October 1851, insurrection broke out in the countryside of the Loire valley. Five communes rose in protest against the arrests of *démocrate-socialiste* propagandists. The insurgents had been promised that the Nivernais and indeed the whole of France was rising. There was no looting, no deaths, the insurrection just faded away at the first signs of resistance, but to conservatives this was an awful warning, the culminating event in a vast series of minor incidents described by officials and journalists, which warned of 'an insurrection of beggars or of peasants'[132] to destroy society.

Conservative attitudes after the restriction of the suffrage had developed increasingly clearly at two levels, one being parliamentary, the other that of the public in general. The relationships between Louis-Napoléon and the conservative majority of the Assembly, between the head of the executive and the political leaders of the country were especially revealing of the attitudes of social conservatives to the possession of political power.

The division of the Assembly, initially into three main groups: Orleanists, Legitimists and Republicans, and with increasingly a more or less committed Bonapartist following, appeared in every political crisis in which it was involved. The basic feature of these crises seems to have been Louis-Napoléon, as a man knowing clearly what he wanted, faced by a divided and indecisive Assembly.

During the summer parliamentary recess of 1850 military reviews had been held at Saint-Maur and Satory, notable because Louis-Napoléon wined and dined officers and men and they in response shouted *Vive Napoléon!* or even *Vive l'Empéreur!* when parading before him.

At Sedan however the infantry passed the President in silence, to his intense annoyance, obeying the orders of General Changarnier, based on the view that acclamations under arms were subversive of discipline.

Changarnier saw himself as the potential saviour of society. He owed no firm allegiance to any dynasty but had grown to distrust Bonaparte possibly because after the suppression of the demonstration of June 1849, to which he owed much of his fame, he had, as Maxime du Camp suggested, offered to direct a coup in favour of Louis-Napoléon, which offer the latter had rejected, because, du Camp further suggested, he wanted power independent of reliance on another.[133]

Changarnier often expressed in public during those summer and autumn months of 1850, a contempt for the President of the Republic,[134] which must have increased any desire on the part of Louis-Napoléon to be rid of a powerful rival.

Castellane felt that Changarnier who had reached so rapidly a position of eminence, now exaggerated his own importance,[135] and Rémusat agreed with this.[136] According to Barrot towards the end of the parliamentary recess, early in October, Changarnier attempted to persuade conservative leaders that Louis-Napoléon ought to be imprisoned. These leaders were frightened at the thought.[137]

The recalcitrant general had established for himself an influential position in the Assembly where various monarchists hoped he would arrange a coup for them, or shared his distrust of Bonaparte. A move by the latter against him, therefore, meant a political crisis.

This was probably inevitable following a summer recess in which Monarchist claims had been re-asserted, and in which Bonapartist propaganda and especially criticism of the Assembly had been constant.[138] Relations which had been quite good immediately following the law on the suffrage were deteriorating under the pressure of competing ambitions, whereas before the law these had been more restrained from fear of the *démocrate-socialistes*.[139]

The storm broke only in January 1851. On the 3 January Louis-Napoléon dismissed Changarnier. The constitution gave him the right to do this, and the legality of the action limited the force of the conservative reaction, but conservatives realizing the importance of control of the army had placed much faith in the intentions and power of this general commanding the Paris region, and conservative leaders had previously seemed to agree that Changarnier must be retained in his command.[140]

The dilemma of conservatives was clearly illustrated by Gustave de Beaumont who in a letter to de Tocqueville said that if the Assembly did not have the courage to meet Louis-Napoléon's challenge over Changarnier it would always give way, but on the other hand seemed worried that any opposition the Assembly might offer could lead to a political crisis with unpredictable consequences.[141] Thiers told the Assembly 'There are only two powers in the State, the executive and the legislative. If the Assembly gives way today there will be no longer more than one, when there is only one power, the form of the government will be changed. . . . The word will come later, when? This matters little to me . . . the Empire is made.'[142]

But the Assembly did cede. It simply passed a relatively weak vote of no confidence in the government. It was too divided itself, too aware of the unwillingness of the conservative public to accept a political crisis, too afraid of the threat from the left. Beaumont himself obscured his awareness of Louis-Napoléon's aims with his fear of socialism.[143] This fear was increased by the general republican reaction to Changarnier's dismissal, which tended to welcome it. One moderate republican, replying to Thiers' demand for action against Louis-Napoléon said that 'We have no great confidence in the devotion of Prince Louis-Napoléon to the Republic; but we have even less confidence in yours and in that of General Changarnier'.[144] Castellane described conservative public opinion following the Assembly's vote of no confidence and concluded that 'The provinces pronounce themselves openly against the Chamber, and this latter begins to be frightened at having had so much courage'.[145]

This quarrel, signified by the vote of no confidence, was seen by contemporary figures as a breach, the beginning of a struggle to the death with Louis-Napoléon according to Beaumont which, paradoxically, conservative leaders were determined to pursue by constitutional means.[146]

Louis-Napoléon allowed his ministry to resign after the vote of no confidence – he needed the vote of a new subsidy to cover his personal expenses, and probably sought to weaken the Assembly's opposition to him by a conciliatory move. He was neither militarily ready for a coup, nor was public opinion ready to accept it.

The element of conciliation was limited. Changarnier was replaced in Paris by an eminent monarchist Baraguey-d'Hilliers, but the new government was badly received; by Beaumont 'as men who present themselves . . . only as very humble clerks'.[147] The bad impression was heightened by the demand for a new subsidy.[148]

This crisis, like subsequent crises, revealed to Louis-Napoléon the weakness of conservative opposition, later crises revealed the continued weakening of what opposition there was. There was a general unwillingness to risk conflict, not only because of the strength of the President of the Republic, but because each faction within the Assembly was afraid of the others, and in particular the conservative groups of the republican, labelled by them as socialist. Thus was the political initiative left to Louis-Napoléon. Even in January 1851 the demand to the Assembly for a subsidy had failed by only 396 votes to 294, the latter were all conservatives indicating this decline in opposition to Louis-Napoléon.

Conservative politicians were anxious to avoid conflict and many were prepared to accept a compromise with Louis-Napoléon by which the constitution would be revised to permit him to stand for re-election and to remain as head of the executive for an indefinite period. This would avoid the unpleasant prospects of any change whatsoever.[149] Even Thiers was prepared to accept a compromise, the establishment of a constitutional monarchy, with Louis-Napoléon as its head if necessary.[150] What is doubtful is whether Louis-Napoléon would have been prepared to accept a compromise restricting his authority.

He does seem to have made an effort in favour of constitutional revision. The administration helped organize petitions in its favour. A new and more prestigious government was appointed, largely that which had resigned on the occasion of the dismissal of Changarnier, apparently to work for revision, although Barrot felt that the ministry appointed, with Faucher at the Ministry of the Interior, was calculated by Louis-Napoléon to irritate the left and ensure its opposition to revision, thus making the three-quarters majority necessary for constitutional changes impossible to obtain.[151]

Other evidence however supports the belief that Louis-Napoléon sincerely desired revision, for example, that of Maupas.[152] It seems quite logical to suppose that a man who would often reveal a distaste for violence,[153] should seek to establish himself in power by the path of least resistance, but additionally that he would require from the conservatives the grant of substantial additional executive powers. Faucher himself confirmed this when in conversation with Nassau Senior, he told him that if only Louis-Napoléon 'would submit to be a parliamentary sovereign. . . . I believe that his reign might be postponed far beyond its legal terms'.[154] Conservatives wanted to restrict his powers, he to extend them, but as de Tocqueville warned 'he does not wish at any price to be, or even to appear to be, the instrument or the agent or the creation of the protégé of a parliamentary majority'.[155] If he favoured revision it was probably as a first step.

446 voted for revision, 278 against, but the constitution demanded 543 affirmative votes. Republicans opposing on principle and intransigent Orleanists hoping for the candidature of Thiers or even the Prince de Joinville in 1852 ensured the bill's failure.[156] However, the size of the majority evinced a further weakening of conservative opposition to Louis-Napoléon's retention of power.

Falloux believed that the rejection of revision only served to further Louis-Napoléon's cause, persuading conservatives in the country as a whole that illegal action to maintain a strong executive was necessary.[157] Indeed with this rejection Louis-Napoléon would have no choice in 1852, but to meekly retire or attempt a *coup d'état*. This was the root of Barrot's criticism of the opponents of revision – in rejecting it 'they did not wish the re-election of Louis-Napoléon as President of the Republic; they made him an emperor'. Revision was the only means of restraining Louis-Napoléon's ambition.[158] From this point he was committed to a coup.

His next major move in this direction was to propose in October 1851, the abrogation of the law of May 1850 restricting the suffrage. The Faucher ministry refused to support this and was replaced by another ministry of nonentities dependent on the President and significantly with Saint-Arnaud at the War Ministry. The personnel of the coup were being gathered. General Lamoricière had already warned that 'when you see Saint-Arnaud in the Government the decisive operation will be close'.[159]

Louis-Napoléon was the elect of the masses. In their votes lay his authority. On the parliamentary scene this proposal could be calculated to intensify the division between republicans and the more conservative and also to remind the latter that Louis-Napoléon had an alternative source of support to them.

The ministry claimed that circumstances had changed since 1850 and the restriction was no longer justified. Barrot suggested that at this point conservatives should have sought to compromise with the left, and strongly criticized the choice of this as an issue on which to stand up to Louis-Napoléon.[160] But hatred and fear were too strong. The government's proposal was rejected by 355 votes to 348, with the left supporting the government and not all conservatives against. Indeed the smallness of the majority against indicated a further decline in conservative opposition to the President.

Through this the Assembly 'once more confirmed the fact that it had transformed itself from the freely elected representatives of the people into the usurpatory parliament of a class'.[161] It could, less than ever, count on mass support in a crisis.

The decisive element in an increasingly tense political situation in which rumours of coups were constant and the threat from the masses for conservatives always menacing, appeared to be the army. In June 1851, Changarnier, although now only a deputy without military command had promised the Assembly that the army would not tolerate any assault on it. With great self-confidence he ended his speech with the words 'Representatives of France, deliberate in peace!'[162] Stirring words, which the now active General de Castellane found both irritating and amusing.[163]

That the army itself was not as sure of what its duty was as Changarnier believed, was evident. General Le Flô, the Questor, responsible for the security of the Assembly, was aware that officers were unsure whether, if conflict occurred, they should obey the Assembly's requisition as the constitution seemed to demand, or the orders of the Minister of War as military discipline required. He requested a clear statement of the constitutional position from the Assembly. To Thiers, at least, this appeared unnecessary. He favoured

273

the simple assertion of the Assembly's right to prove its continued existence. Typically most conservative leaders were afraid that this would precipitate a final conflict with the President, and decided on the middle course of an interpretative motion by the Assembly.[164]

They were right to fear the President's reaction to a move designed to secure their control over the army. Figures close to Louis-Napoléon seem to have viewed this move as a prelude to the arrest of the President, and the establishment of a dictatorship by the Assembly. An immediate coup was prepared in case, as seemed likely, the Questor's proposition concerning requisition was supported by a majority of the deputies.[165]

The proposition was however rejected by 408 votes to 300, figures produced by two factors. Conservatives feared the effect of a divided command upon the army in the case of a mass rising, they opposed any weakening of the President's power.[166] Secondly, most republicans were opposed to the proposition, mainly because the prospect of the army being controlled by the conservative majority in the Assembly had no more attraction to them than that of its control by Louis-Napoléon.[167] The Montagnard, Michel de Bourges, was sufficiently out of touch with public opinion to assert to applause that from the President. 'There is no danger, and I add that, if there was a danger there is an invisible sentinel who protects us. This invisible sentinel is the people'.[168]

Of this action of the Assembly Marx could justifiably write: 'By rejecting the Questers' Bill it made public confession of its impotence'.[169]

Marx lays great stress on the revival of differences between the royalist factions and indeed within each, as a factor weakening the Assembly.

The death of Louis-Philippe in the summer of 1850 had seemed to make the reconciliation of these factions possible, since it left the Orleanist Comte de Paris heir to both his grandfather and to the childless Legitimist pretender, the Comte de Chambord. But more than allegiances to specific royal houses divided monarchists. Legitimists and Orleanists in general had differing conceptions of social existence based on their differing orientations, one to rural society, and other more to the developing urban scene, differences which Marx described simply, too simply, as 'divided class interests'.[170]

Chambord in a manifesto declared that he 'entirely condemned this system of appeal to the people, as implying negotiation of the grand principle of monarchical inheritance'.[171] This politically inept move disappointed many of the more liberal Legitimists and for Orleanists who demanded a constitutional monarchy shattered any hopes of fusion.[172] With the threat from the left less immediate in the summer and autumn of 1850 the old quarrels of principle and personality were reborn. Orleanists envisaged the candidature of Louis-Philippe's son, the Prince de Joinville, in 1852.

Division made Restoration seem unlikely and this drove many conservatives to consider Louis-Napoléon as the only alternative to social conflict.

Louis-Napoléon was in a strong political position given these divisions amongst his only rivals for the support of conservatives in the country as a whole. Barrot felt that members of the respective Monarchist factions would prefer the Empire, as they had preferred the Republic, to the success of the rival faction.[173]

Support in the Assembly for Louis-Napoléon was increasing amongst those tired of division or who from habit expected and desired to follow the lead of strong governments. Rémusat felt that most members of the majority were never as concerned about Monarchist restoration as they pretended, but were expected by their families to so pretend.[174] Orleanists especially, less tied by principle, were prepared to compromise for the sake of social order.[175] They did not like Louis-Napoléon and would not welcome his regime but they could not struggle wholeheartedly to preserve the Republic.[176] In such a situation there were few prepared to take the initiative in opposing the ambitions of Louis-Napoléon, few prepared to risk a conflict. Odilon Barrot later asked himself why so many experienced politicians had let themselves be hoodwinked by Louis-Napoléon, and answered that they saw the danger but felt themselves too weak to oppose it and therefore 'they preferred to appear deceived than to have to combat' and even in the face of clear preparations for a coup, conservatives forced themselves into the belief that the threat was non-existent.[177] Towards the end even Thiers, formerly firm in opposition seems to have given up and adopted this waiting attitude.[178] On the day before the coup Apponyi went to dinner: 'The dinner was not very gay, Molé painted a grim picture, he spoke of the *coup d'état*. . . . The opinion of Molé is that there is nothing more to do for the Assembly if that is not to retire with dignity, and he

275

repeated to us his phrase: that it is better to leave by the door than by the window.'[179]

This attitude can be clearly understood against the background of conservative feeling in the country as a whole.

This feeling was one of fear. This was the dominant emotion in 1851 amongst most middle-class groups and the majority of peasants. Informed opinion believed that there was a distinct possibility of a victory of the left in the legislative elections of 29 April 1852 and even the presidential elections in May, additionally that whatever the election result the masses influenced by socialism would resort to force to avenge their misery, to establish a new form of society. The future was uncertain, and could not be regarded optimistically. France in this year was beset by an economic, social and political crisis, the effect of which was to make men timid.

The Bonapartist propagandist Romieu wrote of 'millions of peasants and workers to whom the newspaper and the peddlar give each morning the poison of envy, of rage, of loathing, no longer against the gentleman who is dead, but against the bourgeois who has succeeded him. . . . The poor full of envy, of hatred, of the thirst for pillage, are ready to ravage, with their millions of arms, the mansions, the luxurious apartments; to disperse, with a loud cry, all that which appears to them as an insult'.[180] If for the social élite Romieu was too crude, he appealed to those for whom he wrote – those middle class groups with some property and something to lose in the socialist holocaust. Moreover ignore the crudity of expression and his views were those of the best social circles, of the most informed opinion.

Castellane at the summit of authority in Lyon, wrote that 'The goal of the "New Mountain" is the division of property; each member swears not to hesitate in the face of any sacrifice to attain this goal, to be ready to do everything to satisfy the legitimate vengeance of the people and achieve social renovation'.[181] He was especially concerned because of information he had received concerning the activities of refugees from various European countries organizing themselves in Switzerland – 'The programme of the association, is to demand, arms in hand, the organization of the Republic for the whole of Europe and the destruction of all institutions which might serve to support monarchy, religion, property and the family.'[182]

This psychosis of fear shared by the administration led it to play safe, to prosecute all hints of *démocrate-socialiste* activity and in so doing to confirm and increase the fears of the worthy middle class citizens of France. As early as May 1850 Gustave de Beaumont had told Nassau Senior that 'if the insurgents succeed, their victory this time will be one of plunder and murder. Two hours of pillage have been promised to them, and will be taken', and of the government which would ensue from a red revolution – 'they would assassinate widely. They would impose progressive taxes on property which would confiscate or drive away capital, they would affect a national bankruptcy, probably by means of an enormous paper currency. Beyond this all is obscurity',[183] but for him this was more than enough.

Not only was a revolution seen to be threatening, but more immediately the economy was again depressed, and if this depression was primarily due to international conditions 'The French bourgeoisie attributed this trade stagnation to purely political causes . . . to the terrifying prospect of the second Sunday in May 1852.'[184] The textile entrepreneurs of Roubaix and of Tourcoing wrote saying exactly this, the depression was due 'to the lack of confidence in the present and of security in the future'.[185] Those of Lyon said the same thing[186] and from Paris 'letters . . . announce that they are plunged into an incredible torpor. . . . Business is almost non-existent. Everyone questions his neighbour; no-one understands'.[187] Above all, 'It is the uncertainty which torments the spirit.'[188]

Uncertainty and consequent torment reached a peak as the year came to an end. In the department of Bouches-du-Rhône an official reported of the population that 'The year which begins appears to them as a menacing and terrible date. There is a sort of religious terror in the emotions which troubles them'.[189]

Marx described, in the second half of 1851, the growing estrangement between the conservative politicians of the Assembly and conservative opinion as a whole. De Tocqueville best described the feelings of the latter when he wrote from Normandy, warning Beaumont and his parliamentary colleagues that the nation 'is mad for peace, stability, power'.[190] According to a writer in the *Gazette de France* the public 'seeing arise so often in Parliament so many tempests, without any result, is taken with an immense disdain for what happens there. . . .'[191]

The pro-Bonapartist *Constitutionnel* was more direct. Its proprietor, Dr Véron, wrote of the conservative parliamentary leaders that 'The habit of rules, of compromise, of parliamentary coalitions, has profoundly depraved their intelligence, which no longer believes

277

in anything except their ambition and their vanity'.[192] Such men could not, he felt, give France order and security. The *Constitutionnel* openly asked whether 'in the state of complete disorganization in which France finds itself order is not more compromised than defended by the Assembly'.[193]

The growing pro-Bonapartist, anti-parliamentary opinion felt that France was being suffocated under constitutional proprieties, such as those which had prevented revision of this constitution. Even the law which had restricted the suffrage, once so warmly welcomed, was now condemned in some sectors as simply providing the *démocrate-socialiste* leaders with an excuse for insurrection in 1852.[194]

There was thus a desire to break free from the restrictions of legality – 'We ask if there is not a solution whatever it is, and from whichever source it emanates, of which the dangers are not infinitely exceeded by the dangers of this legality'.[195]

Louis-Napoléon offered one solution. A deliberate propaganda effort was made to direct the attention of conservatives towards this solution. Writers, of whom Romieu was only one of the most popular, directed their works at the middle classes. The liberties they had demanded were now being used against them. There was only one force preserving society – the army, only one hope for its continued preservation – the establishment of 'the leader' – 'his role is simple. To impose, with a firm hand, the dictatorship the most absolute'.[196]

The President himself was active in this, touring the country, and 'Everywhere . . . he uses the words most appropriate to the state of spirits and dominant sentiments in the locality'.[197] Thus, in the north and east in the summer of 1850, in cities like Dijon and Strasbourg he had denied any intention of a coup though rather ambiguously promising, as he did at Caen, that 'if stormy days were to reappear and the people wish to impose a new burden on the head of government, this head in his turn would be very guilty if he deserted his great mission'.[198] It was noticed that where hostile demonstrations did occur they involved the more wealthy middle classes rather than the lower middle class and workers.[199]

At Dijon in June 1851 after attacking the designs for Monarchist restoration as resulting in social unrest, he bitterly condemned the Assembly as always supporting him in repressive measures but refusing to co-operate when he wished to introduce reforms. He appealed both to the masses and to conservatives, with a promise of better social conditions for the former, and social order for the latter.[200]

278

Administrative measures supported this activity. From the dismissal of the Barrot ministry in October 1849, senior officials had been appointed on the basis of loyalty to the President and had organized pressure for the revision of the constitution and opinion against the Assembly. Barrot himself bemoaned the action of 'the agents of this vast administration who hold the whole of France in a net'.[201] This control of the administration of a centralized state was indeed one of the major elements of Louis-Napoléon's strength.

More devious methods were also used. The Duchesse de luynes complained to Apponyi of Persigny, Louis-Napoléon's closest confidant, who had warned her husband that 'We have in our service 100,000 common people, who would pillage in the rich quarters and in the mansions of people who intrigue against us. As we have no mansions, we have nothing to risk if this happens'.[202] Conservatives had always suspected the socialist inclinations of the President so he could effectively threaten to ally with the masses if they would not support him. The exaggerated reports concerning socialist and democratic secret societies which came from the provinces permitted Louis-Napoléon to continually declare a state of siege somewhere or other to maintain conservative fears at a high pitch.

The noble duchesse's disgust at Persigny exemplified the attitude of the social élite towards Louis-Napoléon's entourage, described elsewhere as 'common adventurers, ruined men or those of ill repute, and the young debauched'.[203]

At all levels those active in the service of the Prince-President were adventurers. With him on his provincial tours went 'as *claqueurs* people from the Society of December 10, that organization of the Paris *lumpenproletariat*',[204] once officially dissolved, but always existing. Beaumont saw this organization as did Marx, as 'the most visible sign and the most devoted agent'[205] of Louis-Napoléon.

In terms of the social composition of this society Barrot lends weight to the accurateness of Marx's description of it as being composed of members of the large semi-criminal element of the Parisian population. Indeed its activity supports this – it existed to organize demonstrations in favour of Louis-Napoléon and to beat up those who showed signs of hostility.[206] To Dijon in the summer of 1851 it was estimated that about one thousand of these gentle souls preceded him. This was officially a charitable society and for Marx so it was 'in so far as, like Bonaparte, all its members felt the need of benefitting themselves at the expense of the labouring nation'. It characterized for Marx, the man and the regime he would create – the man, 'This Bonaparte, who constitutes himself *chief of the lumpenproletariat*, who here alone rediscovers in mass form the interests which he personally pursues, who recognizes in this scum, offal, refuse of all classes the only class upon which he can base himself unconditionally, is the real Bonaparte . . .', his charitable society nothing but a 'party fighting force'.[207]

By the closing months of 1851 this propaganda effort magnifying the elements of social conflict anyway obviously present had to a large extent succeeded.

At the top of the middle-class hierarchy the support of the great financiers was evident in the way the value of the rentes rose with each of Louis-Napoléon's political successes.

If Legitimists were in many cases still openly hostile – the edition of the *Gazette de Languedoc* of 29 November 1851, was seized for an editorial which accused the President of increasing unrest in the country – this opposition was usually restrained to wishful thinking and those whose Catholicism outweighed their Legitimism, like Montalembert were clearly supporters of the President who promised social order and who had supported, even if with reservations, the temporal power of the Pope.

De Tocqueville wrote from Normandy that although people were very reluctant to express themselves freely, both from prudence and their personal confusion, he discerned 'no passion, little taste for the President of the Republic, great tolerance of those who do not like him, but an almost general desire to re-elect him *because he is there*'.[208]

His description of the attitudes of the mass of Orleanist supporters is masterly – 'Most . . . are attached to that house as pigs are attached to the memory of their pigsty and provided they are offered another . . . they will not stir'.[209] Theirs was a less emotional commitment than that of the Legitimists.

Conservatives were above all anxious for social order, for the continued enjoyment of their material wealth and social prestige, and were in this particular moment of crisis prepared to accept a political regime they would not have freely chosen. They were likely to be passive in response to action by Louis-Napoléon.

His tools for any action must be the administration and particularly the army. The former, at all levels, was as might be expected anxious to preserve itself. Individuals with careers at stake were not likely to take risks. Beaumont made fun of them – 'Officials are precipitated into terrible anguish; they write lamentable letters and come to Paris to make enquiries of all parties, trying to guarantee themselves against all eventualities'.[210]

The army was the vital factor. This was throughout the period of Louis-Napoléon's presidency being prepared for use.

Bonapartist propaganda and tradition proved attractive essentially to the rank and file, the officers, especially the more senior, tended to associate themselves with one or other of the two Monarchist parties, as did the social groups of their origin.

These officers were reluctant to follow Louis-Napoléon. Many were promised advancement in return for their allegiance, but few were prepared to commit themselves. A long process of military transfers was necessary to accumulate a sufficient number of officers prepared to support a coup in Paris. To promote Saint-Arnaud rapidly to the war ministry, it was even necessary to arrange a brief campaign in the Kabylie mountains of Algeria. Once this gentleman had arrived then preparations could proceed apace; 'Regiments were systematically brought up to the capital or removed to a distance according to their readiness to utter the cry of "Vive l'Empéreur!" '[211]

The attitude of army officers was clear. Consider the behaviour of one Colonel d'Allonville who had refused to accept the President's invitation to his troops to shout 'Vive Napoléon' at a review at Satory, but had chosen to obey his superior officer, Changarnier, as both the constitution and military law indicated he should. Changarnier, after his dismissal asked for d'Allonville's support for the opposition to Louis-Napoléon, to which the colonel replied 'General, at Satory I was under your orders and ready to do anything you ordered. Today you are no longer my Chief, I have another and I am ready to obey him blindly. . . .'[212]

This was an army trained to obey without question, composed of men who with few exceptions were not prepared to accept responsibility for involving the army in political conflict. But by the end of 1851 some of the few more adventurous spirits were in a position to give the orders. This is one reason no doubt why the coup occurred when it did, taken with the failure of hopes for revision, the evident lack of the will to resist, shown by conservatives both inside and outside the Assembly, and the rumours that a few Orleanists were plotting a coup of their own [213] and the ever more intense level of démocrate-socialiste activity.

The final decision in favour of the coup was apparently taken on

November 27.[214] The National Guard of Paris had been neutralized by the appointment of Bonapartists to its general staff [215] and on the previous day the general commanding the army in Paris, Magnan, had sought to ensure the obedience of his subordinates – 'You will passively obey my orders. All your lives you have practised military duty in this manner. . . . You understand what is necessary. . . . We must save France, it counts on us. But whatever happens, my responsibility will cover you. You will not receive an order which is not written and signed by me. In consequence, in case of failure, whatever the Government which demands that you account for your actions, you have only to show your orders to safeguard yourselves'.[216]

In common with most other men with a vested interest, these senior officers of the army of Paris were concerned above all to safeguard these interests. They would obey their superiors.

VII

The *Coup d'État* of Louis-Napoléon Bonaparte

On 2 December 1851, the coup occurred, planned by a few adventurers with the active participation of the army and bureaucracy, 'under the second Bonaparte ... the state seem(s) to have made itself completely independent. As against civil society, the state machine has consolidated its position so thoroughly that the chief of the Society of December 10 suffices for its head, an adventurer blown in from abroad, raised on the shield by a drunken soldiery, which he has bought with liquor and sausages, and which he must continually ply with sausage anew.'[1]

Crude but effective. Rémusat presented a similar image of the coup, accusing its directors of 'contempt for all principles, absolute indifference to morality', of being concerned primarily to line their own pockets. It was, he said, as much a *coup de bourse* as a *coup d'état*.[2] This expresses a common contempt for Louis-Napoléon's entourage. And the army? Contemporaries did stress its pre-eminent role. Hübner, the Austrian ambassador commenting that 'Louis-Napoléon has become master of France ... with and through the army. In 1830 the bourgeoisie was victorious, in '48 the people, on 4 December 1851, the army.'[3] But if the rank and file tended to be enthusiastic supporters of Bonaparte the officers were not. We have already commented upon the difficulties the conspirators found in gaining the support of senior officers. The officer corps was not in 1851 Bonapartist but Monarchist. It had, however, been trained to passive obedience in the interests of military efficiency and the desire to escape political involvement. It was contemptuous of civilians and particularly politicians, and did have a taste for strong leadership which would help it overcome the shame it still felt from February 1848. In December 1851 it obeyed the orders of its senior commanders and its officers welcomed this assertion of the principle of social order and hoped for promotion in return.

For similar motives the bureaucracy also obeyed, even without much enthusiasm for Bonaparte. Its political loyalties went elsewhere. Even in 1853, according to one report, of the 985 officials in the Haute-Garonne for example, 629 were Legitimists, 241 Orleanists, 53 Republicans and 9 had unknown principles. Only 53 were committed Bonapartists.[4]

In practical terms, the army's attitude meant that an attempt by conservative members of the Assembly to remind soldiers of their constitutional duty to protect this Assembly was met with the response of General Ferry – 'We are soldiers, we only recognize our orders.'[5]

These orders were obeyed almost without exception.[6] According to the Prefect of the Bas-Rhin reporting on December 5, in Strasbourg 'Today some groups tried to harangue the troops; the soldiers replied *Vive Napoléon!*'[7] This was typical.

In a proclamation accompanying the coup, Louis-Napoléon appealed to both the interests of social order and the defence of the Republic against the plots and obstruction of the Assembly.[8] The prefect of the Saône-et-Loire simplified its meaning in a circular which told the village mayors of his department that the President 'desires to found a government as religious as that of the Restoration, as prosperous as that of July, as glorious as that of the Emperor, as virtuous as that demanded by the Republic.'[9] All things to all men – 'the party of Order includes . . . in all social classes, all those afraid of innovations and who can not conceive a society different from that which exists.'[10] Thus the majority of Frenchmen.

Most of the leading conservative figures in Paris had little enthusiasm for the coup, but what resistance they offered was feeble and half-hearted and at best amounted to non-cooperation. In the provinces the attitudes of aristocrats and the upper middle class tended to vary according to the extent to which they felt threatened by the red menace. This was clearest in the Legitimist response where, as in the Gard, and Ille-et-Vilaine, they were socially dominant and tended to protest quite openly against the coup, and in the latter department the leading Legitimist newspaper was suppressed.[11] The Prefect of the Gironde reported that at Bordeaux the workers were enthusiastic for the coup, but the upper classes extremely reserved.[12]

However, attitudes changed. The daily reports of the Prefect of Ille-et-Vilaine complained about Legitimist attitudes until December 12. But on the 14 the news of insurrections in the south had persuaded most of them to rally to Louis-Napoléon in the interests of order – 'Necessity dominates convictions and silences sympathies. Chateaux have been burnt, that is sufficient motive for an alliance, at least temporary as in 1848.'[13] As in 1848 events were seen by Legitimists as a further step towards 'a more acceptable order of things',[14] their restoration.

The most important effect of these insurrections in the south was to appear to confirm the most alarmist Bonapartist propaganda, something which the limited resistance in Paris had failed to do. It now appeared as if indeed the *démocrate-socialistes* had been preparing for an insurrection in 1852, and that the President had taken necessary preventative action. Even those involved in planning the coup seem to have believed this.[15] Others were told how, in preparation for this rising 'the division was decided in advance: to the valets the clothing of their masters, to the labourer the house he has built, to the peasant the farm he exploits, to the vicious the honest woman, to the lazy the wealth of the successful merchant.'[16] The coup was then justified – 'Society has a right to rise against this invasion of savagery, it is a right, it is a duty, everywhere the man of order finds himself alongside the soldier defending civilization: it is the divine right of society in conflict with ... barbarism.'[17] The *Courrier de Tarn-et-Garonne* of December 18 asked the question whether the coup was really necessary? It answered itself – 'The act of the President has preserved the country from the calamities which threatened it ... for 1852.' It admitted that previously it had not really believed in the existence of this threat but the uprisings in the south had convinced it of the real dangers threatening France.[18]

Most conservatives, especially those of the upper middle classes had fewer problems of conscience. Being less concerned than some Legitimists with questions of honour and traditional family allegiance, they tended to intone with the Bonapartist Mayor 'glory to Louis-Napoléon ... 1852 is dead'.[19] They anyway needed little convincing of the reality of the threat to social order. Whatever their ill-feeling regarding the dictatorship about to be created, they accepted the coup because of this promise of dictatorship and not in spite of it. Guizot wrote to Morny 'it is necessary that dictatorship triumph ... We have not known how to preserve free government, let us know how to support the necessary power.'[20] Former liberals and moderate republicans after the initial shock tended to lend support to, or at least not to oppose the new regime.[21] In the Moselle, for example, an opposition newspaper promised to avoid political comment if the administration agreed not to suppress it.[22] The government whipped up fear by means of exaggerated descriptions of the insurrection,[23] and was thus able to justify itself. But it justified itself best, in the eyes of conservatives, by its very success in seizing power and holding it. The *Univers* of December 19, claimed that 'December 2 is the most anti-revolutionary date in the history of the past 60 years. . . . Iniquity trembles in front of justice. . . . Property has no longer the perspective of pillage, the family of dishonour, religion of martyrdom. . . .'

The middle classes from the great financiers to the provincial manufacturers accorded their confidence to Louis-Napoléon. The 5 per cent rente rose from 91·60 on December 1 to 100·90 by December 16.[24] For the *Constitutionnel* this was 'the best news, the news with the most certain effect, that could be sent to the departments'.[25] An editorial in the *Moniteur industriel* representing the opinions of the more important industrialists affirmed – 'Prince, you have restored our confidence! We owe to you the order and work which are the strength and prosperity of States.'[26] This seems to have been the general view of those who made profits from industry or commerce.[27]

The vital ideological link between those relatively wealthy, relatively well informed, influential opinion leaders and the mass of the population was Catholicism.

The attitude of the Church was quite clear, a few republican or socialist clergy, a few Legitimist bishops reaffirmed their principles. The attitude of most was that expressed in a circular letter by the Bishop of Chartres to his clergy – 'We have avoided that 2 May 1852, which opened to France a frightening abyss . . . the abominations, the horrors, the excesses which have occurred are a mere indication of the monstrosities which would have been committed on a large scale in the whole of France if God had permitted the triumph of socialism'.[28] The typical response of those who had a vested interest in the existing state of affairs. Louis-Napoléon was the man who had helped restore the temporal power of the Pope. The clergy willingly sung *Te Deums* to give thanks for his great victory over the unbelievers – 'to call forth the blessings of heaven on the great mission which the French people has confided to the President of the Republic'.[29]

Odilon Barrot commented bitterly on the Church's attitude, explaining it by the fact that 'the Church claims to see, in all force which succeeds, the work of Providence ... A *Te Deum* was celebrated with solemnity in the metropolitan Church of Notre Dame. God had been invoked to witness the oath of loyalty to the Republican constitution. He was called on again to glorify the violation of this same oath.'[30] Once again the Church closely allied itself with the forces of social conservatism.

Although the coup could be seen as fulfilling the needs of the middle classes it would be wrong to suppose that it was welcomed by all. Emile Ollivier reported 'Universal indignation amongst the bourgeoisie . . .'[31] in Paris. It was the liberal elements and those who possessed a share in political power and who were afraid of being deprived of this, who were hostile to the President's action. These more politically aware and involved elements were essentially grouped in Paris, amongst the large middle class of the city and the deputies of the Assembly.

Preventative arrests removed most potential leaders of opposition from the scene and in general, except for lower middle class elements, even when they did not welcome the coup, the middle classes were not prepared to actively oppose it. The National Guard in Paris, again by now, an essentially middle class institution, showed no wish to challenge the patently unconstitutional act of Louis-Napoléon.

Maupas was to a degree correct when he wrote of conservative politicians – that 'They wanted the *coup d'état* as much as we did; they wanted it before we did; if they did not attempt it, it was not scruples which stopped them, it was confidence of success, it was resolution which they lacked.'[32] Scruples though these men did possess. As a point of honour they had to go through the motions of resistance. At the town hall of the tenth arrondissement Monarchist deputies gathered and assumed the executive power granted to them by the constitution in such a situation. This formal act was the limit to which most were prepared to go. 'The general fault was not having taken the Republic seriously. They did not believe themselves to have any duty towards it.'[33] The quality of this resistance can be seen from the practical inaction of this rump of the Assembly and its final surrender, described by Barrot – 'The Vice-President Vitet again declared that we would only cede to force, a sergeant advanced and took him by the arm; then the committee left the town hall, followed by all the members of the Assembly.'[34] They seem to have vied with each other for the honour of undergoing imprisonment, of being proved to have done their duty and furthermore absolved of any further responsibility in the affair.

Armand de Melun reported how at the fort of Mont-Valerien he heard the conservative Buffet tell some fellow prisoners, but republicans 'If the resistance succeeds it will give power to you, and I would still prefer the President's government to yours.'[35] In the difficult position of choosing between an alliance with republicans and socialists against a conservative coup, what else could be expected from those frightened for the safety of society which they believed to be under socialist attack.

Along the boulevards running through the wealthier quarters of the city, crowds of well-dressed men, women and children gathered on December 4 to see the spectacle and to shout defiance at the soldiers. Whether by accident or design these soldiers fired. Republicans tended to see this as by design, an act of terror to quash incipient resistance, and not only republicans, but Barrot, for example, writing that 'a little terror was necessary, if only to magnify the event.'[36]

This, the news of provincial uprisings, and quickly apparent, the easy success of Louis-Napoléon's seizure of power, together with the relief at escaping what was expected to be a general uprising by the left at the time of the elections of 1852, produced a more or less satisfied acceptance amongst most middle class groups – 'the frightened bourgeois throw themselves into the arms of the new dictator.'[37]

Exceptions included Republican deputies who formed a committee of resistance, including the more radical democrats but not socialists, which attempted to harangue groups on the streets and encourage a resistance which was slow to develop.

Most of the Parisian workers on whom, in the first place armed resistance must depend seem initially to have welcomed the restoration of universal suffrage by Presidential decree, or else to have been profoundly indifferent to the political significance of events. They could have had very little sympathy for the fate of this Monarchist assembly, very little attraction to the defence of constitutional principles. Barrot, being transported as a prisoner to Vincennes, described indignantly how in the Faubourg Saint-Antoine workers made a joke of the arrest of the deputies 'Ah! they said . . . those are the 25 francs being put in prison! . . . That's well done!' Twenty five francs being the daily parliamentary salary and an enormous sum for these workers. The experience of June 1848 had anyway served to dampen enthusiasm for insurrectionary experiences and when in the Faubourg Saint-Antoine an attempt was made to rescue deputies from prison vans, and freedom was rejected by these deputies, who preferred the quiet of prison, any ardour was further diminished.

Resistance did occur on December 4, when more militant and politically conscious elements became aware of the arrest of the *démocrate-socialiste* deputies who served as their political leaders. This was not a mass rising and was only possible when troops were concentrated leaving the streets free in the quarters of the east for the construction of barricades. The military commanders intended to proceed as in June 1848 and inflict a smashing defeat on the insurgents. An estimated 1,200 insurgents took part, defending isolated barricades which were soon outflanked. Only 27 soldiers were killed, a figure which indicates the feebleness of the resistance.[38]

Amongst the workers and lower middle class democrats there was little enthusiasm for resistance or for the coup but, as Nadaud found, for many Louis-Napoléon had some positive appeal,[39] whereas no alternative possible at that time did. Bonapartism was still identified with Jacobinism.

The dead in Paris were mainly workers, but the casualty figures were confused by the inclusion of middle class spectators shot on the boulevards. To gain some idea of participation in this resistance we have to turn to the statistics concerning arrests made in the Seine at the time of the coup. This has many drawbacks; most obviously the figures are not limited to Paris, and additionally they included those arrested as suspect of extreme republican sympathies without actually participating in resistance; but the statistics when reduced to proportional terms relating to the professional groups arrested give a fairly clear picture of involvement. Thus of 2,965 individuals arrested 55·06 per cent were clearly workers of one sort or another, 6·78 per cent clerical workers in public or private employ, 15·22 per cent engaged in industry or commerce and 5·63 per cent in the liberal professions, with a further 3·44 per cent classed as *rentiers* and probably mainly retired shopkeepers – in all 31·07 per cent were not workers and would probably be categorized as lower middle class.[40] There is another factor falsifying these statistics in the general police concern to arrest leading militants rather than simple rank and file with a consequent exaggeration of lower middle class participation. Most of those arrested were however workers and more significantly 76·92 per cent belonged to the professions – workers, shopkeepers, etc. identified as the *milieu populaire*, the coalesced urban mass.[41] The low total number of participants, indicates the political rather than social character of this rising in Paris, compared with that of June 1848, indicates also the limited organization and political consciousness of the masses and their discouragement after the series of events from February 1848.

Outside the capital the major cities were quiet except for some minor demonstrations.[42] Obvious military preparedness discouraged many, for example at Lyon.[43] The provinces tended to wait on events at Paris, and on the news of the failure of resistance there, agitation declined of itself.[44] In the new industrial centres, the factory towns like Lille, an illiterate population exhausted by daily labour could not be expected to take much interest in confused political events.[45]

Prefects were generally able to report of industrial centres as did that of the Haut-Rhin: 'The workers of Mulhouse and other industrial centres received the news from Paris without emotion. Work has not been interrupted. . . .'[46] Eugene Schneider the director of the great iron works at Le Creusot similarly reported work continuing as normal[47] and from the Moselle came the report that 'The workers at the Forges at Hayange paraded in triumph today the bust of the President.'[48]

Minor demonstrations perhaps, but industry was relatively prosperous and after years of crisis most workers were determined to make the best of this. Significantly at Anzin, dependent on a rather depressed coal industry an attempt was made to seize arms, held at the town hall, but even here only about fifty men were involved and most of these were shopkeepers, clerks and artisans, indirectly affected by the slump, and politically aware, rather than miners.[49]

The major cities were overawed by troops. Most industrial towns, except in the north, were small and isolated in the countryside. Industrial workers tended to reflect the ideas of the area from which they were recruited, and generally their contacts with the land remained close. This consciousness was usually conservative, but where it was not, and because the workers in the smaller centres escaped to some extent the demoralization caused by life and work in

	Agricultural	Artisan and factory workers (excl. Textile)	Building workers	Day labourers	Textile workers	Transport workers and pedlars	Domestics	Clerical workers	Soldiers	Government officials	Inn and shop keepers	Commercial professions	Liberal professions	Rentiers	Clergy	Students	Diverse	Total
Ain	11	18	11	4	4	3	—	3	—	2	2	2	2	1	—	—	2	65
Aisne	3	8	3	13	6	—	1	2	—	4	4	—	2	1	—	—	4	51
Allier	29	138	48	42	3	18	7	6	3	6	45	10	30	63	—	1	66	512
Basses-Alpes	808	287	107	35	32	18	14	12	3	6	109	21	46	106	4	1	61	1,670
Hautes-Alpes	44	44	11	4	4	—	—	3	3	—	17	2	3	5	—	1	3	144
Ardèche	137	74	25	11	2	4	9	4	4	—	29	7	10	28	2	1	8	355
Ardennes	3	37	1	—	10	3	2	9	—	2	25	10	17	7	1	3	20	150
Ariège	—	10	—	—	—	—	—	1	—	—	3	1	1	2	—	1	1	19
Aube	31	29	7	10	13	1	2	4	—	4	7	6	12	9	—	—	15	151
Aude	29	61	22	5	2	1	—	7	1	2	22	10	24	25	—	1	41	251
Aveyron	19	56	5	—	4	—	4	9	1	—	13	10	19	9	—	—	9	156
Bouches-du-Rhône	123	201	67	56	2	15	9	26	1	2	126	29	26	16	—	2	64	777
Calvados	1	19	7	3	—	—	—	4	—	1	4	3	9	13	—	—	10	76
Cantal	—	—	—	—	—	—	—	—	—	—	—	—	2	1	—	—	1	4
Charente	1	6	2	1	—	—	—	1	—	—	4	1	2	7	1	—	1	28
Charente Inf.	—	4	1	—	—	—	—	—	—	—	—	1	2	—	1	—	—	22
Cher	62	267	88	239	17	11	15	16	11	3	79	15	13	51	1	—	9	938
Corrèze	1	1	1	—	1	—	—	1	—	1	—	1	2	1	1	—	50	16
Côte-d'Or	4	40	7	2	1	2	1	3	1	4	15	4	19	8	1	1	5	121
Côtes-du-Nord	—	—	—	—	—	—	—	—	—	—	—	1	1	—	—	—	12	3
Creuse	4	24	1	—	—	—	—	4	—	7	12	1	13	—	1	1	—	73
Dordogne	8	24	4	2	1	2	3	—	—	1	4	1	13	4	—	—	6	78
Doubs	11	9	1	7	—	—	1	3	1	1	8	3	18	8	—	—	10	89
Drôme	611	278	99	34	44	5	40	5	2	8	123	26	41	117	1	7	16	1,615
Eure	4	22	2	1	5	1	3	6	—	2	11	7	15	7	—	—	175	90
Eure et Loir	3	7	4	3	3	1	—	1	—	—	—	3	4	—	—	1	5	31
Finistère	—	—	—	—	—	—	—	—	—	—	—	—	—	—	—	—	1	—
Gard	95	70	27	13	4	2	4	10	2	3	41	11	28	45	—	4	21	380
Hte-Garonne	1	31	2	—	—	1	—	3	—	3	8	7	20	8	—	—	9	93
Gers	59	127	48	11	14	4	6	10	2	3	60	18	27	41	—	2	32	464

OCCUPATION OF INDIVIDUALS ARRESTED FOR POLITICAL REASONS AT THE TIME OF THE COUP D'ÉTAT OF 2 DECEMBER 1851—cont.

	Agricultural	Artisan and factory workers (excl. Textile)	Building workers	Day labourers	Textile workers	Transport workers and pedlars	Domestics	Clerical workers	Soldiers	Government officials	Inn and shop keepers	Commercial professions	Liberal professions	Rentiers	Clergy	Students	Diverse	Total
Gironde	2	13	3	1	—	1	—	6	1	2	12	6	21	15	1	—	2	86
Hérault	960	487	168	65	319	15	48	43	1	5	158	73	44	134	—	14	308	2,842
Ille et Vil.	—	21	11	—	—	—	—	5	—	2	5	2	14	13	—	—	5	81
Indre	3	4	1	2	—	—	—	—	—	3	5	3	13	1	—	—	1	34
Indre-et-Loire	1	48	14	1	4	2	1	3	—	1	15	6	13	6	—	—	7	132
Isère	156	64	21	14	4	4	4	8	—	2	28	16	30	42	—	2	28	423
Jura	2	8	3	—	1	—	—	—	—	—	2	1	6	6	1	—	5	34
Landes	4	14	—	4	18	2	—	2	—	1	7	—	9	5	—	—	4	46
Loir-et-Cher	6	27	1	1	8	—	—	3	—	5	12	7	9	14	—	—	10	114
Loire	17	10	1	—	8	2	4	3	—	—	9	2	2	5	—	—	3	64
Haute-Loire	—	—	—	—	—	—	—	—	—	—	—	—	—	—	—	—	—	—
Loire-Inf.	—	—	—	—	—	—	—	—	—	—	—	—	—	—	—	—	—	—
Loiret	93	181	32	72	4	13	6	8	—	4	58	18	13	15	—	3	37	557
Lot	5	27	1	4	4	—	—	5	—	—	11	6	22	31	1	1	6	124
Lot-et-Gar.	96	221	101	29	41	11	8	9	4	9	90	19	47	67	4	3	126	885
Lozère	23	10	1	5	—	1	2	1	—	2	2	—	—	3	1	2	—	46
Maine-et-Loire	2	8	3	10	2	—	1	2	1	—	—	—	4	2	—	—	—	32
Manche	—	16	10	5	—	—	—	—	—	—	8	7	8	1	—	—	—	—
Marne	6	15	5	—	5	1	—	1	—	6	4	8	11	—	—	1	7	80
Haute Marne	4	11	1	—	—	2	2	7	—	—	4	1	—	13	1	1	25	109
Mayenne	—	—	—	—	1	—	—	2	—	—	—	—	—	1	—	1	1	23

Department																		Total
Moselle	100	4	386	225	256		38	95	26	20	8	113	16	33	3	47	125	1,503
Nièvre	2		30	3						1		11	4			2	9	69
Nord	4	23	7	16	11			2	1		1	9	7	11		8		107
Oise				1				2	1			1	1	9				3
Orne								1	1				1	1				22
Pas-de-Calais	28	6	1				1	5	1	5		6	2			3	1	197
Puy-de-Dôme	1	53	9		4	1	5	5	5	3	5	15	14	16		38		45
Basses-Pyrénées	7	9	3	1	1	1	3	3	3	3	3	3	4	8		8		37
Hautes-Pyrénées	7	7								2		3	1	8		7		692
Pyrénées Or.	42	123	32	232	12	7	9	8		1		50	24	23	104	21		49
Bas-Rhin	3	10		4	2	1	4	4	2		1	5	4	6		7		42
Haut-Rhin	6	6	2	5	2		6	6	2	1	2	5	4			4	1	465
Rhône	30	102	21	49	91	4	25	4	2		2	40	26	17	11	43		31
Haute-Saône	2	2							2		5		5	7	3			391
Saône-et-Loire	33	137	34	24	4	5	8	6	5		1	45	14	19	31	20	6	187
Sarthe	4	54	16	2	13		7		1			8	15	31	22	10	3	2,965
Seine	15	1160	130	103	84	42	201	114	38		345	106	167	102	330	24		25
Seine-Inf.		5			4	4			1	1	2			3	3	4		196
Seine-et-Marne	21	51	22	38	4	1	2	1			16	7	15	6	2	2		130
Seine-et-Oise	13	39	15	9	4	2	3	2		1	11	5	12	10	5	1		95
Deux-Sèvres	6	23	3	1	1	1	3	1			8	6	17	10	15			14
Somme		2		2								4		2	2	2		73
Tarn	5				26		5			1		5		1	1	1	3	30
Tarn-et-Gar.	6	4					3			1				5	1	3	1	3,149
Var	1253	571	198	261	62	41	14	16	7	7	206	44	50	105		313	7	680
Vaucluse	282	101	44	11	17	7	7	6	2		68	16	16	30		71		
Vendée	No figures available																	
Vienne	"																	
Haute Vienne	"																	
Vosges	"																	
Yonne	"																	
Total	5494	6024	1759	1583	963	355	390	610	103	155	2179	714	1186	1496	31	109	2309	25460

a place like Lille, then they might become involved in political action, but not from a consciousness of class interest, rather from a consciousness shared with discontented peasants and village artisans, of misery and suffering and a concomitant hostility towards the wealthy exploiter. Sharing in the great hope for 1852 workers in some areas would share in the more general resistance to the coup. These were the men engaged in small-scale production and not those of the large factories and mines, the artisans rather than the proletarians.

Over large areas of France armed resistance to the coup did in fact occur, to such an extent that the challenge to the existing social order must have seemed stronger than ever.

Statistics exist which give some idea of participation in this resistance. These statistics suffer from many of the same faults as have been noticed for those concerning the department of the Seine and additionally from the attitudes and actions of officials and officers at departmental level, which varied considerably.

Again, because of the deliberate policy of the administration to deal leniently with the rank-and-file participants it is probable that lower middle-class involvement is exaggerated. First a numerical account of arrests made at the time of the coup and in its interests.[50]

Based on these figures the table below has been constructed. It takes into account only those areas in which sizeable mass demonstrations did occur, and gives some idea of the social groups involved. In a department like the Sarthe significant demonstrations occurred only in one locality. Most of the arrests here were of local political figures and were preventive in intent. The table consequently exaggerates lower middle class participation to a significant extent as a comparison with the figures for the Basses-Alpes, Var or Vaucluse, where widespread mass insurrections occurred, reveals. Except for isolated cases, mass insurrection occurred only in the south-east and here the predominant participants, at least numerically, were peasants and artisans.

There were three main areas in which risings occurred – in the centre, based essentially on the department of the Nièvre, and including the Allier and Cher and some cantons of the Yonne and Loiret, in the south-west in Gers, Lot-et-Garonne and Lot and on the largest scale in departments of the south-east – the Drôme, Basses-Alpes and Var, extending into Languedoc, into the Ardèche, Gard, Hérault and Pyrénées-Orientales. Save occasionally, as for example in isolated cantons in the Sarthe, Jura and Saône-et-Loire, the popula-

	Agricultural	Artisan and factory workers (excl. Textile)	Building workers	Day labourers	Textile workers	Transport workers and pedlars	Domestics	Clerical workers	Soldiers	Government officials	Inn and shop keepers	Commercial professions	Liberal professions	Rentiers	Clergy	Students	Diverse	Total
Allier	5·66	27·28	9·38	8·20	0·59	3·52	1·37	1·17	—	1·17	8·79	1·95	5·86	12·30	—	0·20	12·89	100%
Ardèche	38·59	20·84	7·04	3·10	0·56	1·13	2·54	1·13	1·13	—	8·17	1·97	2·82	7·89	0·56	0·28	2·36	100%
Basses-Alpes	48·38	17·19	6·41	2·10	1·92	1·08	0·84	0·18	0·18	0·36	6·53	1·25	2·75	6·35	0·24	0·06	3·65	100%
Cher	6·61	28·46	9·38	25·48	1·81	1·17	1·60	1·71	1·17	0·32	8·42	1·60	1·39	5·44	0·11	—	5·33	100%
Drôme	37·83	17·21	6·13	2·11	2·72	0·31	2·48	0·31	0·12	0·50	7·62	1·61	2·54	7·24	—	0·43	10·84	100%
Gard	25·00	18·42	7·11	3·42	1·05	0·58	1·05	2·63	0·58	0·79	10·79	2·92	7·37	11·84	—	1·05	5·79	100%
Gers	12·72	27·37	10·34	2·37	3·02	0·86	1·29	2·13	0·43	0·65	12·93	3·88	5·82	8·84	—	0·43	6·90	100%
Hérault	33·78	17·14	5·88	2·28	11·22	0·53	1·69	1·51	0·04	0·20	5·56	2·57	1·55	4·71	—	0·49	10·80	100%
Jura	36·88	15·13	4·96	3·31	0·95	0·95	0·95	1·90	—	0·48	6·62	3·80	7·09	9·93	—	0·48	6·62	100%
Loiret	16·70	32·50	5·75	12·93	0·72	2·51	1·08	1·44	—	0·72	10·41	3·23	2·51	2·69	—	0·54	6·64	100%
Lot-et-Garonne	10·85	24·97	5·31	17·03	4·63	1·24	0·90	1·02	0·45	1·02	10·11	2·15	5·31	7·57	0·45	0·34	14·23	100%
Nièvre	6·65	25·68	14·97	33·53	2·53	6·32	1·73	1·33	0·33	0·53	7·51	1·06	2·20	3·13	0·07	0·60	8·31	100%
Pyrénées-Orientales	6·07	17·77	4·62	6·14	1·73	1·01	1·30	1·16	0·43	0·14	7·23	3·47	3·32	15·03	0·14	—	3·03	100%
Saône-et-Loire	8·44	35·04	8·56	1·97	1·02	1·28	1·54	2·05	—	1·28	11·51	3·58	4·86	7·93	—	1·54	5·12	100%
Sarthe	2·14	28·88	8·56	—	6·95	—	—	3·74	—	0·53	4·28	8·21	16·58	11·76	0·53	1·60	5·35	100%
Var	39·85	18·13	6·29	8·30	1·96	1·30	0·51	0·44	0·22	0·22	6·54	1·59	1·39	3·33	—	0·03	9·96	100%
Vaucluse	41·47	14·82	6·47	1·62	2·50	1·03	0·88	1·03	—	0·29	10·00	2·35	2·35	4·41	—	0·29	10·44	100%
Average	26·86	20·92	7·60	6·62	3·54	1·46	1·23	1·18	0·27	0·40	7·69	2·16	3·02	6·28	0·07	0·34	12·43	102·07%

tions to the north of a line following the middle and lower Loire did not move.[51]

The reports of the *Procureur générals*, military and gendarmerie indicate that most arrests were made for incitement to civil war, insurrection, affiliation with a secret society, seditious words against the person of the President or threatening to the bases of social order – the family, religion and property, detention in the interests of order and mere suspicion without a specific charge.[52] The participants in insurrection themselves had more specific reasons.

For some, and particularly for the leaders, who tended to be drawn from the lower middle classes of small towns and villages – lawyers, doctors, notaries, clerks and inn-keepers – above all for the better educated amongst these, the members of the liberal professions, idealistic political reasons came to the fore – the defence of the constitution and political liberty. The first proclamation of the committee of resistance established in the Basses-Alpes declared that 'the fundamental compact has been brutally torn up by he who had sworn to respect it – Napoléon Bonaparte, traitor, perjurer, wished to satisfy his unbridled ambition, but the people everywhere rises, thwarts his criminal expectations and responds majestically to his attempt; it recalls . . . that the Republic and the Constitution have been confided to its patriotism'.[53] Thus in the hallowed terminology of bourgeois republicanism was an appeal made to the peasant masses of the economically most backward departments in France. In spite of the patent dissatisfaction of these republicans with the constitution, it still meant for them the Republic, it gave them hope for a more satisfactory republic, which a Bonapartist dictatorship would have quashed. A witness of a meeting of republican leaders at Capestang claimed to have seen two emissaries from Béziers give them an order which read 'Article 68 of the Constitution. "The President of the Republic, having dissolved the Chambers, must be prosecuted and put to death." '[54]

But what was sufficient reason for middle class intellectuals would not have secured them a mass following. Few rural artisans or peasants knew much about or cared about the constitution, few were hostile to Louis-Napoléon. The more radical republicans, *démocrate-socialistes* or Montagnards had in their propaganda for two years promised social reform to follow their seizure of power by election or violence in 1852. Now they presented the coup of Louis-Napoléon as a threat to all they had promised. In demanding defence of the republic they demanded the defence of the republic of 1852, not that which existed. In the Basses-Alpes, the only department in which they had sufficient time, they even began to implement their ideals, abolishing indirect taxes and burning tax records. In one commune in the Vaucluse the abolition of usury was proclaimed, free education and the division of communal property promised.[55] To ensure success their political programme had to make social promises. Moreover, many of these lower middle class leaders had a genuine sympathy for the misery of the rural population with which they were in very close contact, and subscribed to a social interpretation of Jacobin ideology, promising substantial social reform.[56]

With this in mind the *procureur générals* at Agen[57] and Paris[58] attacked *démocrate-socialiste* leaders for using exaggerated promises of social change to bring about the political revolution with which they were mainly concerned without thought of the threat to the social structure this might involve, without considering that in all likelihood they would be pushed further than they intended by the pressures from their followers.

It seems likely that most participants in this insurrection involved themselves because the politically committed appealed to an image of the better world they had promised would be created in and after 1852, a world without tax-collectors and usurers, of prosperity and security in the possession of one's land, 'Wait for 1852, say the labourers receiving their wages, it will be our turn then.'[59] Symptomatic, at a minor level, of feelings at this time. This promise had to be defended against the assault of Louis-Napoléon who, supported by the wealthy, was seen to be serving their interests, his coup intended to prevent this promise of 1852 from coming to fruition.

The years of political and economic crisis, of constant propagandizing had served to create and stimulate the feeling of many peasants and agricultural labourers that they were exploited by the wealthy, to such an extent that the *procureur général* at Aix had seen fit to complain that 'There is not a peasant who does not regard the rich man or the bourgeois as the oppressor of the poor, and who does not believe that the workers should be masters of France because they are the only real producers.'[60]

The motives for participation varied between social groups. Peasants of various sorts were involved. Following a period of low prices, those who had previously borrowed even small sums now found it difficult to repay those loans and were faced with the reality or threat of having their land, their source of livelihood and social significance seized. Philippe Vigier stresses the importance of this.[61] Of the requests for the seizure of land for repayment of debts which he was able to trace in the Alpine region, 49 per cent were made by landowners, including both rich aristocrats and hard-saving small-owners, 24 per cent by merchants and bankers, 8 per cent by industrialists and artisans, 7 per cent by officials and 10 per cent by members of the liberal professions: a broad cross-section of the wealthier social groups. For the poor the wealthy money-lenders were uniformly labelled bourgeoisie and, given the threat the legal rights of these over the debtors presented, there could not but be hostility towards them. *Démocrate-socialiste* propaganda therefore had a great appeal to the small and medium peasants.

These were impelled by a sense of necessity. For the departments of lower Languedoc it has been calculated that two-thirds of those deported after the coup were married and eight-ninths of these were fathers. These were not irresponsible elements, but desperate men.[62]

What for the authorities was the result of a socialist plot a repeated 'conspiracy of Baboeuf',[63] was for most insurrectionaries a struggle for survival, which must result if necessary in a real conflict. Their words revealed this. They sang amongst other things:

> *Away with the kings and away with the Cossacks,*
> *Misery has reappeared*
> *The harvest approaches and the peasants*
> *Will come to reap amongst the tyrants*
> *Hunger chases them from the village*
> *They must eat: Jesus has said so.*
> *Misery produces a rage,*
> *And if they complain, they are cursed.*
> *Let them have cause to curse us!*
> *The end must come, as soon as possible*
> *So that the bailif will not seize it*
> *Carry the straw to the château.*[64]

Sentiments of social hostility were everywhere evident, not ideologically based, but part of an age-old hostility, which had already come to the fore before and immediately after the revolution of February 1848 – once again the houses of moneylenders were invaded and their account books destroyed, and similarly tax records[65], but after the disappointments and suffering of the intervening years hostility was greater. Various witnesses in the trials which succeeded insurrection reported that 'in 1852 property would be shared out' and to explain membership of a secret society – 'If I belonged to the society, I would no longer have to pay rent.'[66] Similarly a gardener was reported as saying to those reluctant to involve themselves 'from now, I will ask for nothing, I take the garden of which I am tenant, and while you others, poor devils, you will eat cabbage stumps, me I will be eating apples'.[67] These were practical men.

Some were more bitter – one accused was reported to have said 'What is occurring, is the war of the poor against the rich. There will be much blood spilt . . . It is time that all this finished.'[68] Others simply used the old slogan 'to the guillotine with aristocrats'.[69]

Agricultural labourers took part because often they were unemployed. A large number of small town and village artisans and building workers also took part; the former in particular participating in numbers out of all proportion with their numerical strength because not only of their often greater political awareness, of the unemployment resulting from a reduced purchasing power but also from the fact that, in the south especially, the smaller urban centres were adjuncts of the countryside, inhabited by peasants. The artisan lived in an integrated community dominated by rural concerns, his interest in these being often increased by the fact that he owned a small plot of land. Similarly the keeper of a small shop and the innkeeper owning a small business in economic difficulty, oppressed by high taxes, finding his customers amongst the poor, owning again a small plot of land, he too was one of the poor and oppressed, of those who could be incited to action by the words 'My friends, we are going to march on the *sous-préfecture*, to demand work and bread for our children.'[70]

This was a protest by the poor against the privileged, often taking an anti-clerical direction in protest against the church's authoritarianism and social conservatism. The *procureur général* at Paris complained that in the village of Taingy 'the bandits fouled the sanctuary with sacrilegious songs, indecent dances, shouts in honour of the guillotine, they smashed the confessional where, according to them, the women prostituted themselves to the priests'.[71] The poor protested not simply, though mainly, against economic pressures, but also from a feeling that their dignity as human beings had to be asserted. In all this socialist ideas had a limited part to play. They helped determine the shape and phraseology of the demands made, but the basic social hostility and the demands associated with it were part of the age-old desire of the poor to improve their condition.

As in any crowd action, motives were extremely confused. The motives of individuals presented here are all fairly typical, these examples drawn from reports in the *Gazette des Tribunaux* being selected after reference to the details concerning large numbers of arrests contained in the registers of the departmental and military commissions. In addition to the motives already presented, more personal concerns, scores to pay off, were important and more commonly men were involved because they could not resist the apparent unanimity of the crowd to which they belonged, were persuaded or forced by friends or neighbours.[72]

The *procureur général* at Agen commented that 'without doubt . . . amongst the insurgents, there are those who do not know in what aim they marched, there is no lie that was not employed to excite in them the worst passions. Some believed themselves to be taking up arms in defence of Louis-Napoléon . . . others to demand the reduction of taxes. Others again imagined it to be a question . . . of restoring universal suffrage, and yet others gave in to violent pressure from the most determined, who threatened to shoot them if they refused to follow them.'[73] Taking account of the natural tendency of those on trial to plead ignorance the accounts of the trials of insurrectionaries give this impression of a confusion of motives.

Most admitted to having participated in a secret society previous to the insurrection, whilst ignorant of any revolutionary intentions it might have had. One François Caumette claimed that 'they told me that the society would help the sick and unfortunate, they promised us the right to work'.[74] Etienne André that he had joined 'hoping that if we were sick, my child or me, we would be helped'.[75] Some were promised higher wages.[76]

But once a member of such a society, whatever the motives for joining it might have been, it was difficult to leave. One accused complained that 'Before initiating you, they made many promises; after, they made threats.'[77] The minority of committed members exerted pressure on the others, even to the extent reported of one construction entrepreneur of giving work only to members of the secret society to which he belonged.[78]

On the day of insurrection, force was used to persuade the recalcitrant. A nineteen year old peasant reported that a society member 'knocked on my door, and told my mother that if she stopped me from going, he would cut her throat.'[79] More effective was the pressure of opinion. Jean-Joseph Thibern affirmed that he had recommended inaction. 'The majority were of my opinion but they called us cowards.'[80] Louis-Marie Boudin, another nineteen year old peasant confessed that 'I wanted to do the same as the others.'[81]

A minority were impelled by personal motives, for vengeance – one accused was reported to have shouted at a crowd 'You are cowards; if you had done like me, six months in prison, you would have more courage!'[82] Another admitted of his participation 'It was not in a political gaol. I wanted to kill Bigot, because I had found out that he wished to become my wife's lover.'[83] Such motives minimized inhibitions and men with a lower resistance to the call for action excited others. In a similar manner rumour served effectively to create an excited atmosphere and a willingness to act – 'they said that the revolution was continuing at Paris . . . that a column had left Blois for Paris to come to the aid of the deputies'.[84] Rumours of risings elsewhere maintained the belief that the new society could be created. Men were ready to act because they believed that action against Louis-Napoléon and his supporters, action of the poor against the rich could succeed.[85] In the Basses-Alpes certainly it was believed that the whole of France was rising.[86]

Zola caught the spirit of the moment. In *La Fortune des Rougon* he described the march of a column of insurgents, 'who with that naïvety and illusion of crowds believed in a certain and easy victory. They would have seized and shot as a traitor whoever would have said to them, at this time, that only they had had the courage to do their duty, whilst the rest of the country crushed by terror, cowardly allowed itself to be strangled'.

The precise form which the insurrectionary movement took was due primarily to the form of organization forced on the *démocrates-socialistes* by the repression of preceding years – the secret society.

It is not easy to judge the number and influence of these secret societies. The administration quite naturally exaggerated their numbers whilst republicans later tended to stress the spontaneity and lack of organization of the insurrection. However in the areas in which insurrection occurred, to judge by the rapidity with which a large number of men were gathered together, for example 4–5,000 in the Drôme, 15,000 in the Basses-Alpes,[87] and by their subsequent action, organization must have existed. The willingness of the masses to involve themselves revealed the efficacy of *démocrate-socialiste* propaganda as well as their felt suffering.

The *procureur général* at Paris described the methods by which members of the secret societies had been recruited – each individual appealed to according to his interests – to defend the republic, to end his misery, or to participate in a mutual aid society.[88]

In the Yonne 'The means of seduction varied according to the localities and the persons, here they associated to demand the reduction or even suppression of taxes, notably the tax on drinks. There for the increase of wages and the organization of labour; elsewhere to oppose the re-establishment of feudal dues and the tithe. Richly endowed sinecures were promised ... freedom from debts, to the tenants ownership of the land they farmed. . . . They flattered the passions of all classes and all ages, but especially those of young men of 18–20 years, whose inexperience and generous instincts made them most easy to seduce.'[89] These would be attracted by the very aura of secrecy and power surrounding the societies. One member, a soldier, described the process of initiation into a secret society – on his knees, eyes bandaged, with a knife held to his chest he swore his readiness to defend liberty and avenge the martyrs of the cause, and also an oath of secrecy. There followed his admission to the society and his initiation into its secret means of recognition – a specific form of handshake followed by the use of specific phrases.[90] The formula obviously owed much to freemasonry and to compagnonnage. Those individuals who had agreed to enter what they had thought was a mutual aid society could not fail to be impressed and frightened by their initiation into the society, even if understanding little of its significance.

The authorities tended to agree concerning the vital importance of the secret societies, the *procureur général* at Nîmes going so far as to write that – 'Without the immense influence of these societies, even an attempted insurrection would have been impossible. It is by means of daily relations established between the committees of the chief place of the departments and those of the arrondissements, of the cantons and communes that it was possible to put on foot in 48 hours armed masses.'[91] The secret society was the only organization in existence through which mass support could be mobilized, so that this is conceivable. A mass of evidence supports this view, not the least being that of the registers of the judicial commissions. Most of the accused listed in these admitted membership of secret societies.[92]

In each of the main centres of population in a department were a recognized group of leaders, in close contact with representatives in smaller centres of population and having contacts with regional leaders – in the Midi with those of Lyon and Marseilles in particular.

It appears that risings only occurred in particular localities after the arrival of messages from regional, departmental, arrondissement and cantonal leaders in that order.[93] Concerning the insurrection at Capestang, one of the accused affirmed that 'All the orders came from Béziers,'[94] and then 'assembly notices addressed to the neighbouring villages were written'.[95]

The source of leadership for these organizations can be discerned from the statistics relating to arrests at the time of the coup.

The figures below are national averages calculated on the basis of the number arrested in those departments in which insurrections did nor occur. Arrests were in these essentially preventative in character and directed against the leaders of secret societies or else influential local republicans.

Compared with the table, based on areas of insurrection, there is a far smaller proportion of men involved in agriculture, but a much higher proportion of artisans and a higher one also of clerical workers, inn and shopkeepers and members of the commercial and liberal professions. The difference becomes especially noticeable if comparison is made with the individual departments in which mass insurrections occurred on a departmental scale.

Agricultural	11·14
Artisan and factory workers (excluding textile)	23·59
Building workers	5·97
Day labourers	5·20
Textile workers	4·54
Transport workers and pedlars	0·99
Domestics	1·00
Clerical workers	4·02
Soldiers	0·41
Government officials	1·53
Inn and shopkeepers	10·14
Commercial professions	4·49
Liberal professions	9·90
Rentiers	7·01
Clergy	0·23
Students	0·54
Diverse	9·47
Total	100%

The greater prominence of the more urban professions is obvious, indicative of the fact that political organization began in major urban centres and spread through the lesser centres into the countryside.

In the Loir-et-Cher the authorities saw 10 members of the liberal professions (23 per cent of the total), 4 officials (9 per cent), 12 merchants (28 per cent), 8 artisans (18 per cent), 7 workers (16 per cent) and 2 of diverse employment (5 per cent) as the most dangerous *démocrate-socialiste* leaders[96]. The most important leaders were clearly members of the lower middle classes. Our table above is representative of leadership at a communal level, whilst these conclusions presented by Dupeux hardly reach below the level of the canton. But of all these professions it can be said that professionally and socially they were in close contact with the mass of artisans and peasants.

Initially the deputies of the Montagne in the Assembly had provided leadership, but a process tended to occur, which Vigier describes for the Alpine region, by which their squabbles and ineffectiveness killed much of their local influence and they were replaced by local men, usually members of the liberal professions, often sympathetic towards the poor, often however political opportunists as their rivalries indicated. These rivalries led to a repetition of the process of emergence of new leaders even closer to the people – some schoolteachers but mainly artisans and especially shoemakers, cabinet-makers, masons, tailors and innkeepers and even some peasants.[97] The judicial registers in the military archives are especially revealing of the importance at the level of the commune of the leadership of innkeepers and artisans.

In sum, the more important the centre from which leadership was derived, the more eminent socially the leaders, whilst at the local level leadership was provided by artisans and small merchants to a degree out of all proportion to the part they formed of the local population. Essentially leadership came from the socially dissatisfied so that even at the upper levels "the insurgents had obscure leaders, men with nothing to lose and capable of anything'[98] but, in fact, even these were reluctant to act in an all-out revolutionary manner whether because they lacked confidence in the success of the venture or were ambitious for political advancement rather than social reform.[99]

Christianne Marcilhacy, in her study of the Loiret, concludes that these men were planning an insurrection which the coup prevented, causing in reaction only an insufficiently prepared and badly co-ordinated movement.[100] It seems probable, given the apparent confidence of the *démocrate-socialistes* in their electoral success in 1852 that insurrection would be planned only to meet the possibility of a conservative coup in 1852 designed to obviate the results of the election, and additionally to impose the right of all to vote on the polling day. Certainly though, the collection and illegal production of arms and munitions figures constantly in official reports in the period before the insurrection.

Summoned by messengers, the members of secret societies in various southern departments gathered and marched in columns towards a nearby town which they intended to take, armed with 'guns taken from the town halls . . . hunting rifles, scythes, forks and sticks'.[101] The conservative press tended to describe their acts as a new *jacquerie* of murder, pillage and rape as did the first administrative reports based rather on rumour than investigation. The Prefect of Hérault reporting, for example, of the insurgents that 'They are killing the proprietors.'[102] This was of course precisely what the initiators of the coup needed to win over conservative opinion.

In fact there was very little violence. Some gendarmes were brutally killed at Bédarieux[103], a number of money-lenders and landowners threatened, usually with the aim of securing food for the insurgents.[104] A report of the *procureur général* at Aix of 17 December in fact criticized the exaggerated accounts found in the press – 'There have been none of the murders, the pillages and other horrors that one might justly expect . . .' indeed 'a certain moderation, a certain legality, excuse the word, can be seen in the acts and speeches of the leaders.'[105] These latter seem often to have been afraid of the possible acts of their followers and to have sought to discipline them and maintain some sort of a revolutionary enthusiasm to counteract any tendencies towards exacting vengeance on the local wealthy. Some leaders were then revolutionaries in spite of themselves, succumbing to the crowd's pressure for activity.[106]

Surprisingly, given the constant rumours that a coup was planned, or probably because of this, the actual event seems to have taken republicans of all shades of opinion completely by surprise. Before resistance was thought of, many leaders at all levels had been arrested, the administration having long prepared lists of suspects. At Montpellier on 3 December the *démocrate-socialiste* local leaders for the whole area gathered to consult on the path of action to take. Almost 400 were arrested before a decision was taken.[107]

Repression, allied to internal divisions had already gravely weakened attempts to establish some sort of national co-ordination between secret societies. The whole trend had previously been towards localization. Now preventative arrests reinforced this and even more effectively the major urban centres, on which co-ordinated activity within particular large areas could have been based, were overawed by massed troops, as in Lyon, Marseille, Bordeaux and Toulouse.[108]

According to the *procureur général* at Agen, all this resulted in the fact that the insurrection 'was only the partial, premature execution of a vast plot which would have roused the whole of France in 1852.'[109] This may be so, what certainly did occur was a series of local uncoordinated risings in the countryside and small towns where troops were insufficient in number to offer immediate opposition. The extent of the rising in spite of these difficulties revealed the massive discontent of the rural population but this could not compensate for weakness of organization. Even at the level of a single department, with the exception of the Basses-Alpes, co-ordination between the various secret societies was lacking. This department was the only one entirely taken by insurrectionaries, to a large extent because it was the only one with an adequately centralized organisation, where the masses were not divided by quarrelling lower middle-class leaders and competing organizations.[110]

In most places no risings at all occurred, but rather temporization and inaction as orders from Paris or some other centre were awaited and more especially leaders were concerned to see how events would turn out before committing themselves.[111] Successful resistance to the coup in Paris would have resulted in far more widespread insurrections in the provinces.

Where insurrections did occur it was evident that they lacked clarity of purpose. This was due to the vagueness of the ideology of the left, and the weakness of organization exemplified in part by the varying social origins of its local leaders with the different priorities they accorded to action and inaction, political and social revolution. This could be a source of strength for normal political activity concerned to create a mass organization from people with varying interests, but in such a crisis, the lack of a common goal would be fatal. The rank and file, many of whom had believed they belonged to a form of mutual aid society were even less clear of the aims of their action.

With this sort of material on which to base itself, armed insurrection against the regular forces of the state could hardly succeed. The towns of Marmande and Villeneuve were seized by insurgents who fled on the approach of troops,[112] so was that of Clamecy, where troops routed perhaps 1,500 men, taking 100 prisoners at the cost of one soldier wounded.[113] These insurgents were enthusiasts no longer.

On December 9 about 2,000 insurgents were driven away from the town of Crest leaving 300 dead or wounded at the cost of three dead and one wounded to their opponents.[114] More usually however insurgents faded away at the news of the approach of troops or of the failure of resistance to the coup in Paris. At La Suze in the Sarthe, which had been seized by about 200 insurgents led by one of the few moderate republicans to involve themselves, Trouvé-Chauvel, a former Minister of Finance, an official proclamation was enough to frighten the insurgents into dispersal.[115]

After the first enthusiasm, after the initial belief in a speedy, bloodless victory 'The night was disturbed ... the enthusiasm, the confidence of the preceeding day were as though carried away by darkness. In the morning faces were gloomy, they exchanged sad glances, there were long, discouraged silences. Frightening rumours spread, the bad news which the leaders had succeeded in hiding the previous day circulated without anyone speaking, propelled by that invisible mouth which throws the breath of panic into crowds. They realized that they alone had risen, that they would become rebels; chased with guns like wild beasts. They had dreamed of a great war, the revolt of a people, the glorious conquest for their rights. Then, in confusion, without restraint, this handful of men cried, its faith dead, its dream of justice vanished. . . .'[116] Zola has evoked with great skill the spirit of failure, betrayal and disillusionment.

The regions in which insurrection occurred were essentially those of small property. For ease of analysis France could be divided into three regions, the north with relatively advanced, relatively large-scale agriculture, growing primarily wheat, separated by a mixed zone from the south where the cultivation of the vine and olive assumed prominence – labour – intensive favouring smallholdings – and where in the more isolated mountainous areas dependence on subsistence farming pushed the population into the struggle to acquire land.

In the north farming was more prosperous and the peasant whether owning land or working as a labourer tended to enjoy better material conditions than in the south, and to be more docile in accepting the social *status quo*. Industrial development permitted the absorption of the surplus population. In the south this latter was largely absent and existing urban and rural industry was in decline in the face of competition from the more efficient north as better communications opened up a more nearly national market. Population densities were therefore increasing at a time when the resources necessary to provide this population with a livelihood were declining. Misery and social conflict arising out of this, tended to increase. The areas of resistance to the coup were those which had been most troubled by agrarian troubles in previous years, by forest disorders, the defence of collective rights and resistance to tax-collectors. In their resistance to the coup they hoped to create the new social order they had been promised, to create the conditions for the implementation of the vague ideas of social justice in which they believed. The *démocrate-socialistes* had given them the will for positive action to supplement the previously existing will to resist change.

Social structure tended to vary with economic, though it must not be forgotten that in many cases social structure would still reflect in part some extinct form of production, for example in the north the village structure created by the open-field system continued to exist, where this had been replaced by large-scale industrial farming, but at any rate 'Diversity of evolution, of living standard, of social structure, from which arises differences of mentality' – the basis of a political sociology.

According to André Siegfried the fundamental influence on political relationships in the countryside is the structure of landholding, 'It manifests itself in as much as it lays the foundation for, diminishes or destroys the material or moral liberty of the voter, in as much as it creates the independence of a social class or accentuates its dependence *vis-à-vis* another.'[118] In a rural society only property could make independence possible.

Thus, again following Siegfried, radical political action could be expected to occur amongst the population of a region where small-holdings predominated. Independence was an important, if not an essential or even sufficient pre-condition for action. In large areas of the south it combined with misery and propaganda activity to create a heightened if still rather limited political consciousness. The small and medium landowners had sought to preserve themselves against the attack by the wealthy on customary rights and against the threat of dispossession by the usurer. The fact that the large landowners and bourgeoisie supported Louis-Napoléon was enough to turn the others against him.

But the reactions of the rural masses were not uniform, even where only peasant proprietors are in question. They varied between regions, often small in area. Only the upper and middle classes possessed a national ideology; the lack of uniformity between peasant proprietors was to a large extent the function of the quality of the land exploited and its geographical location. A more complete independence was more likely to exist where the vine was cultivated, where a far smaller area of land was sufficient to provide for the needs of a family in normal times and reduce dependence on alternative sources of income such as common land, forest rights, migration, working as a labourer on someone else's land, or renting an additional plot.

Where farming was carried out primarily on a large scale, then the independence even of the peasant proprietors was limited, by the prevailing communal ethos of subordination determined by those partly or wholly dependent on employment as agricultural labourers.

Most peasants lacked education, lacked contact with new ideas, could not imagine a society differing from that in which they and their fathers lived, could not imagine relationships other than those of dependence and subservience under which they existed. Generally they accepted the lead given by the local landowners, who, particularly if they were old-established aristocrats interpreted for them national events, claimed to defend their interests and in time of need gave real material aid.

The aristocracy enjoyed a genuine prestige and was often willingly obeyed. Often, however, a traditional hostility was maintained, a memory of feudal exploitation, and then obedience must be the product of coercion as well as paternalism.

As for the large number of middle-class landowners and farmers, they possessed the prestige of wealth, intelligence, capacity and authority as employers, but this did not result in bonds of the strength of those created by an older loyalty. Moreover, these bourgeois landowners and farmers were more concerned with making a profit from the land than with maintaining their social eminence. They were far less often paternalistic figures, their contacts with their workers were less close, the links of dependence less strong. They were less concerned with securing obedience in all things than with obtaining labour, and the submission of the peasants and labourers in northern areas was often with resentment and from necessity because of this, but nonetheless real.

Again, though uniformity was less than complete, a shortage of labour in a particular area would tend to increase the independence of the labourers, as would the ownership of a small plot of land. A distinction could also be made between labourers living in the farm, the *domestiques* and the day-labourers living apart, the former would clearly be more closely subject to the employer, and also between labourers in a region of dispersed population and those in a region of villages. In the former, the agricultural labourer would have little choice as to where to work, and would be subordinate because of this. Collective life increased his independence of his employer. This is offered as a partial explanation of the arrests of relatively large numbers of labourers in the departments of the Cher, Loiret, Nièvre, Pyrénées-Orientales and Var.

The distinctions drawn above between regions are extremely simple. They accord to basic types. There was in fact an infinite variety of areas with mixed forms of landholding and exploitation and in consequence an infinite variety of socio-political reactions even within one region. More complicating were influences other than the structure of landholding including the degree of material prosperity and the force of tradition which resulted in peasant proprietors in many areas acting as conservatives and labourers or peasants in some areas of aristocratic large estates acting radically. The absenteeism of proprietors was to increase the latter tendency.

One important explanation of the varying behaviour of what at first glance might appear to be uniform social groups rests on the variation between habitat.

Regions where landholdings were enclosed, the *bocage* areas mainly in the west, were notable for the dispersed character of habitation, each farmer living on or near his fields, in little hamlets containing from two to ten households. This structure meant that only the minimum of collective life could be enjoyed, that a collective consciousness of interest was absent due simply to the lack of contact between men and more often than not that cohesion was supplied by the chateau and Church. Isolation made it difficult for new ideas to penetrate. If they did – because they proved attractive in a period of misery – then they might, as in some areas of the south-west in this period, have great appeal because no collective feeling existed to oppose them. Generally, however, dispersal of habitat made for social conservatism or indifference and the dominance of the only elements with a clear consciousness of interest and social prestige.

Conservatism was generally a characteristic of the peasantry even where living a collective existence in a village or small market town. Most obviously this was true where peasants enjoyed relative prosperity, or were, when misery grew too great, able to escape to the towns, as in the north and north-east. Traditionally in the plains of the north agriculture had been based on the three open fields and community feeling and custom remained stronger than in the south where agriculture and the attitudes it engendered were more individualistic in character, particularly in the case of the vine-grower.

The whole ethos of village life tended to act in order to conserve; the social pressures of the small community in which each man knew intimately his neighbour forced the individual to attempt to conform. It required a great social crisis to effect change in the prevailing social psychology or else a long process of ever more intense questioning of established values, but even then the community's reactions would tend to be uniform. In the north and north-east, the years of the Second Republic had not resulted in a shock sufficient to end their traditional inertia.

Geographical location was of prime importance in influencing political reactions. The urban-rural dichotomy had been reinforced by conservative propaganda which, presenting the urban workers as communists, tended to cause a conservative reaction amongst peasant proprietors in the regions surrounding large urban centres like Paris and Lyon. More generally there were no more efficacious barriers to the spread of ideas than mountains and rivers. In this era of poor communications, mountainous areas like the Lozère, Aveyron and Tarn remained almost as isolated as they had for centuries past. Life was centred on the cantonal capital or larger communes, and the pressures of conformity were all the greater because there were few opportunities for escape. The prestige of those with sufficient wealth to travel, and knowledge of a wider world was increased. Vigier draws a contrast between the Hautes-Alpes which in spite of *démocrate-socialiste* propaganda remained, because of its isolation and the consequent preservation of tradition and especially here its religiosity, far more conservative than the relatively more exposed Basses-Alpes.[119]

In the absence of a crisis stimulating receptivity to new ideas – attitudes to life in the countryside remained a function of the rhythm of labour – a relatively unhurried process by which man linked the pace of his mental and physical activity to that of nature, subordinated himself to his environment, rather than consciously attempting to change it.

For these various reasons most of the rural population either welcomed the coup of Louis-Napoléon, attracted by the whole Bonapartist tradition, especially that part linking the Empire with a prosperous agriculture, or at least accepted it, as they indifferently accepted anything done by the government provided they did not lose by it.[120]

Yet what resistance there was to the coup outside Paris was essentially rural. It tended to occur in those regions which for varying reasons were open to new ideas. Primarily this was because of the shock of economic and social crisis, additionally because the means for the communication of ideas existed in sufficient strength, and also because collective living was important and extensive. If Marx was correct in claiming of the peasantry that they were incapable of acting as a united class because of the absence of a uniform collective consciousness, he grossly exaggerated the lack of collective feelings, without the existence of which, neither village conservatism nor resistance to the coup could be explained.

Because of the factors outlined above, it is possible to contrast an open social structure with the closed types that have already been described.

Geographically *démocrate-socialiste* propaganda penetrated most easily along the plains and river valleys,[121] but because of the other factors, such as economic crisis it is not possible to entirely contrast the populations of the plains and those of the mountains. Indeed Vigier sees this propaganda as having most effect in the Alpine Region in the intermediary area between the plains and mountains, more accessible than the latter, but suffering more severely from low prices, seizures of mortgaged land, and generally more miserable than the former.[122] As compared with the plains this region possessed the added characteristic of a uniform population structure – of peasant proprietors, with relatively few large estates, members of the middle classes or agricultural labourers – and a uniform political response could be expected.[123]

This uniformity was reinforced by the continued importance of the collective aspects of rural life in an area of poor agriculture and by the struggle to retain those fought for since 1846. This was a uniformity and unity grown out of necessity.

Here, and elsewhere in the south, the peasant lived in a village or small town and enjoyed some of the fruits of urban life, leaving the village in the morning for his fields and returning in the evening to spend his leisure in the company of friends, in drinking or playing. Whether because of the older tradition of this civilization, or perhaps because the good weather encouraged sociability, the character of collective relationships differed in their warmth from those of the north. There existed a community of peasants and artisans with a clearly urban character. The combination of individualist farming with collective living produced both a greater awareness of individual interest, and a consciousness of the collective interest of the mass of poor people, prerequisites for uniform action.[124] In the smaller communes, where even the mayor and council were relatively poor, they too would often support the insurrection which followed the coup.[125]

The relative uniformity of social structure was a pre-requisite for the mass action which especially struck the authorities. One military report from the area of Clamecy in the Nièvre complained that for justice to be done it would be necessary to arrest three-quarters of the population.[126] The *procureur général* at Nîmes complained that in the departments of the Gard, Ardèche and Vaucluse even the most honest and politically uninvolved peasants felt that in the last resort they had no choice but to march with their friends and neighbours.[127] Evidence of the pressures of village opinion and the extent of mass discontent. A certain minimum of cultural homogeneity was necessary to permit the communication between a large enough mass of individuals which resulted in collective action. In such a situation, in the village community, an individual would naturally tend to accord his views to that of the group with which he identified himself.

One last factor making insurrection more likely in the south than north was that of topography. A rising was simply more conceivable in hilly, wooded country than on the northern plains. The case of the Alpine Region is significant in this respect, whilst the *procureur général* at Paris explained the failure of insurrection to occur in the arrondissement of Sens (Yonne) by its flatness.[128]

If the forces of insurrection came primarily from the countryside then its organisation was the product of urban action. Large urban centres acted as the bases for the transmission of ideas coming mainly from Paris, and passed these ideas on to small towns and from there into the countryside. What organization there was was established according to a similar pattern.

The typical small or medium-sized town included in its population a large proportion of agricultural labourers and peasant proprietors, of artisans and shopkeepers, and members of the liberal professions. For the lower middle class groups to be politically active, they must be socially and politically discontented and enjoy a degree of independence. The town must then be large enough to escape the overwhelming dominance of the countryside, or else the surrounding area be inhabited by fairly independent peasant proprietors. Even a large town, such as Orléans or Rennes could be dominated by landowners who possessed town houses in it, and provided employment for artisans, shopkeepers, and members of the liberal professions. The town must also be sufficiently akin to the surrounding countryside to share many of its interests and for consciousness of these common interests to exist. The ability of a town based on a particular trade or industry with a fairly uniform population distinguished from that of the surrounding countryside, to extend its influence into the latter would then be severely limited. Thus the case of some mining, metallurgical or textile centres where the labour force was not recruited from an extremely narrow local area.

The lower middle classes with the prestige of greater wealth and education were able to exert a considerable influence on the masses with whom they enjoyed daily contacts. The curé of Ouzouer-sur-Loire in the diocese of Orléans complained that, 'The more prosperous peasant or the worker thinks as the bourgeois with whom they have contacts and in whom they have much confidence.'[129] These 'bourgeois' translated into images, which the artisan and peasant could understand, the ideas of the city. Numerous members of the lower middle classes were socially very conservative, but it was far more likely that a member of this disparate social group would exert a radical influence than that of a member of a more solid and satisfied middle class group.

Official reports support this interpretation. They were full of complaints about the influence of town on countryside in particular areas[130] and tended additionally to associate rural unrest with the presence of a population of workers. It certainly seems true that usually the existence of a group of artisanal workers in a depressed industry made for a more intensely anti-bourgeois and often anti-clerical propaganda as though a more extreme appeal could be made to these more ideologically aware and materially miserable, more willing to renounce the values of the existing society than most peasants.

As we have seen, social behaviour depended not only on the size of the town, on its social structure and that of the surrounding countryside, on the level of discontent, but also on the overall pattern of communications.

To state the obvious – 'the mobility of beliefs . . . depends closely on the mobility of men'.[131] The isolated community would then conserve its traditions more completely than one more open in terms of communication. This factor of communications as contributing to the creation of a mass consciousness can be discussed in terms of links established by trade, by the workers operating the means of communications, and by labour migration, in addition to the factors already considered, like the education of members of the liberal professions, or the links between newspapers.

In terms of trade-links the major cities, Paris, Lyon and Marseille in particular, as major centres of production and consumption, occupied a place of cardinal importance, but given the limited development of the techniques of communication these each served as a regional centre, with Paris paramount but with the other centres assuming a vital importance. Men and material were moved between such cities and smaller towns and the countryside, and with them moved ideas, whether as part of a deliberate propaganda effort, or more significantly for permanent effect through men talking to each other *en route*, in their homes and places of work and especially in the taverns, vital elements in the communications network. Ideas were exchanged not only at the extremities between which trade was occurring, but at all points *en route* – along roads, railways, rivers and at sea ports.

In the Basses-Alpes ideas spread through the department, particularly from Manosque, which acted as a departmental centre of communications, itself being in very close contact with Marseille.[132] In the Var a group of about 2,000 insurgents were actually led by the editors of the Marseille *Journal du Peuple*.[133] The *procureur général* at Grenoble had complained that 'The localities situated on the banks of the Rhône, and peopled in great part with boatmen, in continual relations with the population of Lyon, are particularly noticeable for their turbulent dispositions.[134] Vigier makes the added point that steam navigation on the Rhône was more favourable to political agitation than were the railways, because of the frequency and length of stops.[135]

Geographical position along routeways could to some extent

offset other factors limiting accessibility to new ideas, for example in the Gatinais of Loiret an illiterate, miserable population was vulnerable to simple promises of better days,[136] where populations living in similar conditions, but more isolated would have been subordinate to an age-old routine. In the Seine-et-Oise the population was generally calm after the coup with the exception of elements in Versailles, Corbeil and Etampes 'which occupy an important position on the railway line and serve to link the demagogues of Paris and those of the Loiret'.[137]

Railway workers and men engaged in the construction of railways, often of urban origin, were signalled as elements of unrest in the areas in which they worked,[138] but more commonly it was another kind of travelling workman who frightened officials. These were the very large number of migrant workers, both artisans (the *compagnons* on their *tour de France* to gain experience of their crafts) and the more numerous seasonal and temporary migrants.[139]

The vital characteristic of these was that their migrations were temporary, their links with their homes were not broken and after experience of city life, they would return, often bringing with them new ideas, depending on whether or not the city or countryside in which they had worked as artisans, in building or in the fields had radical traditions. Their sojourn in a society with a social structure differing from that of their homes was 'The kind of contrast that gives people an opportunity to view a different culture at least partially from the inside' which 'gives them a new perspective from which they observe their own culture'.[140] Usually those who did migrate were men with few possessions and relatively little status in their own communities. Their new experience would tend to lead them to question the validity of the existing social hierarchy, to protest against the privileges of people who now began to appear unfairly advantaged. Only a small minority might be so affected but these would spread radical ideas and intensify any latent dissatisfaction. The size of this minority itself would depend on the strength of tradition in their home areas. If this had already been weakened then the migrant would be more likely to succumb to the infection of new ideas. Often significant numbers were involved; from the Creuse it has been estimated 25–30,000 men migrated in search of work each year.[141] The existence of migrant labour provides a partial explanation of the accessibility of some of the most isolated regions to *démocrate-socialiste* propaganda. The Alpine region described by

Vigier was in part radicalized through its position on the main trade routes between the Mediterranean and the north, but additionally, it could be suggested, because poverty induced migration. This most certainly seems to be the case of the department of the Creuse, whereas by contrast Brittany also geographically isolated, did not at this time provide many migrant workers, and when migration did begin from this area it assumed rather a permanent form instead of a continued urban-rural link.

The factor of migratory labour is then a further element in an explanation of variation in political behaviour between regions. Another aspect of this, the other side of the same coin in fact, was the relative strength of traditional ways of life and influences. According to Ernest Labrousse 'we have written until now the history of movements and not sufficiently the history of Resistances'.[142]

Conservatism is the product of satisfaction with the *status quo* or the inability to accept the possibility of an alternative, in which case it borders on apathy, a resignation. The map of religious practice is one means by which it can be determined whether a rural population has partly freed itself from the restraints of custom. Although, as in the case of the peasants of the Beauce, they might even so remain politically conservative, without the initial escape from tradition they could not adopt radical attitudes. There is some concordance between a map of religious beliefs and one of political behaviour, with irreligious areas favouring more radical politicians than the religious. In both cases change tends to follow the ways of communication to begin in and emerge from the cities. Just as Christianity came first to the less isolated areas, so it declined first in them, though important anomalies are evident. It remains true, however, that the regions revealed by the enquiry of 1848 as most irreligious including Hérault, Vaucluse, Bouches-du-Rhône, Aube, Yonne, Nièvre and Cher,[143] were all relatively radical in politics.

The continued strength of religious feeling over large areas was due to a number of factors amongst which all sorts of historical reasons; geographical isolation; or else the influence of religious centres – Paris or Lyon, for example, as well as diffusing socialist ideas were centres for religious propaganda which partly counteracted the former; social structure both in respect of the influence exerted by the upper classes and the form of daily life of the peasant – the routine of his daily life meant that it was more difficult for him than for others to understand and accept criticism of what was established, with the exception as has been said of the vine cultivator, more independent where living in a community of small-owners involved in intensive cultivation, often more prosperous and enjoying more leisure for thought and argument, in the south an urban figure.

The existence of traditional attitudes is something which makes historical explanation extremely difficult. Often the root of tradition is beyond explanation. The varying behaviour and attitudes of the populations of two villages, due perhaps to hostility causing a perverse opposition between them with important political results within the locality, but in terms of cause ascribable simply to tradition, of which an explanation is difficult to find. This is a causal element of immense complexity, this existence of historical influences. 'Historical, because they result from ancient evolution and because the picture they compose does not always accord with the picture which a simple totalization of contemporary economic, professional, or demographic circumstances would tend to create.'[144] The Marxist theory of history is not a 'simple totalization' but the existence of tradition reveals its dangerous simplicity. It provides for example only limited help in an explanation of the Legitimist political allegiance of many workers at Avignon.

Religion tended to be strongest where the social hierarchy went most unchallenged. It and the institutional Church were elements within the existing society, and each political and social crisis tended to increase this identification. Challenges to the Church were aspects of a more general challenge. Those who were challenging in 1851 were lower middle class elements, workers and peasants. Those who were consciously defending the *status quo* were the aristocracy and more established middle-class groups. It was on their local strength, their influence on the masses that the Church to a large degree depended. If the various elements conducive to their social dominance existed, then the Church too found its authority recognized, for many the same reasons, and the parish priest, often of peasant origin, living amongst peasants, thinking like them, but raised above them by his sacred authority, was a man of considerable importance. Here religion remained a part of peasant life, the principal element of diversion from the routine activity of work and family life, a collective activity given the limited scope for nonconformity in the village.

In such a situation religion fortified respect for authority of all sorts and resisted all encroachments upon it. Aristocrats in particular

318

were careful to associate themselves by means of good works with the Church, and so, where religion was strong, it consecrated the temporal authority and strengthened this. Sometimes, as in the case of much of Brittany, the influence of the priest might be greater than that of the noble, but they shared a belief in a common interest and normally cooperated, introducing a moral factor of immense significance into politics. In the everyday life of societies, religious practice tended to sanctify social divisions. In the ceremonies of the Church the rich and powerful were given precedence. This would intensify the deference of the submissive and the anticlericalism of others but clearly identified the Church with the forces of conservatism.

One other religious factor in the events under discussion was the Protestant-Catholic division. Religious fervour was especially strong where these faiths co-existed, particularly if educational levels were also poor, as they usually were. Vigier concluded that in a department like the Drôme, hostility towards Roman Catholics entrained the less prosperous and less well educated Protestants to take part in *démocrate-socialiste* activity.[145] In the Gard and Hérault it seems that the populations of mountainous areas were conservative except where Protestants,[146] resisting Catholic political dominance from traditional hostility, sectarian dogmatism and because of the more egalitarian, more republican character of their Protestantism. This is an added factor of complexity in explaining the greater political radicalism of southern France, although one of lesser importance than economic-class factors as the conservatism of the Protestant wealthy revealed.

The most important factor in our explanation is that of economic crisis, and consequent social misery.

In the last two years of the Second Republic French agriculture was beset by low prices. The effects of this, however, varied. The owners of land, even the peasant-proprietors were not a homogeneous class. The effects of crisis varied according to regions, the amount of land farmed and previous standards of prosperity. In general the large-scale farmers of the north were far more capable of supporting a crisis of declining prices than the peasant-proprietors of the south because of their large-scale production. Throughout France there was a division between the more and the less prosperous proprietors, constituting a hierarchy within the peasantry itself. In the wheat growing plains of the north and Paris Basin even the agricultural labourer was fairly well off – unemployment was low given the good crops, and for the same reason food prices were low. This latter fact was something beneficial to the urban population as well, but often peasants resented the benefit the towns enjoyed from low prices, which meant suffering for them.

The crisis affected most seriously the small and medium peasant-proprietors and those who for one reason or another needed to make cash payments. To escape from the pressure of their creditors was their great hope, and the new society to be created from 1852 promised this. The peasant reacted essentially to his economic position. This is what made it possible to engage in effective political propaganda.

Marx saw that most peasants welcomed the Bonapartist coup but 'The Bonapartist dynasty represents not the revolutionary, but the conservative; not the peasant that strikes out beyond the condition of his social existence, the small holding, but rather the peasant who wants to consolidate this holding, not the country folk who, linked with the towns, want to overthrow the old order through their own energies but on the contrary those who, in stupefied seclusion within this old order want to see themselves and their smallholdings saved and favoured by the ghost of the empire.'[147]

This was, as Marx claims, the revolt of a part of the poor peasantry but their aim was not to destroy the society of small proprietors but to secure its continued existence. This was a struggle of the rural and small town poor and not simply peasantry against the economic pressures of the more wealthy and essentially the wealthy members of the middle class, intended to create a society of small proprietors without bourgeoisie. In some senses this was a reactionary revolt. Indeed in December 1848 these peasants had looked to Louis-Napoléon and the Empire to save them, but had been quickly disappointed by the failure of their situation to improve even with a Bonaparte as President of the Republic.

Not all the poor peasants were involved. Most were too apathetic, but the coincidence between the regions of resistance to the coup and those of resistance to tax collection in 1848 reveals the pressure of poverty. Peasant political loyalties were to notables and Church where isolated from new ideas. Otherwise they went to whoever they felt would best serve their interests. They did not want and could not visualize extensive social revolution. Men are always reluctant to accept change especially of basic elements in their lives. In a rural community the basic element for security and personal significance is possession of land. In a situation where possession was threatened by forcible seizure then extreme political behaviour was to be expected.

Resistance to the coup in isolated areas, uncoordinated and unprepared, was bound to fail. A seal was set on the success of the coup, an attempt to legitimize it, by a plebiscite.

This was presented by the government and conservative press as a choice between anarchy and order.[148] Montalembert wrote in a letter to *Le Constitutionnel* that 'To vote for Louis-Napoléon Bonaparte is not to approve everything he has done, it is to choose between him and the total ruin of France.'[149] And more specifically he warned conservatives of the Meuse in a departmental newspaper *La République de 1848* of 17 December 1851 – 'To vote against Louis-Napoléon is to support a socialist revolution: the only possible heir at the moment to the existing government. It is to call the dictatorship of the reds to replace the dictatorship of a prince who for three years has rendered incomparable services to the cause of order and Catholicism. . . .'[150] Just as after February 1848 conservatives had accepted the Provisional Government as the best guarantee of order in the circumstances so now they would accept Louis-Napoléon, sacrificing liberty if necessary, for security.

The ultra-Catholic *Univers* on December 19 recommended its readers to vote 'Yes. One hundred times yes!' But a clearer example of Catholic conservatism was the pastoral letter of the Bishop of Chartres to his clergy – 'Inspired by the love of country of which Jesus Christ has given us the example, you will, I have no doubt, vote "yes".'[151]

Government pressure was not absent from the plebiscite campaign. The suppression of all expressions of disagreement in the press or elsewhere, the fear resulting from preventative arrests, military operations and court martials made for a very one-sided campaign. The replacement was ordered of all officials who were unwilling to pledge their loyalty to the new regime,[152] although this purge was not carried too far because of the need for competent administrators. In a circular from Morny at the Ministry of the Interior to the Prefects, the latter were warned that 'the administration was expected to exert its influence'.[153] In practice, the amount of pressure varied. The Prefect of Loiret in a circular to the mayors of his department even affirmed the need to avoid putting pressure on voters in order to avoid scandals which would be associated with the government.[154] This was uncommon, compared for example with the circular of the Prefect of Doubs which demanded forceful action in support of Louis-Napoléon.[155] In the Mayenne the Prefect felt compelled to help 'cultivators, artisans, men of labour' to vote wisely.[156]

What pressure there was, however, only served to increase the success of the plebiscite and did not cause it. Louis-Napoléon was immensely popular in all social groups. All had something to hope from him. Already to the most deprived he had restored their right to vote, which seemed to symbolize his concern for them. George Sand wrote to Mazzini of the plebiscite – 'There has been terror, but the people would have voted as it has without this.'[157] The *procureur général* at Paris described the reaction to the results in rural communes in his area – 'In certain communes, music and drums celebrated the counting of the votes; in others they paraded the bust of the Emperor. In one commune where a single "no" was found in the urn the municipal authority had quickly to destroy the ballot, to save its author from the fury of the crowd which was trying to recognize the writing.'[158]

In fact 7,439,216 voters supported the establishment of a Presidential regime; 640,737 voted against and about one and a half million abstained. Opposition came essentially from the larger towns and some republican areas of the east and Midi. In Paris 132,981 voted yes; 80,691 no; and 75,102 abstained, with significant opposition or abstentions in all arrondissements, although less marked in the more wealthy arrondissements of the west, the first, second, ninth and tenth.[159]

In all areas many workers voted in support of Louis-Napoléon but workers, both artisans and factory workers, were not as likely to do so as other social groups. This was revealed by the Parisian results and even more clearly in the department of the Nord where if 224,214 voted in favour and only 13,956 against, in the textile centre of Lille 4,073 voted against compared with the 7,342 for, and in the working class district of Saint-Sauveur 604 yes, and 591 no.[160] In another textile centre, Mulhouse, the no's were in a majority (1,800 against, 1,660 yes) and similarly high proportions of opponents were recorded at Limoges, and Saint-Étienne.[161]

The departments which had resisted the coup by force now voted overwhelmingly in its favour because of administrative pressure, and, in an atmosphere of terror, the desire to appease the authorities.[162]

Indifference and deliberate choice resulted in a large proportion of abstentions in many departments. Many Legitimists chose the latter path which resulted in less than 50 per cent of those eligible voting 'yes' in Finistère, Morbihan, Ille-et-Vilaine, Seine-Inférieure and Bouches-du-Rhône and only 50–60 per cent in Gard, Hérault and Vendée.[163]

The instrument of the coup, the army, voted overwhelmingly in its favour, although in spite of the fact that soldiers voted on open registers, significant opposition, often to the extent of 20–30 per cent of the voters was recorded in the military districts of the east, centred on Metz, Marseille, Montpellier, Perpignan and Toulouse, primarily amongst the urban-derived artillery and engineers and due to their place of origin, and also the influence of the population of the areas in which they were garrisoned.[164] In the Isère where some soldiers voted twice, once openly, once secretly, the prefect complained that a 'battalion of chasseurs which was unanimous with one exception (174 against 1) when voting openly, revoted by secret ballot and only gave 96 for and 54 against'.[165]

A year later another plebiscite gave the consent of the people of France even more overwhelmingly to the establishment of the Empire, but the Republic in all but name had disappeared in December 1851 if not three years before.

What of the man who more than any other single individual had destroyed it? What of the role of the individual in history?

Marxist theory denigrates the importance of historical individuals, and with reference to the particular individual Louis-Napoléon, Marx wrote in his preface to *The Eighteenth Brumaire* that his purpose was to 'demonstrate how the *class struggle* in France created circumstances and relationships that made it possible for a grotesque mediocrity to play a hero's part'.[166] It might appear exaggerated to describe a man who was able to seize power and maintain it for some twenty years, as a 'grotesque mediocrity'. Victor Hugo faced up to this doubt and answered it – 'When one measures the success, and finds it so enormous, it is impossible that the mind should not experience some surprise. One asks oneself: how has he managed? One decomposes the adventure and the adventurer, and making allowance for the advantage he derives from his name, and for certain external facts, of which he made use in his escalade, one finds as the basis of the man and his measures, but two things – cunning and cash.'[167] But the existence of the former and the ability to use the latter surely demand some ability. Similarly if according to another deputy of the left, Victor Schoelcher, 'This deplorable prestige of a name entirely made the incredible fortune of M. Bona-parte',[168] then again the prestige could have been wasted.

Here was a man possessed of certain useful attributes, placed in a social situation in which these could be used to some effect. The significance of the man rests on his ability to exploit these attributes. He took particular decisions, manoeuvred politically in specific ways and was successful.

Louis-Napoléon was variously described by those who knew him well. Leon Faucher believed him to have 'considerable intellect', but felt that 'his imagination predominates over his reason; it is wild, romantic, and irregular'.[169] His life-long friend Madame Cornu saw him as possessing 'in a high degree decision, obstinacy, dissimulation, patience, and self reliance', but on the other hand as being 'indolent and exceedingly procrastinating' and unable to trust subordinates.[170]

De Tocqueville once wrote that, 'A dwarf on the summit of a great wave is able to scale a high cliff which a giant placed on dry ground at the base would not be able to climb',[171] but saw Louis-Napoléon as more than a pygmy, paying compliment to his courage and determination if not to his indecision, his confused ideas and the dissipation of his energies in debauchery.[172] In the last resort, however, he subscribed to the opinion of most of the conservative leaders. If Louis-Napoléon had out-manoeuvred them – 'Although the President had in his heart and even in his spirit certain uncommon qualities, all together, this is the poorest usurper who ever presented himself to a great nation and nothing shows better than the possibility of his success, the scepticism, the enervation, the softness of spirit and of heart in which the 60 years of revolution have left us.'[173] Not a great man, yet greater than his rivals, obsessed by the idea of his mission to strengthen France and end its social divisions. In the context of his time, he was doomed to failure. 'Bonaparte would like to appear as the patriarchal benefactor of all classes. But he cannot give to one class without taking from another.'[174]

He did in all probability wish to satisfy all, but had first to satisfy those who had supported his action, and those social groups who provided the personnel of the state machine. If the upper- and middle-middle class had resigned its political power into his hands it still possessed the power through the wealth, eminence and social authority of its individual members to exert influence. In Marxist terms in continuing to possess economic and social power it retained the means to repossess political power.[175]

The rise in prices on the Bourse was indicative of a widespread middle class opinion concerning the coup. The economic recovery already beginning but which was to be explained by contemporaries in relation to Louis-Napoléon's action seemed to confirm the wisdom of middle class acquiescence and solidify peasant acceptance of the Bonapartist regime. The vast majority of the population were then prepared to welcome the events of December 1851. Some regrets were expressed perhaps for the passing of liberty, but generally the sacrifice seemed worthwhile.

The experience of the Second Republic had to an immeasurable extent aided the development of the political consciousness of all social groups. The possessors were now more determined than ever to maintain a firm hold on their possessions. They were never again to lose their fear of the social revolution which might smash their world.

The less satisfied, many of the small property-owners and workers, relapsed into apathy, but the experience was not forgotten, the republican areas of the early Third Republic were those of the Second. Hostility to the wealthy had been intensified, the desire for social justice increased and also the sentiment that violence might be necessary to secure it. In gaining universal suffrage they had made an institutional gain, which if its principles were to be long perverted by the system of official candidature of the Empire, would, before the end of that Empire, be used as a base from which to launch a further assault on authoritarian political and social principles.

In the meantime, however, 'Though this government established itself by one of the greatest crimes in history, it will survive for a long time unless it precipitates itself towards ruin. Its excesses, its wars, its corruption must make the country forget its fear of the socialists which will take time. God grant that it will not find its end in a manner as prejudicial to us as to itself, in some mad foreign adventure. We know too well in France, that governments never escape from the laws of their origin. What is created by the army is only able to last through the army, which can only be popular or justify its existence through the memory of military glory. This government will be led fatally to wish territorial aggrandisement, exclusive influence, in other words to war. That, at least is what I fear. In war it will assuredly find its end, but its death would then cost us a great deal'.[176]

The mass society of today, the ferment peculiar to it, are creations

325

of techniques capable of rapidly moving men, goods and ideas from place to place. The Second Republic occurred during a period of transition to this from a society characterized by its dependence on agriculture, by poor communcations and the survival of age-old routines.

In this transitional society the towns, always the primary centres of change, were extending their influence as the means of communication were developed. Economic and social change affecting the towns themselves, and inducing structural change in agriculture and rural society led to a growing tendency to question established values.

Those who were satisfied with their lives, because they were relatively prosperous, or remained in isolation from new social forms and new currents of thought, resisted the impulse to change established social relationships. They were the great majority; thus more than a history of change, this is a history of continuity and yet it is also the history of a period of revolution, not only political, but also economic. Human relationships and attitudes towards these were changing and at an ever faster pace. With this speeding up in the rate at which society changed, human uncertainty and fears grew. For many, stability at any price became acceptable, for others, made aware of their misery, further, even more rapid change was wished for. Louis-Napoléon represented essentially those who wanted order – the satisfied and the apathetic. The balance of power in French society was on the side of conservatism. It has remained there to this day, but the fright conservatives received in 1848 has never been forgotten. Indeed it was to be heightened by subsequent crises, all of which bred an insecurity and an immobility in social questions – a desire for strong men to protect property from theft and so preserve the status in society of those who possessed it. To this extent at least the France of the twentieth century has much in common with the France of the Second Republic.

BIBLIOGRAPHY

I. ARCHIVES NATIONALES

Series BB : Justice

BB II 1118 – results of the plebiscite of December 21–22, 1851

BB18 General correspondence of the criminal division:

    1460 Dévastations commises dans les forêts après la Révolution de février

    1461 Diverse disorders

    1462 Poursuites contre les auteurs des rébellions survenues à la suite de la perception des 45 centimes (1848–1849)

    1463 Complot du 15 mai 1848

    1464 Diverse

    1465 Insurrection de juin 1848: répercussions dans les départements

    1469 Dossier sur les clubs (1848–50)

    1471–1473 Dossiers concerning secret societies

    1475–1479 Dossiers concerning strikes and workers organizations

BB24 Requests for pardons:

    361–368 during 1848–1849

    385 during 1850

    401–404 during 1851–1852

BB30 Office of the Minister of Justice

    332 Affaires politiques: correspondance 1848–1849

    334 Affaires politiques: correspondance 1850–June 1851

    335 Affaires politiques: correspondance July 1851–1852

    358–361 Troubles postérieurs à la Révolution de février 1848: correspondance et rapports

    366 Supplementary reports

    391 Affaires politiques (November 1850–February 1851)

    392A Affaires politiques (March–April 1851)

    392B Affaires politiques (May 1851)

    393 Affaires politiques (June–July 1851)

    394 Affaires politiques (August–November 1851)

    395 Événements de décembre 1851

    396 Affaires politiques (December 1851)

    397 Affaires politiques (December 1851 – January 1852)

Series C : National Assembly

C.930 Enquiry into the events of May and June 1848: evidence

C.934 Enquiry into the events of May and June 1848: evidence

C.938–940 Enquiry into the events of May and June 1848: evidence including the correspondence of the delegates of the Club of Clubs (March–April 1848)

C.941–942 Enquiry into the events of May and June 1848: evidence plus a collection of election manifestos published in April 1848

Series F : General Administration

F^{1a} 10 Proclamations et actes publics des préfets à l'occasion des événements de décembre 1851 et janvier 1852

F^{1c} III Esprit public et élections

12 Seine

F^7 Police générale:

2585 Insurrection de juin 1848: liste générale des inculpés

2587 Liste des individus transportés en Afrique par suite des événements de décembre 1851

2595 Événements de 1851: decisions des Commissions mixtes, Statistiques

12654 Dépêches des préfets au ministre de l'intérieur (décembre 1851)

12710–12713 Correspondence concerning individuals condemned after the events of December 1851

F^9 Military Affairs:

1072 Reports concerning the Garde mobile

F^{19} Cultes

5604 Police de cultes. Seconde République

ARCHIVES OF THE PARIS PREFECTURE OF POLICE

A^a 427 Événements divers 1848

428 ditto

429 ditto

432 Concerned with workers' associations and secret societies 1848–51.

433 Events of and subsequent to December 2, 1851

ARCHIVES OF THE MINISTRY OF WAR

F^1 Correspondance militaire générale: République de 1848

9 Correspondance générale June 16–June 30, 1848

16–17 Rapports des cinq jours (1848–1849)

51–54 Correspondance générale December 2, 1851–January, 1852

55 Rapports des cinq jours (1851)

G^8 Justice militaire

194–196 Records of the military and mixed commissions established in December, 1851.

THE PRESS
Systematically utilized

L'Ami du Peuple	Bibliothèque nationale Lc²2133
Le Constitutionnel	Lc²1056
La Gazette de France	Lc²1
La Gazette des Tribunaux	F8
Le National	Lc²1239
La Réforme	Lc²1553
La Révolution démocratique et sociale	Lc²1974
L'Union	Lc²1648
L'Univers	Lc²1368
Voix du Peuple	Lc²1664
La Vraie république	Lc²1748

Isolated numbers consulted:

Journal des Débats	Lc²151
La Liberté (Rouen)	App Aa428
Le Peuple	Lc²1662
La Presse	Lc²1416
Représentant du Peuple	Lc²1663
Revue des Deux Mondes	
Le Siècle	Lc²1418

OFFICIAL PUBLICATIONS

Bulletin des lois de la République française, 1ᵉ Série, vol. 1, Paris, 1848

(1) 'Statistique de la France: Territoire et population. Résultats généraux du dénombrement de 1852', Paris, 1855
(2) 'Résultats généraux du dénombrement de 1861 comparé au cinq dénombrements antérieurs', Strasbourg, 1864
(3) 'Résultats généraux du dénombrement de 1872', Paris, 1873
(4) 'Statistique de l'industrie manufacturière et des exploitations', 2 vols. Paris, 1847
(5) 'Statistique de l'assistance publique de 1842 à 1853', Strasbourg, 1858
(6) 'Statistique de l'industrie à Paris résultant de l'enquête faite par la Chambre de Commerce pour les années 1847–1848', 2 vols. Paris, 1851
(7) 'Statistique de l'industrie à Paris, résultant de l'enquête faite par la Chambre de Commerce pour l'année 1860', Paris, 1864.

CONTEMPORARY WORKS

Anon. (1) *L'Armée et le socialisme, simples réflexions sur la question du moment, par un paysan qui a été soldat*, Paris, 1849
Anon. (2) *Simples avis aux électeurs*, Paris, 1849 (Published by the Réunion démocratique des représentants du Palais National)
Anon. (3) *Simples réflexions morales et politiques*, Paris, 1849 (Published by the Comité électoral de la rue de Poitiers)

Anon. (4) *Le Socialisme c'est la famine!*, Bordeaux, 1849

Apponyi, R. *De la révolution au coup d'état*, Geneva, 1948

Andiganne, A. (1) *Les Populations ouvrières et les industries de la France dans le mouvement social du XIX siècle*, 2 vols, Paris, 1854

    (2) 'L'industrie française depuis la révolution de février', *Revue des Deux Mondes*, Vol. II, 1849

    (3) 'De L'agitation industrielle et de l'organisation du travail', *Revue des Deux Mondes*, 1946

Balzac, H. de (1) *The Atheists' Mass and Other Stories*, London, n.d.

    (2) *César Birotteau*, London, 1896

    (3) *The Peasants*, London, 1899

    (4) *The Country Doctor*, London, 1899

    (5) 'The Girl with the Golden Eyes', in *The Poor Relations*, II, London, 1896

    (6) *The Village Curé*, London, 1899

    (7) *Cousin Bette*, London

    (7) 'Cousin Pons', in *The Poor Relations*, III, London, 1896

    (9) 'Lettres inédites sur le révolution de 1848', *L'Année Balzacienne*, 1960

Barrot, O. *Mémoires posthumes*, II, III and IV, Paris, 1875–76

Benoist, J. *Confessions d'un prolétaire*, Paris, 1968

Bergier, J. *Le Journal d'un bourgeois de Lyon en 1848*, Paris, n.d.

Bertillon, Dr *La Démographie figurée de la France*, Paris, 1874

Blanc, L. *Révélations historiques*, Leipzig, 1859

Blanqui, A. *Textes choisis*, Paris, 1955

Bonaparte, L.-N. *Des Idées napoléoniennes*, Paris, 1860

Boucher de Perthes, J. *Misère, émeute, choléra*, Abbeville, 1849

Brisset, M. J. 'L'Ouvrier de Paris', *Les Français peints par euxmêmes*, V, Paris, 1842

Bugeaud, Maréchal d'Isly *Veillées d'une chaumière de la Vendée*, Lyon, 1849

Camp, M. du *Souvenirs d'un demi-siècle*, 2 vols, Paris, 1949

Castellane, Maréchal de *Journal*, IV, Paris, 1896

Caussidière, *Memoirs*, 2 vols, London, 1848

Chansons, Pierre Barbier and France Vernillet 'Histoire de France par les Chansons', VII, *La République de 1840 et le Seconde Empire*, Paris, 1959

Considérant, V. *Journée du 13 juin, 1849. Simples explications à mes amis et à mes commettants*, Paris, 1849

Flaubert, G. *Sentimental Education*, Harmondsworth, 1964

Falloux, Comte de *Memoirs*, 2 vols, London, 1888.

Hodde, L. de la (1) *La Naissance de la République, en février, 1848*, Paris, 1850

    (2) *Histoire des sociétés secrètés et du parti républicain de 1830 à 1848*, Paris, 1850

Hugo, V. (1) *Napoleon the Little*, London, 1852

(2) *Things Seen*, London, 1964
(3) *Les Misérables*, London, 1965
Hautpoul, Général Marquis A. d' *Mémoires*, Paris, 1906
Kerry, The Earl of (ed.) *The Secret of the Coup d'État*, London, 1924
Lamartine, A. de *Histoire de la Révolution de 1848*, 2 vols, Paris, 1852
Lamennais, *Oeuvres*, Geneva, n.d.
Lavollée, C. 'Statistique industrielle de Paris', *Revue des Deux Mondes*, 1865
L.A.R. *Étude sur l'organisation de la société politique*, Paris, 1849
Ledru-Rollin, *Le 3 Juin*, Brussels, 1850
Lucas, A. *Les Clubs et les clubistes*, Paris, 1851
Magen, H. *Histoire de la terreur bonapartiste*, Brussels, 1852
Martinelli, J. *Un Mot sur la situation*, Bordeaux, 1848
Marx, K. (1) 'The Eighteenth Brumaire of Louis Bonaparte', *Marx-Engels Selected Works*, I, Moscow, 1962
(2) 'The Class Struggles in France, 1848–1850', *ibid.*
Mayer, P. *Histoire du deux décembre*, Paris, 1852
Mauduit, Capitaine H. de *Révolution militaire du 2 décembre, 1851*, Paris 1852
Ménard, L. *Prologue d'une révolution*, Paris, 1849
Montépin, X. de *et al.*, *Le Gouvernement provisoire: Histoire anecdotique et politique de ses membres*, Paris, 1848
Nadaud, M. *Mémoires de Léonard*, Paris, 1948
Normanby, Lord *Journal of the Year of Revolution*, 2 vols, London, 1851
Ollivier, É. *Journal 1846–1869*, Paris, 1961
Pasquier, Chancellier *La Révolution de 1848*, Paris, 1944
Perdiguier, A. *Mémoires d'un compagnon*, Paris, 1964
Pichery, J. L. (1) *Du Gouvernement démocratique*, Paris, 1849
Procès-verbaux du Gouvernement provisoire et de la Commission du pouvoir exécutif, Paris, 1950
Proudhon, P.-J. *Les Confessions d'un révolutionnaire*, Paris, 1929
Rémusat, C. de *Mémoires de ma vie*, IV, Paris, 1962
Renouvier, C. (1) *Manuel républicain de l'homme et du citoyen*, Paris, 1848
Réponses du département du Haut-Rhin à l'enquête faite en 1848 par l'Assemblée nationale sur les conditions du travail industriel et agricole, Paris, 1939
Romieu, M.A. *Le Spectre rouge de 1852*, Berlin, 1851
Schmit, J. P. *Aux Ouvriers : Du pain, du travail et la vérité*, Bordeaux, n.d.
Schoelcher, V. *Histoire des crimes du deux décembre*, London, 1852
Senior, N. W. (1) *Journals kept in France and Italy from 1848 to 1852*, 2 vols, London, 1871
(2) *Conversations with M. Thiers, M. Guizot and other Distinguished Persons during the Second Empire*, 2 vols. London, 1878
von Stein, L. *The History of the Social Movement in France, 1789–1850*, Totowa, N.J., 1964 ed.

331

BIBLIOGRAPHY

Stern, D. *Histoire de la Révolution de 1848*, 3 vols, Paris, 1850, 51, 53
Ténot, E. (1) *Paris en décembre 1851 : Étude historique sur le Coup d'État*
    Paris, 1868
    (2) *La Province en décembre 1851*, Paris, 1868
    (3) *Le Suffrage universel et les paysans*, Paris, 1865
Thomas, E. *Histoire des Atéliers nationaux*, Paris, 1848
de Tocqueville, A. (1) *Souvenirs*, Vol. XII of *Oeuvres complètes*, Paris, 1964
    (2) *Oeuvres complètes*, VI (1); VIII (2); IX, Paris, 1959–67
Vallès, J. (1) *L'Enfant*, Paris, 1963
    (2) *Le Bachelier*, Paris, 1964
de Valori, C. *La Fusion et les Partis*, Paris, 1849
Véron, Dr L. *Mémoires d'un bourgeois de Paris*, V Paris, 1856
Xavier-Durrieu *Le Coup d'État de Louis Bonaparte*, London, 1852
Zola, É. (1) *La Terre*, London, 1967
    (2) *La Faute de l'Abbé Mouret*, London, n.d.
    (3) *La Fortune des Rougon*, Paris, 1966

SECONDARY WORKS

A.H.	L'Actualité de l'histoire
A.H.R.	American Historical Review
A.S.R.	Archives de sociologie des religions
C.D.U.	Centre de documentation universitaire
C.I.S.	Cahiers internationaux de sociologie
E.H.M.C.	Études d'histoire moderne et contemporaine
E.H.R.	Economic History Review
Études	Études de la société d'histoire de la Révolution de 1848
F.H.S.	French Historical Studies
I.R.S.H.	International Review of Social History
J.C.H.	Journal of Contemporary History
J.E.H.	Journal of Economic History
J.H.I.	Journal of the History of Ideas
J.M.H.	Journal of Modern History
M.S.	Le Mouvement Social
R.E.	Revue économique
R.F.S.P.	Revue français de science politique
R.H.	Revue historique
R.H.E.S.	Revue d'histoire économique et sociale
R.H.M.C.	Revue d'histoire moderne et contemporaine
R.S.	Revue socialiste

Aboucaya, C. *Les Structures sociales et économiques de l'agglomération*
    lyonnaise à la veille de la Révolution de 1848, Paris, 1963
Acquaviva, S. S. *L'Éclipse du sacré dans la civilisation industrielle*, Tours,
    1967
Aguet, J.-P. *Les Grèves sous la Monarchie de Juillet*, Geneva, 1954

Agulhon, M. (1) 'La Crise dans un département méditerranéen. Le Cas du Var' in E. Labrousse (ed.) *Aspects de la crise et de la dépression de l'économie française au milieu du* XIXe *siècle, 1846–51*, Paris, 1956
  (2) *La Sociabilité méridionale*, 2 vols, Aix-en-Provence, 1966
Amalric, J.-P. 'La Révolution de 1848 chez les cheminots de la compagnie du Paris-Orleans', *R.H.E.S.*, 1963
Amann, P. (1) 'The Changing Outlines of 1848', *A.H.R.*, 1963
  (2) 'Writings on the Second French Republic', *J.M.H.*, 1962
  (3) 'Karl Marx "Quarante-huitard" Français?', *I.R.S.H.*, 1961
  (4) 'Prelude to Insurrection: The Banquet of the People', *F.H.S.*, 1958–1960
  (5) 'Du Neuf on the "Banquet of the People", June, 1848' *F.H.S.*, 1968
Anderson, E. N. and P. R. *Political Institutions and Social Changes in Continental Europe in the Nineteenth Century*, Los Angeles, 1967
Ariès, P. *Histoire des populations françaises et de leurs attitudes devant la vie depuis le* XVIIIe *siècle*, Paris, 1948
Armand, F. '1848–1851: Grandeur et servitude de l'utopisme petit-bourgeois', *La Pensée*, 1948
Armengaud, A. 'La Question du blé dans la Haute-Garonne au milieu du* XIXe siècle', *Études*, XVI, Paris, 1954
  (1) *Les Populations de l'est-Aquitain au début de l'époque contemporaine (vers 1845–vers 1871)*, Paris, 1961
Arnaud, R. *Le 2 décembre*, Paris, 1967
Aron, R. 'Le Développement de la société industrielle et la stratification sociale', *C.D.U.*, Paris, 1956
  Main Currents in Sociological Thought, I, Harmondsworth, 1965
  La Lutte de classes, Paris, 1964
Augé-Laribé, M. *La Révolution agricole*, Paris, 1955
Balandier, G. 'Tradition et continuité', *C.I.S.*, 1968
Balland, R. 'De l'organisation à la restriction du suffrage universel en France (1848–1850)' in J. Droz (ed.) *Réaction et suffrage universel en France et en Allemagne (1848–1850)*, Paris, 1963
Barber, B. and E. Introduction to *European Social Class: Stability and Change*, New York, 1965
Barral, P. 'Les Mouvements agrariens de l'ère industriel', *R.H.*, 1964
  Les Perier dans l'Isère au XIXe *siècle d'après leur correspondance familiale*, Paris, 1964
Bastid, P. *Doctrines et institutions politiques de la Seconde République*, 2 vols, Paris, 1945
Beau de Lomenie, E. 'Le Trouble intellectuel et moral à la veille de 1848', *L'Esprit de 1848*, Paris, 1948
  Les Responsabilités des dynasties bourgeoises, Paris, 1943
Becheyras, A. 'Lamartine au Pouvoir' in *L'Esprit de 1848*, Paris, 1948

333

Belin-Milleron, J. 'Les Petitions de 1848', *1848*, 1950
'Symbolic Expressions in the Collective Psychology of Political Crises' in R. H. Turner and L. M. Killian *Collective Behaviour*, Engelwood Cliffs, N.J., 1957
Benjamin, W. 'Paris – Capital of the Nineteenth Century', *New Left Review*, 1968
Blanc, A. 'Histoire sociale et géographie humaine' in *L'Histoire sociale. Sources et méthodes*, Paris, 1967
Blanchard, M. *Le Second Empire*, Paris, 1956
Bleton, P. *La Vie sociale sous le Second Empire*, Paris, 1963
Bligny, B. 'Histoire sociale et histoire religieuse' in *L'Histoire sociale . . .*, Paris, 1967
Bloch, M. 'La Répartition des dépenses comme caractère de classe' in *Annales d'histoire économique et sociale*, 1935
'Une Émeute rurale en 1848', *ibid*, 1938
Bois, P. *Paysans de l'ouest*, Le Mans, 1960
'La Crise dans un département de l'ouest: La Sarthe', in Labrousse (ed.) *op. cit.*
Bottomore, T. B. *Élites and Society*, Harmondsworth, 1966
Bouchary, J. 'Économie et Finances' in *1848: le livre du centenaire*, Paris, 1948
Bouillon, J. (1) 'Les Démocrates-Socialistes aux élections de 1849', *R.F.S.P.*, 1956
(2) 'Les Démocrates et l'Armée aux élections de 1849' *Études*, XVIII, Paris, 1955
Boulard, F. *An Introduction to Religious Sociology*, London, 1960
Bourgin, G. 'Les Journées de Juin', *R.S.*, 1946
'France and the Revolution of 1848' in F. Fejtö (ed.) *The Opening of an Era: 1848*, London, 1948
'La Démocratie révolutionnaire en 1850', *Études*, XV, Paris, 1953
'Bibliographie historique de la presse', *Bulletin of the International Committee of Historical Sciences*, 1934
'Un homme de '48: Arnaud de l'Ariège', *1848*, 1950
Revue of Godechot (ed.), 'La Révolution de 1848 à Toulouse et dans la Haute-Garonne', *ibid.*
Revue of Lacroix, 'Vienne sous la 2e République', *ibid.*
'Les Préfets de Napoléon III historiens du Coup d'État', *R.H.*, 1931
Bouvier, J. 'Histoire sociale et histoire économique' in *L'Histoire sociale . . .*, *op. cit.*
'Mouvement ouvrier et conjonctures économiques' in M.S. 1964
Branciard, M. *Société française et luttes de classes*, I, 1789–1914, Paris n.d. (1967?)
Le Bras, G. (1) *Études de sociologie religieuse*, 2 vols, Paris, 1955–6
(2) *Introduction à l'histoire de la pratique religieuse en France*, 2 vols, Paris, 1942–5

Brekilien, Y. *La Vie quotidienne des paysans en Bretagne au* XIXe *siècle*, Paris, 1966

Brodbeck, M. 'Methodological Individualisms' in W. H. Dray (ed.) *Philosophical Analysis and History*, London, 1966

Brown, M. L. *The Comte de Chambord*, Durham, N.C., 1967

Bruchat, M. 'Le Coup d'État de 1851 dans le Nord', *Revue du Nord*, 1925

Brugerette, J. *Le Prêtre français et la société contemporaine*, I, Paris, 1933

Burney, P. 'Implications religieuses de l'évolution sociale', *C.I.S.*, 1968

Byrnes, R. F. *Antisemitism in Modern France*, New Brunswick, N.J. 1950

Carr, E. H. *What is History?*, Harmondsworth, 1961

Carter, E. and Middleton, J. S. 'The Paris National Workshops of 1848', *The Socialist Review*, 1908–9

Cassou, J. *Le Quarante-Huitard*, Paris, 1948

Caute, D. *Communism and the French Intellectuals*, London, 1964

Chaboseau, A. 'Les Constituants de 1848', *La Revolution de 1848*, 1910–12

Chalmin, Commandant P. 'La Crise morale de l'Armée francaise', in *L'Armée et la Seconde République*, Paris, 1955

  (1) 'Une Institution militaire de la Seconde République: La Garde nationale mobile', *E.H.M.C.*, 1948

  (2) *L'Officier français de 1815 à 1870*, Paris, 1957

  (3) 'Quelques repères pour une histoire sociale de l'Armée française au XIXe siècle', *A.H.*, 1958

Chambert de Lauwe, P.-H. 'Dynamique des aspirations et changement des institutions', *C.I.S.*, 1968

Chanut, A. *et al.*, 'Aspects industriels de la crise: Le département du Nord' in Labrousse (ed.), *op. cit.*

Charnay, J.-P. *Société militaire et suffrage politique en France depuis 1789*, Paris, 1964

  Les Scrutins politiques en France de 1815 à 1962, Paris 1964

Chatelain, A. 'Les Migrants temporaires et la propagation des idées révolutionnaires en France au XIXe siècle', *1848*, 1951

  'De l'histoire sociale à la géographie sociale: Les horizons d'une géo-histoire sociale de la bourgeoisie lyonnaise', *Revue de Géographie de Lyon*, 1950

Chauvet, P. 'Le Coup d'État vu par un ouvrier' in *1848*, 1951

  Les Ouvriers du livre en France de 1789 à la constitution de la Féderation du Livre, Paris, 1956

Chevalier, L. (1) *La Formation de la population parisienne au* XIXe *siècle*, Paris, 1950

  (2) *Classes laborieuses et classes dangereuses à Paris pendant la première moitié du* XIXe *siècle*, Paris, 1958

  (3) *Les fondements économiques et sociaux de l'histoire politique de la region parisienne*. Thèse pour le doctorat ès lettres, 1950

  'L'Émigration française au XIXe siècle', *E.H.M.C.*, 1947

'La Comédie humaine: Document d'histoire', *R.H.*, 1964

Chobaut, H. 'La Commission du Travail de Vaucluse (15 mars - 23 mai, 1848)', *1848*, 1949

Clapham, J. H. *The Economic Development of France and Germany 1815–1914*, Cambridge, 1961

Clough, S. B. and Cole, C. W. *Economic History of Europe*, Boston, 1952

Clough, S. B. (1) *France: A History of National Economics*, New York, 1964

    (2) 'Retardative Factors in French Economic Development in the Nineteenth and Twentieth Centuries', *J. E. H.*, 1946

Cobban, Alfred (1) 'Administrative Pressure in the Election of the French Constituent Assembly, April, 1848', *Bulletin of the Institute of Historical Research*, 1952

    (2) 'The Influence of the Clergy and the 'Instituteurs Primaires' in the Election of the French Constituent Assembly, April 1848', *E.H.R.*, 1942

    (3) 'The "Middle Class" in France, 1815–1848', *F.H.S.*, 1967

Cogniot, G. '1848 et ses enseignements', *La Pensée*, 1948

Cole, G. D. H. *A History of Socialist Thought*, vols. I and II, London, 1954

Cole, W. A. and Deane, P. 'The Growth of National Incomes' in *The Cambridge Economic History of Europe*, VI, Cambridge, 1965

Collins, I. *The Government and the Newspaper Press in France, 1814–1881*, London, 1959

Coornaert, E. 'La Pensée ouvrière et la conscience de classe en France de 1830 à 1848', in *Studi in Onore di Gino Luzzatto*, Milan, 1950

Coquerelle, S. 'L'Armée et la répression dans les campagnes (1848)' in *L'Armée et la Seconde République*, Paris, 1955

Cornu, A. *Karl Marx et la Révolution de 1848*, Paris, 1948

Courtheoux, J.-P. 'Naissance d'une conscience de classe dans le prolétariat textile du Nord, 1830–1870', *R.E.*, 1957

Coutrot, A. and Dreyfus, F. G. *Les Forces religieuses dans la société française*, Paris, n.d.

Créveuil, G. 'La Condition ouvrière et la crise de 1847 à Nantes', *1848*, 1948

Crubellier, M. 'L'Événement en histoire sociale' in *L'Histoire sociale . . .*, Paris, 1967

Cuvillier, A. (1) *Hommes et idéologies en 1840*, Paris, 1956

    (2) *Un Journal d'ouvriers: 'L'Atelier' 1840–50*, Paris, 1954

Daniel, Y. *L'Équipement paroissial d'un diocèse urbain: Paris (1802–1956)*, Paris, 1957

Dansette, A. (1) *Deuxième République et Second Empire*, Paris, 1942

    (2) *A Religious History of Modern France*, vol. I, London, 1961

    (3) *Louis-Napoléon à la conquête du pouvoir*, Paris, 1961

Darricau, 'La Vie intellectuelle des archevêques de Bordeaux et de leur clergé au cours du XIXᵉ siècle', *Revue d'histoire de l'église de France*, 1967

Daumard, A. (1) 'Une Source d'histoire sociale: l'enregistrement des mutations par décès – le XIIᵉ arrondissement de Paris en 1820 et 1847', *R.H.E.S.*, 1957

    (2) *La Bourgeoisie parisienne de 1815 à 1848*, Paris, 1963

    (3) *Maisons de Paris, et propriétaires parisiens au XIXᵉ siècle, 1809–1880*, Paris, 1965

    (4) 'Une Référence pour l'étude des sociétés urbaines en France aux XVIIIᵉ et XIXᵉ siècles. Projet de Code', *R.H.M.S.*, 1963

Dauphin-Meunier 'Socialisme doctrinaire et socialisme constructif' in *L'Ésprit de 1848*, Paris, 1948

Dautry, J. *Histoire de la Révolution de 1848 en France*, Paris, 1948

David, M. *Les Travailleurs et le sens de leur histoire*, Paris, 1967

Delépine, M. 'Le Conseil d'état et la Révolution de 1848', *E.H.M.C.* 1948

Desaunais, M. 'Le Commissariat de Jules Grévy dans le Jura (15 mars–29 avril, 1848)', *La Pensée*, 1948

Desert, G. 'Aspects agricoles de la crise: La region de Caen' in Labrousse (ed.), *op. cit.*

Dessal, M. (1) *Un Révolutionnaire jacobin : Charles Delescluze 1809–1871*, Paris, 1952

    (2) Le Complot de Lyon et la résistance au Coup d'État dans les départements du sud-est', *1848*, 1951

Deyon, P. 'Aspects industriels de la crise: Rouen' in Labrousse (ed.), *op. cit.*

Dickinson, R. E. *The City Region in Western Europe*, London, 1967

Dolléans, E. (1) 'Vie et pensée ouvrière entre 1848 et 1871', *R.H.*, 1947

    (2) *Histoire du Mouvement ouvrier*, vol. II, Paris, 1948

    (3) 'Droit au travail et à l'éducation nationale' in *1848 : le livre du centenaire*, Paris, 1948

    (4) 'Organisations ouvrières et Rassemblements populaires', *ibid.*

Dolléans, E. and Dehove, G. *Histoire du travail en France*, vol. I, Paris, 1953

Dominique, P. *Louis-Napoléon et le Coup d'État*, Paris, 1951

Doumenc, Général 'L'Armée et les journées de juin' in *Actes du Congrès historique du centenaire de la Révolution de 1848*, Paris, 1948

Dreyfus, F.-G. 'La Crise dans un département de l'est: Le Bas-Rhin' in Labrousse (ed.), *op. cit.*

Droz, J., *et al. Restaurations et Révolutions (1815–1871)*, Paris, 1953

Droz, J., 'Conclusion générale' in Droz (ed.)
    Réaction et suffrage universal en France et en Allemagne (1848–1850), Paris, 1963

Dubois, J. *La Vocabulaire politique et sociale en France de 1869 à 1872*, Paris, 1962

Dubuc, A. 'Frédéric Deschamps, Commissaire de la République en Seine-Inférieure (Fev.–mai, 1848)', *La Pensée*, 1948
'Les Émeutes de Rouen et d'Elbeuf (27, 28 et 29 avril, 1848)', *E.H.M.C.*, 1948
Duby, G. and Mandrou, R. *A History of French Civilization*, London, 1965
Dufraisse, R. 'A Propos d'une bourgeoisie de province', *R.H.E.S.*, 1956
Dugrand, R. *Villes et campagnes en Bas-Languedoc*, Paris, 1963
Dunham, A. L. *The Industrial Revolution in France, 1815–1848*, New York, 1955
'Unrest in France in 1848', *J.E.H.*, 1948
Dupaquier, J. 'Problèmes de la codification socio-professionnelle' in *L'Histoire sociale . . .*, *op. cit.*
'De l'application de la méthode des sondages à l'histoire sociale', *ibid.*
Dupeux, G. (1) *La Société française 1789–1960*, Paris, 1966
(2) 'Aspects agricoles de la crise: Le Département de Loir-et-Cher' in Labrousse (ed.), *op. cit.*
(3) *Aspects de l'histoire sociale et politique du Loir-et-Cher*, Paris, 1962
Dupeux, E. *et al. Atlas historique de la France contemporaine 1800–1965*, Paris, 1966
Duroselle, J.-B. (1) Les Catholiques et le problème ouvrier en 1848', *Actes du Congrès . . .*, *op. cit.*
(2) 'L'Abbé Clavel et les revendications du bas-clergé sous Louis-Philippe', *E.H.M.C.*, 1947
(3) *Les Débuts du catholicisme social en France, 1822–1870*, Paris, 1951
Dutacq, F. (1) 'Notes et documents sur le complot du sud-est (1850–51)' in *La Révolution de 1848*, 1925–6
(2) 'Les Élections législatives de 1849 à Lyon et dans le département du Rhône', *ibid.*, 1927–8
Duveau, G. 'Les Idéologies de 48' in *1848 : le Livre du centenaire*, Paris, 1948
'Les Hommes du Gouvernement provisoire', *ibid.*
'1848 en France', *ibid.*
'Les Barricades', *ibid.*
(1) *Histoire du peuple français de 1848 à nos jours*, Paris, 1953
Les Instituteurs, Paris, 1961
(2) *1848*, Paris, 1965
(3) *La Vie ouvrière en France sous le Second Empire*, Paris, 1946
'L'Ouvrier de Quarante-Huit', *R.S.*, 1948
'Les Rèlations internationales dans la pensée ouvrière (1840–1865)', *Actes du Congrès . . .*, *op. cit.*
(4) *La Pensée ouvrière sur l'éducation pendant le Seconde République et le Second Empire*, Paris, 1947
'Utopie et planification' in *Sociologie de l'Utopie et autres essais*, Paris, 1961
'Le Poids de l'histoire dans l'action historique', *ibid.*

338

'Protestantisme et prolétariat en France au milieu du XIXᵉ siècle', *Reveu d'histoire et de philosophie religieuses*, 1951

Easterbrook, W. T. 'The Entrepreneurial Function in Relation to Technicological and Economic Change' in Hoselitz and Moore (ed.), *Industrialisation and Society*, The Hague, 1963

Elbow, M. H. *French Cooperative Theory, 1789–1940*, New York, 1953

Ellul, J. *Métamorphose du bourgeois*, Paris, 1967

Emmet, D. *Rules, Roles and Relations*, London, 1966

Epstein, L. *L'Économie et la morale aux débuts du capitalisme industriel en France et en Grande-Bretagne*, Paris, 1966

Evans, D. O. *Social Romanticism in France, 1830–1848*, London, 1951

Eversley, D. F. C. 'Population, Economy and Society' in Eversley and Glass (ed.), *Population in History*, London, 1965

de Fabreques, J. 'Les Catholiques et le Révolution de 48' in *L'Esprit de 1848*, Paris, 1948

Fasel, G. W. 'The French Election of 23 April, 1848: Suggestions for a Revision', *F.H.S.*, 1968

Faucheux, M. and Morauzeau, L. 'Les Débuts du communisme en Vendée et l'affaire Madeline', *Études*, XV, Paris, 1953

Faure, M. *Les Paysans dans la société française*, Paris, 1966

Ferré, M. *Histoire du mouvement syndicaliste révolutionnaire chez les instituteurs*, Paris, 1955

Feuer, L. S. 'Causality in the Social Sciences' in Lerner (ed.), *Cause and Effect*, New York, 1965

Fisher, H. A. L. *Bonapartism*, London, 1957

Folhen, C. 'Bourgeoisie française liberté économique et intervention de l'état', *R.E.*, 1956

    L'Industrie textile au temps du Second Empire, Paris, 1956

    Le Travail au XIXᵉ siècle, Paris, 1967

    Une Affaire de famille au XIXᵉ siècle : Méquillet-Noblot, Paris, 1955

Folhen, C. and Bédarida, F. *Histoire générale du travail*, III, Paris, 1962

Franklin, S. H. *The European Peasantry*, London, 1969

Friedmann, G. (ed.), *Villes et Campagnes*, Paris, 1953

Fussell, G. E. 'The Agricultural Revolution, 1600–1850' in Kranzberg and Purcell (eds) *Technology in Western Civilisation*, London, 1967

Gaillard, J. 'La Question du crédit et les almanachs autour de 1850', *Études*, XVI, Paris, 1954

Garavel, J. *Les Paysans de Morette*, Paris, 1948

Gargan, E. T. *Alexis de Tocqueville: The Critical Years, 1848–51*, Washington, D.C., 1955

Garros, L. 'Le Coup d'État du 2 décembre' in *Toute l'histoire de Napoléon*, 1951

Garvan, A. N. B. 'Effects of Technology on Domestic Life, 1830–1850' in Kranzberg and Pursell (eds.), *op. cit.*

Gerschenkron, A. 'Economic Backwardness in Historical Perspective' in D. S. Landes (ed.), *The Rise of Capitalism*, New York, 1966

Gerth, H. and Wright Mills, C. *Character and Social Structure*, London, 1965

Gille, B. (1) *Les Sources statistiques de l'histoire de France*, Paris, 1964
(2) 'La Concentration industrielle en France, au début du Second Empire', *Bulletin de la Société d'Histoire moderne*, 1952
(3) *Recherches sur la formation de la grande enterprise capitaliste, 1815–1848*, Paris 1959
(4) *Histoire de la maison Rothschild*, I and II, Geneva, 1965–67

Girard, L. *La Garde nationale 1814–1871*, Paris, 1964
La IIe République, Paris, 1968
'Étude comparée des mouvements révolutionnaires en France en 1830, 1848 et 1870–71,' *C.D.U.*, Paris, 1963

Girardet, R. 'Autour de quelques problèmes' in *L'Armée et la Seconde République*, Paris, 1955
La Société militaire dans la France contemporaine (1815–1939), Paris, 1953
'Pour une introduction à l'histoire du nationalisme français', *R.F.S.P.*, 1958

Glass, D. V. and Grebnik, E. 'World Population, 1800–1950' in *The Cambridge Economic History of Europe*, VI.

Godart, J. *A Lyon, en 1848*, Paris, 1948

Godechot, J. 'La Crise de 1846–47 dans le sud–ouest de la France', *Études*, XVI, Paris, 1951

Goguel, F. and Dupeux, G. *Sociologie électorale*, Paris, 1951

Gonnet, P. 'Sondages à travers l'économie française: Le cas de la Côte-d'Or' in Labrousse (ed.), *op. cit.*

Gooch, G. P. *The Second Empire*, London, 1960

de la Gorce, P. *Histoire de la Seconde République française*, 2 vols. Paris, 1904

Gossez, R. (1) Diversité des antagonismes sociaux vers le milieu du XIXe siècle', *R.E.*, 1956
(2) 'A Propos de la carte des troubles de 1846–47' in Labrousse (ed.), *op. cit.*
(3) *Les ouvriers de Paris*, Paris, 1967
(4) 'La Résistance à l'impôt: les quarante-cinq centimes', *Études*, XV, 1953
(5) 'Notes sur la composition et l'attitude politique de la troupe' in *L'Armée et la Seconde République*, Paris, 1955
(6) 'Littérature de Coup d'État', *1848*, 1951
(7) 'Études critiques: un tournant dans nos études', *1848*, 1950
(8) 'L'Organisation ouvrière à Paris, sous la Seconde République', *1848*, 1950

'Presse parisienne à destination des ouvriers, 1848–1851' in Godechot (ed.), *La Presse ouvrière 1819–1850*, Paris, 1966

Grana, C. *Bohemian versus Bourgeois*, New York, 1964

Guérard, A. *Napoléon* III, Cambridge, Mass., 1943.

Guerrand, R. H. *Les Origines du logement social en France*, Paris, 1967

Guichonnet, P. 'William de la Rive: un témoin genévois de la Révolution de 1848', *Études*, XV, Paris, 1953

'Les Projets de la droite monarchique à l'automne 1848', *1848*, 1950

Guillaume, P. 'La Situation économique et sociale du département de la Loire d'après l'Enquête sur le travail agricole et industriel du 25 mai, 1848', *R.H.M.C.*, 1963

Guillemin, H. (1) *La Tragédie de Quarante-Huit*, Paris, 1948

(2) *Le Coup du 2 décembre*, Paris, 1951

Histoire des catholiques français au XIXe *siècle*, Paris, 1947

Guiral, P. 'Le Cas d'un grand port de commerce: Marseille' in Labrousse (ed.), *op. cit.*

Gurvitch, G. *Le Concept de classes sociales de Marx à nos jour*, Paris, 1954

The Spectrum of Social Time, Dordrecht, 1964

Halbwachs, M. *The Psychology of Social Class*, London, 1958

Hamelin, A. 'La Seconde République dans le Loir-et-Cher', *Études*, XVI, Paris, 1954

Hammen, O. J. 'The Spectre of Communism in the 1840s', *J. H.I.*, 1953

Heaton, H. 'The Spread of the Industrial Revolution' in Kranzberg and Pursell (eds.), *op. cit.*

Hérbert, M. and Carnec, A. *La Loi Falloux et la liberté d'enseignment*, La Rochelle, 1953

Henderson, W. O. *The Industrial Revolution on the Continent*, London, 1961

Hertzler, J. O. 'Crises and Dictatorships' in Turner and Killian (eds), *op. cit.*

Higonnet, P. L.-R. and T. B. 'Class, Corruption, and Politics in the French Chamber of Deputies, 1846–1848', *F.H.S.*, 1967

Hilaire, Y.-M. 'La Pratique religieuse en France de 1815 à 1878' in *L'Information historique*, 1963

Hobsbawm, E. J. 'Economic Fluctuations and some Social Movements since 1800', *E.H.E.*, 1952–3

The Age of Revolution 1789–1848, London, 1962

Primitive Rebels, New York, 1965

Hopper, R. D. 'The Revolutionary Process: A Frame of Reference for the Study of Revolutionary Movements' in Turner and Killian (eds), *op. cit.*

Hoselitz, B. F. 'Main Concepts in the Analysis of the Social Implications of Technical Change' in Hoselitz and Moore (eds), *op. cit.*

Hubert, C. F. 'La Question paysanne chez Marx et Engels', *Économie et Humanisme*, 1947

Isambert, F.-A. *Christianisme et classe ouvrière*, Paris, 1961
'L'Attitude religieuse des ouvriers français au milieu du XIXᵉ siècle',
A.S.R., 1958
Janne, H. 'Tradition et continuité dans les sociétés en évolution rapide',
C.I.S., 1968
Johnson, C. *Revolutionary Change*, London, 1968
Johnson, D. *Guizot*, London, 1963
Kahan-Rabecq, M.-M. review of M. Manissadjian, 'La Seconde République en Creuse', *1848*, 1950
L'Alsace économique et sociale sous le règne de Louis-Philippe, Paris,
1939
von Kalken, F. 'Du Facteur topographique en matière de mouvements populaires et de leur repression', *Revue d'histoire moderne*, 1940
Kessel, P. 'Le Prolétariat français', vol. I, *Avant Marx*, Paris, 1968
Kranzberg, M. 'Prerequisites for Industrialisation' in Kranzberg and Purnell (eds), *Technology in Western Civilisation*, London, 1967
Krieger, L. 'Marx and Engels as Historians', *J.H.I.*, 1953
Kuczynski, J. *A Short History of Labour Conditions under Industrial Capitalism: France 1700 to the Present Day*, London, 1946
Kulstein, K. I. 'The Attitude of French Workers towards the Second Empire', *F.H.S.*, 1962
Labracherie, P. 'Le Paysan de 1848', in *L'Ésprit de 1848*, Paris, 1948
Labrousse, E. (1) 'Panoramas de la Crise' in *Aspects de la Crise et de la depression de l'économie française au milieu du XIXᵉ siècle*, Paris,
1956
   (2) 'Comment naissent les révolutions – 1848–1830–1789', *Actes du Congrès . . ., op. cit.*
   (3) 'La Montée du socialisme en France depuis un siècle (1848–1945)'
R.S., 1946
   (4) 'Géographie du Socialisme', *ibid.*
   (5) 'Le Mouvement ouvrier et les idées sociales en France de 1815 à la fin du XIXᵉ siècle', *C.D.U.*, Paris, 1952
   (6) 'Voies nouvelles vers une histoire de la bourgeoisie occidentale aux XVIIIᵉ et XIXᵉ siècles, (1700–1850)' in *Comitato internationale di Scienze Storiche – X Congresso Internationale du Scienze Storiche* vol. IV, Storia Moderna, Firenze, 1955
   (7) Introduction to *L'Histoire sociale. Sources et méthodes*, Paris, 1967
   (8) 'Crise economique et crise politique en France de 1847 à 1851' Communication aux journées Franco-anglaises d'histoire, Sept. 1960
Lambert-Dansette, J. *Origines et évolution d'une bourgeoisie. Quelque familles du patronat textile de Lille-Armentières (1789–1914)*, Lille
1954
Landes, D. S. 'Recent Work in the Economic History of Modern France'
F.H.S., 1958–60

'Technological Change and Development in Western Europe, 1750–1914' in *The Cambridge Economic History of Europe*, VI

Introduction to *The Rise of Capitalism*, New York, 1966

'The Structure of Enterprise in the Nineteenth Century', *ibid.*

Lasserre, A. *La Situation des ouvriers de l'industrie textile dans la region lilloise sous la Monarchie de Juillet*, Lausanne, 1952

Latreille, A., *et al. Histoire du catholicisme en France*, vol. III, Paris, 1962

Ledré, C. *Histoire de la presse*, Paris, 1958
    La Presse à l'assaut de la monarchie, Paris, 1960

Ledrut, R. 'Situation de chomage et analyse sociologique de situation', *C.I.S.*, 1961

Lefebvre, G. 'A Propos d'un centenaire', *R.H.*, 1948
    'Le 24 février 1848', *1848*, 1946
    The Coming of the French Revolution, New York, n.d.

Lefebvre, H. 'Changements dans les attitudes morales de la bourgeoisie', *C.I.S.*, 1961

Leflon, J. *L'Église de France et la Révolution de 1848*, Paris, 1948

Lefranc, G. *Histoire du travail et des travailleurs*, Paris 1957

Lemaire, R. 'Les Sources contemporaines: Les XIXe et XXe siècles en France' in *L'Histoire sociale . . .*, *op. cit.*

Léon, P. 'Une grande thèse sur la bourgeoisie française', *R.H.*, 1965

Leroy, M. *Histoire des idées sociales en France de Babeuf à Tocqueville*, Paris, 1950

Levasseur, E. *Histoire des classes ouvrières en France*, vol. II, Paris, 1867

Levy, C. (1) 'Notes sur les fondements sociaux de l'insurrection de décembre 1851 en province' in *Information Historique*, 1954
    (2) 'Une Journal "rouge" sous la Seconde République: "L'Union Républicaine d'Auxerre"', *Annales de Bourgogne*, 1961

Leys, M. D. R. *Between Two Empires*, London, 1955

Lhomme, J. (1) *La Grande bourgeoisie au pouvoir, 1830–80*, Paris, 1960
    (2) *Économie et histoire*, Geneva, 1967
    (3) *Le Problème des classes*, Paris, 1938
    (4) 'En quels termes se pose le probleme de la suprématie d'une classe' *R.E.*, 1956
    (5) 'Essai de comparaison entre les structures économiques et les structures sociales', *ibid.*

Ligou, D. 'Une Candidature "ouvrière" aux élections législatives de 1848 à Montauban', *R.H.E.S.*, 1963

Lorwin, V. R. 'Working Class Politics and Economic Development in Western Europe', *A.H.R.*, 1957–8

Loubère, L. (1) *Louis Blanc*, New York, 1959
    (2) 'The Intellectual Origins of French Jacobin Socialism', *I.R.S.H.*, 1959
    (3) 'The Emergence of the Extreme Left in Lower Languedoc, 1848–

M

1851: Social and Economic Factors in Politics', *A.H.R.*, 1968

Lucas-Dubreton, J. *Le Culte de Napoléon*, Paris, 1960

de Luna, F. A. *The French Republic under Cavaignac*, 1848, Princeton, N.J., 1969

Marcilhacy, C. (1) 'Les Caractères de la crise sociale et politique de 1846 à 1852 dans le département du Loiret', *R.H.M.C.*, 1959

    (2) *Le Diocèse d'Orlèans au milieu du* XIXᵉ *siècle*, Paris 1964

Marczewski, J. 'Quantitative History', *J.C.H.*, 1968

Markham, F. *Napoléon*, New York, 1966

Markovitch, J. 'La Crise de 1847–1848 dans les industries parisiennes', *R.H.E.S.*, 1965

Mazlish, B. 'Group Psychology and Problems of Contemporary History', *J.C.H.*, 1968

Mayer, J. P. *Political Thought in France*, London, 1949

McClelland, D. C. 'The Impulse to Modernisation' in Weiner (ed.) *Modernisation: The Dynamics of Growth*, New York, 1966

    'The Achievement Motive in Economic Growth', in Hoselitz and Moore (ed.), *op. cit.*

McKay, D. C. (1) *The National Workshops*, Cambridge, Mass., 1933

    (2) 'Le Vicomte de Falloux et les Ateliers nationaux', *1848*, 1930

    (3) 'Un Imprimé "perdu", sur la dissolution des Ateliers nationaux de 1848', *ibid.*

Mellor, A. *Histoire de l'anticléricalisme française*, Paris, 1966

Mendras, H. *Sociologie de la campagne française*, Paris, 1959

Meynier, A., *Les Paysages agraires*, Paris, 1958

Montagne, Capitaine, P. *Le Comportement politique de l'armée à Lyon sous la Monarchie de Juillet et la Seconde République*, Paris, 1966

Moody, J. (ed.), *Church and Society*, New York, 1953

Moore, B. *Social Origins of Dictatorship and Democracy*, Boston, 1966

Moore, W. E. *The Impact of Industry*, Englewood Cliffs, N.J., 1965

Moraze, C. *The Triumph of the Middle Class*, London, 1966

    La France bourgeoisie, Paris, 1947

Mosse, G. L. *The Culture of Western Europe*, London, 1963

Moulin, C. (1) 'La Genèse de 1848 en France' in *1848: Le livre du centenaire*, Paris, 1948

    (2) 'La Vie quotidienne', *ibid.*

    (3) 'Les Clubs et la presse', *ibid.*

    (4) 'Le Visage de 1848 par les textes de l'époque', *ibid.*

Moulin, L. and Aerts, L. 'Les Classes moyennes', *C.I.S.*, 1961

O'Boyle, L., 'The "Middle Class" Reconsidered: A Reply to Professor Cobban', *F.H.S.*, 1967

Olivesi, A. *La Commune de 1871 à Marseille et ses origines*, Paris, 1950

Osen, J. L. 'French Calvinists and the State, 1830–52', *F.H.S.*, 1967

Ossowski, S. *Class Structure in the Social Consciousness*', London, 1963

344

Palmade, G. P. *Capitalisme et capitalistes français au* XIXᵉ *siècle*, Paris, 1961

Parsons, T. 'Some Principal Characteristics of Industrial Societies' in C. E. Black (ed.), *The Transformation of Russian Society*, Cambridge, Mass., 1960

'Cause and Effect in Sociology' in Lerner (ed.), *op. cit.*

Payne, H. C. *The Police State of Louis-Napoléon Bonaparte, 1851–1860*, Seattle, 1966

Perrier, A. '1848 en Creuse', *1848*, 1949

Perrot, M. 'Aspects industriels de la crise. Les régions textiles du Calvados' in Labrousse (ed.), *op. cit.*

Perrot, M. and Maitron, J. 'Sources, institutions et recherches en histoire ouvrière française', *M.S.*, 1968

Pierrard, P. *La Vie ouvrière à Lille sous le Second Empire*, Paris, 1965

Pinton, A. 'La Province' in *1848: Le livre du centenaire*, Paris 1948.

Plamenatz, J. *The Revolutionary Movement in France, 1815–71*, London, 1952

Ponteil, F. (1) 'La Crise alimentaire de 1847 dans le Bas-Rhin' in *La Révolution de 1848*, 1925–6

(2) 'Un Rapport de police sur l'état des esprits à Marseille après les troubles de Juin 1848', *Revue d'histoire modern*, 1930

Les Classes bourgeoises et l'avènement de la démocratie 1815–1914, Paris, 1968

Pourrat, H. *L'Homme à la bêche*, Paris, 1941

Pouthas, C. H. *La Population française pendant la première moitié du* XIXᵉ *siècle*, Paris, 1950

'Complexité de 1848', *1848*, 1949–50

'Les Procès-Verbaux du Gouvernement provisoire et de la Commission du pouvoir exécutif, fev.–juin, 1848', *Bulletin de la société d'histoire moderne*, 1950

Préclin, E. 'La Révolution de 1848 en Franche-Comté (1848–51)', *E.H.M.C.*, 1948

de Pressac, P. *Les Forces historiques de la France : La tradition dans l'orientation politique des provinces*, Paris, 1928

Priouret, R. *Origines du patronat français*, Paris, 1963

Proust, J. 'Histoire sociale et histoire littéraire' in *L'Histoire sociale . . .*, *op. cit.*

Puech, J.–L. (1) Review of Ethel Harris 'Lamartine et le peuple', *1848*, 1948

(2) 'Livres d'images', *ibid.*, 1949–50

Quentin-Bauchart, P. *La Crise sociale de 1848*, Paris, 1920

Rambaud, P. 'Le Travail agraire et l'évolution de la société rurale', *Études rurales*, 1966

Raphael, P. 'La Loi du 31 mai, 1850', *R.H. M.C.*, 1909–10

Reinhard, M. 'Ozanam et la Révolution de 1848', *E.H.M.C.*, 1948

Remond, R. *The Right Wing in France : From 1815 to de Gaulle*, Philadelphia, 1966

Rigaudias-Weiss, H. *Les Enquêtes ouvrières en France entre 1830 et 1848*, Paris, 1936

Robertson, P. *Revolutions of 1848*, New York, 1960

Rosenberg, N. 'The Economic Consequences of Technological Change, 1830–80' in Kranzberg and Pursell (eds), *op. cit.*

Rougeron, G. 'La Situation économique et sociale dans le départment de l'Allier à la fin de la Monarchie de Juillet', *1848*, 1949–50

'La Terreur bonapartiste dans le département de l'Allier après le Coup d'État', *ibid.*, no. 54

Rubel, M. 'Karl Marx et le problème paysan', *R.H.E.S.*, 1954

'Robert Owen à Paris en 1848', *A.H.*, 1960

Karl Marx devant le bonapartisme, Paris, 1960

Rudé, G. *The Crowd in History*, London, 1964

de Saint-Jacob, P. 'La Situation des paysans de la Côte-d'Or en 1848', *E.H.M.C.*, 1948

Schmidt, C. (1) *Des Ateliers nationaux aux barricades de Juin*, Paris, 1948

'Juin 1848', *R.S.*, 1948.

Schnerb, R. (1) *Ledru-Rollin*, Paris, 1948

'La Seconde République dans le département du Puy-de-Dôme' in *La Révolution de 1848*, vols 22, 23, 24, 28

'Les Hommes de 1848 et l'impôt', *ibid.*, 1947

Scriven, M. 'Causes, Connections and Conditions in History' in Dray (ed.), *op. cit.*

Sée, H, (1) 'Quelques aperçus sur la condition de la classe ouvrière et sur le mouvement ouvrier en France de 1815 à 1848', *R.H.E.S.*, 1924

(2) *Histoire économique de la France*, vol. II, Paris, 1942

Séguy, J. 'Les Sectes d'origine protestante et le monde ouvrier français au xixe siècle', *A.S.R.*, 1958

Seignebos, C. (1) *La Révolution de 1848 – Le Second Empire*, Paris, 1921

(2) 'Les Procès-verbaux du Gouvernement provisoire et de la Commission du Poutoir exécutif de 1848', *R.H.M.C.*, 1905–6

Siegfried, A. (1) *France : A Study in Nationality*, London, 1930.

(2) *Tableau politique de la France de l'ouest sous le Troisième République*, Paris, 1913

Simpson, F. A. *The Rise of Louis Napoleon*, London, 1909

Singer, M. 'The Modernisation of Religious Beliefs' in M. Weiner (ed.) *Modernisation : The Dynamics of Growth*, New York, 1966

Slicher, von Bath, B. H. *The Agrarian History of Western Europe*, London, 1963

Smelser, N. J. *Theory of Collective Behaviour*, London, 1962

'Mechanisms of Change and Adjustment to Change' in Hoselitz and Moore (eds), *op. cit.*

Smith, C. S. 'Mining and Metallurgical Production, 1800–1880' in Kranzberg and Pursell (eds), *op. cit.*

Soboul, A. 'The French Rural Community in the Eighteenth and Nineteenth Centuries', *Past and Present*, 1956
  (1) 'La Question paysanne en 1848', *La Pensée*, 18–20, 1948
  (2) 'Les Troubles agraires de 1848', *1848*, 180–81, 1948
  (3) 'La Communauté rurale (XVIIIe–XIXe siècle): Problèmes de base', *Revue de Synthèse*, 1957
  The French Revolution of 1848, London, 1948
  'Description et mesure en histoire sociale' in *L'Histoire sociale . . .*, *op. cit.*

Soltau, R. H. *French Political Thought in the Nineteenth Century*, London, n.d.

Sperber, M. 'Tradition et culture de masse', *Le Contrat Social*, 1966

Spitzer, A. B. *The Revolutionary Theories of Louis-Auguste Blanqui*, New York, 1957

Stearns, P. *European Society in Upheaval*, New York, 1967

Stewart, N. *Blanqui*, London, 1939.

Sullerot, E. 'Journaux féminins et lutte ouvrière 1848–49' in Godechot (ed.), *La Presse ouvrière*

Swart, K. W. *The Sense of Decadence in Nineteenth Century France*, The Hague, 1964

Talmon, J. L. *Political Messianism – The Romantic Phase*, London, 1960
  Romanticism and Revolt, London, 1967

Tchernoff, J. 'Le Rôle politique des sociétés dites secrètes sous la Deuxième République', *Bulletin de la société d'histoire moderne*, 1905
  Associations et sociétés secrètes sous la Deuxième République, Paris, 1905

Tersen, E. 'Juin 48', *La Pensée*, 1948
  'Etudes critiques "L'Esprit de 1848"', *1848*, 1950

Thompson, J. M. *Louis Napoleon and the Second Empire*, London, 1955

Toch, H. *The Social Psychology of Social Movements*, London, 1966

Tudesq, A. J. 'La Crise de 1847, vue par les milieux d'affaires parisiens' in Labrousse (ed.), *op cit.*
  'La Légende napoléonienne en France en 1848', *R.H.*, 1957
  (2) *L'Élection présidentielle de Louis-Napoléon Bonaparte, 10 décembre 1848*, Paris, 1965
  (1) *Les Grands notables en France (1840–1849): Étude historique d'une psychologie sociale*, 2 vols, Paris, 1964
  Les Conseillers généraux en France au temps de Guizot, Paris, 1967
  'L'Élection du Président de la République en 1848 dans l'Hérault', *Annales du Midi*, 1955

Turner, R. H. and Killian, L. M. *Collective Behavior*, Engelwood Cliffs, N.J.,1957

Usher, A. P. 'The Textile Industry, 1750–1830' in Kranzberg and Pursell (eds), *op. cit.*

Varagnac, A. 'La Vie Paysanne au siècle dernier', *Annales*, 1933 de Vaulx, B. and Beau de Lomenie, E. 'L'Arrivée de Louis-Napoléon au pouvoir' in *L'Esprit de 1848*, Paris, 1948

Vauthier, G. 'A Propos de l'impôt des 45 centimes', *1848*, 1929–31

Vicaire, M. H. 'Les Ouvriers parisiens en face du catholicisme de 1830 à 1870', *Schweizerische Zeitschrift für Geschichte*, 1951

Vidalenc, J. (1) 'Les Résultats de l'enquête sur le travail prescrite par l'Assemblée constituante dans le département de l'Eure', *La Pensée*, 1948

(2) 'La Situation économique et sociale des Basses-Alpes en 1848', *Études* . . ., XVI

(3) 'La Province et les journées de juin', *E.H.M.C.*, 1948

'Étude politique et sociale d'un département en 1848: L'Eure au début de la Seconde République', *1848*, 1946

Review of R. Laurent 'Les vignerons de la Côte-d'Or au XIXᵉ siècle', *R.H.*, 1959

Vigier, P. (1) *La Seconde République dans la région Alpine*, 2 vols, Paris, 1953

(2) *La Monarchie de Juillet*, Paris, 1965

(3) *La Seconde République*, Paris, 1967

(4) 'Lyon et l'évolution politique de la province française au XIXᵉ siècle *Cahiers d'histoire*, 1967

Vincienne, M. and Courtois, H. 'La France en 1848 d'après l'enquête cantonale ordonnée par le Comité du Travail', *A.S.R.*, 1958

Walter, G. *Histoire des paysans de France*, Paris, 1963

Warner, S. B. 'Population Movements and Urbanization' in Kranzberg and Purnell (eds), *op. cit.*

Wassermann, S. 'Le Club de Raspail en 1848', *La Révolution de 1848*, 1908–09

Les Clubs de Barbès et de Blanqui en 1848, Paris, 1913

Weber, A. F. *The Growth of Cities in the Nineteenth Century*, New York, 1963

Weil, G. D. *Les Elections législatives depuis 1789*, Paris, 1895

Histoire du Mouvement social en France, Paris, 1911

Weiner, M. Introduction to *Modernisation: The Dynamics of Growth*, New York, 1966

Wright, G. *Rural Revolution in France*, London, 1964

'A Poet in Politics: Lamartine and the Revolution of 1848', *History Today*, 1958

Wylie, L. *Chanzeaux: A Village in Anjou*, Cambridge, Mass., 1966

Zeldin, T. 'The Myth of Napoleon III', *History Today*, 1958

(2) 'Government Policy in the French General Election of 1859', *E.H.R.*, 1959

Zévaès, A. (1) 'La Propagande socialiste dans les campagnes en 1848' in *La Révolution de 1848*, 1934

(2) 'L'Agitation communiste de 1840 à 1848', *ibid.*, 1926–7

(3) 'La Lutte des classes à Rouen en avril 1848', *ibid.*, 1927–8

REFERENCES

The numerals in parenthesis refer to a work cited in the Bibliography.

CHAPTER I: PAGES 5–30
1 See B. Gille (1), *passim.* and Chevalier (pp. 23–40)
2 Marx (2), pp. 148–49
3 Statistique (6)
4 *Ibid.*, table 3
5 Audiganne (2), pp. 992–3
6 Lavollée, p. 1037
7 p. 14
8 *Ibid.*
9 *Ibid.*, and Daumard (1), p. 52ff
10 Marx (1), pp. 294–95
11 Chevalier (2), p. 483
12 Statistique (3), p. 20
13 *Ibid.*, p. 21
14 Weber, pp. 71–4
15 *Ibid.*, p. 71
16 Statistique (1)
17 *Ibid.*, p. 152
18 Statistique (3), pp. 8, 9, 14, 15
19 *Ibid.*, p. 8ff
20 Marx (2), p. 148
21 Marx (1), p. 359
22 Statistique (4) vol. I, pp. 270–71
23 *Ibid.*, vol. II pp. 210–11
24 W. E. Moore, p. 21
25 Priouret, p. 46
26 Gille (3), p. 153
27 Kuczynski, p. 96
28 Sée (2), p. 300
29 Clough (1), p. 193
30 *Ibid.*, p. 153
31 Pierrard, p. 6
32 *Ibid.*, pp. 68–78

[33] Lasserre, pp. 81–103
[34] Vidalenc (2), p. 128
[35] Guillaume, p. 6ff
[36] Vidalenc (1), p. 326ff
[37] Marx (1), pp. 335–7
[38] Statistique (1), p. 142
[39] Marx (2), p. 215
[40] Statistique (1), p. 142
[41] Dupeux (1), p. 157
[42] Soboul (1), p. 59
[43] Dupeux (1), p. 157
[44] Sée (2), p. 323
[45] Vigier (1), p. 18ff; Marcilhacy (2), pp. 43–171
[46] Vigier (1), pp. 35–6
[47] *Ibid.*, pp. 38–40
[48] Duveau (1), p. 41
[49] Soboul (1), p. 55
[50] *Ibid.*, p. 63
[51] *Ibid.*, p. 55ff
[52] Duveau (1), p. 41
[53] Tudesq, (1) vol. I, p. 186
[54] Sée (2), p. 321
[55] Soboul (1), p. 59
[56] Statistique (3), p. 21
[57] *Ibid.*, p. 32
[58] *Capital*, vol. I, London 1962, p. 845
[59] Chevalier (3), p. 632

CHAPTER II: PAGES 31–56
[1] Marx (1), p. 264
[2] Marx (2), p. 140
[3] *Ibid.*, pp. 139–40
[4] p. 140
[5] p. 211
[6] Tocqueville (1), p. 79
[7] Higonnets, p. 222
[8] Tudesq (1), vol. II, pp. 862–3
[9] *Ibid.*, vol. I, p. 323
[10] Armengaud (1)
[11] Tudesq (1), vol. I, p. 475
[12] Aboucaya, Table I
[13] Tudesq (1), vol. I, p. 474
[14] *cf.* Kahan-Rabecq
[15] Pierrard, p. 430ff

16 Vigier (1), p. 161ff
17 Aboucaya, pp. 19–20
18 *cf.* Daumard (2), p. 160
19 Quoted by Fabreques, p. 252
20 Tudesq (1), vol. I, p. 126
21 Higgonets, p. 214
22 Gille (4), vol. I, p. 383
23 Tudesq (1), vol. I, p. 425
24 Gille (4), vol. I, p. 374
25 *On Britain*, Moscow, 1962, p. 345
26 Duveau (1), p. 177
27 Tudesq (1), vol. I, p. 429
28 Guizot *De la Démocratie en France*, quoted by Soltau, p. 48
29 Audiganne (3)
30 Réponses, p. 193
31 *Ibid.*, pp. 48–49
32 Aguet, p. 140
33 Pierrard, p. 172
34 Dansette (2), p. 232
35 Balzac (7)
36 Lasserre, pp. 235–37
37 Marx (1), p. 272
38 *Ibid.*
39 Balzac (4), pp. 201–202
40 Marcilhacy (2), pp. 180–1 quoting l'Abbé Méthivier, *Études rurales*
41 Tudesq (1), vol. I, p. 185
42 Marcilhacy (2), p. 241 quoting the *Mandement pour le Carême de 1829* of Mgr. de Beauregard, Bishop of Orléans
43 Balzac (4), p. 209
44 Falloux, vol. I, p. 157
45 Comte Beugnot in the *Correspondent* of 1844 quoted by Duroselle (3), p. 159
46 Marx (2), pp. 189–90
47 *Ibid.*, pp. 193–94
48 Rémusat, p. 194

CHAPTER II: PAGES 56–82
1 Daumard (2), p. 8
2 *Ibid.*, p. 10
3 Lasserre, p. 141
4 Réponses, p. 54
5 *Ibid.*, p. 237
6 Lasserre, p. 124
7 Pierrard, p. 207

[8] *Ibid.*, p. 209
[9] *Ibid.*, p. 139
[10] Kahan-Rabecq, p. 164
[11] Lasserre, p. 150
[12] Sée (1), p. 583
[13] Chevalier (2), p. 405
[14] Pierrard, p. 122
[15] Chevalier (2), pp. 425–26
[16] Quoted *ibid.*, p. 162
[17] *The Manifesto of the Communist Party*
[18] Chevalier (2), p. 444
[19] Brisset, p. 561
[20] Labracherie, p. 216
[21] Kahan-Rabecq, p. 74
[22] Réponses, p. 197
[23] *Ibid.*, p. 179
[24] *Ibid.*, p. 168
[25] *Ibid.*, p. 227
[26] Nadaud, p. 55
[27] *Ibid.*, p. 132
[28] Marx (2), p. 134
[29] *Ibid.*, p. 222
[30] Quoted by Daumard (2), p. 256
[31] *Ibid.*, pp. 308–11
[32] Daumard (1), pp. 64–5, 78
[33] Chevalier (1), pp. 225–8
[34] Lambert-Dansette, p. 275ff
[35] Marx, *Capital*, Vol. 1, p. 636
[36] Pierrard, pp. 186–7
[37] Aguet, p. 134
[38] *Ibid.*, p. 209
[39] *Ibid.*, p. 300ff
[40] Cuvillier (2), p. 112
[41] *Ibid.*, p. 114
[42] *Ibid.*, p. 90
[43] *Ibid.*, p. 177
[44] Zévaès (2), p. 981
[45] Cuvillier (2), p. 52
[46] Brisset, p. 569
[47] Nadaud, pp. 159–60
[48] W. E. Moore, p. 49

CHAPTER II: PAGES 82–94
[1] Labrousse (8), p. 1

[2] Desert, p. 41
[3] *Ibid.*, p. 47
[4] Dupeux (2), p. 80
[5] Chanut, p. 107
[6] Bouchary, p. 257
[7] Kahan-Rabecq, p. 379
[8] Agulhon, p. 328
[9] Armengaud (1), p. 171
[10] Vigier (1), vol. 1, p. 72ff
[11] Chevalier (2), p. 405
[12] Statistiques (5), p. XIX
[13] *Ibid.*, pp. 9, 12
[14] Chevalier (2), p. 343 – in Paris in 1843, 681 suicides; in 1846, 918
[15] Lasserre, p. 198 – in 1844, 4936 accusations on the Nord; in 1847, 6596
[16] Gossez (2), p. 3
[17] Deyon, p. 144 and 149
[18] Gossez (2), p. 2
[19] Marx (2), pp. 144-5
[20] de la Hodde (2), p. 12
[21] Duveau (1), p. 25
[22] de la Hodde (2), p. 436
[23] Apponyi, p. 5
[24] Rémusat, p. 222

CHAPTER III: PAGES 95-154
[1] de Tocqueville (1), pp. 91-2
[2] Rémusat, p. 255
[3] Archives nationales (hereafter *A.N.*) BB⁶287
[4] Normanby, vol. 1, p. 128
[5] Guichonnet (1), p. 158
[6] Montépin and Calonne
[7] Tudesq (1), p. 994
[8] Dupeux (3), p. 320
[9] *A.N.*, BB³⁰358
[10] *Ibid.*
[11] Marx (2), pp. 144-5
[12] de la Hodde (2), pp. 422-3
[13] Quoted by Puech (2)
[14] Bulletin des lois
[15] Schmidt (1), p. 15
[16] Thomas, p. 142
[17] Dolléans (4), p. 235
[18] Lamartine, pp. 111-12
[19] Marx (2), p. 147

353

[20] See *Procès-verbaux* ...
[21] Bastid, p. 138
[22] Marx (2), pp. 152-4
[23] *Ibid.*, pp. 149-50
[24] *Ibid.*, p. 148
[25] Marx (1), p. 253
[26] Chauvet, p. 178
[27] Barvier and Vernillat pp. 34-35
[28] Duveau (2), p. 236
[29] Lefranc, p. 325
[30] *A.N.*, C. 934
[31] *cf.* Gossez (3), pp. 61-7
[32] Gossez (8), p. 35
[33] Nadaud, p. 196
[34] de la Hodde (2), p. 13; Lucas, *passim.*
[35] Chevalier (2), p. 136
[36] Barrot, vol. VIII, pp. 9 and 53
[37] Barbier and Vernillat, p. 14
[38] Chauvet, p. 41
[39] Moulin (4), p. 296
[40] Lucas, pp. 227-28
[41] *Ibid.*, pp. 80 and 216
[42] Audiganne (1), vol. II, p. 191
[43] Lucas, pp. 122-23 and 216
[44] Chevalier (3), p. 624 and *A.N.*, C. 938-940
[45] Nadaud, p. 185
[46] Wassermann (2), p. 224
[47] Marx (2), pp. 149-50
[48] Blanqui, p. 108
[49] *A.N.*, BB^{18}1460-1461 and gendarmerie reports in *A.H.G.*, F^{1}16-17
[50] Guillaume, pp. 33-4
[51] Duveau (2), p. 95
[52] Wassermann (2), p. 233
[53] Blanqui, p. 112ff
[54] Thomas, p. 95
[55] Causidière, vol. I, p. 21
[56] Bastid, vol. II, p. 168
[57] Soboul (3), p. 304
[58] *A.N.*, BB^{18}1461, report of June 2
[59] Same loc., April 15
[60] *A.N.*, BB^{18}1460 letter of 12 July, 1849
[61] Reports in *A.N.*, BB^{18}1460-1461, BB^{30}359, 362-5, *A.H.G.*, F^{1}16
[62] Soboul (1), p. 62
[63] Cocquerelle, p. 125

[64] Chevalier (3), p. 200
[65] *Ibid.*, pp. 161–3
[66] Bergier, p. 19
[67] Bouchary, p. 258; Tudesq (1), vol. II, p. 1018
[68] Bouchary, p. 261
[69] Dupeux (2), p. 83
[70] Chevalier (3), p. 169
[71] Tudesq (1), vol. II, p. 1019
[72] Bergier, p. 44
[73] Ménard, p. 63
[74] Barrot, vol. II, p. 94
[75] Chevalier (3), pp. 166–67
[76] A.N., BB^{18}1462–1464 and A.H.G., F^{1}16
[77] A.N., C. 939
[78] Barrot, vol. II, pp. 108–9
[79] Marx (2), p. 156
[80] Tudesq (1), vol. II, p. 1053
[81] Barrot, vol. II, p. 1
[82] Flaubert, *Education sentimentale*
[83] Apponyi, p. 41
[84] Tocqueville (1), p. 117
[85] Bergier, p. 65
[86] Lamartine, vol. II, p. 406
[87] A.N., C. 938–940
[88] A.N., C. 938
[89] A.N., C. 938 letter from M. Prat of April 13
[90] Same loc. letter of April 4
[91] de Tocqueville (1), p. 106
[92] A.N., C. 939
[93] Same loc.
[94] A.N., C. 938
[95] Baciot, delegate in the Ain, April 6, same loc.
[96] Marx (2), p. 158
[97] Dupeux (3), p. 328
[98] Tudesq (1), vol. II, p. 1056, 1061 and Chevalier (3), p. 207ff
[99] Declaration of principles of the moderate republican 'Comité centrale des élections' in Lucas, pp. 71–92; see also the press and reports of the delegates of the Club of Clubs, A.N., C. 938–939
[100] Tudesq (1), vol. II, p. 1064
[101] Seignebos (2)
[102] Cobban (1) *passim* and (2), p. 334ff
[103] Falloux, vol. I, p. 243
[104] A.N., C. 940
[105] A.N., C. 938 from St. Cloud

[106] Dupeux (3), p. 333
[107] *A.N.*, F^{19}5604
[108] *A.N.*, C. 938
[109] *A.N.*, C. 939, letter of April 17
[110] same loc. report of the delegate Chavant of April 27
[111] Marx (2), p. 158
[112] Labracherie, p. 234
[113] *A.N.*, C. 940
[114] *A.N.*, C. 930
[115] Fasel, p. 292
[116] *A.N.*, 938–939 and Cuvillier (2), pp. 32–3
[117] *A.N.*, C. 938 and Chauvet p. 190 quoting an appeal of the 'Comité central des ouvriers de la dépt. de la Seine'
[118] Marx (2), pp. 158–59
[119] Seignebos (1), pp. 82–3
[120] Fasel, p. 289–90
[121] Lamartine, p. 377
[122] Tudesq (1), vol. II, p. 1065
[123] de Tocqueville (1), p. 121
[124] Tudesq (1), vol. II, p. 1067
[125] Tersen (1), p. 19
[126] Tudesq (1), vol. II, p. 1065
[127] Normandy, vol. I, p. 346–47
[128] Senior (2), vol. II, p. 44
[129] Tudesq (1), vol. II, p. 1071
[130] e.g., at Rouen, Limoges, Amiens, Castelsarrasin, Rodez and Nîmes
[131] Dubuc, p. 274
[132] Castellane, p. 66
[133] Deyon, pp. 157–58; Dubuc, p. 248ff
[134] Blanqui, pp. 119–21
[135] Wassermann (1), p. 672
[136] *A.N.*, C. 930
[137] *A.N.*, C. 930
[138] Report of the *avocat-général* at Rouen, May 5 in *A.N.*, BB^{30}365
[139] April 30
[140] Thomas, p. 177
[141] *Ibid.*, p. 190
[142] Vidalenc (3), p. 96
[143] Reports in *A.N.*, BB^{18}1461–1464; *A.H.G.*, F^{1}16 and Gossez (4), *passim*
[144] In *A.N.*, BB^{18}1462–1464
[145] Report of the *procureur-général* at Pau, 30 August, 1848 same loc.
[146] Marx (2), p. 160
[147] *A.N.*, C. 934, pp. 9 and 43
[148] *A.N.*, C. 930

[149] Police reports of 3 and 12 May in *A.N.*, C. 930; Thomas, p. 258; Wassermann (1), p. 749

[150] *A.P.P.*, Aa 428

[151] de Tocqueville (1), pp. 134 and 129

[152] Rémusat, p. 301

[153] Barrot, vol. II, p. 202

[154] Proudhon, pp. 137–38

[155] Reports in the *Gazette des Tribunaux*

[156] Thomas, p. 258

[157] Marx (2), p. 160

[158] Tudesq (1), vol. II, p. 1079

[159] May 16 and 17

[160] May 15 and 16

[161] Balzac (9), p. 44

[162] *A.N.*, C. 930 and *A.P.P.*, Aa 428

[163] de Tocqueville (1), p. 144

[164] *Ibid.*, p. 148; Bergier, p. 104

[165] Tudesq (1), vol. II, p. 1234

[166] Bergier, p. 109

[167] Chanut, pp. 121–22

[168] *A.N.*, C. 934

[169] May 20

[170] Tudesq (1), vol. II, p. 1105

[171] Ménard, p. 97

[172] Declaration of principles of the 'Société des répresentants républicains' in Lucas, pp. 200–4

[173] L'Assemblée nationale, 17 May, quoted by Tudesq (1), vol. II, p. 1077

[174] McKay (3), p. 168

[175] Nadaud, p. 194

[176] Report of Prefect of Police of 23 May in *A.N.*, C 930

[177] Report of 12 June, *A.N.*, C. 930

[178] Police reports of May and June, in *A.N.*, 930 and 934, and also the Paris correspondent of *La Liberté*

[179] Reprinted in *La Liberté* of June 18

[180] *Ibid.*, June 14; Blanc, vol. II, p. 141

[181] 'Enquête sur les événements de mai et juin, 1848', p. 41 in *A.N.*, C. 934 and a police report of 3 June in *A.N.*, C. 930

[182] Audiganne (1), vol. II, pp. 193–4

[183] *A.N.*, C. 930

[184] Reprinted in the *Presse* of June 19

CHAPTER IV: PAGES 155–188

[1] McKay (2), p. 34

[2] Duroselle (3), p. 303

[3] Schmidt (1), p. 27
[4] McKay (3), pp. 154–8
[5] de Tocqueville (1), p. 147
[6] Senior (1), vol. I, pp. 14–15
[7] *A.N.*, C. 930
[8] Lamartine, vol II, p. 428; Thomas, p. 324
[9] June 23
[10] Schmidt (1), p. 39
[11] Marx (2), p. 160
[12] Reported in *Le National* of 7 September
[13] *Ibid.*, September 17
[14] *Ibid.*, report concerning Pierre Moulin in *A.N.*, $BB^{24}401$–4
[15] e.g., report of trial of J.-B. Cornu in the *Gazette des Tribunaux*, Sept. 5
[16] Evidence of M. Joubert in 'Commission d'enquête sur l'insurrection...'
Paris, n.d., vol. I, p. 298; de Tocqueville (1), p. 512
[17] e.g., trial of M. Guérin, *Gazette des Tribunaux*, December 8
[18] e.g., trial of F. Jacquet, *Le National*, October 2
[19] e.g., trials of Leharanger and Formage, *Gazette des Tribunaux*, August 2
and October 26
[20] *Ibid.*
[21] Police reports in *A.N.*, C. 930
[22] Lamartine, vol. II, p. 451
[23] Blanc, vol. II, p. 186
[24] Flaubert, *Education sentimentale*
[25] Reported in *Le National* of September 7
[26] *A.N.*, C. 934 – see also Nadaud, p. 185ff and the various reports of trials
[27] Lucas, p. 44
[28] Undated report of the officer commanding the 1st battalion of the 4th
Legion of the National Guard of the banlieu in *A.H.G.*, $F^{1}9$
[29] Trial of L.-A. Raccari, *Gazette des Tribunaux*, August 27
[30] Chauvet, p. 199
[31] Rémusat, pp. 325–6
[32] Marx (2), p. 161
[33] *Marx-Engels Werke*, Band 5, Berlin 1959, p. 112
[34] Daumard (4), p. 185ff
[35] Daumard in Labrousse (7), p. 170
[36] Statistique (6), Table No. 3
[37] Based on *A.N.*, $F^{7}2585$. The category employed in producing 'Articles
de Paris' according to the census report has been subsumed under
various other categories, because of the impossibility of distinguishing its
various professions from the register of arrests
[38] Not including shopkeepers, but including bakers
[39] Report of the military commission of enquiry to the *Procureur-général*
at Paris, 22 August, 1948 in *A.N.*, $BB^{18}1465$

[40] *Ibid.*; Tersen (1), p. 22; Duveau (2), p. 150
[41] Labrousse (7), p. 180
[42] Statistique (6), Table No. 3
[43] Marx (1), pp. 294–5
[44] *A.N.*, C. 934, pièce no. 3198
[45] Morazé, p. 52
[46] de la Gorce, vol. I, p. 391
[47] Based on Statistique (6): 'Nombre des ouvriers non conservés durant les mois de mars, avril, mai et juin, 1848', and 'Résumé du recensement par professions des ouvriers des Ateliers nationaux au 19 mai' in
[48] McKay (1), p. 142ff
[49] Based on *A.N.*, $F^7 2585$
[50] *Enquête . . .*, pp. 82–3, *A.N.*, C. 934; Tersen (1), p. 23
[51] de Tocqueville (1), p. 152
[52] *A.N.*, C. 934, *Enquête . . .*, evidence of Proudhon
[53] *La Liberté*, July 2
[54] Statistique (6), p. 980
[55] Based on *A.N.*, $F^7 2585$
[56] Based on *A.N.*, $F^7 2585$ and Chevalier (1), p. 288
[57] Chevalier (1), p. 18
[58] *Ibid.*, pp. 14–15
[59] *Ibid.*, pp. 15–16, 81ff; Audiganne (1), vol. II, p. 160
[60] Using the estimate of the departments of origin of the Parisian population for 1833 contained in Chevalier (1), p. 285, corrected to allow for population increase and assuming as he does that the nature of this immigration changed hardly at all between 1833 and 1848. The official census does not contain information on the origins of the Parisian population until 1861, by which time the character of migration had to a more significant extent changed
[61] Report of the Minister of War to the Prefect of Police of June 26 in *A.N.*, C. 934
[62] *Enquête . . .*, p. 82, *A.N.*, C. 934
[63] *Ibid.*, pp. 82–3
[64] *Ibid.*
[65] Marx (2), p. 161
[66] Thomas, p. 342
[67] Amann (4), p. 349
[68] *cf.* McKay (1), p. 150
[69] Lamartine, vol II, p. 442
[70] Thomas, p. 53
[71] *A.N.*, $BB^{18} 1465$ dossier 5964^A
[72] July 3
[73] Amann (4), p. 349
[74] Based on *A.N.*, $F^7 2585$

[75] Gossez (1), p. 440
[76] Police report of April 6, in *A.N.*, C. 930
[77] Daumard (3), p. 231ff
[78] A point made by Professor Douglas Johnson
[79] Barbier and Vernillat, pp. 62–3
[80] Stein, p. 399
[81] Gossez (1), pp. 441–50
[82] *Ibid.*, p. 441
[83] Swart, p. 94
[84] Gossez (1), p. 442
[85] June 23
[86] Rémusat, p. 339
[87] June 24
[88] Cuvillier (2), p. 37
[89] Castellane, pp. 52–3
[90] Girardet (1), p. 14; (2), p. 73, 124ff, Chalmin (2), pp. 145–6, 283, 363; Gossez (1), p. 445
[91] Normandy, vol. II, p. 76; Chalmin (1), p. 41
[92] Audiganne (1), vol. II, p. 195
[93] Lamartine, vol. II, p. 97
[94] Report from the general staff of the National Guard to the Minister of the Interior, 13 July, 1848 in *A.N.*, F⁹1072
[95] 'Club de la garde mobile – procès-verbal de séance du avril 5, 1848', *A.N.*, C. 930
[96] *A.N.*, F⁹1072
[97] Lamartine, vol. II, p. 438
[98] Hugo, *Les Misérables*
[99] Castellane, p. 85
[100] 751 were reported killed, wounded or missing out of 12,000 involved. Chalmin (1), p. 69
[101] Schmidt (1), p. 47
[102] de Tocqueville (1), p. 154
[103] Chauvet, p. 201
[104] Marx (2), p. 161
[105] *Ibid.*, p. 160
[106] Rémusat, p. 335
[107] Rémusat, p. 442
[108] Lhomme (2), p. 70

CHAPTER IV: PAGES 189–192
[1] Marx (2), p. 160
[2] Dautry, p. 209
[3] Tudesq (1), vol. II, p. 1109

4 Vidalenc (3), p. 119
5 *Ibid.*, pp. 127–30
6 *A.H.G.*, F¹9
7 Report of the *procureur-général* at Caen of 5 July, 1848 in *A.N.*, BB³⁰359
8 *A.H.G.*, F¹9
9 *A.N.*, BB¹⁸1465
10 Enclosed with a report from the *procureur-général* at Bordeaux of 22 July in *A.N.*, BB¹⁸1465
11 *A.N.*, BB¹⁸1465, dossier 5964ᵃ
12 Vidalenc (3), pp. 125–6
13 Faucheux and Morauzeau, p. 84
14 Act of accusation drawn up by the *procureur-général* at Aix, *A.N.*, BB¹⁸1465
15 *Ibid.*; Ponteil (2), pp. 413–15
16 Report of the *procureur-général* at Reims, 30 June, *A.N.*, BB¹⁸1465
17 Report of the *procureur-général* at Bordeaux, 22 July, same loc.

CHAPTER V: PAGES 194–208

1 Marx (1), p. 256
2 Rémusat, p. 344
3 Speech in the Constituent Assembly, Sept. 20
4 Armand de Melun in a letter of 23 August, 1848 in Duroselle (3), p. 444
5 Castellane, p. 95
6 de Tocqueville (2), vol. VIII, part 2, p. 31, letter to Beaumont, 27 August, 1848
7 Bergier, p. 150
8 de Tocqueville (2), vol. VIII, Part 2, p. 51, letter to Beaumont, 24 Sept., 1848
9 Apponyi, p. 66
10 Castellane, p. 92
11 Letter from Brossette, municipal councillor at Lyon, of 5 July, 1848, in Bergier, p. 141
12 Apponyi, p. 65
13 6 December, 1848
14 Dupeux (2), p. 75
15 Armengaud, p. 185
16 *Réponses . . .*, p. 61, canton of Habsheim
17 *A.N.*, BB¹⁸1462–1464
18 *A.P.P.*, Aa 428
19 Castellane, p. 91
20 Vigier (3), p. 98
21 Dupeux (3), p. 317
22 Castellane, p. 142
23 Circular of 29 July, signed Marie in *A.N.*, BB¹⁸1472

[24] See reports from the *procureur-générals* at Nîmes of 5 August and Lyon of 2 August in *A.N.*, BB[18]1472, and especially a vague report of the *procureur-général* at Paris of 7 August, which largely repeats the ministerial circular in *A.P.P.*, Aa 428
[25] de Tocqueville (1), p. 175
[26] De la Gorce, vol. II, p. 129
[27] Dessal (1), p. 75
[28] *La Réforme* of 21 August, 11 October, 2–3 November and 6 December
[29] Schnerb (1), p. 59
[30] *La Réforme*, 2–3 November, 1848
[31] Pamphlet dated 25 September, 1848 in *A.N.*, BB[18]1472
[32] A series of reports in *A.N.*, BB[18]1473 and *A.H.G.*, F[1]17
[33] De la Gorce, vol. II, pp. 129–30
[34] Loubère (3), *passim*; Chatelain (1), p. 12
[35] *A.N.*, BB[18]1462–1464; Coquerelle, pp. 131–2
[36] Gossez (4), p. 132
[37] de Tocqueville (2), vol. VIII, Part 2, p. 53, letter to Beaumont of 24 September, 1848
[38] Castellane, p. 93
[39] Bastid, vol. II, p. 23
[40] de Tocqueville (1), p. 188
[41] Bastid, vol. II, p. 82
[42] *Ibid.*, p. 93
[43] de Tocqueville (1), p. 192
[44] Marx (2), pp. 170 and 172

CHAPTER V: PAGES 208–225
[1] Police reports on popular feelings in June 1848, *A.N.*, C. 930
[2] e.g., Police report concerning the crowd in the Place de l'Hôtel-de-Ville, 21 June, 1848, same loc.
[3] *Le Constitutionnel*, 14 June, 1848
[4] Dansette (3), p. 228
[5] Tudesq (1), vol. II, p. 1184
[6] Balzac (4)
[7] de Tocqueville (1), p. 279
[8] de Tocqueville (2), vol. VIII, Part 2, letters to Beaumont of 24 September and 20 October, pp. 51 and 71
[9] *Ibid.*, p. 81
[10] Rémusat, p. 366
[11] Senior (2), vol. I, p. 34
[12] Castellane, p. 103
[13] Dansette (3), p. 243
[14] *Gazette de France*, 6 November, 1848
[15] Normanby, vol. II, p. 361

[16] December 5
[17] Normanby's report to Lord Palmerston in Simpson, pp. 314–15
[18] Apponyi, pp. 76–7
[19] B. de Vaulx and E. Beau de Lomenie, p. 207
[20] Senior (1), vol. II, p. 180
[21] Audiganne (1), vol. I, p. 119
[22] *cf.* reports of the *procureurs-générals* at Poitiers of 9 November in *A.N.*, [18]1462–1464 and Bordeaux of 22 September, 1848, *A.N.*, [18]1461
[23] Marx (2), p. 174
[24] Stern, vol. III, p. 342
[25] Normanby, vol. II, p. 160
[26] Amann (5), p. 425
[27] Duveau (3), p. 56
[28] Ménard, p. 224
[29] Normanby, vol. II, p. 272
[30] Apponyi, pp. 73–4
[31] Cuvillier (2), p. 40
[32] October 27
[33] Marx (2), p. 174
[34] Tudesq (1), vol. II, p. 1200
[35] Enclosed with a report from the *procureur-général* at Metz, 1 December, 1848 in *A.N.*, BB[18]1471
[36] Letter from Pagany at Lyon in Bergier, p. 168
[37] Bergier, pp. 163–5; d'Hautpoul, pp. 319–20
[38] 14 January, 1849, quoted by Tudesq (1), vol. II, p. 1175
[39] Letter from Pagany at Lyon of 28 November, 1848, in Bergier, p. 165
[40] Tudesq (2), p. 175
[41] 20 October, November 6, 9 and 16
[42] December 6
[43] December 1
[44] Tudesq (1), vol. II, p. 1172
[45] Barrot, vol. III, p. 20
[46] Chalmin (4), pp. 62–3 and 155; Charnay, p. 177
[47] *La Liberté*, report dated 11 December, 1848
[48] de Tocqueville (1), p. 279
[49] Tudesq (2), p. 151; Cuvillier (2), p. 39
[50] December 12
[51] Bergier, p. 163
[52] *La Liberté* report dated 11 December, 1848
[53] d'Hautpoul, p. 320
[54] *La Liberté* report dated 11 December, 1848
[55] An appeal for pardon forwarded by the *procureur-général* at Amiens, 29 August, 1849, *A.N.*, [24]361–368
[56] *La Réforme*, 11 December

[57] Marx (2), p. 173

[58] Tudesq (2), pp. 206 and 211 supplemented by statistics from *La Gazette de France*, 14 December, 1848

[59] *Gazette de France*, 13–14 December

[60] Figures in brackets are the results of the supplementary elections of September 1848 published in *Le National*, 22 September

[61] Tudesq (1), vol. II, p. 1168–79

[62] Footnote by Godart in Bergier, p. 169

[63] Marx (2), p. 175

[64] *Le Peuple*, 19 December, 1848

[65] December 23

[66] Proudhon, p. 277

[67] Rémusat, pp. 359–60

[68] Apponyi, p. 78

[69] Martinelli, p. 26

CHAPTER V: PAGES 225–245

[1] Marx (1), p. 264

[2] Castellane, p. 123

[3] Falloux, vol. I, p. 322

[4] *Ibid.*

[5] Bastid, pp. 168–70

[6] *Le Constitutionnel*, 10 February, 1849; Falloux, vol. I, p. 384

[7] Report from the general staff of the National Guard, 18 February, 1849 in *A.N.*, F⁹1072

[8] It was thought in some quarters that Changarnier favoured a military *coup d'état*, e.g. Thiers – Senior (2), vol. II, pp. 45–7

[9] Apponyi, p. 130

[10] Telegram of Faucher, Minister of the Interior to the Prefect of the Pyrénées-Orientale, Bastid, p. 245

[11] Armengaud, p. 370

[12] Rémusat, pp. 404–5

[13] *cf.* Cosnac, p. 76

[14] Anon. (4)

[15] Bugeaud; Schmit; *Le Constitutionnel*, 27 January, 8, 10 February, 1849

[16] Anon (1), p. 17

[17] Marx (2), p. 191

[18] e.g. Pichery

[19] Anon. (3) – published by the 'Comité électoral de le rue de Poitiers'

[20] *Le Haro*, 23 January, 1849; Perrot, p. 195

[21] Reports of the Prefect of the Rhône of 13 February and the *procureur-général* at Dijon of 5 March, 1849, *A.N.*, BB¹⁸1472

[22] Zeldin (2), pp. 241–2

[23] Dutacq (2), pp. 144–5

24 *Le National*, 24 April, 23 May, 1849
25 Published in *La Réforme*, 20 April, 1849
26 Dutacq (2), p. 135
27 Armengaud, pp. 369–79
28 Report of the Prefect of the Yonne of 2 March, 1849 and a whole series of similar reports in *A.N.*, BB¹⁸1471–1472
29 29 February, 1849, *A.N.*, BB¹⁸1472
30 Programme of the 'Comité démocrate-socialiste des élections de la Seine' published in *La Réforme*, 20 April, 1849
31 *Le Réforme*, 24 February, 1849
32 *Le Peuple*, 2 September, 1848
33 Marx (1), p. 274
34 Audiganne (1), vol. I, p. 53
35 Reports of the *procureur-général* at Agen, 12 May in *A.N.*, BB³⁰358 and Toulouse, 28 May, 1849 in *A.N.*, BB¹⁸1462
36 Marx (2), p. 192
37 Rambaud, p. 138
38 Charnay, pp. 156–7, quotes an 'Appel du Comité électoral centrale démocratique et du Rhône'; Bouillon (2), p. 112ff
39 *A.N.*, BB³⁰362; see also a report of the Paris Prefect of Police of 2 May, 1849 in *A.P.P.*, Aa 432
40 Castellane, p. 144
41 Report of the *procureur-général* at Rouen, 12 May, 1849, *A.N.*, BB³⁰363
42 Castellane, p. 156
43 Bouillon (1), p. 74ff
44 Dupeux (3), p. 352
45 Bouillon (1), p. 80
46 *Ibid.*, pp. 80–5 and Tudesq (1), vol. II, pp. 1217–24
47 Marx (2), p. 193
48 Girard (1), p. 325
49 Bouillon (1), pp. 81–93; Montagne, p. 276
50 Loubère (3), pp. 1036–39
51 Vigier (1), vol. II, p. 170
52 Letter to the Minister of Justice, 12 July, 1849, *A.N.*, BB¹⁸1460
53 Undated police 'Note sur la propagande de 1849'; report of 25 February, 1848 on 'Propagande démocratique et sociale' and one of 1 September, 1849 'Sur les Associations ouvrieres' in *A.P.P.*, Aa 432; reports of the *procureurs-générals* on policital situation, *A.N.*, BB³⁰358 and gendarmerie reports in *A.H.G.*, F¹16
54 Report of 1 December, 1849, *A.N.*, BB³⁰379
55 Report of 9 January, 1850 in *A.N.*, BB³⁰378
56 Loubère (3), pp. 1037–38; Vigier (4), p. 204
57 Report of the *procureur-général* at Aix of 2 March, 1849, concerning the

town of Tarascon with its 3 Republican and 3 Legitimist clubs all propagandizing in the surrounding region

[58] See e.g. a gendarmerie report covering 5–10 July, 1849 from the 9th Military Division concerning protests against the drink tax at Carcassone, *A.H.G.*, F¹16

[59] Chatelain (1), p. 12; Nadaud, p. 202

[60] *La Réforme*, 17 May, 1849

[61] Armengaud, p. 370

[62] de Tocqueville (1), p. 282

[63] Vigier (1), vol. II, p. 222

[64] Castellane, p. 161, 21 May, 1849

[65] *Ibid.*, p. 156

[66] Montagne, p. 276

[67] Letter to de Tocqueville of 23 May. 1849 in de Tocqueville (2), vol. VIII, Part 2, p. 138

[68] Bouillon (2), p. 119

[69] Kerry, pp. 63–4

[70] *Journal des Débats*, 20 May, 1849

[71] de Tocqueville (1), p. 200; Barrot, vol. III, p. 246

[72] *Ibid.*, p. 245

[73] Bastid, vol. II, p. 209

[74] Marx (2), p. 192

[75] Vigier (1), vol. II, p. 204

CHAPTER VI: PAGES 246–282

[1] de Tocqueville (1), p. 214

[2] Falloux, vol. I, pp. 369–72; Thiers in Senior (2), vol. II, pp. 53–4

[3] Apponyi, p. 135

[4] *Ibid.*

[5] Marx (1), pp. 275–6

[6] de Tocqueville (1), p. 216

[7] Barrot, vol. III, p. 291; Apponyi, p. 140

[8] Falloux, vol. I, p. 373

[9] de Tocqueville (1), p. 213

[10] Considérant, pp. 18–19

[11] *La Réforme*, 12 June, 1849; Article 3 of the 6 propositions of the 'Comité démocrate-socialiste' in Bastid, vol. II, p. 208

[12] Falloux, vol. I, pp. 401–2

[13] de Tocqueville (1), p. 215

[14] Considérant, p. 56

[15] Marx (1), pp. 277–8

[16] Proudhon, p. 330

[17] Marx (2), p. 200

[18] Chauvet, pp. 233–4

19 Marx (2), p. 198
20 Nadaud, p. 208
21 Castellane, p. 172
22 de Tocqueville (1), p. 219
23 Castellane, pp. 165–6 and Guillemin (2), p. 139
24 Considérant, p. 37
25 Montagne, p. 382
26 See the reports of the military divisions, particularly of the 6th and 10th in *A.H.G.*, F^{1}16–17
27 See *A.N.*, BB^{30}366 and gendarmarie reports in *A.H.G.*, F^{1}16–17
28 Tenot (3), p. 19; see also 'Ministère de la Justice – Resumé des documents judiciaires – travail sur le mouvement demagogique antérieur au 2 décembre' in *A.N.*, BB^{30}394
29 *Le National*, 5 March, 1850
30 Dupeux (3), p. 368
31 The *Républicain de Loir-et-Cher*, Dupeux (3), p. 365 *cf. Le National*, 4 February and 3 March, 1850.
32 *A.N.*, BB^{18}1461 and *A.H.G.*, F^{1}16–17
33 Vigier (1), vol. II, p. 61
34 *Ibid.*, pp. 62 and 32
35 *Ibid.*, pp. 62–3
36 Five daily reports, 15–20 September, 1849, *A.H.G.*, F^{1}17
37 Marx (2), pp. 225 and 201
38 Castellane, p. 173, 16 June, 1849
39 Marx (2), p. 218
40 Falloux, vol. I, p. 356
41 Cobban (2), p. 344
42 Seignebos (1), p. 148
43 Castellane, p. 129
44 Falloux, vol. I, p. 359
45 De la Gorce, vol. II, p. 278
46 Thiers quoted by Duveau (1), p. 248 and Hébert and Carnec, p. 40
47 Hébert and Carnec, p. 54
48 Bastid, vol. II, p. 443
49 Hébert and Carnec, pp. 51 and 40
50 Falloux, vol. I, p. 359
51 Guillemin (2), p. 193
52 Seignebos (1), p. 141
53 Falloux, vol. I, p. 356
54 Guillemin (2), p. 193
55 Hébert and Carnec, p. 97
56 Apponyi, p. 171
57 Hébert and Carnec, p. 86
58 27 October, 1849

[59] Proudhon, p. 282 and *Voix du Peuple*, 22 December, 1849

[60] L'Abbé Gaduel, 'De la vocation ecclésiastique chez les enfants et de leur première éducation dans les presbytères', quoted by Marcilhacy (2), p. 226

[61] A parish priest in Lille – Pierrard, pp. 375–6

[62] Audiganne (1), vol. I, p. 237

[63] Castellane, p. 334, 8 September, 1851

[64] Latreille *et al.*, p. 342

[65] Duveau (1), p. 248; Bastid, vol. II, p. 255

[66] Pierrard, p. 327; Duveau (4), p. 130

[67] Pierrard, p. 320

[68] Dupeux (3), pp. 281–2

[69] Ferré, p. 18

[70] 16 March, 1850

[71] 2 May, 1850

[72] Castellane, p. 218

[73] Letter to the Minister of the Interior, 10 March, 1850, in *A.N.*, F¹ᶜIII Seine 12

[74] *Journal des Débats*, 18 March, 1850

[75] Castellane, pp. 221 and 225

[76] Balland, pp. 158–9; Duveau (3), pp. 58–9

[77] 3 June, 1850

[78] Dansette (1), p. 72

[79] Rémusat, p. 429

[80] De la Gorce, vol. II, pp. 334–5

[81] Béchard and Faucher in the Assembly debate, quoted by Raphael, p. 73

[82] *Ibid.*, p. 79

[83] Rémusat, p. 429

[84] Barrot, vol. IV, pp. 30–31

[85] *Ibid.*, p. 35; Rémusat, p. 429

[86] Mme. Cornu remembering a conversation with Louis-Napoléon at the time the suffrage bill was under discussion in the Assembly – Senior (2), vol. II, p. 338

[87] de Tocqueville (1), p. 226

[88] de Tocqueville (1), pp. 226 and 282; Barrot, vol. III, p. 278

[89] *Ibid.*, pp. 227 and 285; Falloux, vol. I, p. 360

[90] Rémusat, p. 422

[91] Falloux, vol. I, p. 399

[92] Marx (2), p. 206

[93] Barrot, vol. III, p. 415; Falloux, vol. I, pp. 440–3

[94] Bastid, vol. II, p. 228

[95] Barrot, vol. III, p. 479

[96] de Tocqueville (2), vol. VIII, Part 2, p. 232, letter to Beaumont, 4 November, 1849; also Barrot, vol. III, p. 403

[97] Véron, vol. v, p. 156
[98] Marx (2), pp. 207–8
[99] Barrot, vol. IV, p. 5
[100] *Ibid.*, p. 38
[101] Falloux, vol. I, p. 473
[102] Rémusat, p. 420
[103] Castellane, p. 204
[104] 23 March, 1850
[105] Dessal (1), p. 147
[106] Marx (1), p. 291
[107] Nadaud, p. 208
[108] Castellane, p. 305
[109] Guiral, p. 219
[110] Report of the *procureur-général* at Agen, 30 March, 1850, *A.N.*, BB³⁰370
[111] Barbier and Vernillat, pp. 119–20
[112] Undated report of the *procureur-général* at Grenoble in *A.N.*, BB³⁰394
[113] Police reports dated 14 November, 1855, concerning the organization of secret societies in Lyon, February, 1848 – December, 1851 in *A.P.P.*, Aa 432; Castellane, pp. 288–89; Dessal (2), pp. 88–9; Dutacq (1), pp. 407–11; de la Gorce, vol. II, p. 543; Vigier (3), pp. 79–86
[114] Castellane, p. 291
[115] *Ibid.*, p. 334, 8 September, 1851
[116] Barbier and Vernillat, pp. 102–3
[117] Report of the *procureur-général* at Grenoble, 27 March, 1851, *A.N.*, BB³⁰366
[118] Vigier (1), vol. II, p. 266
[119] *La Révolution*, 17 September, 1851
[120] Included with the report on secret societies at Lyon of November 1855 in *A.P.P.*, Aa 432
[121] 'Prière des Voraces de la Croix-Rousse', same loc.
[122] Castellane, pp. 289–90, 26 October, 1850
[123] Report of the *procureur-général* at Montpellier, 21 October, 1851, in *A.N.*, BB³⁰394; Castellane, p. 343 entry of 21 November, 1851; Marcilhacy (1), p. 51
[124] Castellane, p. 340, 18 October, 1851.
[125] Report of the *procureur-général* at Montpellier of 9 September, 1851, *A.N.*, BB³⁰488
[126] Castellane, p. 309, 11 May, 1851
[127] Speech made in September, 1851 – Dessal (2), p. 83
[128] Dessal (1), p. 181
[129] Report of the *procureur-général* at Orleans of 7 November, 1851, *A.N.*, BB³⁰382
[130] *Ibid.*, report of 11 November, 1851 in *A.N.*, BB³⁰394

[131] *La Voix du Proscrit*, 27 July, 1851 – Dessal (1), p. 176

[132] Reports of the *procureur-général* at Bourges of 12 and 20 October, 1851, *A.N.*, BB³⁰394

[133] Du Camp, vol. I, p. 104; also Falloux, vol. I, p. 428; de Tocqueville (2), vol. VIII, Part 2, p. 234, letter of 4 November, 1849

[134] Castellane, pp. 271–2, 29 August, 1850

[135] *Ibid.*, p. 290

[136] Rémusat, p. 444

[137] Barrot, vol. IV, p. 61

[138] See Beaumont's letter of 15 November, 1850, in de Tocqueville (2), vol. VIII, Part 2, p. 317

[139] Faucher reported by Senior (1), vol. I, p. 274

[140] Barrot, vol. IV, p. 62

[141] Letter of 16 January, 1851, in de Tocqueville (2), vol. VIII, Part 2, p. 355

[142] Seignebos (1), p. 193

[143] Letter of 16 January, *loc cit.*

[144] Pascal Duprat quoted by Ténot (1), pp. 38–9

[145] Castellane, p. 29

[146] Letter of 26 January, 1851 in de Tocqueville (2), vol. VIII, Part 2, p. 362

[147] *Ibid.*

[148] Barrot, vol. IV, p. 104; Rémusat, p. 459

[149] Conversations with Senior (1), p. 282; Beaumont in de Tocqueville (2), vol. VIII, Part 2, p. 322

[150] Senior (2), vol. II, p. 40

[151] Barrot, vol. IV p. 125

[152] Guillemin (2), p. 275

[153] See Falloux, vol. I, p. 380

[154] Senior (1), vol. I, p. 275

[155] Letter to Beaumont, 4 November, 1849, in de Tocqueville (2), vol. VIII, Part 2, p. 234

[156] Barrot, vol. IV, p. 163

[157] Falloux, vol. II, p. 72

[158] Barrot, vol. IV, p. 163; Beaumont in de Tocqueville (2), vol. VIII, Part 2, p. 414

[159] Bastid, vol. II, p. 300

[160] Barrot, vol. IV, pp. 173–4

[161] Marx (1), p. 326

[162] Guillemin (2), p. 293

[163] Castellane, pp. 327–8

[164] Barrot, vol. IV, p. 187

[165] Letter of the Comte de Flahault to Mme. de Flahault, 18 November 1851 in Kerry, p. 111; see *L'Univers*, 16 November and Véron, vol. V, p. 217

[166] *Le Constitutionnel*, 10 and 24 November, 1851

[167] *Le National*, 17 November, 1851
[168] Ténot (1), p. 75
[169] Marx (1), p. 326
[170] Marx (2), p. 238
[171] Falloux, vol. II, p. 5
[172] Rémusat, p. 439; Beaumont, 25 December, 1850 in de Tocqueville (2), vol. VIII, Part 2, p. 340
[173] Barrot, vol. IV, p. 118
[174] Rémusat, pp. 459-60
[175] Beaumont, 16 February, 1851 in de Tocqueville (2), vol. VIII, Part 2, p. 375
[176] Tocqueville, 28 November, 1851, *ibid.*, p. 252
[177] Barrot, vol. IV, pp. 70, 184-5, 203; Rémusat, p. 476
[178] Rémusat, p. 479
[179] Apponyi, p. 183
[180] Romieu, pp. 14 and 33
[181] Castellane, p. 292, 3 December, 1850
[182] *Ibid.*, p. 343, 21 November, 1851
[183] Senior (1), vol. I, p. 235
[184] Marx (1), p. 321
[185] Letter of the Chambre Consulative at Tourcoing to the Prefect of the Nord in March, 1851, in Chanut, pp. 124-6
[186] Castellane, p. 304, 20 March, 1851
[187] *Ibid.*, p. 339, 29 September, 1851
[188] *Le Constitutionnel*, 19 September, 1851
[189] Vigier (1), vol. II, p. 304
[190] Letter of 9 November, 1850, Tocqueville (2), vol. III, Part 2, p. 310; also Ollivier, p. 76, 2 February, 1851
[191] 16 November, 1851
[192] Véron, vol. V, p. 205
[193] 15 July, 1851
[194] *Le Constitutionnel*, 1 September, 1851
[195] *Ibid.*, 27 August, 1851
[196] Romieu, pp. 42, 33, 60
[197] Barrot, vol. IV, p. 40
[198] Bastid, vol. II, p. 274
[199] *Ibid.*
[200] *Ibid.*, p. 275; Castellane, p. 309
[201] Barrot, vol. IV, p. 219
[202] Apponyi, p. 173
[203] de Tocqueville (1), p. 213
[204] Marx (1), p. 239
[205] Letter of 3 September, 1850 in de Tocqueville (2), vol. VIII, Part 2, p. 288
[206] Barrot, vol. IV, p. 63

[207] Marx (1), pp. 295–6
[208] Letter to Beaumont, 14 September, 1851 in de Tocqueville (2), vol. VIII, Part 2, p. 407
[209] *Ibid.*, p. 410
[210] Letter of 16 February, 1851, *ibid.*, p. 374
[211] Falloux, vol. II, p. 82
[212] Dansette (3), p. 325
[213] Falloux, vol. II, pp. 380–1
[214] Letter of the Comte de Flahault to Mme. de Flahault, 3 December, 1851 in Kerry, p. 120
[215] Girard (1), p. 336
[216] Dansette (3), pp. 338–9

CHAPTER VII: PAGES 283–326
[1] Marx (1), p. 33
[2] Rémusat, pp. 492–3
[3] Seignebos (1), p. 210
[4] Payne, p. 169
[5] Charnay, p. 142; Ténot (1), p. 162
[6] *A.H.G.*, $F^1$52 – at Lille six officers of the 14th artillery were retired for insubordination – report of the General commanding the 2nd Military Division, 10 December, 1851
[7] *A.N.*, $F^7$12654
[8] *A.N.*, F^{1a}10
[9] Circular dated 9 January, 1852 in *A.N.*, F^{1a}10
[10] Armengaud, p. 378
[11] Reports of the Prefect of Ille-et-Vilaine of 5, 7 and 8 December and of the Prefect of the Gard of 2 December, 1851, *A.N.*, $F^7$12654
[12] Report of 5 December, 1851, same loc.
[13] Report of 14 December, 1851; see a similar report from the *sous-prefet* at Ancenis (Loire-Inf.) of 5 December, in *A.N.*, $F^7$12654
[14] De Barante, letter of 12 December, 1851, quoted by Guillemin (2), p. 420
[15] Comte de Flahault to Mme de Flahault, 10 December, 1851, in Kerry, p. 132
[16] Mayer, p. 5
[17] *L'Union*, 30 December, 1851
[18] Held in *A.N.*, $F^7$12654
[19] Mayer, p. 4
[20] 15 December, 1851, quoted by Guillemin (2), p. 420
[21] Various reports in *A.N.*, $F^7$12654
[22] Report of the Prefect in *A.N.*, $F^7$12654
[23] Circular from Morny, Minister of the Interior to the Prefects, 10 December, 1851, quoted by Dansette (3), p. 365 and e.g. circular from

the Prefect of Maine-et-Loire to *sous-prefets* and mayors of 17 December 1851 in *A.N.*, F¹ᵃ10

24 Dominique, p. 302; Dansette (3), p. 367

25 9 December, 1851

26 Priouret, p. 111

27 Letter from the Chamber of Commerce at Gray (Hte.-Saône), 10 December, 1851 in *A.N.*, F¹ᵃ10; Chanut, pp. 124-5

28 Guillemin (2), p. 424

29 Circular of the Prefect of Maine-et-Loire, 2 January, 1852 in *A.N.*, F¹ᵃ10

30 Barrot, vol. IV, p. 240

31 Ollivier, p. 96, 3 December, 1851

32 Guillemin (2), p. 439

33 Barrot, vol. IV, p. 230; also Rémusat, p. 482

34 Barrot, vol. IV, p. 227

35 Guillemin (2), p. 367

36 Barrot, vol. IV, p. 237

37 *Ibid.*

38 Dominique, p. 279

39 Nadaud, p. 213

40 *A.N.*, F⁷2595

41 *Ibid.*

42 Daily reports in *A.H.G.*, F¹51, 52, 54

43 Report of General de Castellane commanding at Lyon, 4 December, 1851 in *A.N.*, F⁷12654; undated report of the *procureur-général* at Lyon in *A.N.*, BB³⁰396

44 Report of the *procureur-général* at Limoges, 7 February, 1852 in *A.N.*, BB³⁰396 and reports in *A.H.G.*, F¹51, 52

45 Telegram from Rouen to Minister of War, 3 December; report from the gendarmerie commander in the Loire concerning St Etienne, 4 December, 1851, in *A.H.G.*, F¹51; Pierrard, p. 432

46 Report of 6 December, 1851 in *A.N.*, F⁷12654

47 Letter of 4 December, 1851 same loc.

48 Report of the prefect of 9 December, 1851 same loc.

49 Reports of the general commanding the 2nd Military Division, 6 and 10 December, 1851, in *A.H.G.*, F¹51; Bruchet, p. 87

50 *A.N.*, F⁷2595

51 *A.N.*, F⁷2595, F⁷12654, BB³⁰396, *A.H.G.*, F¹51, 52, 54, Levy (1), *passim*, Ténot (2), *passim*

52 *A.H.G.*, G⁸195-196.,

53 Vigier (1), vol. II, p. 330; trial of Zanote, a printer at Montargis, reported in the *Gazette des Tribunaux*, 16–17 February, 1852; proclamation of the insurgents at Bédarieux (Hérault) in Ténot (2), p. 182

54 Evidence of A. Maurel, witness at the trial of R. Faubladie at Montpellier, reported in the *Gazette des Tribunaux*, 12–13 April, 1852.

[55] Vigier, (1), vol. II, p. 332
[56] e.g. Evidence of Simon Dudrage, sergeant in the 13th infantry regt. appearing before the IIe Conseil de Guerre of the 6th Military Division at Lyon, reported in the *Gazette des Tribunaux*, 6 June, 1852
[57] Undated report in *A.N.*, BB^{30}396
[58] Report of 26 January, 1852 same loc.
[59] Report of the *procureur-général* at Nîmes, 27 January, 1852, *A.N.*, BB^{30}396
[60] Report of 15 May, 1850, concerning the arrondissement of Forcalquier (Basses-Alpes) in *A.N.*, BB^{30}370
[61] Vigier (1), vol. II, p. 32 and (4), p. 198
[62] Loubère (3), p. 1049. That a large proportion were married is borne out by the registers of the judicial commissions *A.H.G.*, G^{8}195–196
[63] Undated report of the *procureur-général* at Agen in *A.N.*, BB^{30}396
[64] Copy included with a report of the *procureur-général* at Lyon, same loc.
[65] See the gendarmerie reports in *A.H.G.*, F^{1}51, 52, 54
[66] Trial of Jean Carrière, a tanner, by the 2e Conseil de Guerre of the 10e Division militaire, at Montpellier – *Gazette des Tribunaux*, 27 May, 1852
[67] Trial of François Colombier, *ibid.*, 7–8 June, 1852
[68] Evidence of Joseph Lafond at the trial of a watchman called Capelle, *ibid.*, 12–13 April, 1852
[69] Report of the Prefect of the Nièvre concerning events at Clamecy, 8 December, 1852 in *A.N.*, F^{7}12654
[70] Trial of Jean Galibert, *op. cit.*, 22–23 March, 1852
[71] Report of 26 January, 1852 in *A.N.*, F^{7}12654
[72] The registers in cartons *A.H.G.*, G^{8}195–196 indicate the official acceptance of the reality of such pressures
[73] Undated report in *A.N.*, F^{7}12654
[74] A *cultivateur* on trial at Montpellier, *Gazette des Tribunaux*, 28 March 1852
[75] A witness at the trial of J.-J. Thiberin, *cultivateur*, *ibid.*, 20 March, 1852
[76] *Ibid.*
[77] Trial of Isaac Lauze, weaver, *ibid.*, 29 May, 1852
[78] Trial of one Coeurdacier, a building entrepreneur, *ibid.*, 22–23 March
[79] Evidence of Dominique Bellot, *ibid.*, 14 April
[80] *Ibid.*, 28 March
[81] Before the IIe Conseil de Guerre of the 19e Division militaire at Clamecy, *ibid.*, 16–17 February, 1852
[82] Evidence of one Raux at trial of A. Philippon, *agriculteur*, *ibid.*, 12–13 April, 1852
[83] Jean Pech, *cultivateur*, *ibid.*, 10 April, 1852

84 Evidence of Zanote, printer, *loc. cit.*
85 Report of the Prefect of the Dordogne, 5 December, 1851, in *A.N.*, F⁷12654
86 Ténot (2), p. 256
87 Vigier (1), vol. II, p. 327; *cf.* Ténot (2), p. 195
88 Report of 26 January, 1852 in *A.N.*, BB³⁰396
89 *Ibid.*
90 Evidence of Dudrage, *loc. cit.*
91 Report of 27 January, 1852, in *A.N.*, BB³⁰396; see also the reports of his colleagues at Limoges (7 February, 1852), Paris (26 January, 1852) and Agen (undated) same loc., and a report from the 2nd subdivision (Nièvre) of the 19th military division of 9 January, 1852, in *A.N.*, F⁷12710
92 *A.H.G.*, G⁸195–196
93 Report of the *procureur-général* at Dijon, 2 February, 1852 in *A.N.*, BB³⁰396; see also *A.H.G.*, F¹51, 52, 54; G⁸195–196; various witnesses at the trial of Casimir Peret at Montpellier, reported in the *Gazette des Tribunaux*, 22–23 March, 1852
94 Evidence of Maxine Chambert, *agriculteur*, *ibid.*, 9 April, 1852
95 Evidence of one Salettes, a cooper, *ibid.*, 22–23 March
96 Dupeux (3), p. 381
97 Vigier (1), vol. II, pp. 258–61, 328–9
98 Report of the *procureur-général* at Paris, 26 January, 1852 in *A.N.* BB³⁰396
99 See evidence of Maxime Chambert, *loc. cit.*
100 Marcilhacy (1), p. 55 (2), p. 355
101 Report of the *procureur-général* at Nîmes, 27 January, 1852, in *A.N.*, BB³⁰396
102 Report of 5 December, 1851, in *A.N.*, F⁷12654
103 Report of the general commanding the 8th military division, 6 December, 1851, *A.H.G.*, F¹52
104 Reports of the Prefect of Gers, 7 December, 1851; the *procureur-général* at Nîmes, 27 January, 1852, in *A.N.*, F⁷12654; Vigier (1), vol. II p. 337
105 Vigier *ibid.*, p. 334
106 Evidence of Chambert, *loc. cit.*
107 Report from the general-in-chief of the 7th, 8th and 9th military divisions of 3 December, 1851 in *A.H.G.*, F¹51
108 Reports in *A.H.G.*, F¹51–52; undated report of the *procureur-général* at Lyon and one from Dijon of 2 February, 1852 in *A.N.*, BB³⁰396
109 Undated same loc.
110 Vigier (1), vol. II, pp. 325–6
111 Reports of the prefects of the Hérault and Dordogne of 3 and 7 December in *A.N.*, F⁷12654

[112] Reports of the Prefect of Lot-et-Garonne of 7 and 9 December, in *A.N.*, F⁷12654

[113] Report of a *commissaire extraordinaire* of the government of 12 December, 1851 in *A.N.*, F⁷12654

[114] Report of the Prefect of the Drôme of 9 December, 1851, same loc.

[115] Report of the Prefect of the Sarthe, of 6 December, in *A.N.*, F⁷12654; and of the Colonel commanding the 7th Regt. of Dragoons of 7 December in *A.H.G.*, F¹52

[116] Zola (3); *cf.* Ténot (2), p. 222

[117] Marcilhacy (2), p. 44

[118] Siegfried (2), p. 370

[119] Vigier (1), vol. II, pp. 419 and 440

[120] Various reports in *A.N.*, F⁷12654 and *A.H.G.*, F¹52, 53, 54

[121] *cf.* Vigier (1), vol. II, p. 416; Loubère (3), p. 1052

[122] Vigier, ibid, pp. 441–2

[123] *ibid.*, p. 133

[124] *cf.* Agulhon (2), pp. 41–7, 422, 570

[125] Report of the *procureur-général* at Aix, 19 January, 1852, in *A.N.*, BB³⁰396; notes concerning the mayor of Crane, Benoit Ducos, sentenced to transportation to Cayenne by the Commission militaire de la Drôme, *A.H.G.*, G⁸196

[126] Report from the 2nd sub-division of the 1st military division, 9 January, 1852, copy in *A.N.*, F⁷12710

[127] Report of 27 January, 1852, *A.N.*, BB³⁰396

[128] Report of 26 January, 1852 same loc.

[129] Marcilhacy (2), p. 205

[130] *cf.* report of the Prefect of the Vaucluse, 9 December, 1851 in *A.N.*, F⁷12654

[131] Le Bras (2), vol. II, p. 17

[132] Vigier (1), vol. II, p. 422

[133] Reports of the Prefect of the Var of 8 and 9 December, in *A.N.*, F⁷12654

[134] Vigier (4), p. 200

[135] *Ibid.*

[136] Marcilhacy (2), p. 329

[137] Report of the *procureur-général* at Paris, 26 January, 1852 in *A.N.*, BB³⁰396

[138] Two reports from the Prefect of the Nièvre, both of 6 December, and one from the Prefect of the Charente of 21 December, 1851 in *A.N.*, F⁷12654

[139] Chatelain (1), p. 6ff; Vigier (4), pp. 200–1; Loubère (3), p. 1039; Ariès, pp. 54–5

[140] Turner and Killian, p. 520

[141] Chatelain (1), p. 9

[142] Labrousse (7), p. 5

[143] Hilaire, p. 60
[144] Chevalier (3), p. 632
[145] Vigier (1), vol. II, pp. 410–11
[146] Loubère (3), pp. 1032–3
[147] Marx (1), p. 335
[148] *A.N.*, F^{1a}10
[149] 15 December, 1851
[150] Contained in F^{1a}10Meuse
[151] Guillemin (2), p. 424
[152] Telegraphed circular from Morny to the Prefects, 2 December, 1851 in *A.N.*, F^{1a}10
[153] Bruchet, p. 110
[154] Circular of 16 December, 1851 in *A.N.*, F^{1a}10
[155] Circular of 12 December, same loc.
[156] *Ibid.*, 15 December
[157] Guillemin (2), p. 429
[158] Report of 26 January, 1852, in *A.N.*,BB^{30}396 – the section quoted relating events in the arrondissement of Nogent-sur-Seine (Aube)
[159] *A.N.*, BB II 1118
[160] Bruchet, p. 110
[161] Duveau (3), pp. 79, 90, 94
[162] Vigier (1), vol. II, p. 344; Dansette (3), p. 368
[163] *Ibid.*, report of the gendarmerie commander in the Ille-et-Vilaine of December 23 and especially that of the general-in-chief of the 10th 11th and 12th military divisions of the same date in *A.H.G.*, F^{1}54
[164] Charnay, p. 170; Girardet (1), p. 11; Gossez (5), p. 106
[165] Report of 9 December, 1851, copy in *A.H.G.*, F^{1}52
[166] Marx (1), p. 244
[167] Hugo (1), p. 34
[168] Schoelcher, p. 402
[169] Senior (1), vol. II, pp. 244–5
[170] Senior (2), vol. I, p. 257
[171] Letter to Beaumont of 29 January, 1851 in de Tocqueville (2), vol. VIII, p. 369
[172] de Tocqueville (1), pp. 211–13
[173] Letter to Beaumont, 20 November, 1849 in de Tocqueville (2), vol. VIII, Part 2, p. 252
[174] Marx (1), p. 342
[175] *Ibid.*, p. 341
[176] de Tocqueville (2), vol. VI, Part 1, p. 133

INDEX

Pyrénées (Hautes-), department of 145, 146
Pyrénées-Orientales, department of 238, 294, 310

Questors' proposition 273, 274

Raspail 140, 148, 201, 209, 219–23
Reims 122, 191, 192
Religion, attitudes to 48, 49, 52, 53, 75, 101, 132, 194, 195, 229, 253–6, 299, 317–19
Rémusat, C. de 55, 93, 94, 97, 147, 162, 183, 188, 210, 224, 225, 229, 260, 261, 275, 283
Renan, E. 182
Rennes 130, 314
Republicans, men and ideas 55, 56, 93, 95, 137–9, 148; moderate 54, 55, 96, 104, 129, 130, 133, 135, 138, 142, 144, 148–50, 183, 189, 194, 196, 201, 205–7, 216, 217, 219, 226, 227, 230–2, 235, 238, 249, 251, 263, 286, 307; radical 54, 55, 122, 134, 135, 138, 142, 148, 183, 189, 201, 205, 221, 232, 235, see also démocrate-socialistes
Revolution, February 1848 1, 82–94, 99, 122
Rhin (Bas-), department of 85, 88, 118, 218, 240
Rhin (Haut-), department of 59, 85, 88
Rhône, department of 221, 230, 241, 265
Rive, W. de la 98
Rive-de-Gier 116
Rodez 142, 356
Roman expedition 246–8, 261
Romieu 276, 278
Rothschild, James de 14, 42
Roubaix 57, 84, 150, 257, 277
Rouen 88, 115, 122, 137, 142–4, 221, 356
St-Arnaud, General 273, 281
St-Étienne 264, 322
Ste-Marie-aux-Mines (Haut-Rhin), canton of 60
St Malo 137

St Maur 269
Sand, G. 322
Saône-et-Loire, department of 221, 265, 284, 294
Sarthe, department of 294
Satory 269, 281
Schoelcher, V. 323, 324
School-teachers 138, 257
Second Republic, significance of 3, 50, 155, 187–9, 194, 200, 244, 245, 325, 326
Secret societies 201, 232, 264, 267, 268, 301, 302, 306
Sedan 269
Seine, department of 208, 209, 221, 238
Seine-Inférieure, department of 88, 221, 259, 323
Seine-et-Marne, department of 230
Seine-et-Oise, department of 230, 250, 316
Senior, N.W. 141, 156, 213, 214, 272
Sibour, Mgr, Archbishop of Paris 213
Sobrier 112, 146
Social mobility 69, 70, 72, 181
Société des Droits de l'Homme et du Citoyen 113, 177
Société republicain 114, 116, 143
Society of December 10 279
Solidarité républicaine 230, 250
Soult, Marshal 41
Statistics 5, 11, 19, 163, 164, 290, 294, 359
Stein, L. von 181
Stendhal 42
Stern, D. 214
Strasbourg 278, 284
Students 182
Sue, E. 10, 258

Tarascon 366
Tariff questions 14, 36, 40, 41
Tarn, department of 145, 311
Tarn-et-Garonne, department of 145, 228, 232, 237
Taxation: popular hostility towards 120, 121, 366